Colonial exchanges

Manchester University Press

Colonial exchanges

Political theory and the agency of the colonized

Edited by Burke A. Hendrix and Deborah Baumgold

Manchester University Press

Copyright © Manchester University Press 2017

While copyright in the volume as a whole is vested in Manchester University Press, copyright in individual chapters belongs to their respective authors, and no chapter may be reproduced wholly or in part without the express permission in writing of both author and publisher.

Published by Manchester University Press
Altrincham Street, Manchester M1 7JA
www.manchesteruniversitypress.co.uk

British Library Cataloguing-in-Publication Data
A catalogue record for this book is available from the British Library

ISBN 978 1 5261 0564 6 hardback
ISBN 978 1 5261 0565 3 paperback

First published 2017

The publisher has no responsibility for the persistence or accuracy of URLs for any external or third-party internet websites referred to in this book, and does not guarantee that any content on such websites is, or will remain, accurate or appropriate.

Typeset by Out of House Publishing Ltd
Printed in Great Britain
by TJ International Ltd, Padstow

To D. F. B., and to the memory of B. C. H.

Contents

List of contributors

Deborah Baumgold is Professor Emerita of Political Science at the University of Oregon and a member of Wolfson College and Clare Hall of the University of Cambridge. Her research focuses on European political thinkers, particularly seventeenth-century natural law thinkers including Thomas Hobbes, Hugo Grotius, and John Locke. She is especially interested in the relationship between textual composition, context, and political contestation. She is the author of *Hobbes's Political Theory* (1988) and *Contract Theory in Historical Context* (2010), along with work on slavery discourse in the seventeenth century. She is the editor of *Three-Text Edition of Thomas Hobbes's Political Theory: The Elements of Law, De Cive and Leviathan* (2017).

Burke A. Hendrix is Associate Professor of Political Science at the University of Oregon. His research focuses on the political agency of indigenous peoples in the United States and Canada, with cognate interests in Australia and New Zealand. He also works on normative analytic questions surrounding the political status of these peoples. He is the author of *Ownership, Authority, and Self-Determination* (2008), and is currently completing a book on the ethical character of indigenous political action. Future work will examine American Indian political thinkers in relation to central currents in American political thought, from the period of the American Revolution to the 1930s.

Yasmeen Daifallah is Assistant Professor at the University of Massachusetts-Amherst, where she holds a joint appointment in Middle East Studies and Political Science. She specializes in modern and contemporary Arab political thought, as well as postcolonial theory, comparative political theory, and Middle East politics. She has a special interest in the ways that religio-cultural traditions orient their subjects towards politics. Her current work focuses on contemporary trends in Arab and Islamic political thought, especially the work of Abdullah Laroui, Hassan Hanafi, and Mohamed Abed al-Jabiri, while future projects will engage the politics of affect in the context of the Egyptian revolution of January 2011.

Johnhenry Gonzalez is Assistant Professor of History at the University of South Florida. His scholarship grapples with the complex history of Hispaniola – the initial site of European conquest and African slavery in the New World. His scholarship draws from archival work in the United States, France, Haiti, and the Dominican Republic. His forthcoming book, *Maroon Nation: A History of Early Haiti*, focuses on systems of land ownership and crop production devised by the former slaves who overthrew the plantation system of colonial Saint-Domingue. In particular it focuses on unauthorized settlements of runaways and squatters that emerged amid the violence and upheaval of the Haitian Revolution and that subsequently shaped the culture, demographics, and economics of the Haitian countryside.

Bonny Ibhawoh teaches African, global, and human rights history in the Department of History at McMaster University, where he is Associate Dean of Graduate Studies and Research for the Humanities. He formerly taught at universities in Africa and Europe. He is the author of *Imperialism and Human Rights* (2007) and *Imperial Justice: Africans in Empire's Court* (2013). The latter examines judicial governance and the adjudication of colonial difference in British Africa, with a focus on the Judicial Committee of the Privy Council and the regional Appeal Courts for West Africa and East Africa. His work examines the tensions that permeated the colonial legal system in upholding standards of British justice while at the same time allowing for local customary divergence.

Murad Idris is Assistant Professor of Politics at the University of Virginia, specialising in political theory. He has wide-ranging interests in political theory and the history of political thought, including war and peace, language and politics, postcolonialism, political theology and secularism, comparative political theory, and Arabic and Islamic political thought. His current research examines competing idealisations of 'peace' across canonical works of ancient and modern political thought in thinkers including Plato, al-Farabi, Aquinas, al-Mas'udi, Ibn Khaldun, Erasmus, Gentili, Grotius, Hobbes, Kant, and Sayyid Qutb. A cognate study focuses on linguistic constructions of 'Islam', particularly contention over its meaning in relation to peace, war, violence, and submission in Euro-American and Arabic thought.

Jimmy Casas Klausen is a faculty member in the Institute of International Relations at the Pontifical Catholic University of Rio de Janeiro. His research focuses on modern and contemporary European political theory in a global frame. He is the author of *Fugitive Rousseau: Slavery, Primitivism, and Political Freedom* (2014), as well as articles on political theory and the British Empire, including settler-colonialism in Locke, concepts of life and harm in Gandhi's and Ghose's writings against the British Raj, Dalit disobedience in Ambedkar's thought and practice, and race and epistemology in J. S. Mill's writing on India. Current research focuses on national policies with respect to 'uncontacted' tribes in Amazonia and elsewhere.

Inder S. Marwah is Assistant Professor of Political Science at McMaster University. His work examines the ways that traditions of political thought respond to human diversity and pluralism. He is currently completing a book entitled *Millian Liberalism*, which argues against the overwhelming influence of Kant and neo-Kantianism in contemporary liberal political theory, defending instead John Stuart Mill's liberalism. His research also explores the influence of Darwin and Darwinian evolutionary theory on late nineteenth and early twentieth-century political thinkers who resisted colonialism, imperialism, and political domination. This work focuses on a range of non-Western thinkers and activists (particularly in India and Egypt) who marshalled Darwinian and evolutionist arguments to resist British imperialism.

Tim Rowse is Professorial Fellow in the School of Humanities and Communication Arts and in the Institute for Culture and Society at Western Sydney University. He has taught at Macquarie University and Harvard University, and has held research appointments at several other institutions, including the University of Melbourne and Australian National University. He is a Fellow of the Australian Academy of the Humanities and the Australian Social Science Academy. He is the author of multiple books on indigenous history and contemporary politics in Australia, including *White Flour, White Power* (1998), *Indigenous Futures* (2002) and, most recently, *Rethinking Social Justice* (2012).

Megan C. Thomas is Associate Professor of Politics at the University of California at Santa Cruz. Her work focuses on the ways in which scholarship in the human sciences is taken up by political thinkers and movements, especially the ways that Orientalist and ethnological research and thinking informed nationalist, socialist, and anarchist thought at the end of the nineteenth century. In her book, *Orientalists, Propagandists, and Ilustrados: Filipino Scholarship and the End of Spanish Colonialism* (2012), she argues that Filipino intellectuals used Orientalist genres, methods, and societies for anti-colonial scholarly and political ends. Current work focuses on nineteenth-century anarchist Mikhail Bakunin's conceptions of enlightenment and education, and on contests of sovereignty in the Philippines during the British occupation of Manila (1762–64).

Lynn Zastoupil is Professor of History at Rhodes College. His work focuses on the intellectual encounters produced by European imperialism. His first book, *John Stuart Mill and India* (1994) examines Mill's career in the London offices of the East India Company, and traces parallels between his views about administering

India and his own intellectual development. This book was followed by *J. S. Mill's Encounter With India* (1999), edited with Douglas Peers and Martin Moir, in which his own contribution argues that the submerged voices of Indians can be found in the imperial discourse that influenced Mill's thinking on education, public opinion, and the role of women. His most recent book is *Rammohun Roy and the Making of Victorian Britain* (2010), which examines Rammohun's status as an intellectual celebrity in Britain and the American republic in the 1820s.

Acknowledgements

An edited volume is by nature a collective endeavour and that is especially true in this case. It is difficult to imagine a more interesting, energetic, and collegial set of contributors, who have been a joy to work with from the early envisioning of chapters to this final product. They have, in turn, helped us to conceptualize what this type of volume should contain and to recognize the depth of possibility that inquiries of this kind open up. We are grateful to them for their chapters, conversation, and company. We hope readers will get some sense of this intellectual richness as they read the volume.

We would like to thank colleagues at the University of Oregon for conversation about the enterprise at various stages of construction. These include Tuong Vu, Anita Chari, Dan HoSang, Craig Parsons, Sebastián Urioste, Michael Fakhri, Lindsay Braun, Arafaat Valiani, Andre Djiffack, Erik Benjaminson, and Carlos Aguirre. We especially thank Dennis Galvan for his encouragement and support throughout.

In October of 2014, the College of Arts and Sciences at the University of Oregon, in conjunction with several departments and programmes, provided us with funds to gather the contributors for a conference and workshop on the developing papers. This was enjoyable and intensive – a weekend in which we all learned a great deal. We thank Sue Peabody, Jonathan Katz, and Lindsay Braun for their excellent work as discussants, and Sankar Muthu for his generous contributions to these conversations. The Oregon Humanities Center later contributed pre-publication funding for the project. In addition to those who could attend the conference, we wish to thank Jennifer Pitts, Adom Getachew, Jeanne Morefield, Julia Gaffield, Navid Hassanzadeh, Christopher Bayly, and Frederick Cooper for their suggestions and support. At ANU, Katherine Curchin, Tim Rowse, and Tim Bonyhady provided insights from Australia's colonial experience.

Our thanks to Caroline Wintersgill for shepherding the volume to publication, along with Ally Jane Grossan, under whose editorship the volume began. David Estrin helped to bring the chapters towards final form as copy-editor, while

Chris Steel gave them their final polish. Michelle Chen designed the volume's cover and located the interesting image of cross-colonial advertising that adorns it.

Chapter 7 of the volume draws on some materials from 'The Uses of Ethnology: Thinking Filipino with "Race" and "Civilization"' in Chapter 3 of Megan C. Thomas, *Orientalists, Propagandists, and Ilustrados* (Minneapolis: University of Minnesota Press, 2012). We thank University of Minnesota Press for permission to include them. Chapter 6 by Tim Rowse previously appeared as 'The Indigenous Redemption of Liberal Universalism', *Modern Intellectual History*, 12:3 (2015). We thank Cambridge University Press for permission to reprint the chapter here.

Introduction: when ideas travel: political theory, colonialism, and the history of ideas

Burke A. Hendrix and Deborah Baumgold

Ideas travel. The history of political thought as it has generally been studied is deeply interested in these forms of travel and in the transformations that occur along the way. Ideas of a social contract first crystallize in the England of Hobbes and Locke, and then travel in branching ways to Jefferson's North America, Robespierre's France, Kant's Prussia, and elsewhere. In their travels, these ideas hybridize with others, are repurposed in new social contexts, and often take on political meanings deeply divergent from what their originators intended. Students of the history of political thought are acutely aware of these complexities in the development of European political ideas during the early modern and modern eras, given the centrality of such ideas for shaping the political worlds in which we now live.

These European countries were not only engaged in processes of political debate and transformation among themselves, however. They were also, at the same time, expanding their colonial reach outward into the lives of peoples in other continents, who were themselves deeply immersed in ongoing political debates and transformations. European bodies, products, and social institutions brought with them explicit or implicit political arguments; their superiority commonly asserted by threats of physical violence or other patterns of domination. Along with patterns of political expansion, and often intended to buttress them, there travelled a by-now familiar set of ideas: claims of civilizational superiority, technological progress, and racial superiority intended as justification of these political transformations to the colonized, and, often, to the colonizers themselves. Other ideas travelled in these colonial channels as well, often with a more ambiguous relation to patterns of domination: claims of personal freedom, popular sovereignty, legal proceduralism, and political toleration. European colonialism altered the world both politically and intellectually.

The colonized were never mere spectators in these processes. They were instead active agents, seeking to sort through the barrage of European ideas and

practices for tools of resistance or reform, or alternatively to shore up local hierarchies and to entrench themselves within global patterns of violence and profiteering. Their exercises of agency were sometimes ambiguous, partaking both
of resistance and acceptance at once. The space for political agency among the
colonized was often profoundly constrained, and for that reason often exercised
in peculiar and unexpected ways depending upon the political gaps available for
action. Often their efforts sought to reach back to the metropole; usually these
efforts failed, but sometimes they succeeded in surprising or unintended ways.
These acts of intellectual agency were often deeply hybrid, in the sources invoked,
arguments made, and rhetorical stances adopted. In some cases, however, they
were surprising exactly for their lack of hybridity, as European ideas were taken
up with little change at all. Ideas travel, often transforming as they go, and sometimes not transforming at all.

This volume presents acts of hybrid theorization from across the world, from
figures within societies colonized by the British, French, and Spanish empires
who sought an end to their colonial status or important modifications to it.
Historians of colonialism have paved the way in studying the impact of Western
ideas abroad, but political theorists have increasingly given attention to colonialism as well. The study of canonical Western political theorists' arguments
in favour of empire constitutes a well-developed subfield, as represented in the
work of Uday Mehta, Jennifer Pitts, and Karuna Mantena among others.[1] The
still-developing field of 'comparative political theory' seeks to give attention to
political thinkers beyond the Western canon, but it remains protean in form.
While there are exceptions, much of this scholarship has sought to recognize the
character of political ideas that explicitly come from outside of Western traditions, either to engage in conceptual comparison with Western ideas or to show
the integrity of non-Western ideas on their own terms. The present volume
represents an approach to comparative political theorizing that focuses explicitly
on the interactions created by colonialism.[2] With the developed literature on
canonical theorists and empire, we are interested in the history of European
colonialism in the realm of ideas; with other strands of comparative political theory, we are interested in the agency and intellectual production of non-European
thinkers. At the intersection between the two lies the 'colonial exchanges' that
are our subject.

We follow in the footsteps of historians such as the late C. A. Bayly who
studied how colonized, activist individuals used, adapted, and rejected Western
ideas that colonial rulers brought with them.[3] More strongly than historians,
however, political theorists have an interest in the ideas themselves, beyond
the ways in which they played out in affecting particular regimes at particular moments. As an intellectual enterprise that colonialism made necessary
across the world, what was distinctive about the actions of political thinkers
in colonized societies? Answering the question, we think, calls for comparing
examples from a variety of countries and colonial regimes as well as a variety

of intellectual traditions. This volume includes a diverse array of case studies as a step towards conceptualizing the character of these exchanges, including instances in which the colonized sought to reverse the direction in which ideas flowed.

Parochial universalisms

The chapters in this volume are written by a mix of political theorists (five chapters) and historians (four chapters), all of them concerned with colonialism and political agency. The chapters are intended to illustrate a diversity of forms of intellectual agency with resultant hybrid ideas. The volume's chapters cover broad geographical and temporal ranges, though no effort has been made at anything like a full accounting of the colonized's agency. We focus on a range of case studies rather than seeking to be comprehensive. There are two chapters on the use of European ideas in nineteenth-century India and one on an obverse case, the suspicious neglect by J. S. Mill of the work of the influential Indian thinker, Rammohun Roy. Other chapters on British colonialism discuss the highest court of appeal in the British Empire (the Judicial Committee of the Privy Council) as the embodiment of tension between universalism and colonial otherness and the impact of Western ideas on indigenous thinkers in North America, Australia and New Zealand. The impact of European ideas in North African settings arises in discussions of Egyptian and Moroccan theorists, while a Philippine case brings in Spanish colonialism. This volume also covers the well-known case of the Haitian Revolution. The rebel slaves of Saint-Domingue formed ideological alliance with the Jacobin regime during the most radical phase of the French Revolution and directly adopted much of their rhetoric of liberty, equality, and '*résistance à l'oppression*.' But, as the chapter will show, the full picture must also include their response to the failure of revolution at home and in the metropole.

The figures in this volume held a variety of social positions in relation to colonial structures. They were judges, editors, political 'extremists', educators, and armed revolutionaries. They were sometimes active in the metropoles as well as the colonies. They produced theoretical work in a variety of genres, and met a range of responses from colonial powers. Their work drew on a wide variety of European intellectual resources alongside those from their own societies. Sometimes these European resources are specific thinkers from colonizing countries, such as Thomas Paine, Herbert Spencer, or Karl Marx. In others, they are broader patterns of discourse, including British legal debates, Orientalist texts, proclamations of rights, Christian claims of equality, and scientific studies. The theorists consider a wide range of questions stretching beyond simply the character of colonialism. These include the status of women, the nature of domestic domination, the criteria of social progress, and the legitimate forms of political rule. Each articulates a map (more or less complete) of the social and political world, describing both the most important empirical features of its present and the normative features that it should have in the future. Each, in other words, engages in acts of political theorizing about the context in which they live and about how one should act in those conditions.

There are many things to learn from these case studies. Many of them can be learned only through reading each chapter and engaging with the characters described there, but other themes emerge across the volume as a whole. Perhaps most centrally, these theorists can shed light on the contingency and parochialism of many European political ideas. Western political thinkers have often claimed to understand the true character of political life, and to offer clear guidance that all people, European or not, should eventually come to emulate. Those who disagreed were often framed as hopelessly parochial, mired within their own cultural limitations and unable to progress alongside the more advanced portions of humanity. The ideas of the colonizers, on this familiar description, were universal in scope; those who resisted them were simply narrow-minded and particularist. Yet European ideas could also carry anti-colonial possibilities that would be used by dissident thinkers to proclaim universal truths that held the promise of a less domineering and imperial world. Colonized intellectuals hardly saw themselves to be articulating particularistic – rather than universal – values or to be endorsing cultural or societal relativism. They often chose to speak in the name of universal values as a way to challenge the parochialism of their colonizers.

Overall, our cases suggest a different, more global way of thinking about the binary of universal and particular. They demonstrate the multiplicity of claims to universalism and the reality that erstwhile universalisms are simultaneously transnational and parochial. Five universalizing paradigms rank large in this volume: British liberalism, French Republicanism, Christianity, Social Darwinism, and Marxism. The vast differences among them, starting with obvious differences in the relative weight given to ethical versus analytic components, are balanced by a fundamental similarity: all are general paradigms that are also clearly tied to specific intellectual and political contexts. A different collection might highlight other paradigms, but we believe that would only serve to demonstrate further that there are multiple universalisms and that 'parochial universalism' is a ubiquitous feature of social thought, made especially visible when examined at the global level.

This reframing puts Western paradigms in their proper place within a larger, indeterminate set. Kantian and Utilitarian brands of liberalism, for example, are simply schools of thought specific to a particular period of intellectual history in particular cultures. Thinking of them this way, we might go on to speculate about whether, and why, some Western paradigms might have attracted non-Western intellectuals more than others. In recent years, the involvement of particular European theorists, such as John Locke, in colonial domination has been extensively studied. Perhaps the racism apparent in the failure of colonial regimes to extend Western ideals of the period to colonized people made certain sets of ideas unattractive to non-Western thinkers. We see relatively limited use of the language of natural rights in this volume, for example, perhaps because colonized intellectuals were aware of the hollowness of the language of natural right and social contract in the world they actually experienced. If so, it may be that the Haitian Revolution is something of an aberrant case, the revolutionaries' appeal to the 'rights of man' a matter of joining an immediate revolution in the metropole. But we want to be cautious about hypotheses of this kind, as well. The relative absence of eighteenth-century deontology from the present collection may be insignificant and the prominence of Social Darwinism simply the result of the predominance of nineteenth-century theories. In other words, there is a great deal of important work for political theorists to do in this area.

The prominence of Social Darwinism points to a further common feature of the acts of hybrid theorizing seen here: these theories often surprise us by upending twenty-first century expectations about the arguments of apparently anti-colonial thinkers. As Megan Thomas observes of the Filipino intellectual Pedro Paterno, 'His writings demonstrate how colonial appropriations of European thought can unsettle our expectations of them; they invoke political claims that are neither repetitions of European supremacism nor challenges to presumptions of racial inequality' (Chapter 7). Nor is Social Darwinism a unique case: liberalism, Christianity, monarchism, and abolitionism all appear in unexpected translation in the volume. Taking the hybrid renderings seriously prompts reflection on what about them accounted for their attraction for colonized intellectuals. Possibly, where we see the racism of Social Darwinism, many nineteenth-century colonial subjects saw science and an ideology of progress. Rejecting Europeans' racist application of the paradigm, it could be adapted to valorize a 'modern' understanding of their own societies. Nonetheless, the paradigms carried their own intellectual straightjackets, separate from specific applications, as illustrated by the elitist ways in which Social Darwinism was commonly deployed.[4]

The theories covered here also share a further bias: from a twenty-first-century perspective, they are often non-democratic or inegalitarian in their conclusions. The relative lack of democratic arguments may be related to specific features of case selection, but it may also be related to circumstances common among an otherwise diverse range of thinkers. On some levels, the figures in this volume varied a great deal, coming from different societies and time periods, writing on a range of topics using a diverse set of sources, and experiencing a variety of reactions from colonial powers to their work. Yet their biographies tend to be similar in several crucial respects. To engage in conversation with imported European ideas presupposes an education in the schools of the colonizer or, at least, unusual educational resources of some variety. Given the additional reality of gender bias in the opportunity for education, it is unsurprising that the thinkers in the collection are – with a single exception in Chapter 6 by Tim Rowse – uniformly male. Due to gender and class bias, some elitist presumptions may be expected, as well as a tendency to equivocate about colonialism. Still, these hybrid theories are hardly uniform in these regards, and we need to remember that ideas can have an independent effect on the conclusions reached. Some paradigms, like Marxism, may naturally support a more critical perspective than, say, British liberalism, which often pretended that equal treatment existed where it clearly did not, or Social Darwinism, which lent itself to justifying existing hierarchies within the colonized society.

By extension, reflecting on gender and class bias suggests a hypothesis about the likely, and unlikely, locales for hybrid theorizing. Likeliest locales were colonial regimes that relied upon, or at least permitted, the existence of a local, educated and professional elite class. Such was India under British indirect rule. In this light, it is unsurprising that the volume includes several chapters (Chapters 1, 2, 3) on Indian thinkers and that these thinkers drew on a variety of ideas; indeed, the richness of the documentary record enables identification of missing conversations such as Mill's neglect of his internationally celebrated Indian colleague, Rammohun Roy.

Patterns of gender, class, and differential uptake of European ideas could all contribute to closing off other forms of thinking about politics, whether traditional to a particular society or held by specific disempowered groups within it. Political theorists have much to learn from historians and anthropologists about the displacement of 'subjugated knowledges' in communities subjected to colonial and other forms of domination. Although that is a different subject from hybrid political theorizing, the volume incorporates an important example. In Chapter 4, Johnhenry Gonzalez narrates the return of an older outlook on politics in Haiti after Napoleon's rise, which had brought an end to the egalitarian politics of radical republicanism in the colony as well as the metropole. The older outlook was the creation of generations of individuals who escaped new forms of forced labour by resorting to the centuries-old practice of *marronage* or runaway settlements. This pattern of evasive, decentralized social conflict had a far different character from the ideas associated with revolutionary France: more fragmentary, non-literate, and based in practice. Doubtless there are many experiences of this kind for political theorists to examine in future work.

Engaged political theory

We also want to call attention to the value of this kind of comparative work to our understanding of 'political theory' as an enterprise. The theorists here can help us recognize once again the character of what political theorizing is, and therefore shed light back on to more canonical works as well. There are several ways in which this is so. Consider, first, genre presumptions about political theory. For those working in the Western canon, there is a tendency to regard a particular genre of writing as coterminous with political theory as such: the 'systematic' essay or tract. The discussions of social contract theory that form a central axis of much modern European theorizing, for example, have a particular reiterated form that is taken to signal a high degree of moral and intellectual seriousness surrounding a unifying trope. In actuality, these works often combine disparate theoretical elements, often in uncertain relationship to one another, and often related to specific debates of the times. Nonetheless, the genre gives an impression of boundedness and coherence, characteristics that have come to exemplify 'political theory' as such.

Some of those described in this volume undertook systematic works of political theory of this form. Qāsim Amīn's *The Liberation of Women* and *The New Woman*, discussed in Chapter 8 by Murad Idris, seem clearly recognizable as fitting the model. Yet they are also intended to have popular effects, and are constructed in hopes of calibrating styles of argument correctly for particular audiences. As Idris shows, Amīn's attention to reception makes it difficult to see these texts as separate, discrete works and neatly bounded wholes; they are instead structured in conversation with audiences both real and presumed, across multiple times and locations. Works by Abdullah Laroui, Jotirao Govindrao Phule, and Pedro Paterno (by Yasmeen Daifallah (Chapter 9), Jimmy Casas Klausen (Chapter 3), and Megan Thomas (Chapter 7) respectively) also appear to fit the model of 'political theory' as traditionally conceived. But alongside their focus on political ideas, these works are also layered with discussions that might be thought distinctive to other disciplines, such as theology, ethnology, sociology, and evolutionary biology.

Two other kinds of texts emerge as central to the chapters by Inder Marwah and Bonny Ibhawoh: political journals and legal cases. As Marwah describes in Chapter 2, Shyamji Krishnavarma's political writings are found largely in the journal *The Indian Sociologist*, which was published in England, France, and Switzerland to aid the cause of Indian decolonization. Similarly, the legal cases and accompanying debates that are the subject of Bonny Ibhawoh's writing in Chapter 5 on 'imperial justice' do not, in themselves, articulate a free-standing conception of political life or seek to answer many of the kinds of questions that might concern political theorists. Nonetheless, these texts represent careful, nuanced attempts to grapple with ideals of the rule of law, political and cultural difference, fair proceduralism, civilizational change, and other issues of importance to political theorists. Other kinds of texts appear within this volume as well, including the letter written by Haitian insurgents Georges Biassou, Jean François, and Charles Bélair to the French National Assembly that is described in the chapter by Johnhenry Gonzalez (Chapter 4). Altogether, these various works remind us that acts of political theory need not take the form of systematic tracts in order to be understandable or important. They may be fragmentary in appearance but nonetheless fruitful in substance; indeed, their form may often add rich layers to their substance. This is political theorizing in an active mode, which attempts to describe the world correctly so that it can be changed, and which is carried out in political worlds structured by unpredictable patterns of power and beset with power struggles.

It can be useful to think of the relationship between treatises and other kinds of political texts as a translation between praxis and theory as much as between divergent genres of writing. Writers in the European canon were often responding with works we now call 'political theory' to works of a much different variety: pamphlets, public speeches, court cases, biblical interpretations, private letters, and so on. Their works often sought to influence these other kinds of writing in turn: to render certain kinds of political speeches unpersuasive, for example, or to alter the decisions of courts or monarchs. The figures we see in these chapters are equally concerned with ongoing political struggles, seeking to persuade and to intervene, while also seeking to clarify portraits of the political world for their own distinctive intellectual purposes. They are translating ideas from one area of social practice into another, or from theories into the revision of old practices or the creation of new. Theoretical and practical purposes are often difficult to separate even in principle in these contexts.

As we suggested at the outset, translation of a second variety – of ideas being carried from one political context to another – is as characteristic of the European canon as it is definitive of hybrid theorizing under colonialism. The history of canonical European ideas is a story of continual translation and retranslation, with meanings shifting in complex ways throughout this process. The transfer of a concept between different political contexts or theoretical traditions often led to deeply divergent intellectual results, as for example the familiar transition of the constitutionalist contractualism of Locke to the more democratic contractualism of republican France indicates. Texts themselves often circulated from one country to another in altered editions and as altered by translation, to be taken up in divergent and often contradictory ways, as with circulating notions of the 'rights of man' in British, French, and North American debates. Theoretical hybridization of this kind is endemic to the process of political communication and theorization.

Intellectuals in colonized societies were continually engaged in such of acts of transference and translation in obvious ways, often in conditions that created complexities which European theorists did not have to confront. They were frequently dealing with translations between intellectual traditions with much deeper gulfs between them; consider, say, the encounter between Hindu ideas about virtue and purity and Christian-inflected European ideas. When ideas, for example of British liberalism or the common law, came in contact with the political traditions of a India, China, or North Africa, they were entering the unsteady confluence of discursive traditions with millennia of depth, made up of inherited frameworks for understanding the character of the political world and appropriate political action. Intellectuals in the colonies who wished to make sense of their political world, and to act as agents within it, were required to navigate these intellectual complexities over and over again, translating notions back and forth between languages and the much deeper well of reasoning, metaphor, and presumption thus entailed. Because all traditions are themselves amorphous, protean, and sometimes deeply divided, the prospect of finding one's footing is potentially dizzying. The works that are produced are often hybrids that draw from certain elements of each side, but they are often more innovative or fractured than this as well, since the 'sides' are themselves not steady structures. In some cases the results are simply colonial ideas redressed in new terminologies; in others they may be the obverse – old domestic ideas recast in new clothing; in many cases, they are something else entirely, new ideas that have not emerged anywhere before.

These acts of translation vary in their results based not only on the individuals involved, but also on the contexts of power in which they found themselves. In colonial conditions, the space for intellectual innovation, and the resources available for it, were deeply structured by colonial patterns of power. Sometimes, individuals who regarded themselves as undertaking radical acts of agency were achieving nothing like this, but instead were merely replicating colonial expectations or longstanding patterns of domestic domination, whether of gender, class, caste, religion, or nationality. In this volume, many of the chapters present more ambiguous figures: thinkers who were deeply alive to liberatory possibilities in some ways and deeply opposed to many kinds of social change in others. Of course the experience of colonial domination encouraged many to use the leverage of European radicalism; revolutionaries in Haiti and Marxists in the Arab world are notable examples being covered here. Yet radical beginnings did not always lead reliably to radical conclusions.

It would be a mistake to reduce the individuals in these pages simply to products of fields of power, however. To the contrary, all of them struggled to exercise intellectual agency in the widest way possible, and many surely succeeded. Reducing the colonized – even those strongly associated with colonial machinery – to mere outcomes of power politics will lead us to misunderstand them and their theoretical productions. It can also lead us to forget how difficult finding the political space to intervene into patterns of colonialism can be even for those who exercise robust agency over their own thinking. However elite their background, colonial writers often had little room to operate: their works were threatened with suppression and the political stakes of their arguments were high. A badly framed idea might not only endanger oneself, but one's community or nation as well, either by provoking colonial powers to react or by stimulating risky action. Intellectuals who produced acts of political theorizing in colonial conditions could never be speaking just for themselves, whatever they wished. So they had profound reason to exercise great care in the ideas that they produced and promulgated, and – sometimes – reason to take great risks.

The circumstances surrounding hybrid theorizing make interpretation especially complicated in several dimensions. To start with, colonial domination makes intentionality particularly opaque insofar as it encourages strategic action generally. In the realm of ideas, we must be attentive to the reality that arguments can serve a range of goals above and beyond intellectual inquiry in and of itself. Sincerity should not be assumed. Looking for acts of strategic communication in conditions of power will also keep us alive to the shifting and ambiguous nature of the audiences that these intellectuals expected. Writing with one audience in mind often led to quite different arguments, images, or illustrations than would be directed to another. In this volume, we see the question of audience arising in several chapters, but most strongly, as was noted above, in the chapter by Murad Idris on the writings of the late nineteenth-century Egyptian social theorist, Qāsim Amīn (Chapter 8). The arguments seem to shift between the works, but Idris makes clear that the nature of these shifts is predictable: writing for a French audience, Amīn sought to defend the integrity of Muslim societies; addressing a domestic audience, he gave a different analysis of Muslim societies and advocated social and religious reforms needed for their survival. This pattern of divergent texts for divergent audiences is replicated in colonial conditions across the world, with works targeted to the colonizers and the colonized often having a very different nature. The enterprise created special difficulties for authors because the uptake of their arguments could not be controlled and might go in directions they hardly intended. As Idris demonstrates, Qāsim Amīn failed to secure the dialogic ends for which he aimed: his works in Arabic were instead taken up by European Orientalists and missionaries in ways that he could not control and did not want, so that he is now often interpreted as a supporter of colonialism.

For these multiple reasons, the thinkers covered in this volume need to be read both for the substance of their arguments and for the contextual limitations on those arguments. We cannot see them appropriately as agents if we focus only on their potentially compromised positions in relation to European ideas; but we cannot understand the workings of power if we set colonialism aside either. Thinking politically requires that we keep both in mind, and that we engage deeply with the details of each. It is in this richness of detail that we have the best chance for understanding. This is perhaps another way to say that general programmatic statements cannot do justice to the richness of the chapters in this volume. They will, on their own, speak much more powerfully.

As we noted earlier, these works can remind those of us who work primarily on the Western canon of the contingency and vibrancy of political theories, when seen not as timeless, free-standing texts but as acts of intellectual and political agency. Studying the political theorizing of the colonized can revise our conception of the European canon, as different Europeans come to the fore. Figures such as Charles Darwin and Herbert Spencer take on a greater centrality, while others like Thomas Paine turn out to have resonances beyond the revolutions and other events with which they are most familiarly associated. Sometimes the most important intellectual figures for the colonized are not members of familiar European canons at all; these include the now-obscure French biological theorists discussed by Megan Thomas and Qāsim Amīn's interlocutor d'Harcourt. No doubt some hardly merit reclamation beyond their own time and context but, in the long run, continued engagement with the efforts of colonized intellectuals will transform the shape of the canon. In our engagements with colonial intellectuals, as in their engagement with European ideas, nothing is in the end likely to remain unchanged.

Situating the volume

We have waited until this stage to discuss existing literatures on this topic, since it seemed more useful to readers to introduce more substantive matters first. We would not, however, want to suggest that the contents of this volume are entirely unprecedented. Broadly speaking, as was remarked at the outset, there have been two kinds of responses by political theorists to the history of colonialism to which the volume relates. One response, represented by the work of Mehta, Pitts, Mantena and others including Sankar Muthu, Daniel O'Neill, Anthony Pagden, Barbara Arneil, James Tully, and Jeanne Morefield, focuses on imperial – and, less-commonly, anti-imperial – presumptions within the work of canonical thinkers in the European political tradition.[5] This literature often focuses closely on a small set of thinkers, to elucidate often-overlooked colonial references within their familiar texts, or focuses on their less familiar texts to illuminate routinely ignored colonial (or anti-colonial) themes. In other cases, this scholarship focuses on European figures (e.g. Henry Maine in the work of Mantena) who deserve much greater attention in understanding how colonialism was structured and justified.[6] This research is intended to fill out and correct our understanding of colonialism and canonical European thinkers. Insofar as political theory is likely to continue to focus on canonical figures, it is essential that their colonial presumptions are recognized. Yet colonized intellectuals rarely appear in this literature. The range of responses to canonical figures by the colonized needs be examined and understood, so that we can better separate the beneficial and the brutalizing in their thought. The chapters in this volume extend scholarship in this direction.

A second broad area of scholarship often goes by the name of 'comparative political theory', though debate about the term continues. The present volume falls within this developing literature. Given the new and relatively protean character of this subfield, however, our approach is closer to some understandings of comparative political theory than others. As illustrated in the seminal work of Fred Dallmayr, comparative political theory often seeks to understand the political thought of non-European societies on its own terms, to show the ways in which the political thinking of Europe is not synonymous with political thinking itself.[7] This version of comparative political theory is not oriented primarily towards tracking the travel of ideas associated with European colonialism, but with opening intellectual space to recognize ideas that have their origins and development elsewhere. When operating in a conceptually comparative style, this approach often examines in parallel ideas from European and non-European thinkers who did not have (and, indeed, could not have had) any direct influence on one another, as seen, for example, in Stuart Gray's recent work comparing Niccolo Machiavelli with the ancient Indian thinker Kautilya.[8] In other cases, works in this style seek to escape the intellectual hegemony of the West entirely by examining debates within non-European intellectual traditions simply on their own terms.[9] These approaches do not directly focus attention on colonialism, or to the hybrid and ambiguous ideas that it produced.

Our volume is closer to a different branch of comparative political theory that focuses explicitly on the circulation of colonial and anti-colonial ideas.[10] Our volume combines an interest in how colonialism impacted political theorizing in the European tradition with a focus on non-European discussions, adaptations, rejections, and acts of agency. We largely set aside questions of conceptual comparison, and focus on tracing the flows and counterflows of ideas more directly. Our presumption is that understanding canonical ideas requires appreciating how these were used, adapted, and/or set aside by political thinkers in circumstances outside the European orbit. As the volume indicates, intellectuals in colonized societies often found valuable tools of self-defence against both colonial and domestic forces of domination and often deployed these intellectual frameworks in creative and sometimes surprising ways. Sometimes their efforts even fed back into European ideas themselves, reshaping their character in certain ways; there were both intellectual flows of ideas and counterflows, even if the latter were less common. A fair evaluation of European political ideas thus requires close investigation of this kind, as does necessary respect for the difficult political action undertaken by colonized intellectuals, often at great personal risk and requiring great effort. Insofar as political theory will continue to teach the ideas of Europe's 'great thinkers', it is essential to see how these ideas were received and appropriated elsewhere. Insofar as it seeks to take the colonized seriously, it should also take their engagement with these and other materials seriously.

From outside of political theory, there is a background in the extensive work of historians of ideas who have investigated colonized societies. David Armitage, Samuel Moyn, Andrew Sartori, Frederick Cooper, Laura Ann Stoler, Bernard Cohn, Lauren Benton, to name but a few in addition to C. A. Bayly, document the dense layers of intellectual and other exchanges characteristic of specific colonial periods and of colonialism in general, and have vividly portrayed the ways in which the colonized sought to assert their agency.[11] To take only one example, Bayly's investigation of the development of liberalism in India foregrounds a surprising application of Mill's *On Liberty*: despite the work's disparaging language about the 'less civilized', it was nonetheless picked up and deployed by Indians seeking to claim greater rights for themselves.[12] As we suggested at the outset, however, political theorists are interested in the enterprise of hybrid theorizing in and of itself in ways that differ from the interests of historians: political theorists often focus on a small number of intellectual figures and texts and emphasize textual interpretation and exegesis. Given this contrast in typical approaches, but in view of the overlap in substantive concerns, we hope historians will find general utility in our approach to investigating political theorizing in colonial regimes as well as utility in the specific case studies.

A second cognate intellectual field is represented by postcolonial theory, as produced by scholars working in literary studies and related fields. Many aspects of this work overlap with our concerns here, though some of its elements move at a higher level of abstraction and with a more explicitly critical focus. While encompassing an array of analytic styles, postcolonial theory generally seeks to describe the ideological structures by which the colonizing conceptualized the colonized, and the hold that these colonial ideological apparatuses exercised over the colonized themselves. Certain figures loom large in this scholarship, especially Edward Said and Gayatri Spivak.[13] Some of the chapters in this volume are inflected by this scholarship (e.g. those by Murad Idris and Jimmy Casas Klausen), with varying degrees of foregrounding. Given differing genre practices, this literature is not always easily accessible to political theorists working on canonical thinkers, nor does it generally focus on interpretation of specific intellectual figures in the extended ways characteristic of political theory. In its concern for the experiences of the colonized and the importance of intellectual production, however, it is a fruitful interlocutor for the approach found in this volume. We hope that those working in the area will find in these case studies much that is of interest.

An overview of the chapters

Read as a body, the case studies in this volume provoke reflection on both the difficulties and the possibilities of intellectual agency in colonial contexts. With that in mind, we conclude with an outline of the chapters that highlights themes stretching across them. Readers will no doubt identify others that we have missed.

The volume begins not in the colonies, but in London, with a figure familiar to political theorists for his involvement in colonial projects: John Stuart Mill. Lynn Zastoupil has written a great deal on Mill's involvement with India and, separately, on Bengali reformer Rammohun Roy. In Chapter 1, Zastoupil discusses a missed colonial exchange between the two. When Rammohun arrived in Britain from India in 1831, he was already internationally famous as a theologian, reformer, and advocate of press freedom and other liberties. He was so well known, in fact, that the aged Jeremy Bentham sought Rammohun out immediately after his arrival, and others later encouraged him to stand for parliamentary election. As Zastoupil shows, Mill and Rammohun travelled in close social circles, including as participants in the international movement for freedom of the press, so that Mill could scarcely have avoided knowledge of the eminent Bengali. Moreover, Mill was at this time deeply taken with the Herderian notion of *Einfühlung*, which emphasizes the importance of imagining oneself within the minds of those from different civilizational traditions. Yet there is complete silence in Mill's work about Rammohun and his achievements, and years later in *On Liberty* Mill would notoriously deny freedom of the press and other liberties to 'barbarian' peoples. Despite the personal and philosophical connections that should have energized an intellectual exchange, none occurred. Zastoupil's essay prompts us to keep in mind that colonial exchanges did not always occur as might be predicted. There is much room for future work in tracing and understanding these spaces of surprising absence.

Inder Marwah focuses in Chapter 2 on another Indian expatriate in Britain. Given both a traditional Sanskrit and an English education in Gujarat, as a young man Shyamji Krishnavarma became known in India as a Sanskrit scholar, and this reputation would eventually bring him to England. Yet he was no simple Anglophile: deeply committed to the reformist Hindu Arya Samaj movement, he became a radical voice for anti-colonialism through the pages of his journal *The Indian Sociologist* (1905–22), which was published by turns in London, Paris, and Geneva to wider international circulation. As Marwah makes clear, Krishnavarma scorned the passivity of India's moderate nationalists in favour of violent opposition to British rule, yet he also avoided the spiritualism and romantic attachment to violence of many of India's 'extremist' leaders. Krishnavarma turned, instead, to the social theory of Herbert Spencer as the inspiration for a cosmopolitan anti-colonialism. In his work, we see the uptake of Spencer's British anti-colonialism for Indian purposes. But we also see that, far from simply echoing Spencer or British liberalism, he was an active adapter and creator, with a particular goal of putting theoretical conceptions drawn from those sources into political practice.

The volume's third chapter, by Jimmy Casas Klausen, treats an Indian writer who ultimately, seemingly paradoxically, endorsed British colonialism, which he saw could be an instrument for overcoming Brahmin domination at home. Jotirao Govindrao Phule, often called 'the other Mahatma', drew on writings of Thomas Paine and the experiences of the American Civil War to argue for the rights of Sudras and other non-Brahmins to govern themselves as a people free of Brahmin domination. Phule was profoundly influenced by Paine's claims regarding the constituent authority of the people to choose their own form of political life. Yet, in his view, the long intellectual domination of Sudras by Brahmins had left them far less ready for freedom than recently-freed American slaves, unable even to conceptualize the need for their freedom. Curiously, given his admiration for the anti-monarchical Paine, this led Phule to appeal to Queen Victoria to improve British rule by freeing it of corruption and error. Klausen describes this, not as a naive monarchism, but as a canny one, which appeals to – and calls to account – the one figure in a position to end both British abuses and deeper, more abiding patterns of Brahmin domination. The movement and hybridity of ideas here is both clear and surprising: the anti-monarchic Paine is wedded with the epitome of monarchy, Queen Victoria.

Chapter 4 by Johnhenry Gonzalez takes us from British colonialism to the revolution that itself informed the work of Thomas Paine. Gonzalez's chapter focuses on the Haitian Revolution and its brief moment of impact in France's National Assembly. As Gonzalez makes clear, Haitian revolutionaries – former slaves – asserted their claims to the 'rights of man' in strong and direct ways, following up on their successful military action with petitions to the new government in France. For a moment in the middle of the two revolutions, the idea of the 'rights of man' really did reach across boundaries of race and geography, as the National Assembly voted to end slavery in Haiti and other colonies. These thin transatlantic bonds did not last long, however, as the rights of man were overridden by racism, violence and, finally, the resumption of slavery. The flow of ideas back to the metropole was thus profoundly incomplete. Gonzalez illustrates, moreover, the dangers in interpreting the Haitian Revolution too strongly through these French terminologies. The Haitian revolutionaries who adopted the language of the rights of man were themselves few in number and unrepresentative. A far larger portion of the Haitian population identified much more strongly with a different kind of universal practice, one lacking its own theoretical canon: the process of *marronage*, of running away from enslaving and domineering social structures to live on their own terms in any way possible.

Appeals to the metropole of a much more extended kind form the subject of Bonny Ibhawoh's discussion of the British imperial rule of law in Chapter 5. The ideal was embodied in a supreme right of appeal to the Judicial Committee of the Privy Council, which right continues in force even in a few locations today. During its more active periods, the Privy Council drew conflicted reactions from those who lived under its authority, many seeing in it simple colonialism, but others seeing a real attempt to develop a meaningful system of legality across differing cultures and societies. It saw itself as the instantiation of the idea of rule of law across the empire, and therefore as a profound force towards world-spanning legality and social order. Yet this universal aspiration towards the rule of law did not lead towards simple assertions that all peoples throughout the empire should immediately adopt British social forms. Instead, the judges sought to assimilate existing patterns of social life to a shared juridical order. Theirs was a universalism that did not insist upon the same rights for everyone, regardless of who and where they might be, but rather emphasized the submersion of all local legal orders to the rule of the empire's central court. As Ibhawoh notes, many of the questions that occupied the Privy Council continue to matter today as developing systems of international law replay many similar, difficult debates.

Tim Rowse focuses in Chapter 6 on the uptake of liberal universalism by indigenous thinkers in the settler societies of Canada, the United States, Australia, and New Zealand. He focuses on thinkers – namely Peter Jones (Canada), Charles Eastman and Zitkala-Ša (US), Apirana Ngata (New Zealand) and William Cooper (Australia) – who accepted the Christian faith and belief in the perfectibility of human beings of their settler overlords. Here, we see the ideas of the colonizers taken up literally and directly, with little revision: where there was little chance that the colonizers might go away, they turned the colonizers' ideas on their head. They took the principle of human perfectibility seriously, more seriously than Europeans did, by saying that it applied truly universally – to all human societies, their own and the colonizers' alike. 'What was important about liberal universalism', Rowse concludes, 'was that every branch of humanity, including those that colonized, must be measured against a civilized standard.'

In Chapter 7, Megan Thomas shifts our attention away from the more familiar cases of India, Haiti and Anglophone settler societies to the nineteenth-century Philippines. Where the chapters by Zastoupil and Gonzalez document missed or incomplete patterns of exchange, the chapter by Thomas, like that of Klausen, illustrates the odd or troubling directions in which these exchanges could sometimes develop. Focusing on Pedro Paterno, one of a group of *ilustrados* who were educated in colonial Spanish schools and, in the case of Paterno and others, travelled to Europe, the chapter demonstrates ways in which ethnological research from France could be used to contest colonial domination. Paterno's work described waves of past colonization through which the current people of the Philippines came to be, beginning with the (dark-skinned) Ita people, and followed by two subsequent waves before the Spanish arrived. Paterno drew on French ethnology in the school of Jean-Baptiste Lamarck to argue that the 'hybrid' character of some people of the Philippines made them especially suited to social progress. At the same time, however, he reinforced many of the racially troubling features of European Social Darwinism by portraying the remaining unmixed Ita people as primitives with no hope of progress. Thus Paterno engaged in the same racializing move as his European sources. As this chapter illustrates, arguments that championed colonized peoples were not always appealing in their details, even as they may also be explicable.

Some related evolutionary themes are picked up in the chapter that follows. In Chapter 8, Murad Idris examines the complex and ambiguous thought of Egyptian jurist Qāsim Amīn. His work is fraught with issues of gender and freedom, which are occasioned by ideas about the sociological conditions of modernity that include the premise of natural selection in the competition between societies. Amīn worried that Egypt had made itself unable to compete fully in the evolutionary conflict between societies and linked the competition to normative questions about individual freedom and, especially, the position of women in society. At the same time, Amīn also sought to counter the universalist claims of certain interpreters and critics of Islam. Thus he sought to navigate unsteady terrain in describing the meaning of a progressive society without simply reproducing European ideas. Idris's chapter demonstrates the difficulty of writing in ambiguous and profoundly asymmetric colonial circumstances. Seeking both to defend and reform Islamic societies – and both admiring and fearing colonial power – Amīn wrote divergent texts for different audiences: in French, he made defensive arguments; in Arabic, reformist. The conclusion of the chapter power-fully illustrates the ways in which the strategy could misfire: European commenta-tors would in the end deploy Amīn's Arabic language work as support for further imperial entrenchment.

The volume's final chapter, by Yasmeen Daifallah, brings the book up to the present day with an investigation of the contemporary Moroccan scholar Abdullah Laroui, who has been active since the late 1960's in a variety of works and genres. Daifallah demonstrates that Laroui's thinking has continued to use Marxism as an anchoring tool for thought up to the present, even as it has become less explicit about that source over time as shifting political and intellectual circumstances left Marxism with less visibility across the Arab world as a whole. Throughout his prolific corpus, Daifallah argues, Laroui deploys Marxist forms of historicism as a tool for envisioning a more appealing future that bypasses the colonizing and other problematic tendencies of liberalism. In this way, Laroui seeks to sensitize readers to the contingency of their current circumstances and to open space for envisioning new, heretofore novel, possibilities for a world free of colonialism and domination. This future, Laroui suggests, will adopt many of the 'principles and dreams' of European thought, while shaking free of its brutality, domination, and exploitation. Laroui's Marxism illustrates the continuing fecundity of rival univer-salisms, and demonstrates that debate about the stakes of divergent social theories is by no means concluded in the contemporary world.

Altogether, as we see it, the chapters demonstrate the ubiquity, vitality, and high stakes of political theorizing across the world. In the complex and ambigu-ous interplay of colonial exchanges, ideas and agency come alive, as does the tenuous character of erstwhile universalist arguments that otherwise are com-monly framed as timeless and unquestionable. We can see anew the difficulty of political theorizing and the myriad forms in which it can occur. Political theory is enriched, in multiple ways, by examination of these conversations.

Notes

1   Jennifer Pitts, *A Turn to Empire: The Rise of Imperial Liberalism in Britain and France* (Princeton, NJ: Princeton University Press, 2006); Uday Singh Mehta, *Liberalism and Empire: A Study in Nineteenth-Century British Liberal Thought* (Chicago: University of Chicago Press, 1999); Karuna Mantena, *Alibis of Empire: Henry Maine and the Ends of Liberal Imperialism* (Princeton, NJ: Princeton University Press, 2010). See also Sankar Muthu, ed., *Empire and Modern Political Thought* (Cambridge: Cambridge University Press, 2014).

2   For similar approaches to those in this volume, see for example Roxanne Euben, *Journeys to the Other Shore: Muslim and Western Travelers in Search of Knowledge* (Princeton, NJ: Princeton University Press, 2008); Margaret Kohn, 'Afghānī on Empire, Islam, and Civilization', *Political Theory*, 37 (2009), 398–422.

3   C. A. Bayly, *Recovering Liberties: Indian Thought in the Age of Liberalism and Empire* (Cambridge: Cambridge University Press, 2011); C. A. Bayly, 'European Political Thought and the Wider World in the Nineteenth Century', in Gareth Stedman Jones

and Gregory Claeys, eds, *The Cambridge History of Nineteenth-Century Political Thought* (Cambridge: Cambridge University Press, 2011), 835–63.

4   Mike Hawkins, *Social Darwinism in European and American Thought, 1860–1945: Nature as Model and Nature as Threat* (Cambridge: Cambridge University Press, 1997).

5   Mehta, *Liberalism and Empire*; Pitts, *Turn to Empire*; Mantena, *Alibis of Empire*; Sankar Muthu, *Enlightenment Against Empire* (Princeton, NJ: Princeton University Press, 2003); Daniel I. O'Neill, *Edmund Burke and the Conservative Logic of Empire* (Oakland, CA: University of California Press, 2016); Anthony Pagden, *Lords of All the World: Ideologies of Empire in Spain, Britain and France c.1500-c.1800* (New Haven, CT: Yale University Press, 1998); Anthony Pagden, *The Burdens of Empire: 1539 to the Present* (Cambridge: Cambridge University Press, 2015); Barbara Arneil, *John Locke and America: The Defence of English Colonialism* (Oxford: Clarendon Press, 1996); James Tully, *Strange Multiplicity: Constitutionalism in an Age of Diversity* (Cambridge: Cambridge University Press, 1995); Jeanne Morefield, *Covenants Without Swords: Idealist Liberalism and the Spirit of Empire* (Princeton, NJ: Princeton University Press, 2004). This work is itself much more diverse than we can indicate here.

6   Mantena, *Alibis of Empire*. See also Morefield, *Covenants Without Swords*.

7   Fred Dallmayr, 'Beyond Monologue: For a Comparative Political Theory', *Perspectives on Politics*, 2 (2004), 249–57; Fred Dallmayr, ed., *Comparative Political Theory: An Introduction* (New York: Palgrave 2010).

8   Stuart Gray, 'Reexamining Kautilya and Machiavelli: Flexibility and the Problem of Legitimacy in Brahmanical and Secular Realism', *Political Theory*, 42 (2014), 635–57. See also Jon D. Carlsen and Russell Arben Fox, eds, *The State of Nature in Comparative Political Thought: Western and Non-Western Perspectives* (New York: Palgrave, 2013) for approaches of this kind among others.

9   There are deep disagreements about the costs and benefits of 'comparison' as fundamental to this developing academic field. See e.g. Andrew March, 'What is Comparative Political Theory?', *Review of Politics*, 71 (2009), 531–65; Farah Godrej, 'Response to "What is Comparative Political Theory?"', *Review of Politics*, 71 (2009), 567–82; Leigh Kathryn Jenco, '"What Does Heaven Ever Say?" A Methods-Centered Approach to Cross-cultural Engagement', *American Political Science Review*, 101 (2007), 741–55. Both Jenco and Godrej are concerned with how European colonialism was understood within the idioms of Chinese and Indian traditions respectively.

10 As seen especially in the formative work of Roxanne Euben, e.g. *Enemy in the Mirror: Islamic Fundamentalism and the Limits of Modern Rationalism: A Work of Comparative Political Theory* (Princeton, NJ: Princeton University Press, 1999). See also Euben, *Journeys to the Other Shore*. Euben's approach remains more focused on conceptual comparison than our own approach, but her work informs many contributions to this volume. See also Kohn, 'Afghānī on Empire'.

11 David Armitage, *The Declaration of Independence: A Global History* (Cambridge, MA: Harvard University Press, 2007); David Armitage and Sanjay Subramanyan, eds, *The Age of Revolutions in Global Context, c. 1760–1840* (New York: Palgrave MacMillan, 2010); Samuel Moyn and Andrew Sartori, eds, *Global Intellectual History* (New York: Columbia University Press, 2013); Samuel Moyn, *The Last Utopia: Human Rights in History* (Harvard, MA: Belknap Press, 2012); Andrew Sartori, *Liberalism in Empire: An Alternative History* (Berkeley: University of California Press, 2014); Frederick Cooper and Laura Ann Stoler, *Tensions of Empire: Colonial Cultures in a Bourgeois World* (Berkeley: University of California Press, 1997); Bernard S. Cohn, *Colonialism and Its Forms of Knowledge: The British in India* (Princeton, NJ: Princeton University Press,

1996); Lauren Benton, *Law and Colonial Cultures: Legal Regimes in World History, 1400–1900* (Cambridge: Cambridge University Press, 2001).

12 Bayly, *Recovering Liberties*, 200–3.

13 Edward Said, *Orientalism* (New York: Vintage, 1979); Gayatri Chakravorty Spivak, 'Can the Subaltern Speak?', in Cary Nelson and Lawrence Grossberg, eds, *Marxism and the Interpretation of Culture* (Urbana: University of Illinois Press, 1988); Gayatri Chakravorty Spivak, *A Critique of Postcolonial Reason: Toward a History of the Vanishing Present* (Cambridge, MA: Harvard University Press, 2009); Ranajit Guha and Gayatri Chakravorty Spivak, *Selected Subaltern Studies* (Oxford: Oxford University Press, 1988).

1

Intellectual flows and counterflows: the strange case of J. S. Mill

Lynn Zastoupil

Samuel Moyn and Andrew Sartori recently argued that there are many ways to explore global intellectual history. One approach addresses the circulation of ideas and the factors that facilitate or hinder this. Attention to individuals who traverse(d) cultural borders was an early contribution. A large body of scholarship is now available on the travellers, intermediaries, translators, and go-betweens who, in 'crossing seemingly insurmountable borders[,] learned how to make intellectual cultures mutually intelligible'. Related to this are studies of the role of translation itself in 'forging a global concept history'. As with go-betweens, issues of incommensurability and misunderstanding arise here, as does the more specific question of what gets lost in transmission. These problems, however, cannot obscure the 'circulation of concepts and their material vehicles' that has long taken place across the world. Scholarship on transnational intellectual networks forms the final piece of this approach to the globalisation of ideas, according to Moyn and Sartori. These studies have examined different types of networks such as those forged by religious groups or those devoted to the propogation of philosophical systems or economic theories. This scholarship tends to emphasise the specific conditions – book markets or intellectual networks, for instance – that make possible the transnational circulation of ideas. Studies of an early modern European 'republic of letters' anticipated this line of investigation.[1]

What Moyn and Sartori outline here is familiar to scholars of colonialism. One of the important features of modern empires was the circulation of people, ideas, and texts between Europe and the world. These 'circuits of knowledge and communication', as Ann Laura Stoler and Frederick Cooper noted, were multi-directional, creating networks of exchange and influence that linked the world in multiple, complex ways.[2] Gandhi provides ample confirmation of this. A colonial subject for nearly his entire life, Gandhi lived in British territories spanning three continents. He moved freely among India, South Africa, and Britain and formed transnational friendships, intellectual bonds, and activist networks. Influenced by campaigns, writers, activists, and texts from across the British Empire and beyond,

Gandhi came to wield a global influence, fuelled partly by his personal travels but more so by the circulation of his ideas and news of his campaigns. His doctrine of non-violent resistance exemplifies all this. Inspired in part by the passive resistance of British suffragette hunger strikers, Tolstoy's *The Kingdom of God Is Within You* (which he read in South Africa), Thoreau's essay on civil disobedience, and Indian traditions such as *hartals, dharna,* and peasant desertions – and inspiring in turn civil rights and non-violent resistance movements in South Africa, the United States and elsewhere – *satyagraha* is testament to the flow and counterflow of ideas engendered by modern imperialism.[3]

Intellectual exchange was part of the colonial enterprise from the start. European expansion led to encounters with foreign societies that rendered necessary cross-cultural understanding. Cultural brokers became an integral part of the early colonial landscape, transmitting information and fostering sensitivity between Europeans and indigenous peoples. Often they were local women who entered into intimate or familial relationships – real or fictive – with European men. These 'go-betweens' relayed everything from basic linguistic skills to vital cultural and religious information to complex ideas about social and political organisation. In the process they shaped as well as facilitated the exchange of ideas.[4]

In British India these intellectual encounters were intensified by many factors. For one, India was home to an ancient, complex, and evolving civilisation with 'a brilliant and enduring tradition of indigenous scholarship'.[5] Also important were the highly developed precolonial political system – which thrived on gathering and disseminating information – and the equally vibrant public arena where religious and political debating skills, as well as other intellectual talents, were prized.[6] The introduction of Western education by the British was another factor, as was the manner in which Indians embraced this education both in India and in Europe. The unusual nature of imperial rule played a role too. The British East India Company (EIC) evolved from a mere trading venture into the paramount power in India by the early nineteenth century in large part because it drew upon the talents of countless Indians. Among those who entered its service were learned elites, intellectuals, and others with knowledge and skills related to the local information order or venerable scholarly traditions. These knowledge-rich individuals and groups grew in importance as the expanding British Raj required ever more knowledge of regional languages, dynastic matters, political affairs, revenue sources, local history, religious customs, popular culture, and the like. Many of these knowledge brokers became part of what Bernard Cohn appropriately described as the veritable army of Indians who 'ran the everyday affairs of the Raj'.[7]

A vast and growing body of scholarship exists on the flow and counterflow of ideas spawned by these circumstances. The Raj's long duration and the intense exchanges it created means that there is an almost inexhaustible list of Britons and Indians who can be studied for how ideas were borrowed, adopted, embraced, altered, challenged, contested, or rejected. The literature on these encounters resists categorisation, although Shruti Kapila recently suggested that much of the recent scholarship tends to fall into one of two competing schools of interpretation, one investigating 'the power of colonial knowledge', and the other stressing the vigor of Indian agency. Representative of the two schools are important works by Cohn and C. A. Bayly.[8] William Pinch has highlighted the key differences in their interpretive frameworks. Cohn saw the British colonising Indian forms of knowledge and inventing ones of their own useful for the imperial project. Bayly meanwhile stressed the British ability to adapt to their own purposes Indian means of gathering and disseminating information, although these were later subverted by the use of new, scientific forms of intelligence gathering. Cohn's argument leads to the conclusion that 'the colonial state [was] the main author of politics and political meaning', whereas Bayly's emphasises the vitality of Indian processes and local agency.[9] Kapila and Pinch both make a case for moving beyond these interpretive frameworks, each pointing in the direction of the emerging field of global intellectual history.

In fact, significant work has already been done on British–Indian intellectual encounters that anticipates this call for a transnational approach. These studies have tended to reject the notion that colonial encounters were one-sided affairs in which Britons imposed their intellectual will and that Indian intellectuals were passive victims or mere informants marginalised by a colonial state that invaded their epistemological space.[10] In 1994, for instance, Eugene Irschick explored the dialogic process of cultural formation and knowledge construction in colonial south India. This process involved both British administrators and Indian interlocutors, Irschick insists, who 'participated equally in constructing new institutions with a new way of thinking to produce a new kind of knowledge'. The result was cultural formations that were neither European nor Indian, but heteroglot constructions so multi-authored that it is 'impossible to locate any real provenance for them'.[11] Norbert Peabody makes similar claims about early British censuses in Rajasthan. These were similar to precolonial surveys because colonial officials relied upon local informants who used household lists prepared for previous rulers. Colonial discourse, in other words, involved Indian agency and was formed 'by way of *bricolage*'.[12]

Suggestions of transnationality are also rife in scholarship on early British engagement with Sanskrit studies. Rosane Rocher and Ludo Rocher eschew notions of colonial impositions and stress the interactions between EIC officials and Indian pandits that led to the foundation of modern Indology.[13] Along with others, they note how early British Sanskritists worked closely with *pandits* and were deeply indebted to the Indian scholarly tradition, defending both against German Sanskritists. The latter favoured the classical philological methods developed in Europe and most had only limited use for indigenous Sanskrit studies.[14] It is thus fair to speak of an Indo-British school of early Indology. H. H. Wilson became its chief exponent in Europe after returning from India in 1833 to become the first Boden professor of Sanskrit at Oxford. He criticised European scholars who undervalued Indian authorities on Sanskrit and argued that the Boden chair must be held by someone who had learned Sanskrit in India and was familiar with classical Sanskrit literature and its grammar as studied in India.[15]

A word of caution is in order, however. Although colonialism produced exchanges that enabled a global intellectual culture to emerge, the transmission and reception of ideas was uneven, ambiguous, and not always fruitful or long-lasting. George Orwell's critique of empire, for example, owes a deep debt to his experiences as a police officer in Burma. Yet, in his famous essay 'Shooting an Elephant' and the autobiographical passage on his imperial service in *The Road to Wigan Pier*, Orwell displays little interest in and perhaps even less sympathy for Burmese views on British rule. Cases easily come to mind, too, of individuals who came into contact with foreign ideas, texts, or individuals and were seemingly unchanged intellectually by those encounters. Thomas Macaulay's infamous comment on South Asian literature and learning – 'a single shelf of a good European library [is] worth the whole native literature of India and Arabia' – suggests that nearly a year in India had done nothing to alter his confidence in the 'intrinsic superiority of the Western literature'.[16]

There are instances as well where intellectual exchange never transpired despite very favourable circumstances. This essay will examine one notable case of this: J. S. Mill's neglect of the Bengali reformer, Rammohun Roy. Mill's silence about this transnational celebrity renowned on three continents is striking, given the opportunities they had to meet, their shared networks of intellectuals and activists, and their similar views on key political and social matters. This neglect is even more remarkable when one considers Mill's embrace of *Einfühlung*, an underappreciated intellectual move on his part that reflects the influence of his colonial career. Although he owed a manifest debt to an EIC ethos promoting sympathetic understanding of Indians, Mill apparently remained unsympathetic to the famous Rammohun Roy who captivated many people that Mill knew and admired.

J. S. Mill's *Einfühlung*

During his period of intellectual ferment in the 1830s, J. S. Mill wrote as if he had imbibed Herder's influential notion of *Einfühlung*. In 1832, he indicated the benefits of transporting oneself into the minds of other people in order 'to know and feel' what they are, how the world paints itself to them, 'still more to decipher in that same manner the mind of an age or a nation, and gain ... a vivid conception of the mind of a Greek or Roman, a Spanish peasant, an American, or a Hindu'.[17] Such an act of genius, he wrote a few years later, was possessed by historical writers such as William Ware, who had the 'power of throwing his own mind, and of making his readers throw theirs, into the minds and into the circumstances of persons who lived far off and long ago'.[18] This is why great history writing was a form of poetry, as in the case of Schiller's *Wallenstein* and Thomas Carlyle's history of the French Revolution. Those two writers presented historical figures as flesh and blood individuals, as 'real beings' with desires, ambitions, and fears. This ability to transport readers into the minds of others, to make readers understand what others thought and felt, was lacking in most historical accounts. Hume's *History of England* was a case in point.

> Does Hume throw his own mind into the mind of an Anglo-Saxon, or an Anglo-Norman? Does any reader feel, after having read Hume's history, that he can now picture to himself what human life was, among the Anglo-Saxons? ... what were [an Anglo-Saxon's] joys, his sorrows, his hopes and fears, his ideas and opinions on any of the great and small matters of human interest?[19]

This brings to mind a passage in *The Spirit of Hebrew Poetry* where Herder wrote that in order

> to judge of a nation, we must live in their time, in their own country, must adopt their modes of thinking and feeling, must see, how they lived, how they were educated, what scenes they looked upon, what were the objects of their affection and passion, the character of their atmosphere, their skies, the structure of their organs, their dances and their musick.[20]

The notion of *Einfühlung* has a complex history, although many would agree that its origins can be traced back to Herder.[21] Although it is tempting to see Mill using the homegrown concept of sympathetic imagination employed by Coleridge, Shelley, Keats, Hazlitt, and others,[22] the parallels in these two passages are so striking that a chain of influence must be supposed. Michael Forster argues that Mill owes more to the German intellectual tradition, including Herder, than what is suggested in *On Liberty* and elsewhere regarding Wilhelm von Humboldt and other influences. Forster identifies areas of 'striking agreement between Mill and Herder', including Mill's use of Herderian concepts (*Zeitgeist* as the title of his 1831 essay 'The Spirit of the Age' and *Humanität* in his idea of a 'religion of humanity'). It is unfortunate that Forster overlooks Mill's interest in *Einfühlung* and does not trace how Mill acquired his Herderian views, noting only his suspicion that it was through the indirect means of Herder's general influence on European thought.[23] This suspicion proves correct, with an important correction, when one follows the iterations of Herder's *Einfühlung* – or something akin to it – that crossed Mill's private and official desks.

Mill drew upon two distinct sources in framing his version of *Einfühlung*. One was his reading of European authors. Although familiar with Herder, it seems certain that Mill did not absorb the concept from its *Ur*-source. He rarely mentioned the German in his writings,[24] and then mostly as a pioneer of a new scientific approach to history that had caught on among French historians, but not yet with the British.[25] Also unlikely sources are those German thinkers known to Mill who were influenced by Herder's doctrine, such as August Wilhelm Schlegel and Friedrich Schleiermacher. Although Mill owned or knew of some of their works in this period, he gives no indication that he came to *Einfühlung* directly through their writings.[26] Instead, the evidence points to Thomas Carlyle.

Carlyle was instrumental in introducing German literature and thought to British audiences in the 1820s and 1830s. The favourable reception of Goethe in this period, for instance, is almost solely due to Carlyle, who attracted a circle of 'young men' newly interested in German intellectual life.[27] Among these was Mill, who came to admire Carlyle during the winter of 1831–32 when the Scot resided in London.[28] The German intellectual influences to which Carlyle exposed Mill included a version of *Einfühlung*.

Suzy Anger notes that Carlyle was 'the principal representative of romantic hermeneutics in nineteenth-century Britain'. Central to Carlyle's hermeneutics was his conviction 'that the ability to see and feel from another's perspective is crucial to understanding'.[29] Anger adds that it is not certain that Carlyle was directly familiar with German hermeneutic theory.[30] His early writings, however, indicate knowledge of some version of *Einfühlung* from the German tradition, if not from Herder himself. In an important 1827 essay – where he listed Herder among the great intellectual figures of Germany – Carlyle wrote approvingly of how Germans seek not to judge, but to understand other nations in their own peculiarities, so that they 'may see [each nation's] manner of existing as the nation itself sees it, and so participate in whatever worth or beauty it has brought into being'.[31] Two years later he recommended Novalis to all those readers who valued careful study of an author's works, of 'work[ing] their way into his manner of thought, till they see the world with his eyes, feel as he felt and judge as he judged, neither believing nor denying, till they can in some measure so feel and judge'.[32] In an 1832 essay on biography, Carlyle added that it was 'inexpressibly comfortable' to know another person, 'to see into him, understand his goings-forth, decipher the whole heart of his mystery: nay, not only to see into him, but even to see out of him, to view the world altogether as he views it'.[33]

Mill knew all of these essays. He even held up the last passage in an 1833 essay as indicative of what could be accomplished with a perfect biography. The perfection of history, he added, 'would be to accomplish something of the same kind for an entire nation or an entire age'.[34] As we have already seen, this was that act of genius, of poetic insight, that Mill was praising in his other writings from this period. Clearly, then, Mill developed an appreciation of *Einfühlung* through Carlyle.

But this is not the entire story of Mill's attraction to the concept. Mill noted in private letters and his *Autobiography* that initially he found these early essays of Carlyle 'consummate nonsense' – 'a haze of poetry and German metaphysics'. The letters suggest that Mill's admiration for Carlyle grew as the two became acquainted in London. In his memoir, however, Mill indicates a lesser influence.

Carlyle's ideas were appealing because he was already coming across similar ones from other quarters; moreover, he could only appreciate Carlyle's insights 'in proportion as I came to see the same truths, through media more suited to my mental constitution'.[35] Mill does not name those other sources or media. His 1832 essay 'On Genius' – with its praise for the power of transporting oneself into the mind of a Hindu (among others) – offers a clue that his India House work was important here.

As I have argued elsewhere, when Mill entered the EIC's service in 1823 the dominant ethos of adminstration was one closer to the Romantic views he would adopt in the 1830s than to the Utilitarian views he had inculcated in his youth. This was clearly the case with a set of policies suggestive of *Einfühlung*. Influential colonial officials had made it a point of pride, and de facto EIC policy, to develop 'a sympathetic understanding of Indian thought, feelings, opinions, and prejudices'. Their outlook was tied to pragmatic concerns. Without such a sympathetic understanding, fostering allegiance to British rule would be difficult, if not impossible. This required attention to traditional practices, habits, and customs, as well as religious and political loyalties, even nationalist sentiments.[36] John Malcolm expressed this ethos in an influential set of instructions to officers under his authority. For the Raj to last, British officials must carefully cultivate, and act upon, an ability to 'judge [Indians], without prejudice or self-conceit, by a standard which is suited to their belief, their usages, their habits, their occupations, their rank in life, the ideas they have imbibed from infancy, and the stage of civilization to which the community as a whole are advanced'.[37]

Penned in 1821, Malcolm's instructions were printed and circulated by order of government for the use of British civil servants in India.[38] During the 1820s, other important officials echoed its sentiments. William Chaplin, in charge of recently annexed Deccan territories, wrote a similar memo to subordinates. Referring his officers to Malcolm's instructions, Chaplin reminded them that the British had in India an 'empire of opinion' that required careful attention to public sentiments and tolerance 'of all native habits and prejudices'. A sympathetic ear was thus a must for every British official in India, who ought to bear in mind Lord Chesterfield's advice to his son: 'many a man would rather you heard his story than granted his request'.[39] John Briggs, who held key posts in several princely states under British authority, expressed similar thoughts in letters of advice to two young officers new to India. In 1828, he published these letters in a London volume dedicated to Malcolm and containing the latter's 1821 instructions. Briggs described those instructions as a 'code' and offered his volume as an introduction to its principles.[40] In his letters, Briggs offered detailed insights into the nuances of Indian customs, habits and perspectives, a respectful understanding of which was essential for maintaining what he too called an empire of opinion. '[I]t is impossible', he advised, 'we can study the prejudices of the natives too much'.[41]

Mill began supporting this administrative position at roughly the same time that he embraced a version of Herder's doctrine in his published works. A good example occurred in 1837 when he was charged with drafting a dispatch on political events in Jaipur. Violent events in that Rajput state brought to the fore competing imperial visions among British officials. One stressed advancing good government through direct British rule, the other maintaining national governments enjoying popular support (called indirect rule because it depended on Indian rulers as intermediaries). The argument for preserving a Rajput government in Jaipur was made by Charles Metcalfe, the acting governor-general. Metcalfe supported his arguments with repeated appeals to the Indian perspective. The EIC would acquire considerable odium through anything that amounted to naked conquest, as this would confirm what Indians already thought was the real aim of British policy: 'They detest us as strangers and conquerers, and look on all our proceedings with jaundiced eyes'. States possessing 'national pride and feelings', such as Jaipur, will not submit quietly to loss of their national governments. The British must heed public opinion, listen to the 'national voice', take into account 'national indignation', recognise when 'national expectation has been disappointed', acknowledge the 'national will', and avoid offending 'popular feeling'. Lest anyone missed the point, Metcalfe used an imaginary situation to elicit sympathy for the Rajput perspective, citing as an example the EIC's recent annexation of part of Jaipur's territory. Suppose a foreign country were to use the pretext of social and political turmoil in Ireland to annex that island, severing its connection to Britain: 'Such as our feelings would be on such an occasion, those of the people of Jypoor may now very naturally be'.[42]

Mill threw his support behind Metcalfe's decision to uphold a national government in Jaipur. This was a reversal of the position that Mill had previously taken, along with his father, of criticising indirect rule and recommending direct British rule wherever possible. As his father had claimed, any patriotic sentiments on the part of Indians could be disregarded because attachment to British rule would inevitably develop by providing an efficient government that protected property rights and promoted prosperity. Now Mill shared Metcalfe's view that Indians – or some of them – did not see things that way, harbouring strong national feelings that must be acknowledged. An 1866 letter confirms this. Clarifying his stance on the numerous annexations of Indian territories during the administration of Governor-General Dalhousie, Mill noted that he approved all of these, except where there existed 'a nationality, & historical traditions & feelings, which is emphatically the case (for example) with the Rajpoot states'. Although his letter denied national legitimacy or popular support for other Indian dynasties, Mill held firm to Metcalfe's insight into the Rajput perspective.[43]

Another telling example of Mill's concern for seeing things through Indian eyes was his response to organised violence in the region of Kathiwar. Mill initally pushed for direct British rule to overcome the social, fiscal, and political problems arising from, or exacerbated by, the EIC's efforts to prop up the local rulers in Kathiawar. Among those problems was *bahirwattia*, a type of organised plunder and banditry that formed part of the local political culture. Beginning in 1834, Mill abandoned the idea of direct rule in Kathiawar, favouring instead policies that recognised the power of public opinion and the need to work through those elites who could mould it. He also advanced a proto-anthropological view of *bahirwat-tia*, projecting the empathetic understanding that Malcolm, Briggs, and others had advocated. As a threat to law and order, the practice had to be suppressed, but Mill urged using gentle means. It was 'the custom of the country' and those who engaged in it had 'the sanction of immemorial custom'. What might be a barbaric practice in the colonial view, had a different significance to people of the region.[44]

Mill held to some version of this perspective to the end of his days. In his 1868 essay *England and Ireland*, Mill drew upon his India House work to argue that the British needed to recognise that 'the opinions, feelings, and historical anteced-ents of the Irish people are totally different from, and in many respects contrary to those of the English'. EIC administrators had done this with India and Mill lauded them for demonstrating how it was possible to shake off 'insular prejudices, and [govern] another country according to its wants, and not according to com-mon English habits and notions'. The 'work of stripping off their preconceived English ideas' was difficult and many mistakes were made, but over time the EIC succeeded and thus India (or so he thought) was now governed 'with a full per-ception and recognition of its differences from England'.[45] The emphasis here is different – the need to step outside the parochial nature of one's own perspec-tive – but the concern for sympathetic understanding is still apparent.

This sensitivity to Indian perspectives is strongly suggestive of Mill's theoreti-cal interest in throwing oneself into the minds of others, of attempting to see the world as others see it. The timing indicates mutual influence, or a concurrent working out of the possibilities of *Einfühlung* in his philosophical and colonial activities. The passage in the *Autobiography* on Carlyle's limited, belated influence raises the possibility that the philosophical insight – or at least the clarity of that insight – might have occurred only, or largely, because of the colonial environ-ment in which Mill operated. The first enunciation of that insight – throwing oneself into the mind of another is an act of genius – came after nearly a decade of daily exposure to an administrative ethos stressing the need for a sympathetic understanding of Indians. This may explain why a key phrase in that initial articu-lation of *Einfühlung*, where Mill wrote of attempting 'to know and feel what the man is, and how life and the world paint themselves to his conceptions', concludes with the example of a Hindu.[46] The passages just cited from *England and Ireland* add to the sense that it was as a colonial administrator that Mill first grasped the importance of empathy. Theory, in a word, may have followed praxis.

J. S. Mill and Rammohun Roy

When Mill published in 1832 his musings on throwing oneself into foreign minds, a celebrated Indian visitor was then the talk of London. Arriving in the middle of the reform bill agitation of April 1831, this famous Bengali was besieged with visitors and requests for meetings from the day he arrived. Newspapers traced his whereabouts and published his hotel information for the benefit of readers anxious to meet him. He was presented to King William, invited to the royal tent for the opening of the new London Bridge and seated among the foreign dignitaries at William's coronation. Other royals hosted him at grand gatherings and introduced him to the House of Lords. Nobles and commoners invited him to their theatre boxes or social gatherings. His presence at reform debates in Parliament was reported in the press, as were his visits to public sites or attendance at meetings of learned societies. A portrait of him sent a decade earlier from Bengal was re-engraved and circulated widely. Religious, political, and intellectual figures were particularly keen to converse with this important guest, whose views on matters ranging from the Bible to the reform bill interested the many Britons who kept their guest from India occupied in long and deep discussion. The list of notables who met or tried to meet him included Robert Owen, James Mill, William Godwin, Benjamin Disraeli, Lord Brougham, William Wilberforce, and Thomas Macaulay. Also on this list was Jeremy Bentham who, due to advanced age, seldom left home by this date, yet was so eager to meet the Bengali that he found his way to what he thought was the right hotel on the night the latter arrived in London.[47]

This renowned visitor was Rammohun Roy. Famous as a key figure in the so-called Bengal Renaissance, Rammohun is justly celebrated for his multiple contributions to Indian modernity. A religious and social reformer, he criticised image worship, campaigned against *sati*, and defended women's inheritance rights. In these efforts, he was among those Indians leading the way in the use of the new medium of the printed page, which was just gaining currency in India. He was also a pioneer of Indian journalism, founding or supporting several Bengali newspapers and campaigning for a free press. He challenged the colonial authorities on political matters such as press laws, Indian jurors, and free trade. He criticised Christian missionaries and satirised their religious views. A critical admirer of the ideas and learning of the West, he promoted Western education and the English language. He also helped create modern Bengali prose writing. Small wonder then that, in the politically incorrect language of an earlier generation, he was described as the father of modern India.[48]

Why then his celebrity status in Britain? Rammohun's various religious, political, and intellectual interests intersected with those of many reformers in Britain, Europe, and the United States. Those common interests were helped along by the introduction of print media into India, the global circulation of information and individuals, and emerging international networks of activists, all made possible or enhanced by empire. Rammohun became a transnational celebrity as Europeans and North Americans read his published works, or accounts of him, and found that this distant Bengali shared many of their views. Many entered into direct correspondence with him.[49] In the case of constitutional liberals, as C. A. Bayly has shown, Rammohun belonged to a global network of activists attentive to political events in places such as Greece, Spain, and Portugal, who celebrated liberal advances around the world, and who employed common ideas about the virtues of ancient constitutions, a free press, separation of powers, and the like. Rammohun's achievement was to localise these ideas in the context of colonial India, paving the way for the creation of an indigenous liberal tradition.[50] This contribution to the globalisation of liberalism helps explain why Bentham and other British reformers suggested that Rammohun stand for Parliament during the reform crisis of 1831–32, and why Rammohun gave serious consideration to the matter during his visit to Britain.[51]

None of this seemed to attract the attention of J. S. Mill, however. Although many people he knew met the Bengali in London, it does not appear that Mill did so. This may have something to do with the fact that Rammohun was on official business too, representing the Mughal Emperor (or King of Delhi as the EIC titled him) Akbar II in his financial claims against the East India Company. These negotiations dragged on for a long time and Rammohun resorted to tactics – apparently drawn from the dark side of British journalism – that Mill's superiors at the EIC surely did not welcome.[52] A meeting with Rammohun might therefore have been unseemly for Mill, although this did not prevent James Mill and Rammohun from discussing Irish politics at a social gathering in 1833.[53] If meeting the famous Bengali was out of the question, this does not, however, explain the near silence on Rammohun in Mill's voluminous works. The thirty-three volumes of Mill's collected works apparently contain one paltry reference, a letter written to Thomas Carlyle ten years after Rammohun's death where Mill passed on the latter's signature, along with other ones, so that Carlyle could forward these to a Prussian autograph hound.[54]

This silence is even more interesting given that the major reason for Rammohun's celebrity status in Britain was his engagement with Christian Unitarianism. Rammohun first became known in the West through his Vedanta publications and their rationalist criticisms of popular Hinduism. These led some to call him the Luther of India. In the 1820s he embraced Unitarianism and became a skilled biblical exegete and controversialist. This manifested itself in a famous dispute with Trinitarian missionaries in a series of Calcutta publications. These were quickly republished by Unitarians in Britain and the United States as proof that an independent investigator had demonstrated that the Bible did not support orthodox doctrines. Some put Rammohun in the first rank of Christian theologians; others claimed that his writings could be found in every decent theological library. One neutral writer noted that the Church of England's luminaries would surely have to take up the Bengali's challenge to orthodoxy. In general, Anglo-American Unitarians proclaimed Rammohun a celebrity convert – a trophy for their cause, as Ralph Waldo Emerson put it – touting him as a major intellectual figure, along with Locke, Newton, and Milton, who shared their views.

When Rammohun arrived in Britain, Unitarians – especially Unitarian women – thronged to his side. Among those singing his praises were early Unitarian feminists, including William J. Fox, who would later eulogise Rammohun in a funeral sermon at his London chapel. In 1830, Fox, it should be recalled, had introduced Mill to his future wife, Harriet Taylor, a Unitarian whose first husband, John, was a leading member of Fox's congregation. After her marriage to John Taylor, Harriet became very close to several women in Fox's congregation. One of these was Harriet Martineau, who was deeply moved when she first met Rammohun and composed a hymn for the chapel service on the day that Fox delivered his funeral sermon on the Bengali reformer. Fox also enticed Mill to publish some articles in the *Monthly Repository*, a Unitarian organ that he was transforming into a non-sectarian journal soon noted for its feminist essays. The September 1832 issue of that journal contained a review of two recent works that Rammohun had published in London: one his written testimony to Parliament on the affairs of the East India Company; the other a volume reprinting some of his Calcutta works on religion, *sati*, and the inheritance rights of women. The first part of this review was written by Martineau, the second by Fox.[55] The very next month Mill published in Fox's journal his rhapsody about the act of genius involved in throwing oneself into the minds of Hindus and other foreigners.

These circumstances become more intriguing when one considers that Mill and Rammohun once participated in a transnational political campaign. In the 1820s both men took up the pen to defend liberty of the press when that cause was under threat from a Tory government in the period following the Napoleonic wars. The attempt to muzzle the British press during a long agitation for a free and cheap press is well known thanks to such classic works as E. P. Thompson's *The Making of the English Working Class*.[56] Recent scholarship has begun to explore linkages between those events and a crackdown on the press in Bengal at the same time. Among these ties were the circulation to India of news, ideas, and texts from Britain regarding the free press agitation and Tory repressions; an attempt to silence particular editors (Richard Carlile, for example, through imprisonment and fines in Britain, and James Silk Buckingham through expulsion from India); secret collusion between the Tory government and the directors of the East India Company on reining in the Indian press; and the emergence of Buckingham's case as a cause célèbre among many proponents of a free press in Britain.[57] Among Buckingham's supporters was Bentham, who was at the centre of his own global network of political radicals stretching from Russia across Europe to North Africa, Central America, and India. The Utilitarian philosopher lent moral and financial support to Buckingham's journalistic ventures in Britain. He also groomed (with the aid of James Mill) the radical editor for a possible run at a seat in Parliament. This was in line with Bentham's thoughts on the importance of political editors for the functioning of the public opinion tribunal.[58]

These overlapping circles of free press advocates and Benthamite radicals connected J. S. Mill and Rammohun in multiple ways. In his earliest newspaper writings, Mill was, as Stefan Collini notes, little more than a 'mouthpiece' for the ideas of his father. Ann Robson adds that of Mill's twenty-five newspaper contributions for 1823, at least seventeen were applications of the principles of Bentham and James Mill. Carlile's persecution, for instance, provided an opportunity for a defence of liberty of the press based on James Mill's essay on that topic. Mill also applied Bentham's views on sinister interests, publicity, English law, and logical fallacies to the campaign for a free press and other topical matters.[59] Although Rammohun was never really Bentham's disciple – and certainly not a youthful one – the latter did try to recruit him for a panopticon project in Bengal and recommended one of his Central American admirers to Rammohun. The two also had mutual Unitarian contacts. Bentham used these and other individuals to approach Rammohun in an apparent attempt to win the Bengali over to his projects.[60]

One of the things that attracted Bentham, and many others in Britain, to Rammohun was the Bengali's outspoken support for liberty of the press. Buckingham's banishment from India in 1823 was accompanied by new press regulations, including a return to licensing and prohibiting discussion of sensitive topics. (The EIC also wished to reintroduce censorship, but this was nixed by the Tory ministry, which wanted to avoid further inflaming public opinion in Britain.) In response, Rammohun filed a memorial to the Supreme Court in Bengal, asking that the new press regulations not be registered into law. The memorial stressed the importance of a free press for diffusing knowledge, encouraging social progress, and informing the government of public opinion and mismanagement of its affairs. These were all familiar arguments of the day. New here was Rammohun's claim that Indian loyalty to British rule could be endangered if this boon was taken away. After the memorial failed to sway the Supreme Court, Rammohun closed down his Persian-language newspaper, publicly claiming that the new press regulations were the reason. He then took the lead in drafting a petition to the Privy Council asking that body to overturn the new regulations. The petition elaborated on the issue of loyalty, noting that Bengali Hindus viewed the British as liberators who freed them from Muslim tyranny. The British had treated Bengalis equitably, extending to them the love of liberty and promotion of social progress that distinguished Britain. Now, fearful of publicity and out to suppress public criticism of government officials, the EIC had revoked a legal privilege that Bengalis cherished as an important consolation for the loss of political privileges under British rule.[61]

Buckingham returned to Britain shortly after J. S. Mill published his newspaper articles on Carlile's case and freedom of the press. The exiled editor began agitating at once against his banishment and the new press regulations, finding a receptive audience among Britons opposed to the Tory crackdown on the press at home. As Buckingham's cause became a celebrated one, word also spread of Rammohun's opposition to the press regulations in Bengal. Various individuals praised Rammohun as a champion of a free press in political speeches, remarks before the Privy Council, and assorted publications. Among those doing so were people well known to James and J. S. Mill – Joseph Hume, for instance – or moving in Bentham's circle, particularly Leicester Stanhope, James Young, and Buckingham.[62] There was also William J. Fox, a passionate advocate of freedom of expression who wielded arguments that anticipated those of *On Liberty* and who was deeply familiar with Rammohun's writings.[63] In short, J. S. Mill began his publishing career by taking up a cause that he could not help but know that he shared with a very famous Bengali.

This neglected relationship deserves further scrutiny. Here I will focus on one aspect of it. The argument for a free press was localised in the Indian context by its defenders to stress its importance for helping improve a society seen as backward, ignorant, and superstitious. The dissemination of new information and advanced ideas was deemed vital for such social conditions and a free press likened to a great engine of social progress. Missionaries made this case, as did Buckingham and Rammohun in their Calcutta periodicals prior to 1823. Rammohun also reiterated it in his protests against the new press regulations. After Buckingham's expulsion, numerous individuals took up this argument in Britain. Rammohun's name was often invoked as an example of the great intellectual progress underway in India but now threatened by the EIC's restrictions on the press. These references drew their strength from his celebrity status in Britain as an intellectual versed in the arts of biblical criticism and religious controversy, as well as his growing fame as a social reformer leading the campaign against widow burning, which was then just beginning to captivate the public mind.[64] These and other examples of what was deemed the march of intellect were cited as proof that liberty was not a consquence, but a cause of social progress. Rather than a gift reserved for those enjoying an advanced level of civilisation, liberty was a precondition for achieving such a state. Joseph Hume argued along these lines in a speech before the EIC's Court of Proprietors, as did James Young in an 1825 essay in the *Westminster Review*. Buckingham also used the famous Rammohun Roy as evidence of the intellectual progress made possible by a free press in India, warning of the threat to that progress by the new press regulations. In his *Sketch of the History and Influence of the Press in British India* (1823) Leicester Stanhope argued at great length that a free press was an essential condition of social progress, pointing to Rammohun – someone 'perfectly well known' in Britain – as evidence of the fact.[65]

Stanhope's work was directed at the EIC and its supporters who argued that the expulsion of Buckingham and the new press regulations were necessary given the colonial situation in Bengal and, as they saw it, the backward state of Indian society. These arguments were presented in stark fashion by Robert Spankie in 1825 when Buckingham's petition for redress of his grievances against the EIC was heard by the Privy Council. Representing the EIC, Spankie noted that freedom of the press might be appropriate for a free nation, but not so for a conquered people unprepared for such advanced liberties. 'It will require the lapse of a thousand years for the people of [India], if at all capable of it, to arrive at any thing like a European civilization, and the enlightened freedom of mind Europeans enjoy.' Thomas Denman, Buckingham's lead counsel before the Privy

Council, answered this using ideas akin to those of Stanhope and the others. Liberty of the press was a great source of moral and social improvement, and there was no reason to assume that it would not work in India as elsewhere. Denman also chided the EIC for assuming that the benefits of moderate and just government would not be felt in India as elsewhere, because Indians could only respond to 'power, power, power alone'.[66]

The comments of Denman, Stanhope, and the others are striking when one recalls Mill's (in)famous opening argument in *On Liberty* that his defence of individual liberty was intended only for those living in advanced societies.[67] Karuna Mantena notes that this claim raises the theoretical question why liberty and free institutions are not equally needed in less advanced societies.[68] A better question, I think, is why Mill turned his back on what was to him the familiar notion that liberty is a precondition of intellectual and social progress. Not only had this been widely used during the agitation for a free press in the 1820s, he himself had used a version of the argument in a contribution to that agitation. In his 1825 essay for the *Westminster Review*, Mill noted that critics of free discussion argued that 'the incapacity of the people to form correct opinions' was reason alone not to have a free press. But, Mill asked, if the people seem incurably ignorant, why is this so? There is only one answer: 'if they are ignorant, it is precisely because that discussion, which alone can remove ignorance, has been withheld from them'. History affords abundant proof, he added, that free discussion 'produces change: change, not indeed in any thing good, but in every thing that is bad, bad laws, bad judicature, and bad government'.[69]

Why Mill rejected this universalist view of liberty in favour of a more restrictive one in 1859 is a topic for another essay. Such a study would also explore the contrast between Mill's defence of Rajput nationalism at his India House desk with his largely negative assessment of linguistic and ethnic identities in *Considerations on Representative Government*.[70] It would examine as well why his interest in throwing himself into the minds of Hindus and others evaporated by the time of some of his later publications. In works such as *Considerations* and 'A Few Words on Non-Intervention', as Uday Mehta and Jennifer Pitts argue, Mill displayed little of the sympathetic imagination that characterised Edmund Burke's intellectual engagement with India.[71] Pratap Mehta rightly notes that the lack of appreciation for other cultures in these late works is puzzling because of Mill's stated interest in throwing himself into the minds of others.[72] As we have seen, that interest manifested itself in the 1830s when Mill was under the sway of Carlyle's version of German hermeneutics and coming into his own as a member of a colonial bureaucracy with pragmatic reasons for sympathetic understanding of others. But something happened to render *Einfühlung* seemingly invisible by the time Mill wrote key works in his mature period. An investigation of that apparent disappearance would need to address Mill's intellectual break with Carlyle, which erupted into the open when the Scot voiced a strident, racist imperialism in writings on Ireland and Jamaica that Mill could not tolerate. It would also need to be mindful of Mill's enduring debt to the EIC's administrative ethos in his late thoughts on Rajput and Irish nationalism, where the principle of cultural empathy is still evident.[73]

Above all, such a future study would need to explain why Rammohun Roy's ideas, career, and contributions appear to have made no impact on Mill's thought. As the multiple pathways for interaction examined above indicate, this lacuna in the story of Mill's intellectual career is astounding. It acquires additional significance when recent criticisms of Mill's liberal imperialism are considered. Dipesh Chakrabarty argues that Mill – by claiming that Indians and others were not yet ready for representative government and individual liberty – had consigned these peoples 'to an imaginary waiting room of history'. In this historicist consciousness, colonised peoples were asked to be patient until they reached the destination that others, notably Europeans, had already reached.[74] Mantena adds that Mill stressed so many difficulties and pitfalls in the process of social advancement that this waiting room of history might seem a permanent location for those trapped in it.[75] This notion of a long waiting period, of course, carries with it the idea of a lengthy, if not permanent, period of tutelage under colonial rule. Francis Hutchins long ago explored this facet of imperial ideology in British India.[76] Mill's evocation of it, as rephrased by Chakrabarty and Mantena, recalls Robert Spankie's comments before the Privy Council in 1825: India is a thousand years away from being fit, if ever, for such liberties as civilised Europeans enjoy. What makes Mill's endorsement of this view so striking is that it required forgetting or dismissing the celebrated example of Rammohun Roy, as well as the widely used argument that Rammohun proved that liberty was a universal engine of social and intellectual progress.[77] When one thinks of the many people Mill admired who celebrated Rammohun's intellectual talents and progressive views on religion, politics, women's rights, and related matters, this is a very curious case of inattention.

This neglect is also relevant to Mill's views on social development. Bhikhu Parekh, Uday Mehta, and Pitts argue that Mill presented stark binaries of civilisation and barbarism – of progressive and stagnant societies – and claimed that despotism, including colonial rule, was therefore essential for advancing out of the stage of barbarism.[78] Inder Marwah and others counter that Mill was more subtle than this, recognising heterogeneity within nations at different stages of development, divergent paths for social development, and a multitude of contingent factors – such as the international political system, economic structures, national culture, and local traditions – affecting a given society's stage of development and potential for future progress or regression.[79] Both interpretations find support in Mill's works, yet each leaves one wondering why the example of Rammohun Roy never comes into view. As the evidence considered in this essay suggests, that omission is striking given Mill's intellectual passions and social networks. The fact is, in writing about social progress, Mill overlooked Rammohun's role in abolishing *sati* and promoting women's legal rights that British feminists admired; disregarded the brilliant contributions to theological controversies and rational religion that William J. Fox and Unitarians praised; and ignored the efforts on behalf of a free press that inspired Bentham's confidence that Rammohun ought to be in Parliament to help reform the British constitution. What this neglect – or forgetting – reveals about Mill's theory of social development – and any supposedly essential role for despotism in that theory – is an important matter awaiting investigation.

Conclusion: an unfinished project

J. S. Mill was situated like few other major Western intellectuals to participate in cultural and intellectual exchange with the non-Western world. His imperial career brought him into nearly daily contact with the ideas, beliefs, customs, history, institutions, and other features of Indian society. Although filtered through the pens of local British officials, a different intellectual world was opened to Mill for some thirty-five years, years in which he wrote some of his most important works, or began developing the ideas for them. Living in the metropole of a vast empire also exposed Mill (and his contemporaries) to increasing numbers of Asians, West Indians, and above all South Asians, who came to London during the course of the nineteenth century.[80] Some of those Indian visitors met Mill or attended his public lectures. In the case of Keshab Chandra Sen, Mill was invited to a public reception for the Bengali social and religious reformer in 1870. Unable to attend, Mill nonetheless sought out Sen to inquire about Indian political affairs.[81] In a word, at his India House desk and in his private life in London, Mill came into contact with worlds foreign to his own experience and views.

Accompanying these close encounters was nearly simultaneous exposure to intellectual and pragmatic imperatives for cross-cultural understanding. Through Carlyle, Mill came to key insights of German hermeneutics at the same time that his daily work brought home the need for a sympathetic understanding of Indians. These imperatives, alongside his official engagement with Indian affairs, placed Mill in a situation rich with potential for cross-cultural understanding, the exchange of ideas, and the development of transnational perspectives.

Finally, Mill's personal situation – disciple of Bentham, lover of a Unitarian woman, and advocate of liberty of the press, women's rights, and other liberal causes – brought to his attention one of the leading intellectual figures and social reformers of modern Indian history. Surrounded by a multitude of Britons celebrating Rammohun Roy's many contributions to both Indian and British intellectual, political, and religious life, Mill had a unique opportunity to incorporate the famous Bengali's ideas and perspective into his own, and modern European, thought.

Exploring what transpired with this potential for intellectual influence across cultural borders during the course of Mill's intellectual career is an unfinished project. The issues are important and the results yet puzzling, as this essay suggests: Mill's interest in *Einfühlung* evaporated in key respects but lingered in empathy for Rajput nationalism and Irish alterity, whereas shared intellectual networks, political passions, and social agendas were not enough to render a transnational celebrity of Rammohun Roy's stature worthy of Mill's pen. Elsewhere I have indicated areas where the impact of Indian ideas and examples can be detected in Mill's writings, such as his criticism of Bentham for ignoring the importance of political loyalty and his argument for the capacity of women to hold political office.[82] Others have also investigated South Asian influences in Mill's thought. Jonardon Ganeri, for instance, has traced a debt to ancient Indian Emergentism in Mill's philosophy of the mind, arguing that Mill (and other British Emergentists) came to know of this materialist doctrine through the work of the pioneering Indologist, H. T. Colebrooke.[83] More investigations of this sort are needed to assess fully the impact on Mill of the intellectual exchanges engendered by colonialism. This impact has additional significance because, as recent studies remind us, Mill's writings in turn influenced Indian liberals and nationalists.[84] Ideas, texts, and people moved in multiple directions. Mill participated in this phenomenon of empire, but we do not yet know the full significance of the fact.

Abbreviations

CW: *The Collected Works of John Stuart Mill*, gen. ed., J. M. Robson (Toronto: University of Toronto Press, 1962–91), 33 vols.

Notes

1 Samuel Moyn and Andrew Sartori, eds, *Global Intellectual History* (New York: Columbia University Press, 2013), 9–16.
2 Ann Laura Stoler and Frederick Cooper, 'Between Metropole and Colony: Rethinking a Research Agenda', in Frederick Cooper and Ann Laura Stoler, eds, *Tensions of Empire: Colonial Cultures in a Bourgeois World* (Berkeley and Los Angeles: University of California Press, 1997), 28–9.
3 For these and related issues see Anthony J. Parel, ed., 'Editor's Introduction', in M. K. Gandhi, *Hind Swaraj and Other Writings* (Cambridge: Cambridge University Press, 1997), xiii–lxii; David Hardiman, *Gandhi in His Time and Ours: The Global Legacy of His Ideas* (New York: Columbia University Press, 2003); David Arnold, *Gandhi* (Harlow: Pearson Education, 2001); and Eugene F. Irschick, 'Gandhian Non-Violent Protest: Rituals of Avoidance or Rituals of Confrontation?', *Economic and Political Weekly*, 21 (19 July 1986), 1276–85.
4 I explore many of these issues in my article, 'Intimacy and Colonial Knowledge', *Journal of Colonialism and Colonial History*, 3: 2 (2002).
5 Rosane Rocher, 'British Orientalism in the Eighteenth Century: The Dialectics of Knowledge and Government', in Carol A. Breckenridge and Peter van der Veer, eds, *Orientalism and the Postcolonial Predicament: Perspectives on South Asia* (Delhi: Oxford University Press, 1994), 234.
6 C. A. Bayly, *Empire and Information: Intelligence Gathering and Social Communication in India, 1780–1870* (Cambridge: Cambridge University Press, 1996), Introduction, chs 1 and 5.

7   Bernard S. Cohn, *Colonialism and Its Forms of Knowledge: The British in India* (Princeton, NJ: Princeton University Press, 1996), 21.

8   Shruti Kapila, ed., *An Intellectual History for India* (Cambridge: Cambridge University Press, 2010), v–vi; Cohn, *Colonialism*; and Bayly, *Empire and Information*.

9   William Pinch, 'Same Difference in India and Europe', *History and Theory*, 38 (1999), 393–8. The implications of Cohn's approach are manifest in many of the essays in Breckenridge and van der Veer, *Orientalism*.

10 The notion that the British invaded an indigenous epistemological space, subverted it to colonial ends and marginalised Indian informants is advanced by Cohn in 'The Command of Language and the Language of Command', in Cohn, *Colonialism*, 16–56. For a more nuanced view of how Indian informants and their contributions to British administrative discourse were eventually marginalised or lost, see Nicholas B. Dirks, 'Colonial Histories and Native Informants: Biography of an Archive', in Breckenridge and van der Veer, *Orientalism*, 279–313.

11 Eugene F. Irschick, *Dialogue and History: Constructing South India, 1795–1895* (Berkeley and Los Angeles: University of California Press, 1994), 6, 193. Irschick challenges the views of Edward Said (*Orientalism* [New York: Vintage, 1979]), but his arguments apply equally well to the work of Cohn.

12 Norbert Peabody, 'Cents, Sense, Census: Human Inventories in Late Precolonial and Early Colonial India', *Comparative Studies in Society and History*, 43 (2001), 819–50 (quotation, 842). For examples of the scholarship Peabody challenges, see Bernard S. Cohn, *An Anthropologist among the Historians and Other Essays* (Oxford: Oxford University Press, 1987), ch. 10; Nicholas B. Dirks, 'Castes of Mind', *Representations*, 37 (1992), 61, 67–9, 74; Dirks, 'Colonial Histories'; and Arjun Appadurai, 'Number in the Colonial Imagination', in Breckenridge and van der Veer, *Orientalism*, 314–39. Cohn and especially Dirks acknowledge Indian contributions to British information gathering, but both suggest that these contributions were appropriated, and the Indian contributors marginalised, by the colonial regime (Cohn, *Anthropologist*, 245–7; Dirks, 'Colonial Histories').

13 Rosane Rocher and Ludo Rocher, *The Making of Western Indology: Henry Thomas Colebrooke and the East India Company* (London: Routledge, 2012), esp. 200–1; Rosane Rocher, *Alexander Hamilton (1762–1824): A Chapter in the Early History of Sanskrit Philology* (New Haven, CT: American Oriental Society, 1968), 123; Rocher, 'British Orientalism', 215–49; Rosane Rocher, 'The Career of Radhakanta Tarkavagisa, an Eighteenth-Century Pandit in British Employ', *Journal of the American Oriental Society*, 109 (1989), 627–33; and Rosane Rocher, *Orientalism, Poetry, and the Millennium: The Checkered Life of Nathaniel Brassey Halhed, 1751–1830* (Delhi: South Asia Books, 1983), 241–3.

14 Rocher, 'British Orientalism', 240; Rosane Rocher and Ludo Rocher, *Founders of Western Indology: August Wilhelm von Schlegel and Henry Thomas Colebrooke in Correspondence, 1820–37* (Wiesbaden: Harrassowitz, 2013), Introduction; Michael S. Dodson, 'Contesting Translations: Orientalism and the Interpretation of the *Vedas*', in Kapila, *Intellectual History*, 35–43; Michael S. Dodson, *Orientalism, Empire, and National Culture: India, 1770–1880* (New York: Palgrave Macmillan, 2007), ch. 2.

15 H. H. Wilson, 'Review of [A. W. von Schlegel's translation of] Bhagavad Gita', in Reinhold Rost, ed., *Works of the Late Horace Hayman Wilson*, 12 vols (London: Trübner, 1862–71), vol. 5, 127; A. W. de Schlegel, *Réflexions sur l'Étude des Langues Asiatiques …* (Bonn: Weber, 1832), 201.

16 Thomas Macaulay, 'Minute [on Indian Education] … dated 2 February 1835', in Lynn Zastoupil and Martin Moir, eds, *The Great Indian Education Debate: Documents Relating*

to the Orientalist-Anglicist Controversy, 1781–1843 (Richmond, Surrey: Curzon, 1999), 165.

17 J. S. Mill, 'On Genius' (1832), CW 1: 333.

18 J. S. Mill, 'Ware's Letters from Palmyra' (1838), CW 1: 459.

19 J. S. Mill, 'Carlyle's French Revolution' (1837), CW 20: 133–8.

20 J. G. Herder, *The Spirit of Hebrew Poetry*, trans. James Marsh, 2 vols (Burlington, VT: Edward Smith, 1833), 1, 28.

21 Magdalena Nowak, 'The Complicated History of *Einfühlung*', *Argument*, 1 (2011), 303; John Zammito, 'Herder and Historical Metanarrative: What's Philosophical about History?', in Hans Adler and Wulf Koepke, eds, *A Companion to the Works of Johann Gottfried Herder* (Rochester, NY: Camden, 2009), 65.

22 M. H. Abrams, *The Mirror and the Lamp: Romantic Theory and the Critical Tradition* (New York: Oxford University Press, 1953), 245–7, 331–2. Walter Jackson Bate distinguishes a British 'sympathetic imagination' from *Einfühlung*: 'The Sympathetic Imagination in Eighteenth-Century English Criticism', *English Literary History*, 12 (1945), 144–5, and *John Keats* (Cambridge, MA: Harvard University Press, 1963), 256.

23 Michael N. Forster, *After Herder: Philosophy of Language in the German Tradition* (Oxford: Oxford University Press, 2010), ch. 7, esp. 267–8 n10.

24 See the sparse references in the indexes to Mill's collected works: CW 33: 211.

25 J. S. Mill, 'Armand Carrel' (1837) and 'Guizot's Essays and Lectures on History' (1867), CW 20: 185, 261; Mill, 'Coleridge' (1840), CW 10: 139. See also Mill's article in the *Examiner* for 22 April 1832, CW 23: 448, and John C. Cairns, 'Introduction', CW 20: lxviii, lxxix.

26 Mill owned a copy of the 1825 German edition – as well as the 1846 London edition – of Schlegel's *Ueber dramatische Kunst und Litteratur* where *Einfühlung* is presented in the opening pages as a guiding principle of literary criticism (see the list of Mill's private library at: www.some.ox.ac.uk/4055/all/1/Special_collections.aspx, accessed 20 January 2015). But there is no mention of Schlegel or the lectures in the general index of CW. Mill came to know of Schleiermacher's works only in 1833 – after he had published 'On Genius' – and mostly admired him for his philological work on Plato: F. E. Sparshott, 'Introduction', CW 11: xix–xx; J. S. Mill, 'The Protagoras', and 'The Apology of Socrates', CW 11: 41n and 151n; J. S. Mill to John Sterling, 12 July 1833, CW 12: 167–8.

27 Rosemary Ashton, *The German Idea: Four English Writers and the Reception of German Thought, 1800–1860* (Cambridge: Cambridge University Press, 1980), Introduction, ch. 2 and 105–11 (quotation, 105). Ashton demonstrates that Coleridge also played an important role in the diffusion of German thought, but there is little reason to think that Mill discovered *Einfühlung* through that channel.

28 See Mill's letters to John Sterling (20–22 October 1831 and 24 May 1832), CW 12: 85, 101, as well as his *Autobiography* where he wrote of becoming 'one of [Carlyle's] most fervent admirers' (CW 1: 183). For a brief account of the evolving nature of Mill's famous relationship with Carlyle, see John M. Robson, *The Improvement of Mankind: The Social and Political Thought of John Stuart Mill* (Toronto: University of Toronto Press, 1968), 80–95.

29 Suzy Anger, 'Carlyle: Between Biblical Exegesis and Romantic Hermeneutics', *Texas Studies in Literature and Language*, 40 (1998), 78, 85–6.

30 *Ibid.*, 93n5.

31 Thomas Carlyle, 'The State of German Literature', in H. D. Traill, ed., *The Works of Thomas Carlyle in Thirty Volumes*, Centenary edn (New York: Charles Scribner's Sons, 1896–1901) 26: 44–5, 50, 52–3, 55.

32 Thomas Carlyle, 'Novalis', in H. D. Traill, ed., *The Works of Thomas Carlyle in Thirty Volumes*, Centenary edn (London: Chapman and Hall, 1896–99) 27: 50.

33 Carlyle, 'Biography', *Works of Carlyle* (London) 28: 44.

34 J. S. Mill, 'Alison's History of the French Revolution', CW 20: 114.

35 J. S. Mill to John Sterling, 20–2 October 1831 and 24 May 1832, CW 12: 85, 101; Mill, *Autobiography*, CW 1:181–3.

36 Lynn Zastoupil, *John Stuart Mill and India* (Stanford, CA: Stanford University Press, 1994), ch. 3 (esp. 76–8).

37 John Malcolm, *A Memoir of Central India*, 2 vols (London: Kingsbury, Parbury and Allen, 1823) 2: 437 (Appendix 18).

38 John Briggs, *Letters Addressed to a Young Person in India* … (London: John Murray, 1828), 187–8.

39 William Chaplin, Circular Letter to Collectors in the Deccan, 28 May 1823, Deccan Commissioner's Files, vol. 424, #6609, Pune Archives, Pune, India. Chaplin quotes Chesterfield's advice without mentioning his name.

40 Briggs, *Letters*, iii–iv.

41 *Ibid.*, 64 (quotation), 67–75, 96–108, 179–80, *passim* (references to an empire of opinion are on 139 and 186).

42 Minutes by H. T. Prinsep (31 July and 13 October 1835) and Charles T. Metcalfe (14 August 1835), British Library, Asia, Pacific and Africa Collections, F/4/1575, Board's Collection 64255, 105–211 (for the views of Metcalfe cited here, see 130, 134, 139, 147, 149–50, 151, 154).

43 Zastoupil, *Mill and India*, 51–5, 152–4.

44 *Ibid.*, 107–16.

45 *Ibid.*, 184–5. Very similar sentiments can be found in Briggs, *Letters*, 158–62, 184–6.

46 Mill, 'On Genius', 333.

47 Lynn Zastoupil, *Rammohun Roy and the Making of Victorian Britain* (New York: Palgrave Macmillan, 2010), Introduction.

48 *Ibid.*, *passim*.

49 *Ibid.*, *passim*.

50 C. A. Bayly, 'Rammohan Roy and the Advent of Constitutional Liberalism in India, 1800–30', in Kapila, *Intellectual History*, 18–34; Bayly, *Recovering Liberties: Indian Thought in the Age of Liberalism and Empire* (Cambridge: Cambridge University Press, 2012), chs 2–3 (esp. 42–60).

51 Zastoupil, *Rammohun Roy*, ch. 9.

52 *Ibid.*, 148–50.

53 *Ibid.*, 4, 181n53.

54 CW 32: 66, and 33: 340. Where Mill got the signature is a mystery. He may have received a letter from Rammohun. Or he may have acquired the signature from a letter addressed to someone he knew well, which, as the next paragraphs indicate, could have been any one of many individuals.

55 Zastoupil, *Rammohun Roy*, chs 2–3, 5, Appendix A and 227n37. For the joint authorship of Martineau and Fox of the review essay, see Francis E. Mineka, *The Dissidence of Dissent: 'The Monthly Repository', 1806–1838* … (Chapel Hill: University of North Carolina Press, 1944), 407, 417; for Mill, Fox and the Taylors, see Michael St. John Packe, *The Life of John Stuart Mill* (New York: Macmillan, 1954), 116–28.

56 E. P. Thompson, *The Making of the English Working Class* (New York: Vintage, 1966), ch. 16.

57 Zastoupil, *Rammohun Roy*, ch. 6; Bayly, *Recovering Liberties*, 73–82.

58 Zastoupil, *Rammohun Roy*, 156–9.

59 Stefan Collini, 'Introduction', CW 21: xl; Ann P. Robson, 'Introduction', CW 22: xxvii–xxx, xxxii–xl. For specimens of Mill's contributions, see 'Law of Libel and Liberty of the Press', CW 21: 2–34, and various newspaper writings on religious persecution, freedom of discussion, oaths and the libel laws in CW 22: 6–18, 21–4, 30–3, 46–8, 91–4.

60 Zastoupil, *Rammohun Roy*, 153–7.

61 *Ibid.*, 101–2.

62 *Ibid.*, 103–9.

63 *Ibid.*, 16–17; [William J. Fox], 'Religious Prosecutions', *Westminster Review*, 2 (July 1824), 1–27.

64 For the relationship between these issues and Rammohun's celebrity, see Zastoupil, *Rammohun Roy*, chs 3–5.

65 *Ibid.*, 105–9.

66 *Ibid.*, 103–5.

67 J. S. Mill, *On Liberty* (1859), CW 18: 224.

68 Karuna Mantena, 'Mill and the Imperial Predicament', in Nadia Urbinati and Alex Zakaras, eds, *J. S. Mill's Political Thought: A Bicentennial Reassessment* (Cambridge: Cambridge University Press, 2007), 306.

69 Mill, 'Law of Libel and Liberty of the Press', 10–11.

70 J. S. Mill, *Considerations on Representative Government* (1861), CW 19: 546–9, 551.

71 Uday Singh Mehta, *Liberalism and Empire: A Study in Nineteenth-Century British Liberal Thought* (Chicago: University of Chicago Press, 1999), 93–6, 106–12, 159–66, 212–17; Jennifer Pitts, *A Turn to Empire: The Rise of Imperial Liberalism in Britain and France* (Princeton, NJ: Princeton University Press, 2005), 136, 140.

72 Pratap Bhanu Mehta, 'Liberalism, Nation, and Empire: The Case of J. S. Mill', in Sankar Muthu, ed., *Empire and Modern Political Thought* (Cambridge: Cambridge University Press, 2012), 234.

73 Without directly addressing *Einfühlung*, Inder Marwah locates an ongoing regard for cultural diversity and national character in Mill's philosophy of history: Marwah, 'Complicating Barbarism and Civilization: Mill's Complex Sociology of Human Development', *History of Political Thought*, 32 (2011), 345–66; Marwah, 'Two Concepts of Liberal Developmentalism', *European Journal of Political Theory*, 15 (2016), 97–123.

74 Dipesh Chakrabarty, *Provincializing Europe: Postcolonial Thought and Historical Difference* (Princeton, NJ: Princeton University Press, 2000), 8.

75 Mantena, 'Mill and the Imperial Predicament', 308.

76 Francis G. Hutchins, *The Illusion of Permanence: British Imperialism in India* (Princeton, NJ: Princeton University Press, 1967).

77 There is reason to think that Mill came to dismiss, rather than forget, the claim that a free press was an engine of progress: see his 1852 testimony before Parliament where he stated that 'both the dangers and the advantages of the free press in India have been very much overrated' (CW 30: 70).

78 Bhikhu Parekh, 'Decolonizing Liberalism', in Aleksandras Shtromas, ed., *The End of 'Isms'?: Reflections on the Fate of Ideological Politics after Communism's Collapse* (Oxford: Blackwell, 1994), 87–8; Mehta, *Liberalism and Empire*, 104–5; Pitts, *Turn to Empire*, 136–46.

79 Marwah, 'Complicating Barbarism and Civilization' and 'Two Concepts'. See also Mark Tunick, 'Tolerant Imperialism: John Stuart Mill's Defense of British Rule in India', *Review of Politics*, 68 (2006), 586–611.

80 For more on this phenomenon, see Peter Fryer, *Staying Power: The History of Black People in Britain* (London: Pluto, 1984); Rozina Visram, *Ayahs, Lascars and*

Princes: Indians in Britain, 1700–1947 (London: Pluto, 1986); Rozina Visram, *Asians in Britain: 400 Years of History* (London: Pluto, 2002); Michael H. Fisher, *Counterflows to Colonialism: Indian Travellers and Settlers in Britain, 1600–1857* (Delhi: Permanent Black, 2004); and Michael H. Fisher, Shompa Lahiri, and Shinder Thandi, *A South-Asian History of Britain: Four Centuries of Peoples from the Indian Sub-Continent* (Westport, CT: Greenwood, 2007).

81 S. Ambirajan, 'John Stuart Mill and India', in Martin I. Moir, Douglas M. Peers, and Lynn Zastoupil, eds, *J. S. Mill's Encounter with India* (Toronto: University of Toronto Press, 1999), 243; Sophia Dobson Collet, ed., *Keshub Chunder Sen's English Visit* (London: Strahan, 1871), 3–4.

82 Lynn Zastoupil, 'India, J.S. Mill, and "Western" Culture', in Moir, Peers, and Zastoupil, *Mill's Encounter with India*, 111–48, esp. 131–41.

83 Jonardon Ganeri, 'Emergentisms, Ancient and Modern', *Mind*, 120: 479 (2011), 671–703, esp. 676, 683–4.

84 Ambirajan, 'John Stuart Mill and India', 240–53; Bayly, *Recovering Liberties*, 9–13, 200–3.

2

Rethinking resistance: Spencer, Krishnavarma, and *The Indian Sociologist*

Inder S. Marwah

In recent years, political theorists and intellectual historians have begun to examine the impacts of empire in shaping the conceptual frameworks of late modern political thought, and more particularly, the ways that ideas were absorbed, integrated, synthesized and refracted in colonial contexts situated at the intersection of local and global knowledge systems.[1] This chapter aims to contribute to these efforts by excavating a philosophically distinctive line of anti-colonial political thought developed by Shyamji Krishnavarma between 1905 and 1913. Krishnavarma was, among other things, a self-made industrialist, a one-time prime minister of an Indian state, a lawyer, Oxford University's first Indian MA, and, from 1905 until his death in 1930, an ardent anti-imperialist. While his resistance to empire adopted many guises – from founding and presiding over the Indian Home Rule Society, to funding scholarships and lectureships advancing the cause of Indian independence, to inaugurating London's infamous India House – this chapter will focus on *The Indian Sociologist* (IS hereafter), a radical anti-colonial journal created, edited and published by Krishnavarma from 1905–14 and 1921–22 that, for a time, was an important mouthpiece of the early (pre-Gandhian) Indian nationalist movement's extremist faction at the international level.[2]

I will argue that, in the pages of the IS, Krishnavarma developed an anti-colonialism that was deeply critical of the quietism of Indian liberalism (espoused by early Congress moderates), avoided the nativism of his fellow extremists, and resisted the romanticized violence of the nationalist movement's terrorist faction by drawing on 'the Social Science'[3] developed by Herbert Spencer in the latter half of the nineteenth century. Beyond endorsing his own scathing critique of British imperialism, I will contend that Krishnavarma's anti-colonialism was shaped by three distinctive features of Spencer's political sociology. First, Krishnavarma adopted Spencer's view of empire as a given *sociological* condition, characterized by distinctive and recurring features; this recognition of the commonalities binding all colonized states, I will suggest, animated the cosmopolitan bent of his anti-imperialism. Second, both Spencer and Krishnavarma treated the imperial condition as predicated on, and sustained by, a distinctive set of affects and sentiments; drawing on Spencer's evolutionist account of social change, Krishnavarma understood his own activism (and, more broadly, the ascendant nationalist movement to which it contributed) as effecting the *affective* shifts preceding India's political liberation. Finally, I will argue that Spencer's analysis of 'militant' societies informed (and contextualizes) Krishnavarma's advocacy for political violence in resisting empire, the apotheosis of such a 'militant' condition. In total, then, Krishnavarma's turn to Spencerian sociology animated an anti-colonialism that was distinctively *political* (rather than nativist), *cosmopolitan* (rather than inward-looking), and *sociological* (rather than romantic or anti-modern).

In Section 1, I begin by briefly sketching out the unusual heterodoxy of Krishnavarma's early intellectual development, shaped by the confluence of Eastern and Western influences. In Section 2, I situate him in relation to the moderate, extremist and terrorist factions of the early Indian nationalist movement and Indian National Congress (INC), sketching out their respective accounts of the means and ends required to achieve political independence and the historical contexts in which their positions developed. I here focus on two distinctive features of Krishnavarma's nationalism: its explicitly political – rather than romantic, providentialist, spiritualist, or nativist – orientation, and its cosmopolitanism. In Section 3, I delve into the philosophical foundations of his political thought, as elaborated in the pages of the IS, and on its intellectual debts to Spencer. Finally, I conclude by suggesting that Krishnavarma's distinctive strand of anti-colonialism is worth recovering for both historical and philosophical reasons. From a historical perspective, despite having fallen into relative obscurity, Krishnavarma helped to develop and propagate the ideals of the early nationalist movement's extremist faction, which became central to Gandhi's political thought and activism, and so, ultimately, to India's political independence. From a philosophical standpoint, his turn to Spencer informed a nuanced analysis of imperial domination and of its endemic violence that sharpens our vision of the colonial condition, and more broadly, of the productive transmission and translation of ideas across colonial borders. In total, then, Krishnavarma's political thought comprises a philosophically distinctive and in many respects particularly fruitful analysis of the harms of colonialism and political domination.

1 Intellectual foundations

Shyamji Krishnavarma was born to a poor family in Mandvi, a town in the state of Kutch, in 1857.[4] He was by all accounts a particularly adept student, and was fortunate to have had his primary and secondary school educations (both English-language) financed by (respectively) his father and Mathuradas Lavaji, a wealthy Kutchi patron.[5] Krishnavarma concurrently attended a *pathsala*, a traditional Sanskrit school, through which he developed a profound knowledge of both Sanskrit and of seminal texts in the Hindu tradition. As Harald Fischer-Tiné notes, Krishnavarma drew an astonishing level of support from patrons and donors in his caste community, whose reformist inclinations (in conjunction with the rise of organized philanthropy and public spiritedness among the Bhatia caste) made them particularly receptive to sponsoring so proficient a student. He was thus the beneficiary of 'parallel education systems' – the English focusing on the humanities, the Hindu on the rote learning typical of Brahminical pedagogy.[6] With the support of another Gujurati benefactor, Krishnavarma attended Elphinstone College, where he was introduced to Bombay's economic and political elites and to the Hindu reform movement gaining ground in the 1870s.

Most importantly, Krishnavarma's immersion in Bombay's reformist circles brought him into contact, in 1875, with Swami Dayananda Saraswati, founder of the Arya Samaj, a Hindu reformist organization that militated against caste hierarchies and outdated social practices (such as child marriage, idol worship, and enforced widowhood).[7] Saraswati saw India's rejuvenation in a return to the Vedas, issuing a profound critique of what he saw as rising idiosyncratic and unjust cultural practices and 'reconcil[ing] his individual reformist visions with the claim to scriptural authority through the systematic purification of Hindu tradition from later accretions, the apodictic selection of texts as canonical and a reinterpretation of the scriptures based on the rigorous application of his own very peculiar understanding of Sanskrit and Vedic grammar'.[8] Krishnavarma was profoundly taken with Sarawasti's vision; as Har Bilas recounts, 'Shyamji came more and more under his influence, and fully assimilated his teachings based on his rational interpretation of the Vedas … Shyamji accepted Swami Dayanand's teachings and became his pupil',[9] ultimately taking up employment with Bombay's Arya Samaj in 1876. Even thirty years later, Krishnavarma remained steadfast in acknowledging the depth of Saraswati's influence, describing his studies in England as 'a collateral culture … our original training having been purely Oriental, under the guidance of the late Svami Dayananda'.[10]

Alongside his engagements with the Arya Samaj, Krishnavarma continued to 'ma[k]e use of the "western knowledge" he had acquired'[11] to integrate himself into the colonial milieu, through which he met Monier Williams, an Oxford professor of Sanskrit, in 1877. Williams was sufficiently impressed by Krishnavarma's knowledge of Sanskrit and of the Vedas to invite him to Oxford as an assistant. Krishnavarma had, by this point, come into considerable renown as a Sanskrit scholar, both within India and beyond.[12] Through the Arya Samaj, he became known to Helena Blavatsky and Colonel Henry Steel Olcott, founders of the Theosophical Society and devotees of Sarawasti;[13] Blavatsky in fact addressed Krishnavarma (all of twenty-one years old at the time), as 'one of the most prominent and promising members of the Arya Samaj'.[14] Both the theosophists and local elites that valued his expertise in Sanskrit opposed Krishnavarma's move to Oxford, attesting to the considerable reputation that he had developed as a scholar and orator.

Krishnavarma nevertheless made his way to England in 1879, where, under Williams' tutelage, he further developed both his oriental and Western studies and — most significantly — was introduced to Herbert Spencer's philosophy.[15] Spencer was the second pillar of his intellectual formation; Krishnavarma would describe him, in a 1909 interview with *L'éclair*, as 'the great philosopher, my master ... the man whom I admired and esteemed most in the world, and of whom I consider myself an humble disciple'.[16] Spencer's influence over Krishnavarma is difficult to overstate. Beyond the IS's innumerable references to Spencer's work, quotations from his *Principles of Ethics* and *Study of Sociology* adorned the journal's masthead; Krishnavarma's account of its very *raison d'être* — 'to inculcate the great sociological truth that "it is impossible to join injustice and brutality abroad with justice and humanity at home"'[17] — borrowed from the *Principles of Sociology*. Still more profoundly, Krishnavarma's anti-imperialism was shaped by Spencer's sociological analysis of empire, by his critique of its 'militant' nature, and by his recognition of its endemic violence. And yet, Spencer was hardly the only Western thinker on which Krishnavarma's political philosophy drew; the IS cites an extraordinary range of classical and contemporary authorities, from Cicero's Second Philippic Oration, to Plato's *Apology* and *Republic*, to Burke, Voltaire, Cromwell, Shakespeare, Montesquieu, Washington, and countless others.[18] He also absorbed the political traditions of his day, integrating aspects of socialism, positivism, liberalism, and anarchism in his anti-colonialism and developing personal relationships with prominent activists in each of them.[19]

In total, then, Krishnavarma's unusually heterodox intellectual trajectory enabled him to synthesize a broad range of philosophical influences, Eastern and Western, drawing on what Fischer-Tiné describes as 'two different cultures of knowledge'.[20] Far from acting as a 'passive carrier of "subaltern knowledge"',[21] supplanting one intellectual tradition with another, or submitting to any kind of epistemological violence, Krishnavarma drew on a unique ideational constellation to develop an anti-colonialism that avoided the tendencies endemic in the early Indian nationalist movement's three factions — namely, the quietism of the moderates, the nativism of the extremists, and the romanticism of the terrorists.

2 Moderates, extremists, and terrorists: Krishnavarma and the nationalist constellation

(i) The 'unknown patriot'

Despite having fallen into relative obscurity, Krishnavarma was among the leaders of the early nationalist movement's extremist faction whose better-known exponents include Aurobindo Ghose, Bal Gangadhar Tilak, Lala Lajpat Rai, and Bipin Chandra Pal. '[T]hough highly influential and well-known during his lifetime', notes Harald Fischer-Tiné, Krishnavarma, 'does not figure among the celebrities of the official versions of the Indian independence struggle ... he ha[s] fallen victim to a profound amnesia of both professional historians as well as the representatives of the postcolonial Indian state'.[22] This amnesia has several roots. First, Krishnavarma's work as an anti-colonial thinker and activist was undertaken outside of India, at a considerable remove from much of the nationalist movement. As an unapologetic seditionist, from 1905 until his death in 1930, Krishnavarma lived in exile in London, Paris, and Geneva. Second, Krishnavarma's writings are largely contained within the short articles of the IS – a monthly four-page broadsheet – rather than in any cohesive work of political philosophy, such as Gandhi's *Hind Swaraj*. He was among those turn-of-century Indian thinkers who, as Maia Ramnath puts it, were 'creative, flexible, and eclectic freethinkers, rather than systematic followers of a watertight body of philosophy'.[23] Finally, Krishnavarma's associations – real and perceived – with turn-of-century anarchist radicalism and the terrorist faction of the nationalist movement contributed to his marginalization, both within the extremist camp and beyond it.

And yet, from 1905 until the outbreak of the first world war, he was 'one of the major figures of India's anti-colonial freedom struggle',[24] in direct contact with the extremist leadership (including Pal, Tilak, and Rai) and personally responsible for drawing Har Dayal and Vinayak Savarkar (both of whom contributed to the IS) to London's India House. Pal described Krishnavarma as 'the founder and principal spokesman in England' of 'the movement for the promotion of Home Rule or autonomy in India',[25] while Tilak lauded his 'self-sacrificing spirit' and 'efforts on behalf of India'.[26] Krishnavarma was equally enthusiastic about the extremists' political work; he characterized Pal's and Tilak's addresses to the 1906 Congress as 'exhilarating' and sought to enlist them in his 'Society of Political Missionaries'[27] to spread nationalist sentiment in India (to which Pal agreed).[28] Along with Dadabhai Naoroji, the 'Grand Old Man of India', Rai attended the opening of Krishnavarma's India House in July 1905 and supported his resolution advocating Home Rule at the 1905 meeting of the National Democratic League in London.[29]

Krishnavarma was, thus, well-established in the nascent extremist movement and, as Manu Goswami, Maia Ramnath and Harald Fischer-Tiné observe, was particularly prominent at the international level.[30] The IS's 'transnational perspective' reached well beyond India's borders, propagating the central elements of the extremist creed across a global anti-colonial network stretching from Ireland, to Egypt, to the United States, to Japan, and beyond. The Parisian daily *L'éclair* recognized Krishnavarma as 'one of the leaders of the Indian nationalist movement … one of the most eminent chiefs of those whom the English call by the redoubtable name of "Indian Extremists"',[31] while *L'Humanité* chronicled his 'enormous influence among the rising Indian generation'.[32] This international renown was predicated on his extraordinarily prolific political agitation. In addition to editing and publishing the IS from 1905–14 (and, in a final gasp, from 1921–22), Krishnavarma funded multiple scholarships and lectureships at British and Swiss universities, in addition to 'travelling lectureships' in India; inaugurated and presided over the

Indian Home Rule Society in London (until 1907); created a Society of Political Missionaries; and launched London's India House, which rapidly became a centre of Indian revolutionary activism. Each of these initiatives contributed both to the rising visibility of the extremist faction and to the development of its central platforms – namely, the 'adamantine rock-pillars of (1) self-government; (2) the promotion and encouragement of Swadeshism; (3) boycotting foreign goods … [and] (4) national education along national lines'.[33] Krishnavarma was thus among the earliest progenitors of non-cooperation, self-reliance, and passive resistance that, through Gandhi, would become integral facets of the Indian independence movement. And yet, his conception of *Svarajya*[34] (*swaraj*) was distinctively economic and political in its orientation; he advocated a politics of 'dissociation' that aimed to paralyze British rule through (i) non-investment in British securities; (ii) repudiating India's public debt; (iii) inciting Indian public servants to strike; (iv) boycotting all English goods, educational institutions, lawyers, and journals; and (v) inculcating a love of political independence in Indians.[35]

Krishnavarma thus exerted a considerable influence over both the substance and the spread of the extremists' political ideals, particularly at the international level. T. Sriramulu, editor of *The Carlylean*, credited the IS with 'the dissemination of Home Rule ideas and ideals', going so far as to suggest that 'Home Rule ideas and ideals were thus let loose here [in India] from abroad in the beginning of 1905 … the movement found its expression for the first time rather abroad'.[36] I now turn to examine this movement's roots, and to situate Krishnavarma's views in relation to its three main factions: the moderates, extremists and terrorists.

(ii) The nationalist constellation I: moderates

The Indian National Congress formed in 1885 and in its early years was led by Dadabhai Naoroji, Surendranath Banerjea, Pherozeshah Mehta, Gopal Krishna Gokhale and Mahadev Govind Ranade, 'uncritical admirers of western political values'[37] whose commitments to English liberalism pervaded their conceptualizations of the means, ends and direction of India's political future.[38]

Broadly speaking, the moderates sought a better incorporation of Indians into the country's governing structures, rather than outright political autonomy. '[W]e appeal to England gradually to change the character of her rule in India, to liberalise it', Banerjea urged in his 1895 INC presidential address, 'so that in the fullness of time, India may find itself in the great confederacy of free states, English in their origin, English in their character, English in their institutions, rejoicing in their permanent and indissoluble union with England'.[39] The moderates aimed to push India towards this 'great confederacy' through non-violent, law-abiding, constitutional agitation, reflecting what Sankar Ghose describes as 'a touching faith at once in the intrinsic reasonableness of their cause and the British sense of justice'.[40] Like England's, India's movement towards self-government would (and should) proceed gradually, through the democratic learning – the 'laborious process of training in the art of parliamentary self-government'[41] – that constitutional agitation, along with British tutelage, would provide. In this, their liberalism was tinged with Burkean trepidations regarding radical political change, revolutionary activism, and aspirational political idealism; 'politics is a practical art', Banerjea maintained, 'and it cannot deal with principles in the abstract'.[42] As Sumit Sarkar observes, the moderates' political agenda thus 'fell far short of self-government or democracy';[43] the liberalism and gradualism framing their methods of political agitation lent themselves to both elitism and conservatism, reflected in their pursuit of piecemeal improvements of the colonial architecture. Rather than aspiring to political independence, the moderates aimed at democratic self-government within the empire – to have Britain 'grant India a constitution on the Canadian model'.[44] Far from wanting to divest India of its ties with Britain, the moderates sought to maintain the colonial relationship; political reforms aimed, rather, to generate a greater parity between Indians and Britons within it. Gokhale in fact petitioned to place Indian representatives in the British Parliament to secure a permanent position from which to defend India's rights within the empire.

The moderates also reproduced the civilizational hierarchies and stage-based accounts of social, political, and moral progress underlying nineteenth-century liberal imperialism.[45] Reflecting an implicit – and at points, explicit – acceptance of the developmental historicism justifying the empire's civilizing mission, the moderates' gradualism was sustained by their 'uncritical faith … in the providential mission of the British',[46] most evident in their insistence on India's incapacity for self-rule. In Banerjea's words, 'we do not wish to see installed in our midst anything like a democratic form of government. We do not think India is ripe for it yet; nor do we want Home Rule … We want something much less than an English House of Commons'.[47] In light of their 'endless divisions, feeble public spirit, and other national defects, the Indians were unfitted for immediate self-government', Gokhale argued; 'only mad men outside lunatic asylums could think or talk of independence'.[48] Britain's ties to India were not merely fortuitous; 'the British connection', Gokhale asserted, was 'ordained in the inscrutable dispensation of Providence, for India's good'.[49] The moderates' commitments to liberal politics, values, and ideals were, then, enmeshed with the broader civilizational hierarchy justifying the empire's pedagogical – and providential – function of nudging India from 'Asian despotism' to a society of rights, rules, and laws.

Krishnavarma was unsparingly critical of every facet of the moderate view. Beyond his more inflammatory attacks on their mendicancy and sycophancy (branding them 'traitors to their country',[50] 'chain-kissing slaves',[51] and, most colourfully, 'loathsome invertebrata'[52]), he argued that the moderates 'act merely as Indian tools of British tyranny, and their utterances will be quoted against patriotic Indians and others as showing that the people of India are really quite contented'.[53] Not only were the moderates incapable of achieving meaningful political reforms, they in fact extended political domination through piecemeal concessions that merely softened colonial domination, 'and so help to keep back the Indian revolt against intolerable oppression'.[54] Their collusion with colonial authorities could only '[retard] the progress of the ideal of Indian independence'[55] by mollifying resistance and turning Indians away from the more forceful methods required to claim political liberty. He opposed Gokhale's advocacy for Indian representation in British institutions on the same grounds: 'a few Indians' admission into the British Parliament', he argued, 'will afford an argument against a representative form of government in India in as much as the people of this country will naturally say that India needs no Home Rule or Self-Government since it is already represented in the House of Commons'.[56]

More profoundly, Krishnavarma criticized the moderate contention that political change was even possible through constitutional agitation, pointing out that 'the fight in India cannot be fought "constitutionally", for the very sufficient reason that India has no constitution, and its people have no political rights'.[57] Reversing the moderate argument that India should emulate England's slow, gradual ascent to democratic self-government, Krishnavarma questioned

> in what country the principles of liberty have ever prevailed except through the use or display of force. Certainly not in England, for Magna Charta was not wrung from King John by peaceful argument, but by an array of armed barons who imposed it on him by threats of force; while the Parliamentary rights enjoyed by the English people to-day were won in the battles between the Roundheads and the Royalists at Marston Moor and on other fields. The Hungarians did not win their autonomy from Austria by peaceful methods, nor was Italian liberty and unity the result of constitutional agitation. The truth is that liberty everywhere has been won by the use or threat of force.[58]

Gradualism, constitutional agitation, petitioning authorities: these were the tools of a fundamentally different sociological and political condition, within which recourse to the law and constitutional protections were possible.[59] Those conditions, Krishnavarma saw, did not obtain in the colonial context, characterized by relations of domination, rather than by the forms of sympathy that Krishnavarma understood as a precondition for justice. England's own political history attested to the fact that constitutions, liberty, and justice were not themselves achieved by constitutional means.

Finally, Krishnavarma was profoundly critical of the civilizational hierarchies, historicism, and providentialism underlying the moderates' liberalism. Against the contention that Indians' fitness for democratic self-government would require a long acculturation, he questioned

> the connection between education and self-government. What has the one to do with the other? The only test of fitness for self-government which the British Constitution recognises is the possession of a stake in the country ... An educational qualification

has never formed the test of fitness within the British dominions ... going another century or two back, the people of England, man and boy, high and low, with the exception of a mere handful were steeped in the grossest ignorance, and yet there was a House of Commons.[60]

By exposing the tenuous relationship between education and self-government – and their lack of congruence in England's own political development – Krishnavarma undermined the historicism sustaining what Dipesh Chakrabarty describes as the 'not yet' of empire.[61] He also drew on social and natural sciences – and in particular, on evolutionary theory – to refute deterministic accounts of human advancement more broadly. Against Banerjea's claim that 'progress is the order of Nature in the dispensation of Divine Providence, and the Asiatics, as well as Europeans, under the immutable law of progress must, in the course of time, acquire the habits of self-government', Krishnavarma argued that

[e]volution has proved ... that there is no law of progress – only an utterly careless and non-moral law of 'ordered change' ... Thus, there being no immutable law of progress as Mr. Banerjea holds, it is evident that Indians will have to make a supreme effort before they achieve an autonomous self-government by ridding their country of the foreign despotism which fools or knaves regard 'as ordained in the inscrutable dispensation of Providence for India's good'.[62]

Still further, he criticized 'the puerile racial vanity of the English'[63] that blinded colonists into treating a far older, and far more sophisticated, Indian civilization as inferior to their own. Behind the evident prejudice underlying the 'civilizing mission' lay the more cynical truth that Britain's imperialism was, at bottom, little more than profiteering: 'India was civilized many centuries before the discovery of England. The primary object of England in conquering India was not civilization, but plunder'.[64]

Krishnavarma was, therefore, profoundly critical of the moderates' methods, aims, and historicist framework, pushing him squarely into the extremist camp of the early nationalist movement; and yet, his anti-colonialism diverged from both extremists and their terrorist offshoots in important ways.

(iii) The nationalist constellation II: extremists and terrorists

The INC's extremist faction became cemented in 1907, following a spectacularly fractious split with the moderates (the Congress dissolved into chaos after Banerjea was hit in the face with a shoe flung from the gallery) and came to be led by Ghose, Rai, Tilak, and Pal. The group began to take shape in 1905, when the moderates' political agitation protesting the partition of Bengal – initiated by Lord Curzon to divide the Bengali population, increasingly the centre of political radicalism – fell on deaf ears.[65] Their frustrations with the INC's ineffectuality led them to adopt diametrically opposed aims, methods and values; as Tilak asserted, '[m]ere protest, not backed by self-reliance, will not help the people ... It is impossible to expect that our petitions will be heard unless backed by firm resolution ... Three P's – pray, please and protest – will not do unless backed by solid force'.[66] Political change would not be achieved by mendicancy and constitutional agitation, but by the forms of direct (and, if need be, violent) action through which Indians would take control of their economic, social, and political lives – namely, by boycott, *swadeshi*, national education, and *swaraj*.

This shift in political methods stemmed from the moral and political ends of *swaraj* – freedom, understood as self-reliant autonomy.[67] The *swadeshi*, boycott, and national education campaigns were anchored in the ideal of *swaraj*: freedom as self-dependence, rather than as (liberal) negative liberty. Pal treated *swarai* 'not [as] *non-subjection* which would be a literal rendering of the English word independence but self-subjection which is a positive concept',[68] incorporating the term's moral-psychological and political valences. *Swaraj* was not only an ideal of political self-government, but rather a wider conceptualization of positive freedom, understood as self-sufficient and self-dependent autonomy – economic, political, and spiritual. The *swadeshi*, boycott, and national education movements comprised a comprehensive strategy aimed at developing the social, economic, and industrial foundations sustaining this broad-ranging ideal of self-government. *Swaraj*, Tilak famously claimed, was a birth right; without it, 'there could be no social reform, no industrial progress, no useful education, no fulfilment of national life'.[69] The ideal of complete self-dependence – political and otherwise – thus further distinguished the extremists from the moderates: far from accepting the need for England's political tutelage, they understood British domination as the *source* of India's economic, civilizational, and political decline.

This rejection reflected a broader turn away from liberalism and Western values, and towards Indian traditions, ideals and religiosity. The extremists 'drew upon values rooted in Indian culture and civilization',[70] eschewed the Western division between religious and political life, and harnessed Hinduism to galvanize nationalist sentiment. Much of the extremist faction drew on neo-Vedantic philosophy, the *Gita*, and Hindu imagery to generate a powerful cultural nationalism intended to bridge India's cultural, religious, and linguistic divides. This turn to Hinduism imparted two distinctive features to much of the extremists' nationalisms: their spiritualism and their nativism.

In Pal's view, nationalism was 'a movement for the spiritual, social, ethical and political regeneration of the Hindu people'.[71] 'This new National Movement in India', he argued, 'is essentially a Spiritual Movement. To regard it as either a mere economic or political movement is to misunderstand it altogether'.[72] The nationalist movement not only dissolved the distinction between spiritual and national evolution, but in fact treated them as co-dependent; the country's political progress both reflected, and was contingent on, the spiritual awakening implicit in neo-Vedantism. Still further, Ghose understood nationalism as a vehicle for humanity's spiritual transformation; India's 'highest and most splendid destiny, the most essential to the human race', was to 'send forth from herself the future religion of the entire world, the eternal religion which is to harmonize all religions, science and philosophies and make mankind one soul'.[73] For Ghose, the nationalist movement's political significance was ancillary to its broader spiritual purpose, framed in relation to India's manifest destiny in the regeneration of the human race. Tilak similarly 'used mystical quasi-religious appeals to energize the nationalist movement ... [and] revived the Maratha politico-religious tradition'.[74] The extremists' nationalism was, therefore, distinctively religiously inflected; as they understood it, India's movement towards political independence was inexorably enmeshed with its broader spiritual renewal.

Not unrelated, it was also steeped in a thoroughgoing nativism that 'fuelled the Hinduization of Indianness and the Indenisation of Hinduness'.[75] Tilak, Pal, Rai and Ghose harnessed religious festivals to propagate a nationalist consciousness built on Hindu history, traditions and cultural identity; Tilak in fact inaugurated the Ganapati and Shivaji festivals to engraft political nationalism to Hindu revivalism.[76] 'The Hindu system', Pal maintained, 'is at once both national and universal, and, as an ethnic system ... has directly reached the universal stage'.[77] This kind of universalization conflated Hinduism and Indian identity under the banner of a distinctively Indian ethos. As Manu Goswami observes, '[s]wadeshists transposed a specific Hindu religious-philosophic schema – one that emphasized the originary unity of organic wholes and apparently discrete parts – on to the terrain of everyday political contention. They thus provided explicit philosophical-religious content to popular nativist understandings'.[78] Their nationalism comprised 'a paradigmatic instance of a territorial nativist vision of nationhood',[79] replete with its concomitant exclusions and hierarchies, directed, in particular, towards India's seventy million Muslims. The extremists' spiritualism and nativism thus led them to conceive of nationalism less in terms of political liberation than as an epiphenomenal by-product of the Hindu-Indian nation's broader evolution. Both the problem of colonialism and their nationalist resistance to it were framed in relation to the specificities of Hinduism, and to its place in humanity's progress.

The terrorist faction of the nationalist movement, associated with revolutionaries such as Vinayak Savarkar and Har Dayal, shared in the extremists' political vision but also unambiguously endorsed political violence, drawing inspiration from Russian, Irish, and Italian revolutionaries.[80] Savarkar founded a chapter of Abhinav Bharat at London's India House (following Krishnavarma's exile to Paris) and, along with his brother Ganesh, smuggled weapons into India to undertake political assassinations. But beyond engaging in political violence, much of the terrorist faction was animated by a romantic devotion to revolutionary resistance; '[m]ore than just a tactical instrument', Ramnath argues, the bomb 'manifested for them as the focus of a viscerally intense cult of devotion to annihilation that shaded imperceptibly into sacrificial devotion to the mother goddess-as-nation'.[81]

Har Dayal's 'Shabash! In Praise of the Bomb' exhibited precisely such a romanticism, celebrating the bomb as the 'benefactor of the poor', and exhorting the people to '[w]orship it, sing its praises, bow to it'.[82] This romanticized appeal to the purifying force of violence recurred in his three-stage theory of development through which 'an enslaved people' gained its freedom; '[t]he debris of the old regime must be removed', he argued, and 'the only agent that can accomplish this work is the sword. No subject nation can bring freedom without war'.[83] Certain members of the terrorist faction also adopted Russian revolutionaries' anti-modernism in idealising traditional Indian village life, which was 'for Indian extremists and Russian populists a proudly essentialising rejection of Western elements ... [shared by] European Romanticist and cultural Pan-Asianist anti-liberal critics of modernity'.[84]

Krishnavarma was, then, a clear exponent of the extremist creed, and his willingness to countenance political violence (under certain conditions) also led to his association with the terrorist faction of the nationalist movement. And yet, his anti-colonialism is distinguishable from theirs in two important respects.

First, he eschewed the extremists' spiritualism, religiosity, and providentialism, focusing explicitly on India's *political* emancipation. From the very first lines on the IS's masthead – Herbert Spencer's dictum that 'every man is free to do that which he wills, provided he infringes not the equal freedom of any other man'[85] – he announced the journal's mandate as pursuing the '[a]bsolute freedom of my country without any restrictions, and the establishment of an Indian National Government'.[86] Political freedom was both independent of, and a precondition for, any other form of emancipation; without it,

> life was not worth living ... a man might be a great philosopher, an ardent social reformer or a fervid religious preacher, but all his philosophy, his zeal for social reform, or his religious fervour would not avail an iota, if he were tied down and chained to a post by a despot. Every effort ought, therefore, to be primarily directed towards the all-important goal of political freedom.[87]

While sharing in the extremists' political aims and methods, Krishnavarma's nationalism drew on Spencerian philosophy and social science, rather than on neo-Vedantic spiritualism, generating an anti-colonialism that took aim at the sociological foundations of empire.[88] This focused on the psychological foundations underlying all imperial states and on the systemic violence – political, social, and sociological – that both Spencer and Krishnavarma understood as pervading imperial politics. Where Pal's, Tilak's, and Ghose's rejections of Western values led them to treat *swaraj* in spiritualist terms, Krishnavarma's advocacy for Home Rule was framed in relation to Mazzini's revolutionary nationalism and John Robert Seeley's 'great sociological truth' that subjection 'to a foreign yoke is one of the most potent causes of national deterioration'.[89]

This explicitly political orientation was equally evident across Krishnavarma's multifarious anti-colonial agitations, each intended to propagate the 'advantages of freedom and national unity'.[90] His 'Indian Travelling Fellowships' drew young Indians to England

> to give them a chance of seeing for themselves what political freedom and free insti-
> tutions in general have done toward raising the people of these islands. The despotic
> form of government and tyrannical rule in India have left no trace of freedom of any
> sort in that unfortunate country. Although some Indians there read in English books
> all about liberty and political freedom, none has any real notion of what they are.[91]

Krishnavarma's absorption of Spencerian social science attuned him to the social and affective foundations of political freedom so evidently lacking in India; political freedom required a *sense* of how to govern oneself and a *desire* for it cultivated, inculcated, and developed by particular sociological circumstances. This political sociology led him to found (and fund) the Society of Political Missionaries (*Desa-bhakta-samaj*) with the object of generating the conditions – and particularly, the sentimental dispositions that Spencer understood to sustain given political states – for Home Rule through the propagation of written materials, lectures and conferences throughout India:

> The ideal of a Free and United India has been intellectually appreciated by a large major-
> ity of our countrymen. But the moral force which is necessary for embodying it in
> actual movements and institutions is wanting. Let us hasten to supply this want ... It is as
> necessary to convince the intellect as it is to inspire the heart and rouse the conscience.[92]

Where Tilak turned to religious festivals and Hindu revivalism – to the 'dynamite of religion'[93] – to generate the affective sway for political transformation, Krishnavarma's appeal to the 'moral force' of nationalism remained explicitly political. While acutely conscious that 'not merely the thought but the *feeling* of common nationality'[94] was integral to the success of anti-colonial agitation, his proselytizing was directed towards the Home Rule sentiment sustaining self-government. Far from framing India's independence in spiritualist or providentialist terms, Krishnavarma's anti-colonialism was self-consciously social-scientific and political.

The second distinctive feature of Krishnavarma's political thought was, not unrelatedly, its outward-looking cosmopolitanism, manifested in several ways. First, his extensive entanglements in a transnational network of anti-imperial activists made him 'a central figure in the construction of what can perhaps best be called a global anti-imperialist ecumene'.[95] But beyond his personal engagements, Krishnavarma's political philosophy was itself globally oriented and cosmopolitan, in marked distinction from the extremists' often narrower political vision. Manu Goswami notes the 'profound anxiety invoked by *swadeshi*'s nativism' in India's Muslim population, whose merchants and professionals were at times subject to *swadeshi* boycotts;[96] Fischer-Tiné similarly notes that the extremists 'indulged in a rhetoric laden with Hindu symbolism and sometimes openly discriminated against the Muslim minority'.[97] In contrast, Krishnavarma took aim at Muslims' and Hindus' common subjection under colonial rule, expressing his 'desire to see the two races of India united together against their oppressors';[98] Muslim-Hindu antagonisms were, he maintained, largely produced by colonial subjugation itself. He published a speech by Manchershah Sohrabji Master arguing that Parsis' and Muslims' centuries of existence in India 'has made us as much Indians as the Hindus themselves', celebrating their fraternity and amity, and cautioning all alike against the 'attempts … now being made … to keep us aloof from the present political movement in India'.[99] Krishnavarma's nationalism explicitly avoided the nativist framework conflating Indian and Hindu identities; Parsis and Muslims should become 'united with the power of the whole Indian people and … effect a reconciliation with Indians of every race and religion'.[100]

But more broadly, his anti-colonialism perceived the common cause of *all* colonized peoples and took aim at the colonial condition itself, rather than at India's alone. In his 'proposal for an alliance of England's oppressed', he suggested that

> [i]f the Indian Home Rule Society, the Swadeshi Organizations in India, the Young Egypt movement, the discontented in South Africa, and the powerful organization of the Sinn Fein Party of Ireland join hands, much effective work can be done against England by their movements being united and acting in accord, exchanging ideas and suggestions, and all making a forward move along the same lines at the same psychological moment.[101]

The colonized stood to benefit from mutual engagement because they inhabited the same sociological and political condition of subjection and powerlessness, sharing in a 'fraternity of the enslaved nations of the orient'.[102] Rather than focusing on the specificities of the Indian (or Hindu) nation, Krishnavarma's cosmopolitan anti-colonialism both recognized the common foundations binding disparate colonial regimes and agitated for their liberation. He advocated for the Egyptian liberation movement, proclaiming at a 1906 meeting of Egypt's Pan-Islamic Society 'that Indians sympathized with the Egyptian Mahommedans as heartily as they did with their fellow-countrymen the Mahommedans of India'.[103] Krishnavarma also sought to develop a Pan-Asian Union and Pan-Asian Parliament, uniting 'educated Indians, Osmanlis, Egyptians, Japanese, Chinese, Arabs, Armenians, Parsis, Persians, Siamese and others', to 'coordinate the ambition and policy of an Emancipated East'.[104] His anti-colonialism was, however, neither orientalist nor anti-Western. He frequently militated for Ireland's independence, and – perhaps best illustrating his departure from the extremists' inwardness and nativism – adopted two Irish nationalists as moral exemplars: Michael Davitt, whose 'sense of justice was so keen that he could not be persuaded to secure an advantage even for his own country by depriving others of their just rights',[105] and Patrick Ford, whose 'sympathies were very broad, not being confined to his own country but extending to all who were the victims of the greed of stronger and more foxy countries'.[106]

In total, then, Krishnavarma's anti-colonialism comprises a unique political vision that avoided both the quietism of the moderates' liberalism and the extremists' spiritualism and nativism (as well as, as we will see below, the terrorists' romanticism of violence). He neither blindly accepted the historicist freight of liberal imperialism, nor rejected Western thought; he adopted the extremists' political aims and methods without succumbing to their inwardness. In so doing, Krishnavarma developed an explicitly political and cosmopolitan anti-colonialism, whose philosophical foundations I now turn to consider.

3 A state of violence: Spencer, sociology, and the sentimental foundations of empire

The depth of Spencer's influence over Krishnavarma is indisputable; beyond adorning the IS's masthead with quotations from the *Principles of Ethics* and *The Study of Sociology*, Krishnavarma described him as 'the scholar with the generous heart, who understood India and pitied it. Nearly all of my arguments are based on his works. His spirit guides me'.[107] And yet, the more precise contours of that influence over his anti-colonialism remains subject to interpretation. Fischer-Tiné, for instance, treats Spencer's 'political and economic liberalism'[108] as most profoundly shaping Krishnavarma's political philosophy, which he understands as unstintingly liberal. And yet, this might cast the liberal net somewhat widely, given Krishnavarma's lifelong associations with prominent socialists (such as H. H. Hyndman) and anarchists (such as Guy Aldred and Walter Strickland), to say nothing of his scathing criticisms of Indian liberalism. While Krishnavarma adopted many of Spencer's liberal commitments – to individual liberty, to civil and political equality, and to self-government – he remained caustic towards the 'Liberal Imperialist who relies on his civilising services to justify his conquering aggressions',[109] and deeply sceptical that 'the present revival of the spirit, instincts and traditions of Liberty and Liberalism'[110] would lead to any political advancement in India. Shruti Kapila, conversely, treats Spencer's extreme individualism – his 'valuation of the self'[111] – as animating Krishnavarma's critique of (Indian) liberalism, which, she contends, he understood as 'primarily statist and hence oriented towards the colonial order'.[112] She argues that Spencer's anti-statism led Krishnavarma to reject political authority altogether, as 'it was precisely Spencer's distrust of the state and the belief in the powers of the social order that had an interesting potential for a radical nationalist agenda'.[113] And yet, Krishnavarma's resistance to the colonial order did not entail a broader critique of political authority, and neither did he harbour libertarian or anarchist sensibilities; beyond his own explicit rejection of anarchist anti-statism, Krishnavarma agitated 'not for the suppression of order, but for the creation of a national Government, whatever it be, monarchy or republic'.[114]

I would like to suggest that Krishnavarma's most profound debt in fact lay in his adoption of Spencer's sociology, as both a diagnostic tool (for properly understanding the colonial condition) and a normative one (for resisting its political domination). This influence is discernible at several junctures in his work.

Most directly, Krishnavarma appealed to Spencer's own relentless criticisms of British imperialism, predicated on his broader libertarian opposition to all but the most necessary forms of political authority. Spencer's critique took aim at several dimensions of the colonial condition. At one level, colonialism entailed an unwarranted violation of the rights of both colonists (who were subject to the authority of a distant government) and citizens of the home country (who footed the bill for colonial adventuring).[115] But more troublingly, Spencer argued, 'in proportion as liberty is diminished in the liberties over which it rules, liberty is diminished within its own organization';[116] the ever-increasing costs of controlling a colonized population inevitably required ever-increasing resources – and labour – from the home country, and '[l]abour demanded by the State is just as much *corvée* to the State as labour demanded by the feudal lord was *corvée* to him'.[117] Still further, these domestic harms 'look insignificant when compared with those it inflicts upon the aborigines of the conquered countries'.[118] The colonial legal architecture was doubly damnable; beyond the naked injustice and perversion 'allow[ing] the machinery of law to be used for purposes of extortion',[119] the unchecked power it accorded to colonists ensured that a 'brutality will come out, which the discipline of civilized life had kept under'.[120]

Spencer's critique shaped Krishnavarma's anti-colonialism in several ways. Spencer did not treat imperialism as a political form comparable to others, and neither did he treat its harms and injustice as the failings of an otherwise viable political state or civilizing power. Colonialism was, in his view, a particular *sociological* condition, with its own distinctive, endemic, and recurrent features. His critique was directed not at any particular imperial venture, but rather, at 'the general truth that militancy and Imperialism are closely allied – are, in fact, different manifestations of the same social condition'.[121] Empires were, in his view, particular social and sociological systems that entailed equally particular conditions for colonist, colonized, and home country: ever-expanding systems of taxation, loss of individualism and personal liberties in both colony and mother country, distortions of the rule of law, and – worst of all – 'these cruelties, these treacheries, these deeds of blood and rapine, for which European nations in general have to blush, [which] are mainly due to the carrying on of colonization under state-management'.[122] These harms were neither failures nor instances of misgovernment amenable to redress, but were rather implicit in the fabric of the colonial condition, 'in that concentration of power which is the concomitant of Imperialism'.[123] Echoing Hegel, Spencer aimed 'to show those who lean towards Imperialism, that the exercise of mastery inevitably entails on the master himself some form of slavery',[124] both in the form of enchainment to an ever-growing state apparatus, and in the psychological deterioration that accompanied it; '[s]o long as the passion for mastery overrides all others', he argued, 'the slavery that goes along with Imperialism will be tolerated'.[125] Spencer thus treated colonialism not as a viable form of politics perverted by given circumstances, but as a distinctive sociological condition in which those pathologies were, in fact, inherent. A clear-sighted analysis of the colonial order – as of any other sociopolitical formation – had to be predicated on 'those sociological truths which have nothing to do with particular nations or particular races'.[126]

Krishnavarma's cosmopolitanism was animated by precisely this Spencerian 'sociological truth': as subjects of a given sociological condition, all colonized peoples shared in the same set of social and political pathologies. His anti-colonialism thus consistently took aim at imperialism's sociological foundations – the 'truths' that, Spencer argued, had nothing to do with particular races or nations – rather than at the specificities of Hindu or Indian nationalism. His recognition of, and advocacy for, the common cause binding Irish, Egyptian, South African, and Indian nationalists, his advocacy for a Pan-Asian Union and Parliament, his 'alliance of the oppressed' – these all reflected a Spencerian consciousness of colonialism as a distinctive sociological state whose features, and injustices, recurred in them all. 'The story of English treachery, perfidy, and savagery behind a mask of civilization and religion, is spread broad over every page of Ireland's history', Krishnavarma argued; '[t]hat the same characteristics should mark English rule in India was, therefore, only to be expected'.[127] Still further, Krishnavarma's anti-colonialism aimed beyond the British Empire; he regularly publicized Ernest Douwes Dekker's campaign to wrest Java from Dutch colonialism and celebrated Japan's 1905 defeat of the Russian empire in the pages of the IS. In contrast with the extremists' inward turn, Krishnavarma's advocacy for all anti-colonial movements – his appeal to '[a]ll friends of conquered and oppressed races throughout the civilized world'[128] – reflected his conceptualization of colonialism as a particular, and shared, sociological condition.

For Krishnavarma as for Spencer, this condition was both predicated on, and sustained by, an equally distinctive set of affects and sentiments. Rather than treating it in primarily political terms, Spencer saw imperialism as characterized by the widespread diffusion of sentiments of loyalty, servility, and obedience. This was anchored in a larger evolutionist framework (that he would, in later years, develop in conjunction with Darwin's theory of natural selection) that understood social advancement as shaped by the congruity and adaptation between a people's mental/sentimental attributes and its sociological conditions. Any given population's affective, mental, and sentimental state – broadly understood – was, Spencer argued, initially shaped by (and adapted to) its particular sociological circumstances. Early, primitive societies, for instance, were characterized by the sentiments of deference, obedience and loyalty – all products of a generalized awe of power and willingness to submit to authority – required to preserve themselves against the instability and conflict of their sociological condition. The primitive state was, therefore, accompanied by a particular set of mental and affective dispositions conditioned by, and adapted to, its setting. But over time and through further adaptive change, both sociological circumstances and mental states evolved, without which social progress would be impossible; 'only by giving us some utterly different mental constitution', Spencer averred, 'could the process of civilization have been altered'.[129]

Sentimental and sociological evolution did not, however, progress in lock-step: while societies developed the social and political conditions enabling greater individuation and self-realization, the inertia of our mental and affective states generated a mismatch between governing structures and social sentiments. Political violence, domination, and tyranny were the result of this mal-adaptation between a population's affective constitution and its sociological structures:

> the manifold evils which have filled the world for these thousands of years – the murders, enslavings, and robberies – the tyrannies of rulers, the oppressions of class, the persecution of sect and party, the multiform embodiments of selfishness in unjust laws, barbarous customs, dishonest dealings, exclusive manners and the like – are simply instances of the disastrous working of this original and once needful constitution, now that mankind have grown into conditions for which it is not fitted – are nothing but symptoms of the suffering attendant upon the adaptation of humanity to its new circumstances.[130]

The egoism and violence animating political domination were, at an earlier evolutionary stage, necessary to defend societies against external threats; and yet, as social and political structures became increasingly stabilized, and as populations' moral sentiments adapted to them, these predilections for violence and domination ceased to fulfil the sociological role previously required of them. This adaptation was, however, far from complete; humanity remained caught between civilizing inclinations towards sympathy and the 'anti-social characteristics'[131] of barbarism. While civilization's advance represented the steady progress of a new sentimental regime, it remained an adaptive work in progress, subject to regression, variation and – as we will see below – even 'rebarbarization'. In contrast with the eighteenth and nineteenth century's more self-assured developmental teleologies, which understood societies to move through fixed stages of advancement as aggregated wholes, Spencer's evolutionism conceptualized progress as highly uneven – pitching forward, lapsing back, and even unfolding differently within a single sociopolitical entity (such as an empire).[132]

And yet, humanity's general tendency was towards greater sympathy, individuality and independence. '[A]s there arises a perception that these subjugations and tyrannies are not right', Spencer argued, 'as soon as the sentiment to which they are repugnant becomes sufficiently powerful to suppress them, it is time for them to cease'.[133] Thus, at an early stage of civilization, '[w]hilst the injustice of conquests and enslavings is not perceived, they are on the whole beneficial; but as soon as they are felt to be at variance with the moral law, the continuance of them retards adaptation'.[134] Less-advanced social states were characterized by a blind and unquestioning deference to authority rendering, in Spencer's words, the injustice of conquest and enslaving imperceptible; and yet, as the 'loyalty-producing faculty'[135] declined, populations came to see – and more importantly, to *feel* – the injustice of political domination, at which point it became retrogressive. Increasing social and political cohesion enabled citizens to develop their individual interests, capacities and faculties, diminishing their submission to authority and their willingness to tolerate repression. '[C]onduct during each phase of civilization being determined by the relative strength of the two feelings'[136] – obedience and loyalty, on the one hand, and the anti-authoritarian spirit of individualism and critique, on the other – social advancement proceeded through a progressive loss of sentiments of loyalty and servility, and a rise in critical thinking, individualism and respect for rights.

Spencer's account of the relationship between sentiment and sociological conditions – and more particularly, between obedience, loyalty and domination – directly informed Krishnavarma's analysis of India's colonial subjugation. Krishnavarma drew on Spencer's *Social Statics* to 'remind the contemporary reader that there is an intimate relation between loyalty and barbarism ... [autocracy] has ever been the repressor of knowledge, of free thought, of true progress ... organs of public opinion in India ... are addicted to slavish tendencies'.[137] India's prostration to colonial domination was predicated on its population's sentimental proclivities towards servility, docility and obedience, reflecting the 'great sociological truth' that 'submission to tyrannical rule [was] "associated with a defect of moral sense"'.[138] India sat at the precise juncture of sentimental maladaptation that Spencer identified: sufficiently mired in the deference to authority sustaining colonial rule, and yet at the cusp of sensing political oppression as 'at variance with the moral law'. Spencer's 'sentimentalist' framework informed not only Krishnavarma's analysis of India's sociological state, but also his conceptualization of how India might progress beyond the colonial order. Spencer argued that

the aids given to civilization by clearing the earth of its least advanced inhabitants, and by forcibly compelling the rest to acquire industrial habits, are given without moral adaptation receiving any corresponding check. Quite otherwise is it, however, when the flagitiousness of these gross forms of injustice begins to be recognised. Then the times give proof that the old regime is no longer fit. Further progress cannot be made until the newly-felt wrong has been done away or diminished. Were it possible under such circumstances to uphold past institutions and practices (which, happily, it is not), it would be at the expense of a continual searing of men's consciences. The feelings whose predominance gives possibility to an advanced social state would be constantly repressed – kept down on a level with the old arrangements, to the stopping of all further progress.[139]

Colonial India sat at this precise juncture: labouring under a condition of imposed barbarousness in which Indians were beginning to *feel* the gross injustice – the 'newly-felt wrong' – of domination, while still retaining traces of the loyalty and obedience sustaining it. The 'old regime', Krishnavarma saw, was fraying; the sentimental dispositions of 'an advanced social state' were rising and being 'constantly repressed', 'kept down on a level with the old arrangements'. And nowhere were those feelings more pronounced and more clearly articulated than in the nationalist movement. The nationalist movement was the articulation of a new sentimental regime both giving voice to Indians' nascent consciousness of themselves as capable of freedom, self-government and progress and inciting them to resist colonial domination. And Krishnavarma was himself, self-consciously – through the propaganda of the IS, the scholarships, the lectures, the political missionaries, the Home Rule Society, and so on – at the forefront of the effort to propagate those sentiments. 'What India requires', he asserted, 'is education of the heart more than that of the head. People must learn to *feel* and not simply to think that slavery or the loss of political freedom is "the worst of all evils"'.[140] The Society of Political Missionaries aimed precisely 'to create in the people of India a real desire for emancipation', recognizing that 'in order to make their desire effective, we must enlist the sympathies'.[141]

The nationalist movement was, Krishnavarma saw, developing the political sentiments required to transcend the barbarism born of the mismatch between India's governing institutions and its population's nascent moral consciousness. He even embraced 'every act of tyranny and oppression perpetrated by [India's] foreign masters, since what is absolutely necessary for the emancipation of that country is to make the Indian people *feel* that they are ill-treated and oppressed under an alien yoke';[142] colonial violence would only awaken Indians' consciousness of, and resistance to, the injustice of political domination. Indians' 'natural' loyalty was in fact sociologically and circumstantially conditioned, and 'the rapid growth of Home Rule sentiment [was] bound to destroy any such feeling'.[143] Home Rule thus represented the rise of an affective regime that would ultimately make colonial domination unsustainable by exacerbating the mal-adaptation between Indians' moral consciousness and the sociopolitical conditions of empire. '[D]eciduous institutions imply deciduous sentiments', Spencer argued, '[d]ependent as they are upon popular character, established political systems cannot die out until the feeling which upholds them dies out'.[144] Both Krishnavarma's diagnosis of the colonial condition and the nationalist agitations that he championed aimed to precipitate the demise of the colonial order by undercutting its sentimental foundations.

Spencer's sentimental-sociological argument informed his broader distinction between 'industrial' and 'militant' societies, which he understood as distinctive sociological entities marked by particular affective, social and political attributes – and the latter of which was, he argued, pervaded by systemic violence. The 'social structure evolved by chronic militancy is one in which all men fit for fighting act in concert against other societies',[145] he averred, and was characterized by '[g]raduated subordination, which is the method of army-organization, [and which] becomes more and more the method of civil organization where militancy is chronic'.[146] The militant society's primary sociological trait – and in Spencer's view, its most deleterious – was the individual's subordination to the state, such that 'chronic militancy tends to develop a despotism';[147] the demands of military rigor and ongoing warfare (or preparedness for it) produced a society whose social, economic and political institutions revolved around a powerful and centralized political-military apparatus. Far from remaining confined to military or political life, however, militant societies' social structures were equally characterized by rank, hierarchy and status, a 'process of regimentation' that penetrated into the deepest recesses of the social body. '[A] necessary relation exists between the structure of a society and the natures of its citizens',[148] Spencer argued, explaining the pervasive violence, subordination, and submission to authority internalized by militant states' populations. The conjunction of sentiments of obedience and patriotism was particularly pernicious, as the patriot's blind willingness to visit violence on those beyond his borders also suffused domestic social order: 'acting at home on the law of retaliation which they act on abroad, they similarly, at home as abroad, are ready to sacrifice others to self'.[149] This unthinking patriotic zeal entailed an '[u]nlimited confidence in governmental agency'[150] and a concurrent loss of individual initiative and enterprise; hence, 'the mental state generated is that of passive acceptance and expectancy'.[151] The militant state thus 'presuppose[d] a despotic controlling agency',[152] leading to a degradation of intellectual culture and a citizenry equally bereft of capacities for mental exertion and political criticism.

In more than any other type of society, militant traits were 'shown by imperial Rome, by imperial Germany, and by England since its late aggressive activities'.[153] Empire was, unsurprisingly, the apotheosis of the militant society: an ever-expanding, all-consuming sociopolitical order whose centralization, hierarchy and graduated subordination shaped not only its military and political institutions, but its domestic and foreign social structures as well. Spencer saw no clearer instantiation of imperial despotism than 'that furnished by our own society since the revival of military activity',[154] which he understood as leading Britain's 're-barbarization', its slide from an industrial society into a militant one. He recognized, with considerable perspicacity, the ways that violence pervaded every facet of the imperial system and that '[t]he diffusion of military ideas, military sentiments, military organization, military discipline, has been going on everywhere':[155]

> The destructive passions directed towards 'the enemy', as the principle of evil is called, are easily directed towards an enemy otherwise conceived ... there has been a perpetual shouting of the words 'war' and 'blood', 'fire' and 'battle', and a continual exercise of the antagonistic feelings.[156]

Imperial violence was neither contained in isolated instances, nor was it limited to political or military contexts; it was, rather, endemic, a pervasive feature of the affective regime and social structures sustaining the imperial order. It was irrevocably lodged within the fabric of the militant sociological condition, and all the more so in the imperial formation comprising its most developed form. Spencer saw this violence manifested in churches, schools, the Salvation Army, Cambridge University, the 'training-camps of the Volunteers, and the annual rifle-competitions now at Wimbledon', the rising valuation of athleticism, and even in animal-fighting rings – all 'showing the utter change of social sentiment'.[157] He bemoaned '[t]he temper generated by these causes [resulting] in outbursts of violence occurring all over England ... showing how widely the traits of coer-civeness, which is the essential element in militancy, has pervaded the nation'.[158] Under Britain's militancy, even journalism, the arts and literature – traditionally, the conscience of a state – 'reek[ed] with violence'.[159]

And of course, this violence was still more pronounced in the far outposts of the empire. Spencer described colonists as 'schoolboy[s], made overbearing by the consciousness that there is always a big brother to take their part', in whom a 'brutality will come out, which the discipline of civilized life had kept under; and not unfrequently, they will prove more vicious than they even knew themselves to be'.[160] And yet, these more evident instances of violence – the direct military repression of Indians – were only the tip of the iceberg, the clearest manifestations of a broader violence that suffused every facet of the colonial condition, domesti-cally and abroad. These were merely symptomatic of the sentiments of aggression, vengefulness, rapine, obedience, loyalty, and subordination sustaining the imperial order. In the Empire, Spencer argued, 'an aggressive tendency is encouraged by all – a tendency which is sure to show itself in acts, and to betray the colonists into some of those atrocities that disgrace civilization'.[161]

It is in this context that we best understand Krishnavarma's infamous advocacy for political violence. Krishnavarma's views shifted from 1905, when he explicitly rejected violent methods of resistance, to 1907, when he was 'not opposed on principle to an armed rebellion',[162] and finally, to 1908, from which point onward he treated 'a rebellion or revolution [as] the only remedy to overthrow a despotic government',[163] Much of the commentary on Krishnavarma – during his own time, as now – treats his turn to violence as either politically expedient, accelerat-ing India's movement towards independence, or as romantic. Naoroji, for example, criticized his 'impatience' in turning to revolutionary violence to achieve what constitutional agitation would – albeit at a slower pace. Numerous English news-papers branded Krishnavarma as a primary exponent of 'Indian Anarchism' and as 'devoted to the glorification of murder'[164], while contemporary commentators such as Maia Ramnath associate him with the terrorist faction's sentimentalist idealization of violence, bombs and revolution.[165]

And yet, Krishnavarma's accounts of political violence in fact appear to draw on Spencer's conceptual framework; the colonial condition's endemic violence made it unresponsive to the constitutional and legal mechanisms enabling political change in 'industrial' societies. He was acutely conscious of the broad-ranging violence pervading every facet of the 'militant' colonial order's social, political, and affective constitution – from Indians' loyalty and obedience, to the unbridled brutality of colonial officers – rendering it responsive to force alone. Krishnavarma drew on Spencer to make sense of violence in relation to India's condition:

> when that great English philosopher [Spencer] condemns the spread of anarchism or revolutionary methods, he really deprecates violence or the use of physical force in those countries which already enjoy a national or representative form of government, but in the case of a country like India, which is despotically governed by aliens, he favoured the rising of an oppressed race, so much so that he saw no crime in the endeavour of the Indians to throw off the English yoke.[166]

Far from romanticizing violence (he had, as he put it, 'nothing to do with the so-called Indian anarchism. I am not bloodthirsty')[167] or treating it as simply expedient, Krishnavarma understood it as *circumstantially* necessary, in light of India's sociological circumstances. Citing Spencer further, he argued that the 'existence of a government which does not bend to the popular will – a despotic government – presupposes several circumstances which make any change but a violent one unavoidable … We must look on social convulsions as on other natural phenomena which work themselves out in a certain inevitable, unalterable way'. As a result, '[t]he possibility of a peaceful revolution is now, we fear, very remote, seeing that England is bent upon destroying every vestige of political freedom in India'.[168] While legal and constitutional agitations might alter India's governing structures, they were powerless to extirpate the deeper sociological foundations sustaining India's state of imperial violence. Krishnavarma recounted two instances of abuse that he'd received at the hand of British officers in India, echoing Spencer's observations on the violence pervading England's social fabric under the aegis of empire: from the highest reaches of political administration to the lowest foot soldiers, from England to India, from churches to schools, violence was the *lingua franca* of the imperial condition. And like Spencer, he saw that within such a sociological condition, violence alone was audible, leading him to argue for 'the necessity for a revolution under circumstances applicable to a case like that of India with purely an autocratic and despotic form of government'.[169] Under these circumstances, 'to suppose that … moral suasion can be employed, or, if employed, would answer, is to overlook the conditions'.[170] Moral suasion, legal argument and constitutional agitation were not merely slower, less expeditious, or less effective mechanisms for achieving political change; they were altogether incapable of it. Imperial violence was a *sociological* violence that penetrated the deepest recesses of Irish, Egyptian, Indian, and all other colonized states. As such, Krishnavarma saw, violence alone stood to undermine the sentimental and sociological bases supporting India's political domination.

Conclusion

While Krishnavarma remains an obscure figure in India's struggle for independence, his political thought is worth recovering for several reasons.

From a historical perspective, he was, for a time, an important exponent of the nationalist movement's extremist faction – particularly at the international level – whose activism helped to shape and propagate the ideals of *swadeshi*, boycott, national education, and *swaraj* pivotal to India's eventual political emancipation. Moreover, his anti-colonialism broadens and complicates our view of their conceptual genealogy: far from partaking in the extremists' rejections of liberalism and Western values, Krishnavarma's *Svarajya*, his conceptualization of Home Rule, was profoundly influenced by nineteenth-century social and political science. And yet, in contrast with the moderates, he also remained deeply critical of liberalism's historicist and racist conceits, drawing on a vast intellectual repertoire to develop an anti-colonialism that, I have argued, was distinctively political, cosmopolitan, and sociological. Krishnavarma's political thought, then, reveals both the greater complexity of the intellectual strands converging in India's anti-colonial struggle and the ways in which ideas were translated across colonial borders.

From a philosophical standpoint, Krishnavarma's incorporation of Spencerian sociology generated a sophisticated anti-colonial politics as acutely conscious of the foundations – sentimental, political and sociological – of British imperialism in India as it was critical of political domination more broadly. As with Fanon, Césaire, and other anti-colonial thinkers, Krishnavarma not only sharpens our comprehension of the colonial condition, but also articulates a political vision that bridges theoretical insight and direct activism. It both exposes the forms of violence pervading the colonial order and confounds the distinction between high theory and its more prosaic applications. Beyond developing our understanding of empire, this kind of *dépaysement* also unsettles presumptions within political theory itself – distinctions between theory and practice, between ideal and non-ideal theorizing, and between discrete ideological positions. These are all confounded in Krishnavarma's political vision, which incorporated elements of socialism, liberalism, positivism, anarchism, and reformist neo-Vedantism; economic, political, and social sciences; and unrelenting political activism. The result is certainly a more eclectic and less systematic body of political thought than those proffered by more canonical political thinkers, but one that perhaps better captures the breadth of political experience to which these are often blind.

Notes

1 As Jennifer Pitts observes, political theorists have been remarkably late to develop their study of empire; nevertheless, the last decade or so has witnessed rising scholarly interest in the subject. For pioneering work on empire and modern political theory see Jennifer Pitts, 'Political Theory of Empire and Imperialism', *Annual Review of Political Science*, 13: 1 (2010), 211–35; Jennifer Pitts, *A Turn to Empire: The*

Rise of Imperial Liberalism in Britain and France (Princeton, NJ: Princeton University Press, 2005); Uday Singh Mehta, *Liberalism and Empire: A Study in Nineteenth-Century British Liberal Thought* (Chicago: University Chicago Press, 1999); Bhikhu Parekh, 'Decolonizing Liberalism', in Alexander Shtromas, ed., *The End Of 'Isms'?: Reflections on the Fate of Ideological Politics after Communism's Collapse* (Oxford: Blackwell, 1994); Bhikhu Parekh, 'Liberalism and Colonialism: A Critique of Locke and Mill', in Jan Nederveen Pieterse and Bhikhu Parekh, eds, *The Decolonization of Imagination: Culture, Knowledge and Power* (London: Zed Books, 1995); Thomas McCarthy, 'Multicultural Cosmopolitanism: Remarks on the Idea of Universal History', in Stephen Schneck, ed., *Letting Be: Fred Dallmayr's Cosmopolitical Vision* (Notre Dame, IN: University of Notre Dame Press, 2006): 188–213; Thomas McCarthy, *Race, Empire, and the Idea of Human Development* (Cambridge: Cambridge University Press, 2009); Karuna Mantena, *Alibis of Empire: Henry Maine and the Ends of Liberal Imperialism* (Princeton, NJ: Princeton University Press, 2010); Barbara Arneil, *John Locke and America: The Defence of English Colonialism* (Oxford: Clarendon Press, 1996); James Tully, *An Approach to Political Philosophy: Locke in Contexts* (Cambridge: Cambridge University Press, 1993); James Tully, *Public Philosophy in a New Key: vol. 2, Imperialism and Civic Freedom* (Cambridge: Cambridge University Press, 2009); Georgios Varouxakis and Bart Schultz, eds, *Utilitarianism and Empire* (Lanham, MD: Lexington, 2005); and David Armitage, 'John Locke, Carolina, and the *Two Treatises of Government*', *Political Theory*, 32: 5 (2004), 602–27. For defences of twentieth-century/contemporary imperialism, see Niall Ferguson, *Empire: How Britain Made the Modern World* (London: Penguin, 2004) and Michael Ignatieff, *Empire Lite: Nation-Building in Bosnia, Kosovo, Afghanistan* (London: Vintage, 2004); for a critique of these defences (and of contemporary liberal imperialism more generally), see Jeanne Morefield, *Empires Without Imperialism: Anglo-American Decline and the Politics of Deflection* (Oxford: Oxford University Press, 2014). For recent work in global intellectual history, see Shruti Kapila, *An Intellectual History for India* (Cambridge: Cambridge University Press, 2010); Darrin M. McMahon and Samuel Moyn, eds, *Rethinking Modern European Intellectual History* (Oxford: Oxford University Press, 2014); Samuel Moyn and Andrew Sartori, eds, *Global Intellectual History* (New York: Columbia University Press, 2015); and Christopher Bayly, *Recovering Liberties: Indian Thought in the Age of Liberalism and Empire* (Cambridge: Cambridge University Press, 2011).

2 All references to *The Indian Sociologist* will be given as: IS, year: page.

3 Herbert Spencer, *The Study of Sociology* (London: Henry S. King & Co, 1873), 47 (cited as SS hereafter).

4 While Krishnavarma's political thought is subject to a paucity of scholarly attention, a few intellectual histories and biographies provide a relatively clear sketch of his background, upbringing, and development. The earliest of these are Har Bilas Sarda's *Shyamji Krishna Varma: Patriot and Perfect* (Ajmer, Rajasthan: Vedic Yantralaya, 1959) – Bilas was a personal friend of Krishnavarma's – and Yajnik Indulal's *Shyamaji Krishnavarma: Life and Times of an Indian Revolutionary* (New Delhi: Lakshmi Publications, 1950). Recent years have seen the publication of Ganeshi Lal Verma's *Shyamji Krishna Varma, the Unknown Patriot* (New Delhi: Publications Division, Ministry of Information and Broadcasting, Govt. of India, 1993) and Harald Fischer-Tiné's *Sanskrit, Sociology and Anti-Imperial Struggle: The Life of Shyamji Krishnavarma (1857–1930)* (New Delhi: Routledge, 2014), the latter comprising by far the most sustained and rigorous engagement with Krishnavarma's intellectual contributions to the early Indian nationalist movement. Shruti Kapila, Dipesh Chakrabarty and Rochona Majumdar touch on Krishnavarma's thought in the context of broader arguments on the early Indian nationalist movement; see Shruti Kapila, 'Self, Spencer and Swaraj: Nationalist

Thought and Critiques of Liberalism, 1890–1920', *Modern Intellectual History*, 4: 1 (2007), 109–27; and Dipesh Chakrabarty and Rochona Majumdar, 'Gandhi's Gita and Politics As Such', *Modern Intellectual History*, 7: 2 (2010), 335–53. The brief biography sketched out here draws on Bilas, Fischer-Tiné, and Verma.

5 Lavaji's and others' support (Krishnavarma received financial assistance from several members of his caste community over the course of his education) is explained somewhat differently in the literature. Verma attributes the Gujurati merchant class's willingness to finance Krishnavarma's Brahminical learning to its enthusiasm, in the mid-1870s, for the Hindu reform movement embodied in the Arya Samaj – effectively, to their interest in modernizing certain elements of Hinduism. Harald Fischer-Tiné, conversely, attributes the patronage to the prestige it traditionally bestowed upon benefactors, 'who were otherwise at the forefront of "modernising" endeavours' (6).

6 Fischer-Tiné, *Sanskrit*, 7.

7 Fischer-Tiné, *Sanskrit*; Bilas, *Patriot and Perfect*, 24–42; Varma, *Unknown Patriot*, 5–6.

8 Fischer-Tiné, *Sanskrit*, 12.

9 Bilas, *Patriot and Perfect*, 26. Fischer-Tiné still further describes Krishnavarma's adoption of Sarawasti as 'his personal guru' (14).

10 IS, 1909:9. Krishnavarma would also go on to fund a scholarship in Saraswati's name in 1905.

11 Fischer-Tiné, *Sanskrit*, 16.

12 An article in the *Times of India* from May 22, 1877, lays out an expansive list of Krishnavarma's admirers – both Eastern and Western, and including Williams, M. G. Ranade and others – attesting to his considerable national reputation. See Bilas, *Patriot and Perfect*, 30–1.

13 Fischer-Tiné, *Sanskrit*, 17; Varma, *Unknown Patriot*, 8–9.

14 Letter from Helena Blavatsky to Shyamji Krishnavarma, 1878; cited in Bilas, *Patriot and Perfect*, 36–7.

15 Harald Fischer-Tiné nicely illustrates the tensions underlying Krishnavarma's position at Oxford. As would be the case at different points (and under different circumstances) throughout his life, Krishnavarma sat at the uncomfortable juncture of being both a reputed Oriental scholar *and* an object of Orientalist fantasy: while developing his own scholarship at Oxford, Williams also regularly 'presented' Krishnavarma to English audiences for 'theatre recitations' of Vedic chanting and practices. As Fischer-Tiné puts it, he thus qualified as both 'Oriental expert' and 'native informant'.

16 IS, 1909: 3–4.

17 IS, 1905: 1. Spencer's quotation is from *The Principles of Sociology* (New York: D. Appleton and Co., 1898), 642 (cited as PS hereafter).

18 This is not to suggest that Krishnavarma abandoned or supplanted one body of (Eastern) knowledge for another (Western) one; the IS is equally rife with references to Hindu figures such as Manu, Saraswati, Patanjali, Visnusarman, and many others.

19 The limits of this chapter unfortunately prohibit a more expansive exploration of these influences. For IS articles drawing on positivist critiques of empire (and, more specifically, on Richard Congreve, founder of the Positivist Society), see 1905: 13, 1905: 37–8; for socialist critiques of empire (frequently issued by H. H. Hyndman, founder of the Socialist Party and a close personal acquaintance of Krishnavarma's), see 1905: 23; for Krishnavarma's (complicated) relationship to anarchism, see Maia Ramnath, *Decolonizing Anarchism: An Antiauthoritarian History of India's Liberation Struggle* (Oakland, CA: AK Press, 2011); for his indebtedness to liberalism, see Section 2 below.

20 Fischer-Tiné, *Sanskrit*, 25.

21 *Ibid.*, 35.

22 *Ibid.*, xv.

23 Ramnath, *Decolonizing Anarchism*, 124. Fischer-Tiné similarly alludes to Krishnavarma's 'openness to cultural bricolage and wholesale borrowing' (84).

24 Fischer-Tiné, *Sanskrit*, xvi.

25 IS, June 1914: 2 (I here include the month due to Krishnavarma's abandoning yearly serialized pagination in 1914).

26 Letter from Tilak to Krishnavarma, 10 July 1905.

27 IS, 1907: 9. I treat Krishnavarma's 'Society of Political Missionaries' below, at 48 and 55.

28 IS, 1907: 19.

29 IS, 1905: 30–1.

30 Ramnath, *Decolonizing Anarchism*, 60; Manu Goswami, *Producing India: From Colonial Economy to National Space* (Chicago: University of Chicago Press, 2004: 246–7); Fischer-Tiné, *Sanskrit*, 53–109.

31 IS, 1909: 3.

32 IS, 1909: 18.

33 IS, 1908: 4.

34 IS, 1907: 11.

35 IS, 1907: 41–2.

36 T. Sriramulu, cited from the 'International Review' (July 1908) in IS, 1909: 20.

37 Bidyut Chakrabarty and Rajendra Kumar Pandey, *Modern Indian Political Thought: Text and Context* (New Delhi: Sage, 2009), 24.

38 A voluminous literature addresses the history of the INC; for just a few, see Sumit Sarkar, *Modern India, 1885–1947* (New Delhi: Macmillan, 1983), Bayly, *Recovering Liberties*, Chakrabarty and Pandey, *Text and Context*, and Sankar Ghose, *Political Ideas and Movements in India* (New Delhi: Allied Publishers, 1975).

39 Surendranath Banerjea, cited in Chakrabarty and Pandey, *Text and Context*, 24.

40 Ghose, *Political Ideas*, 11.

41 *Ibid.*, 18.

42 Report of the 11th Indian National Congress, cited in Ghose, *Political Ideas*, 23.

43 Sarkar, *Modern India*, 90.

44 Surendranath Banerjea, *The Trumpet Voice of India: Speeches of Banerjea* (Toronto: University of Toronto Libraries, 2011), 105–6.

45 For recent treatments of liberal imperialism, see Pitts, *A Turn to Empire*, Mehta, *Liberalism and Empire*, Parekh, 'Decolonizing Liberalism' and 'Critique of Locke and Mill', Mantena, *Alibis of Empire*, McCarthy, *Race, Empire*, and Dipesh Chakrabarty, *Provincializing Europe* (Princeton, NJ: Princeton University Press, 2000).

46 Chakrabarty and Pandey, *Text and Context*, 25.

47 Surendranath Banerjea, cited in Ghose, *Political Ideas*, 15.

48 G. K. Gokhale, cited in Ghose, *Political Ideas*, 18.

49 G. K. Gokhale, quoted in IS, 1905: 43–4.

50 IS, 1909: 11.

51 IS, 1913: 16

52 IS, 1913: 31.

53 IS, 1908: 21.

54 IS, 1908: 18.

55 IS, 1909: 5.

56 IS, 1906: 1.

57 IS, 1909: 8.

58 IS, 1909: 8.

59 For an acute analysis of the impossibility of just laws and of the just administration of law in colonial contexts, see IS, 1906: 18.

60 IS, 1906: 34.

61 Chakrabarty, *Provincializing Europe*, 8.

62 IS, 1907: 38.

63 IS, 1911: 36.

64 IS, 1912: 39.

65 An extensive literature catalogues the impact of Bengal's partition over the early nationalist movement; see Chakrabarty and Pandey, *Text and Context*, Ramnath, *Decolonizing Anarchism*, Ghose, *Political Ideas*, Sarkar, *Modern India*, and Vishwanath Prasad Varma, *The Life and Philosophy of Lokamanya Tilak* (Agra: Lakshmi Narain Agarwal, 1978).

66 B. G. Tilak, cited in Varma, *Tilak*, 189.

67 The subtler philosophical, ethical and political inflections of *swadeshi* and *swaraj* developed by Ghose, Pal, Tilak and Gandhi are subject to extensive commentary; I here provide little more than a thumbnail sketch in order to situate Krishnavarma's views in relation to the extremists'.

68 Bipin Chandra Pal, cited in Ghose, *Political Ideas*, 32.

69 B. G. Tilak, quoted in Chakrabarty and Pandey, *Text and Context*, 10.

70 *Ibid.*, 14.

71 Bipin Chandra Pal, *Swadeshi & Swaraj, the Rise of New Patriotism* (Calcutta: Yugayatri Prakashak, 1954), 80. For more on Pal, see Amalendu Prasad Mookerjee, *Social and Political Ideas of Bipin Chandra Pal* (Calcutta: Minerva, 1974). For more on religion, secularism and politics in India, see Romila Thapar, 'Is Secularism Alien to Indian Civilization?', T. N. Madan, 'Secularism Revisited: Doctrine of Destiny or Political Ideology?', and Rajeev Bharghava, 'The Distinctiveness of Indian Secularism', all in *Indian Political Thought: A Reader*, eds Aakash Singh and Silika Mohapatra (London: Routledge, 2010).

72 Pal, *New Patriotism*, i.

73 Aurobindo Ghose, cited in Ghose, *Political Ideas*, 45.

74 *Ibid.*, 45. For more on Tilak's spiritualism, see Varma, *Tilak*, 444.

75 Goswami, *Producing India*, 269.

76 Urmila Sharma and S. K. Sharma, *Indian Political Thought* (New Delhi: Atlantic, 1996), 116.

77 Pal, *New Patriotism*, 107.

78 Goswami, *Producing India*, 257.

79 *Ibid.*, 269.

80 The distinction between extremists and terrorists is somewhat fluid, given their many shared ideological commitments; the terrorists are perhaps best understood as a more radical wing of the extremists. For treatments of the divisions between moderates, extremists and terrorists, see Ghose, *Political Ideas*, 53, and Ramnath, *Decolonizing Anarchism*, 78–9.

81 Ramnath, *Decolonizing Anarchism*, 68.

82 *Ibid.*, 68.

83 Cited in Ramnath, *Decolonizing Anarchism*, 83.

84 *Ibid.*, 74.

85 Herbert Spencer, *The Principles of Ethics* (Indianapolis, IN: Liberty Fund, 1978). Cited hereafter as PE.

86 IS, 1909: 18.

87 IS, 1907: 12.

88　This sociological critique of empire is elaborated below, in Section 3.

89　IS, 1907: 21.

90　IS, 1905: 10.

91　IS, 1905: 17.

92　IS, 1907: 19.

93　Ghose, *Political Ideas*, 46.

94　IS, 1907: 30.

95　Fischer-Tiné, *Sanskrit*, 90.

96　Goswami, *Producing India*, 266.

97　Fischer-Tiné, *Sanskrit*, 64.

98　IS, 1912: 22.

99　IS, 1907: 48.

100　IS, 1913: 48.

101　IS, 1907: 41.

102　IS, 1909: 8.

103　IS, 1906: 32.

104　IS, 1909: 16.

105　IS, 1906: 25.

106　IS, 1913: 43–4.

107　IS, 1909: 4.

108　Fischer-Tiné, *Sanskrit*, 88.

109　IS, 1906: 19.

110　IS, 1907: 14.

111　Kapila, 'Self, Swaraj', 111.

112　*Ibid.*, 116.

113　*Ibid.*, 114.

114　IS, 1909: 3.

115　Herbert Spencer, 'Government Colonization', in *Social Statics* (London: John Chapman, 1860), 357–9 (cited as GC hereafter).

116　Herbert Spencer, 'Imperialism and Slavery', in *Facts and Comments* (New York: D. Appleton and Co., 1902), 159–160 (cited as IS hereafter).

117　Spencer, IS, 168.

118　Spencer, GC, 366–7.

119　*Ibid.*, 368.

120　*Ibid.*, 369.

121　Spencer, IS, 159.

122　Spencer, GC, 368.

123　Spencer, IS, 167.

124　*Ibid.*, 158.

125　*Ibid.*, 170.

126　Herbert Spencer, 'Bias of Patriotism', in SS, 205.

127　IS, 1907: 48.

128　IS, 1905: 19.

129　Spencer, SS, 413.

130　*Ibid.*, 413.

131　*Ibid.*, 415.

132　For example, Spencer describes British colonists' tendencies as 'retrograde on being placed in circumstances which call forth the old propensities' (SS, 412); while sympathetic social sentiments might well gain in the metropole, the same state's colonists regress toward anti-social forms of violence and domination.

133 Spencer, SS, 417–18.
134 Spencer, SS, 419. Far from reproducing the liberal imperialist hierarchy of civiliza-
     tions crowned by Europeans, Spencer's sociological account of barbarism and civili-
     zation treated 'the assassinations of Italy, the cruelties of the Croats and Czechs, and
     the Austrian butcheries' (SS, 421) as signs of their under-development.
135 Spencer, SS, 422.
136 Spencer, SS, 427.
137 IS, 1906: 21–2.
138 IS, 1907: 7.
139 Spencer, SS, 418.
140 IS, 1906: 34.
141 IS, 1907: 12.
142 IS, 1907: 21.
143 IS, 1907: 31.
144 Spencer, SS, 419.
145 Spencer, PS, 659.
146 Spencer, 'Rebarbarization', in *Facts and Comments*, 172.
147 Spencer, PS, 662.
148 *Ibid.*
149 *Ibid.*, 228.
150 *Ibid.*, 226.
151 *Ibid.*
152 *Ibid.*, 228.
153 *Ibid.*
154 *Ibid.*, 222.
155 Spencer, 'Rebarbarization', 178–9.
156 *Ibid.*, 178.
157 *Ibid.*, 180.
158 *Ibid.*, 180–1.
159 *Ibid.*, 185.
160 Spencer, GC, 368–9.
161 *Ibid.*, 369.
162 IS, 1907: 30.
163 IS, 1908: 7.
164 IS, 1909: 10.
165 Ramnath, *Decolonizing Anarchism*.
166 IS, 1909: 42.
167 IS, 1909: 19.
168 IS, 1907: 46.
169 IS, 1909: 41.
170 IS, 1909: 41.

3

The other Mahatma's naive monarchism: Phule, Paine, and the appeal to Queen Victoria

Jimmy Casas Klausen

To commemorate the US president's visit in November 2010, Chhagan Bhujbal, deputy to the chief minister of Maharashtra, presented Barack Obama with the book *Slavery* by Jotirao Govindrao Phule. Published in 1873, *Slavery (in the Civilized British Government under the Cloak of Brahmanism)* was Phule's passionately argued case against Brahman supremacy, which had been articulated through interpretations of spiritual texts and practised in caste orderings and exclusions, including restrictions on access to the sacred word. By reinforcing hierarchy and maintaining a conception of purity, Brahmans repressed Sudras and Atisudras – members of the lowest of the four varnas and those below/outside the varna system altogether.[1] This much was clear even to Indian critics of British rule who, conceding to racist British missionaries that Indian religion was decadent and cruel, believed that Indians' political autonomy from Britain would not be granted without serious religious reform.

However, in Phule's more radical analysis, cruelty was constitutive of Brahmanic religion: Brahmins could only demand that Sudras and Atisudras serve all twice-born persons because Brahmans had many centuries ago invaded and defeated the latter in war. In short, the prior condition of possibility for their slavery was conquest. Sudras and Atisudras did not thus owe their servility to a lowly status in an eternal order of things (as Brahmins maintained): they were not essentially abject but had been historically abjected through domination of their ancestors. Indeed, Phule argued, Sudratisudras were abased, maltreated, and reviled as slaves proportionally to the fierceness with which their native warrior ancestors had resisted outside invasion. And, most unexpectedly, Phule held that *further* British intervention was necessary to correct this injustice. At a moment when some Indian elites were developing a critique of alien rule and arguments for greater political autonomy from Britain, Phule was appealing to Queen Victoria. The Sudratisudras, declared Phule, 'will never forget the obligations of the Queen, who alone can remove the bond of slavery tied around their necks by the wily brahmans'.[2]

Given this specific context, why might Phule's tract deserve the honour of a presidential gift? Active in Maharashtra in the second half of the nineteenth century, Phule (1827–90) was an untiring social reformer and political thinker, chiefly known for his projects for the empowerment of two of the most disadvantaged segments of Indian societies: members of the lowest castes and those subject to 'untouchability' (together, the Sudratisudras), and women, especially Sudratisudra girls but also Brahmin widows. Phule's main point of intervention for promoting substantive equality was education. With his wife Savitribai, he established a number of schools at a time when the education of women and the lower classes was considered unnecessary or even dangerous to Maharashtra's social order. Moreover, in radical defiance of rules about defilement, he famously invited Untouchables to use the household's well in 1868. As unrelenting a campaigner as Mohandas Gandhi, Phule might be called the *other* Mahatma, because he, too, had been publicly honoured with this title.

Touched by what he understood to have been the justification for the American Civil War, Phule had dedicated *Slavery* to

> the good people of the United States as a token of admiration for their sublime disinterested and self-sacrificing devotion in the cause of Negro Slavery; and with an earnest desire, that my countrymen may take their noble example as their guide in the emancipation of their Sudra Brethren from the trammels of Brahmin thraldom.[3]

Connecting struggles in this way, between those enslaved in nineteenth-century Maharashtra and those recently enslaved, but now legally free, in the United States, *Slavery* thus seemed a symbolically appropriate gift to the first African-American president: even if Obama himself is not the descendant of slaves, his wife and children are. The gift of Phule's book was only the latest in a series of transactions between South Asians and African-Americans since the nineteenth century, from B. R. Ambedkar's exchange of letters with W. E. B. Du Bois to Bayard Rustin's and Martin Luther King Jr.'s advancing Gandhian strategies. As historians Daniel Immerwahr and Nico Slate have documented, it was through such exchanges that affinities between South Asian and African-American experiences of racism, casteism, and/or colonialism were drawn and critically affirmed.[4]

There is, though, another, deeper, affinity between Phule's Sudratisudras and as yet unemancipated African-American slaves in the United States: both engaged in a political phenomenon that has been dubbed 'naive monarchism'. As Ranajit Guha and Steven Hahn noted regarding the peasant insurgencies of colonial India and strategies of resistance by African Americans to slavery,[5] the lowest strata of peasants and slaves sometimes claimed a mantel of legitimacy for their opposition to dominating social and political systems by claiming that the highest authorities – Queen Victoria or President Lincoln – had authorized their resistance to oppressive intermediate authorities. The sovereign executive power had affirmed subalterns' rights, but the *sarkari, sahukari, zamindari* (government official, moneylender, landlord), and slave-owners were deliberately ignoring higher authorities out of selfish concern to guard the privileges and emoluments they had hoarded. Being so distant from local circumstances, however, neither queen nor president was aware that these intermediate powers were flouting sovereign commands. Thus, it was up to the peasants and slaves to press their rights themselves. *If Victoria only knew* of these local elites' recalcitrant rejection of her command, the empress would surely bless subaltern insurgency and revolts as justified in the spirit of the law if not its letter. Or, as some American slaves even *before* the Emancipation Proclamation believed, the Confederacy's war itself proved that Southern slaveholders insisted on defying a directive to free the slaves that Lincoln either had already or would very soon issue, and so slaves were right to rebel or flee.

As a nameable phenomenon, naive monarchism is a product of twentieth-century radical historiography. For the most part, critical social historians have reconstructed subaltern agency from records written from the standpoint of law and order. Despite the partiality of perspective, the juridical record provides nearly the only archive available for reconstructing naive monarchism: although social elites and political officials generated accounts of insurgency ex post facto, often for punitive purposes, the peasant and slave voices upon which they reported were usually anonymous and often illiterate, and the subaltern archives (such as they were) therefore oral and immaterial. These archives from below were also ephemeral and highly mutable, for, often based in rumour, the object of knowledge was modulated by and for each hearer.[6]

Although mentioned by scholars of subaltern resistance, naive monarchism has yet to be explored in analyses of Phule. Certainly there are differences: Phule's literacy and relative prosperity marked him off from his low-caste or outcaste fellows. Thus *Slavery* is a unique record of naive monarchism by someone who both shared and pushed the Sudratisudra political perspective, yet at the same time, Phule's access to scholarly learning and its publics allowed him to register its paradoxes in a more sustained way than its anonymous, illiterate expositors. Nonetheless, or perhaps consequently, *Slavery's* very complexity as an argument allowed it to mimic the adaptability of the rumour-genre while retaining the (presumptively more) stable form of a published text. Phule's text's many facets could call a counter-public into being for common action by adapting itself to discrete audiences, learned and otherwise. In this sense, Phule could invoke both Paine as an anti-colonial American patriot critical of alien rule, monarchy, and priestly superstition and, simultaneously, Victoria as an empress-redeemer who could set things to right.

Though naive monarchism is hardly the key that solves all of *Slavery's* riddles, it nonetheless does elucidate some of the text's puzzling moves. I start by first tracing out the substance of Brahman domination and Sudratisudra slavery, especially by way of the analogies Phule draws to American slavery. In the second section, I analyse the influence of Thomas Paine's writings on Phule's diagnosis of Brahman oppression by conquest and priestcraft as well as Phule's representation of Sudratisudras as the once and future constituent power of Maharashtra. If, however, the Sudratisudras are the real constituent power, then why would Phule argue that they need British rule? Phule answers that Sudratisudras have been denatured and deculturated by slavery. The character of Britain's imperial governance usefully counteracts such degeneration (see third section). In the fourth section, I explore the politics of supplication and sentimentality in Phule's writing, and especially how these come together – by way of his naive monarchist critique of intermediary authorities – in the appeal to Queen Victoria. Finally, as I argue in closing, the simultaneously real and surreal character of *Slavery*'s political intervention, whose agency could only have arisen under British imperialism even as it points beyond it, derives from Phule's position between critique and catachresis.

Slaveries and conquests

Slavery diagnoses a relationship among three groups – Brahmans, Sudratisudras, and Britons – in hopes of altering the balance of powers among them. As such, the comparison and subsequent contrast between Sudratisudra and African-American slaveries is nearly incidental – yet at the same time the comparison and contrast of slaveries makes the subcontinental triangulation a global concern. It both invites solidarity between the abjectly oppressed groups in the American South and South Asia and ups the moral ante for the British by inserting them in a different triangulation. Placing the British between Americans and Brahmins, Phule suggests that the British are the more promising imperial ruler than the Brahmins yet could nonetheless fail to follow the Americans' lead in declaring emancipation and thus vitiate their reputation for humanitarianism. (I return to this moral appeal to the British in the third and fourth sections.)

Although Phule builds his case for the cruelty of Brahmin domination by drawing a series of parallels to the sufferings of African-American slaves at the hands of their white masters, he also is careful to note some substantive differences. Unlike African slaves in the Americas, the Sudratisudras were not made slaves by violent captivity and forcible removal through an intercontinental, transatlantic slave trade. Rather, they were enslaved on native soil.

> Now the only difference between them and the slaves in America is that whereas the blacks were captured and sold as slaves, the shudras and atishudras were conquered and enslaved by the *bhats* [priests] and brahmans. Except for this difference, [Phule insists] all the other conditions in which they lived were the same.[7]

From a critical multiracial perspective on the United States and other settler-colonial, slave-owning societies in the Americas, however, the difference that Phule concedes makes all the difference. The historical experience of Sudratisudras, being slaves and aborigines, shares features with African-Americans and Native Americans both. Indeed, Phule mentions that '[t]he cruelties which the European settlers practiced on the American Indians on their first settlement in the new world, had certainly their parallel in India on the advent of the Aryans and their subjugation of the aborigines'.[8] This may be the only reference to indigenous Americans in Phule's major writings, although he does speculate, in *Cultivator's Whipcord* (1883), that the Americas were prehistorically peopled by Sudras who had fled the Aryan invasion and refers to ancient indigenous Americans as 'American shudras'.[9] Nonetheless, Phule's references to Native American genocide are sparse, perhaps because, by specifying Europeans' 'first settlement', he consigns it to the past rather than understanding it to be ongoing.

However, Phule seems at least implicitly aware that Sudratisudra subjugation does not just share features with the violations of African-American slaves and Native Americans but, more direly, owes its unique extremity to the fact that it *compounds* the two groups' experiences of violence. It is perhaps for this reason that he repeatedly insists that Sudratisudra experience *exceeds* that of African-American slaves: 'In the days of rigid Brahmin dominancy ... my Sudra brethren had even greater hardships and oppression practised upon them than what even the slaves in America had to suffer.'[10] 'All the calamities suffered by blacks were endured by the shudras and the atishudras who probably,' Phule notes, 'suffered more but not less at the hands of the Brahmans.'[11] The superlative oppression of Sudratisudras by comparison to African-American slaves is a consistent theme in Phule's texts even after *Slavery*; he reiterates Sudratisudras' excess suffering in *Cultivator's Whipcord* a decade later.[12] Thus, Phule argues for the particular brutality of Brahmin domination: it was similar to, but quantitatively more intense than, that of white American slave-owners over African-American chattel, because it was qualitatively different, combining conquest with enslavement.

What makes the conquest so total is that the Brahman invaders succeeded in effacing the memory of their foreign provenance. The Brahmans

> had come originally from distant lands, outside India, invaded it, attacked the original inhabitants of this land, conquered and forcibly turned them into slaves and oppressed them in several different ways. Then, after their memories had somewhat been blunted and blurred, the brahmans, very skilfully, concealed from them all the true facts: that they themselves had come from outside, defeated the original inhabitants and turned them into slaves.[13]

The Brahmans' conquest was so complete that it could not be known as such by its victims – and being unable to know that their subordination was a human artifice, the latter could therefore neither resist nor overturn it. Without knowledge of the historicity of their subjugation, the Sudratisudras could only accept their lot as natural, part of a divine order.

The secret of the Brahmans' foreign status was so well-kept in India that it would take other outsiders to reveal the truth to the Sudratisudras. The preface to *Slavery* begins by mentioning the work of European comparative linguists and racial theorists:

> Recent researches have demonstrated beyond a shadow of doubt that the Brahmins were not the aborigines of India. At some remote period of antiquity, probably more than 3000 years ago, the Aryan progenitors of the present Brahmin Race descended upon the plains of Hindoo Koosh, and other adjoining tracts.[14]

This became known as the Aryan Invasion thesis. Phule was one of several thinkers from the Indian subcontinent who drew on European Orientalist scholarship in the nineteenth and early twentieth centuries, and throughout *Slavery* he creatively employs etymological methods inspired by Indo-European philology. Some British writers redeployed the findings of Orientalist scholars such as Max Müller in order to build racial distinctions out of ethnolinguistic difference between speakers of Indo-Aryan languages and more 'primitive' or 'negroid' speakers of Dravidian and other languages. Constructing such a racial difference had a political purpose, especially after the Revolt of 1857: Reverend John Wilson had sought to reconcile the British with Indian upper castes as belonging to the same racial family.[15] Although not always inclined to weigh in on racial supremacy or imperial governance, some Indian scholars, such as R. G. Bhandarkar, in his *Wilson Philological Lectures on Sanskrit and Derived Languages* (1877), certainly saw in the thesis of common Indo-European origin a legitimation for considering India a great culture, cousin to ancient Greece and Rome.[16] Others saw merely a proof of how far modern India had fallen from the heights of Sanskrit civilization. Mahadev Govind Ranade, writing in the last decade of the nineteenth century, believed that a period of high civilization came to an end because, during a period of stagnation internal to Aryan civilization, non-Aryan aboriginal influences definitively took hold, with the result that struggling, adulterated Aryan civilization finally succumbed to Muslim rule under the Mughals.[17] Many elites of Ranade's generation concluded that India required a national renewal, necessitating a reform or transformation of the imperial relationship with Britain.

That British imperialist missionaries could have recourse to the same arguments as Brahmin nationalists (albeit mostly moderate nationalists) – even if they drew opposed conclusions – suggests how malleable the Aryan Invasion thesis could be. Even still, Phule commandeered the thesis to an entirely surprising end. Despite the fact that, in the estimation of Mahadev Deshpande, 'Phule presents a picture of history, which is not different in substance from the one seen in the works of the Brahmin authors like Bhandarkar, [Mahadeo Moreshwar] Kunte, and Ranade', Phule completely inverts the elements of this history and therefore subverts the Brahmins' findings.[18] Or, perhaps it should be said that they invert the elements of Phule's history, for Rosalind O'Hanlon insists that 'Phule was very much the earliest' of the Indian writers to extrapolate Aryan and pre-Aryan antiquity.[19] Whereas these later, upper-caste, mostly nationalist writers traced all that was great in India – whether still present in sacred books or nearly lost as a living tradition – to the Aryan race, Phule inversely and subversively considered the Aryans' advent the origin of India's decline. The Aryan invaders 'appear to have been a race imbued with very high notions of self, extremely cunning, arrogant and bigoted', whereas those 'aborigines whom the Aryans subjugated, or displaced, appear to have been a hardy and brave people from the determined front which they offered to these interlopers'.[20] Even if he published his lower-caste interpretation of the Aryan past before his upper-caste counterparts did theirs, Phule was nonetheless inverting – or, in his view, *re*inverting – a dominant scale of values.

Yet if the ancestors of the Sudratisudras were such brave and determined warriors, then how could they have been defeated and kept under? Phule's answer is twofold. In part, the foreign invaders were more vicious (i.e. dishonourable) warriors. In part, the Aryans perfected a priestly form of power that installed a new system of values that succeeded in subjugating the aborigines.

Certainly Maharashtra's indigenous population had been mighty, and Phule reserves the name Kshetrias (or Ksatriyas) only for them[21] rather than identifying it with the second highest warrior/ruler division in Brahmanic tradition. However, the indigenous Ksatriyas were overpowered by the Aryans because these invaders' force was especially cruel. Phule contrasts the natives and invaders as warriors by reference to stories that Brahmans themselves tell of the legendary Parashuram, 'one of the chiefs of the brahmans'. Whereas the Ksatriya warriors deserve to be considered valiant, Parashuram is, by the admission of Brahmanic accounts, relentlessly inhumane, tyrannical, and cruel: 'Obviously, nobody boasts of their own shameful deeds,' Phule ventures, 'It is therefore quite surprising that [Brahmans themselves] have described in their books all the gruesome details of the killings of the kshatriya infants.' Parashuram had not only killed Ksatriya adult men in battle; he also attacked indigenous infant boys as well and therefore victimized their mothers. 'When he heard of widowed, pregnant and helpless kshatriya women, desperately running away to save the lives of their unborn babies, he chased them like a hunter and captured them. The moment he heard of a boy being born to the unfortunate captive, he would kill the infant instantly.'[22] More than war, this was 'wholesale extermination' and 'genocide'.[23] So incensed by the fearless resistance of the Ksatriya and apparently affronted by indigenous honour in contrast to their own infamy, the Brahmans were driven to even more dishonourable methods. They committed 'atrocities'.[24]

Having overcome aboriginal, valiant might by cruel force, the Brahmans then succeeded in subordinating the aborigines permanently. This they could not do by force alone. As Orlando Patterson argues, '[n]o system of total power can ever hope to rely solely on naked force for the maintenance of power'.[25] Patterson's assessment rings especially true in the case of Brahman power, for, as we shall see, Phule argues that the Sudratisudras are the fount of power in Indian society. Slavery's system of total power can only maintain itself by 'supplement[ing] the use of force with a minimum of consensual mechanisms'.[26] Certainly genocidal war went a long way in destroying the base of Sudratisudra power, but only Brahmin priestcraft could ultimately usurp native power permanently. Elaborate superstitions endlessly thwarted Sudratisudras from rebuilding a power base for themselves. Although ancient conquest deprived the aborigines of their freedom historically, therefore enslaving them as a people, it was the practice of dominating the aborigines as Sudras and Atisudras through 'that weird system of mythology, the ordination of caste, and the code of cruel and inhuman laws' that perpetuated in the daily performance of rituals the enslavement of their individual 'minds' – a 'psychological slavery' – by way of their bodies.[27]

Moreover, and crucially, the Brahmans secured Sudratisudra subjection by not only having 'produce[d] crafty and cunning books and built, as it were, a strong fortress of these books', which 'justified' Sudratisudra slavery 'even in the eyes of God'. They also restricted access to the sacred word from the very people condemned by it.[28] Maintaining general Sudratisudra ignorance of Brahmanic religion and political history was key to their ongoing slavery: the Brahmans 'were scared that if the shudras remembered their superiority in the past, they would trample them under their feet. They weren't satisfied by this; they even went on to forbid the shudras from listening to even a word of anyone reading a religious book.'[29] Thus, the Sudratisudras were not only enslaved everyday by caste injunctions, but also disabled from questioning this caste subordination as an artifice of historical conquest and religious tyranny. Not only coercive force, nor even coercive force combined with consensual mechanisms, but both of these also combined with intellectual impairment by the Brahmans are what enslaved the Sudratisudras.

Paine in Phule's Indian context

Phule clearly judges the Brahmans' domination of Sudratisudras as vicious, and their enslavement probably worse than that of white slave-owners over African-American slaves, but what precisely were the mechanisms and conditions of continued Brahman dominance? Surprisingly, perhaps, Phule's answer bears the influence of Thomas Paine. Admittedly in the two cases (quoted below) in which Phule explicitly mentions Paine in *Slavery*, Paine functions more as a generic emblem of equal human rights than a sophisticated analyst of political relations. Yet it is wrong to reduce Phule's borrowing from Paine simply to a general commitment to individual rights, as Rochana Bajpai would have it.[30] For Phule's – and Paine's – analysis is more radical than a liberal reading, and Phule's own vague citations of Paine, would allow. However, Phule's invocation of Paine does place him in difficulties because Paine was both too radical and also, in a crucial respect, wrong. These difficulties are what necessitate a naive monarchist analysis: in correcting Paine, Phule had to invoke the Queen, as we shall see.

Reportedly Phule was strongly affected by reading *The Rights of Man* in 1847–48,[31] and, although he never cites it specifically, its analysis seems to undergird Phule's own in *Slavery*.[32] Phule certainly agrees with Paine that humans enjoy rights guaranteed by nature against arbitrary usurpations by contingent social arrangements, but, as O'Hanlon judiciously puts it, '[t]here are other areas of Paine's work [besides the natural rights thesis], especially in *Rights of Man*, which may have helped to shape Phule's thought, or to which at least it shows strong parallels'.[33] In particular, Paine argues that 'governments arise either *out* of the people, or *over* the people', and he develops a tripartite scheme 'of the several sources from which governments have arisen and on which they have been founded': 'government of priestcraft', founded on 'superstition'; 'government of conquerors', founded on sheer might; and the government 'of reason', founded on 'the common interests of society, and the common rights of man'.[34] The Aryan conquest of the aborigines was doubly vicious because it combined both priestcraft and conquest. This duplicity explains why Phule felt compelled to write *Slavery* as an exposé. Although evidence abounded that the Brahmans dominated those whom they designated Sudras and Atisudras, two facts needed to be exposed: that the Brahmans exercised government *doubly* 'over the people' and that this compounded government arose historically from irrational human arrangements. *Slavery* aimed to expose these facts because the Brahmans' victims neither perceived Brahman government as double nor assumed it to be secular. Priestcraft had converted coercion (i.e. force) into consent (i.e. 'consent' to an abject state) by rendering Sudratisudras so ignorant that not only was their faculty of perception impaired but also they were prevented from developing any faculties that could lead them to perceive their lot more sharply and critically.

Obversely, Phule's way of discussing 'the people', that is, the once and future potential of the Sudratisudras, owes something to Paine, I would argue. In the end, however, Phule makes a critical correction to the role of humble 'society' in *Rights of Man*. Paine insists that a constitution, like society itself, precedes a government: 'a government is only a creature of a constitution. The constitution of a country is not the act of its government, but of the people constituting a government'.[35] This distinction between the constituting, or constitutive, power and the constituted power was well elaborated by Paine's French revolutionary colleague Abbé de Sieyès in *What Is the Third Estate?*, and Paine advances it here to make a more recognizably Painean point about popular sovereignty. According to Paine, constitutive power derives from the people functioning as a society, which he identifies in *Rights of Man*, adopting the idiom of Sieyès and French Revolutionary discourse more broadly, as 'the nation'.[36] The constituted power, the government, is to be limited by the constituting power; the creator continues to constrain its creation: '[t]he final controlling power, therefore, and the original constituting power are one and the same power'.[37] Origin and end, the constituting and the limiting power, must coincide in Paine's vision of popular sovereignty.

For Paine, it is *natural* that constituting and limiting powers coincide. He notes that 'the nation … has a natural ability' to 'regulat[e] and [restrain]' the governmental power it constitutes.[38] This is in part because '[f]ormal government makes but a small part of civilized life'[39] because, as their natural faculties are developed, and as they realize the 'reciprocal benefits' therefrom, humans become so 'habituated … to social and civilized life' that 'there is always enough of its principles in practice to carry them through any changes they may find necessary or convenient to make in their government'.[40] In sum, humans naturally control government because humans' natural capacity for association exceeds government, as Paine illustrated by reference to the American Revolution:

> For upwards of two years from the commencement of the American war, and a longer period in several of the American states, there were no established forms of government. The old governments had been abolished, and the country was too much occupied in defense to employ its attention in establishing new governments; yet during this interval order and harmony were preserved as inviolate as in any country in Europe. There is a natural aptness in man, and more so in society, because it embraces a greater variety of abilities and resources to accommodate itself to whatever situation it is in. The instant formal government is abolished, society begins to act. A general association takes place, and common interest produces common security.[41]

In the scheme of civilized life, government ought to be a rather minor creature, hence easy to control, because, here again, origin coincides with end; human nature converges with the interests of society. Of course, it was possible to pervert nature, and Paine made his career writing against such barbarous perversions by aristocrats, monarchs, and priests. Nonetheless, although from *Common Sense* onward he aimed to reorient his diverted citizens to natural right, it was in his view impossible to lose sight of it.

In Phule's view, however, it was indeed possible to *lose* such a natural ability and, likewise, one's civilization. The Brahmans' system of caste enslavement so denatured and brutalized the Sudratisudras that it effaced their cultural memory and past nature as Ksatriyas. As such, they could no longer orient themselves to the possibility of freedom and right on their own but would require emancipation from the outside against equally alien oppressors. Paine might have been unable to acknowledge the phenomenon of denaturing because he never confronted transatlantic chattel slavery, instead identifying 'slavery' with monarchic despotism.[42] Phule, however, acknowledges degeneration, noting how American slaves 'helplessly await[ed] death in a highly degenerated state of mind' until the British and American abolitions of slavery had restored them to life and kin.[43]

For this reason, Phule would effectively correct Paine. For example, Paine waxes lyrical about the resilience of humble society subjected to 'discouragement and oppression': '[u]nder all discouragements, [man] pursues his object and yields to nothing but impossibilities'.[44] Whereas Paine suggests that labouring people advanced materially, even if not morally, *despite* the despotism of their governors, Phule shows that for centuries the Sudratisudras enjoyed neither moral nor material progress. Against Paine's celebration of resilience against all odds, Phule attributes to Sudratisudras just sheer persistence. Yet even mere persistence was on the verge of expiring at the moment of the British advent. Hence, although it is the case that '[s]udras are the life and sinews of the country' and, unlike the false Brahmins, are the *true* support, 'financial as well as political', for the British in the wake of the Revolt of 1857,[45] it is nonetheless the case that the British delivered the Sudratisudras from extinction.

> And then, as luck would have it, God took pity on them and the British rule was established in India. The shudras heartily thank the British for this and are exceedingly grateful to them. They will never forget the obligations of the British on them. It is the British who have liberated them from the prisons of the brahmans and showed them and their offspring these days of comfort. Had the British not been there, the brahmans would have ground them to dust.[46]

The very basis of society, its productive material base, was nearly starved and killed off by unproductive Brahmans. The theme of the unproductive class of Brahmans living off of the productive class of Sudratisudras is thoroughly elaborated in *The Cultivator's Whipcord*, but Phule already alludes to it in the introduction of *Slavery* just quoted and in Part XI, which presents Brahmin ceremonies as vicious parasitism perpetrated through superstitious ruses on Sudras made gullible by ignorance.[47] India owes centuries of 'stagnation' to priestcraft, 'this system of selfish superstition and bigotry'.[48] Extractive ritualism, that is, Brahmins' performing 'necessary' rituals in order to extract *daksina* from humble Sudratisudra cultivators, was leeching Sudratisudras of their force.[49]

Thus, even if the arrival of the British had, at the eleventh hour, interrupted the Brahmans' certain destruction of Sudratisudras, it only delivered them from physical slavery. Yet they 'still remain ignorant and captive in the mental slavery which the brahmans have perpetuated through their books'.[50] Indeed, extractive ritualism perpetuates 'consensual' physical slavery through mental slavery. Because Sudratisudras are incapacitated from questioning the web of rituals in which priestcraft has entangled them, they must 'voluntarily' labour harder in order to be ready at any moment to pay Brahmins for rituals performed. Sudratisudras' enforced ignorance and captivity to superstition compel them to participate in their own exploitation.

More significantly, though, Phule corrects Paine by suggesting that mental slavery is what most denatured and deculturated the Sudratisudras. Consequently, having forgotten freedom, they actively resist emancipation:

> The arguments of the brahmans have been imprinted so firmly on the minds of the shudras that they, like the Negro slaves in America, oppose the very people who are willing to fight for them, and free them from the chains of slavery. It is very surprising that the oppressed people choose to remain resigned to their despicable state of existence; they proclaim that they have no complaints about their circumstances ... Not only do they reject the offer of help, they are willing to fight those very people who want to help them.[51]

Phule may be alluding here to political circumstances he analyses more explicitly later in *Slavery*. Whereas, during the era before Britain's empire in India, the Brahmans incited the Sudras against each other through the creation of sub-caste distinctions and untouchability,[52] the Brahmans now incite them all together against the British because of the threat that the new invaders pose to Brahman dominance, especially through direct exposure of Sudratisudras to Christian missionaries' egalitarian ideas.[53]

In Phule's view – a suspicion that Ambedkar would continue to harbour even past Independence – the high-caste argument for national unity was simply another ruse. The Brahmans' new cant about Hindu unity across castes and their newfound motivation to reform upper-caste excesses amounted to 'selfish advice' given for the sake of preserving hierarchy:[54] the result would simply be that interpersonal exploitation would be converted into elite dominance in national politics. Moreover, in Phule's view, Indian nationalism aimed to erode lower-caste Anglo-patriotism because the Brahmans

> are afraid that if we, the shudras, really become the brothers of the English, we will condemn their wily religious books and then these *bhats* who are so proud of their caste will have to eat dust; the lazy idlers will not be able to gorge themselves on the food produced by the sweat of our brow.[55]

The intense suspicion Phule maintained of Brahman political motives led him to suspect (ultimately unfairly) that even the Revolt of 1857 was nothing more than Brahmans' directing gullible Sudratisudras to rebel against the 'benevolent government' of the British.[56] The incitement against the British, the stoking of disloyalty,[57] and the promise of the Brahman masters' self-reform merely served to keep the Sudratisudras within the Brahman camp, loyally subordinate in a kinder slavery. Giving now not *daksina* for the asking but unquestioning political support, they would still be subservient – no longer as objects of extractive ritualism but in the mode of passive nationalism.

The British: better invaders?

Perhaps the strangest irony in the formation of Phule as political thinker, in his formation as thinking subject of both early Indian nationalism and British imperialism, is that he notes that it was precisely such Brahman proponents of cross-caste unity who had first introduced him to Paine. They had supported their argument for national unity against British oppression 'with quotations from Thomas Paine and others'. He recalls: 'As a young boy, I was impressed by the logic of this argument, and I was crazy enough to think along the same lines. But when I reflected deeply upon the same books they quoted from, the hidden meaning of the selfish advice of these so-called enlightened *bhats* dawned on me.'[58] Having cultivated the skills of critical reflection, Phule disrupts the smooth transmission of elite citations of Paine. Phule wants to maintain and amplify Sudratisudras' patriotism towards England and pre-empt its substitution with patriotism for the 'Indian nation'.

But why does he not use Paine's *Common Sense* as an alibi to go further, to advocate throwing off both Brahman and British yokes and argue for Sudratisudra nationalism or self-rule? How might Anglo-patriotism enhance rather than degrade Sudratisudras' position as 'foundation of all [the] nation'?[59]

Certainly the imperial domination of subject peoples is not equivalent to the domination of masters over slaves, but one political strategy in response to the latter might be to uproot and pre-empt any and every mode of domination between persons whether the alibi for subjection be racial, caste, national, or civilizational superiority. Being neither the radical anti-imperialist nor social revolutionist argument that Paine's writings were reputed to be, however, *Slavery* would make two moves to correct Paine for the Indian context. First, as explored in the prior section, Phule explained why government cannot yet 'arise out of the people', why, that is, the Sudratisudras could no longer naturally found their own freedom and return to self-rule. Second, he would have to articulate the terms on which government, especially foreign rule, '*over* the people' is sometimes unobjectionable. The ultimate question, to be explored in the next section, is what political tactics are left to a people so abjected that they must rely on outsiders for help.

Although Phule occasionally mentions the Mughal invaders – and even notes (mostly in later writings) that the Muslims were, to Sudratisudras, preferable for at least promoting the equality of all believers, which undermined caste[60] – the British are the only remaining contenders for political influence in India against the Brahmans. So what makes the British better invaders? *Slavery* provides two sets of criteria, corresponding to the two dimensions of Brahman domination. First, Britain's empire in India was not necessarily the result of domination. Although Phule mentions 'the cupidity of the Western nations … attracted', like the Aryans long before them, by the 'extreme fertility of the soil in India, its rich productions, the proverbial wealth of its people, and the other innumerable gifts which this favoured land enjoys', he nevertheless allows that there is a difference between emigration 'with peaceful intentions of colonization' and conquest.[61] *Slavery* does not explicitly call the British mere colonists rather than conquerors. Importantly, though, it acknowledges a variety of ways that outsiders might come to India: not all involve brutal force, or might. In any case, whether the British invaded India by force is moot from the standpoint of Sudratisudras, because they were not the ones conquered. Having long ago been conquered, their lot could not worsen and, on the point of death, could only improve.

However, the British are the better outsiders less because of how their invasion may have been closer to colonialism than to conquest and more because of the way that British ideological commitments, namely a scientific rationality and an inclusive religion, counter Brahman priestcraft. Phule notes that 'English scholars have produced books on history' which debunk, from a perspective developed 'impartially and objectively, without selfish interests', the 'self-serving' supremacist treatises of Brahman religion which declare 'that God had deliberately created the shudras for the sole purpose of providing eternal service to the brahmans'.[62] European scholars of religion, employing techniques of historical philology, could disprove 'that only one author composed the four Vedas'.[63] Phule adopts the tactics of scientific rationality to argue against specific fabulous claims of the *Bhagawata* and other books sacred to nineteenth-century Brahmins.[64] From his pen, the science of hermeneutics functions in the mode of disarmingly naive literalism. How, for example, could a religious text claim that Matsya, an avatar of Vishnu, had been born of a fish? Jotirao answers in the dialogue,

> Do you see any similarity between fish and man? … Even in these days of tremendous scientific and medical advancement which has produced brilliant experts in medicine in Europe and America, no doctor, however brilliant, will dare to claim that he can transfer a fish egg on to the land and recover a live [hybrid human-]fish baby from it.[65]

Importantly, though, Phule uses this disarming scientific rationalism merely to argue against cunning impiety, not against religion per se, nor truly godly devotion. For the most lyrical passages of *Slavery* are devoted to outlining the inclusive, egalitarian tenets of the religion of Baliraja, the leader of the ancient kingdom of indigenous Ksatriyas. Against the mystifications and superstitions of the Brahmans, Baliraja was a 'great sage and lover of Truth'. Against caste oppressions supposedly rooted in the divine word made available only to Brahmins, Baliraja was the 'great champion of the downtrodden' because he 'realized that the great Almighty God, our great Father and Creator, had given us the true and holy knowledge and had granted everyone an equal right to it'.[66] Followers of Baliraja included the great '[r]ational sages' like Buddha and were not confined to India: Jesus was the 'Baliraja in the West', whose followers notably included the '[a]ncestors of great scholars like Thomas Paine'.[67] Baliraja included any religion that promoted human equality and a simple rational morality that did not impose intermediary priests or scholars between a person and God or Truth.

Phule associated Baliraja with the British government and Scottish and American missionaries. As such, the Brahmans, besides directly inciting the Sudratisudras against the British, had to find novel ways to protect perquisites they amassed in their hereditary role as arbiters. In the new political context of a British Empire in India, they would extract benefits from serving as political intermediaries, that is, government clerks controlling access to law, rather than only priests and scholars controlling access to sacred order and knowledge. As intermediaries, they controlled access above and below, that is, of the British to the lower castes and of the lower castes to the imperial governors. Thus, Phule despairs of the possibility that Sudratisudras could successfully go over the head of a Brahman clerk and complain of clerical malpractice to conscientious British officers: the Brahmans use bureaucratic feints to bury the latters' desks in paper. Brahmans now enjoyed, and actively employed, a doubly obfuscating role to such a degree that British 'officer[s] generally view men and things through Brahmin spectacles'.[68] Consequently, explaining how slavery can occur (and as *Slavery's* subtitle '*the Civilised British Government under the Cloak of Brahmanism*' also suggests), Phule writes:

> Today it is the *bhats* again who rule though under the name of the British. They are not only harming the interests of the shudras but also of the British themselves; and nobody can say that they won't do so in future as well. Not that the 'sensible' British government is not aware of this fact! Yet they deliberately turn a blind eye towards them and function in accordance with their interests.[69]

Although Phule is clear that the Brahmans have proven themselves absolutely bad – both lustful for domination and ideologically committed to it – *Slavery* is ambivalent about the British. Although the British government represents at least the promise of aspects of Baliraja religion – equality, the rule of law, careers open to talents rather than caste – some of the British neglect to enact, deliver, and enforce their declared political commitments.[70]

Phule provides so much evidence that the British condone Brahman domination, that it is not clear why he maintains faith in British goodness. It is a faith that makes him seem naive. However, he is not naive about how to exploit a divergence between de jure and de facto right. The Brahmans were incorrigible dominators committed to no right, de jure or de facto. The British at least could claim 'political acumen and wisdom' even if they seemed to lack the political will to 'prohibit oppressive practices' and indeed, it seems, actively 'allows them to continue'.[71] Naming the divergence opened a tactical inroad that even the most politically abject could pursue – for, if they could but situate themselves to find the right constellation of circumstances, even they could intervene in a political field.

Authoritative and authority-wielding interlocutors who acknowledged justice even if they did not always enforce it could at least be positioned as benefactors and held to account by those who insisted on being grateful supplicants. Such
self-positioning as supplicants was a provocation to would-be benefactors, a claim
that the supplicants knew that their would-be deliverers knew right (and not just
that they knew it cognitively but, as we will see, that they *felt* it almost irresistibly).
Thus, when Phule writes that 'shudras heartily thank the British for this and are
exceedingly grateful to them', and that '[t]hey will never ever forget the obligations of the British on them',[72] he is not merely describing the present state of
Sudratisudra gratitude. He is instead deploying a power of supplication to incite
those whose political claims position them as discomfited by human abjection; he
is calling a supposedly receptive audience to account.

Phule's claims, in other words, are ethico-political performatives. By positioning Sudratisudras as humble petitioners vis-à-vis the British, Phule designates the
latter as a people who must deliver justice in their empire. Phule compels the
British to recognize themselves in the discourse of humanitarianism that they
themselves circulate, as emblematized by the Slavery Abolition Act of 1833, by
which they dared to contradict national interest in international affairs.[73] Through
his ethico-political performative utterances, Phule made the British accountable not so much to regulatory norms (because humanitarianism is not liable to
enforcement, when, as in Phule's time, construed only as voluntary) as to reputa-
tional norms. Indeed, in light of this incitement to reputation, Phule's distinction
between colonialism and conquest, mentioned above, therefore takes on a conditional quasi-performative dimension in that it suggests that *if* the British wish to
reinscribe their presence in India as peaceful colonization, then they must prove
in practice, repeatedly for as long as they are present, that their political conduct
does not victimize Sudratisudras.

Supplication, sentimentality, and the Queen

It is important that the audience for supplication be, on some construal or evidence,
positioned as open to hearing as well as of higher social status: the same speech
to Brahmans would fall on deaf ears. In fact, because Phule portrayed Brahman
cunning as so pervasive that it fooled both Sudratisudras and local British agents
to assume the Brahman point of view, Phule severely eroded his own authoritative standing. He could not accuse Brahmans of injustice to local representatives
of British law and order if the latter could see only what the former wanted them
to see. Moreover, even if he found a sympathetic British ear, it would undermine
his case if fellow Sudratisudras were convinced that they deserved their abjection
or that it was, anyway, eternal and unquestionable. Thus, Phule had to pursue a
strategy of aligning the two classes of victims of Brahman obfuscation with each
other: in order to build up an authoritative case to accuse Brahmans of crime
and therefore implore British deliverance, he needed to generate Sudratisudra

solidarity and British sympathy. (It bears emphasising that, given how disempowered Sudratisudras were, on Phule's diagnosis, by many generations of degeneration, solidarity alone could not yet deliver them from Brahman oppression.)

Phule's tactic for piercing through cunning and conjuring the reality of the solidarity-sympathy-crime triangle was sentimentality. It is no surprise that he mentions, in *Satsar II*, several years after *Slavery*, the irrepressible effects of that monument of Anglo-American abolitionist sentimentalism, Harriet Beecher Stowe's novel: 'One American woman has written a book called *Uncle Tom's Cabin* in order to expose the cruelty of men. Anyone who reads the book ... will have to sigh and sob.'[74] *Slavery*, too, especially its Introduction, strove for a similar effect:

> And we feel that if merely remembering those calamities causes such intense anguish to our hearts, what must have been the state of mind of those people who actually experienced them? A very good example regarding this can be found in one of the books written by the brahmans themselves. This book describes how Parashuram, one of the chiefs of the brahmans, acted towards the original inhabitants of this country, the kshatriyas. He not only killed several kshatriya men but also snatched from the arms of their orphaned wives their innocent infants and mercilessly sent them to a cruel death ... [Pregnant women] had to run for their lives through little known pathways, under the scorching sun, bearing the burden of their unborn babies ... they must have tripped and fallen and dashed against the boulders on the way or the rocky mountain by the sides of the roads and bled profusely through the several wounds caused by the fall on their arms, foreheads, knees and ankles. On hearing that he was in hot pursuit, they must have stumbled on, desperate for their lives; their delicate feet torn by the thorns in the path, and their clothes shred to pieces by the spiky trees. Their bodies, lacerated by the sharp branches, must have left long trails of blood oozing out of the gashes. Their feet must have been burnt in the scorching sun and their delicate, lotus-like blue skin burnt crimson. Their mouths must have been parched dry in the burning sun and because of the lack of water and constant running, they must have felt sick. Their mouths must have frothed with fear and the tiny lives inside their bellies must have rolled frantically, causing them unendurable, acute pains.[75]

The only way to convey Phule's tactic of deploying florid prose as the antidote to cunning is to quote at length, but Phule's depiction of past and present Sudratisudra suffering continues for pages. And although Phule is a renowned early defender of gender equality in British India, his striving for sentimentality compels him to embody 'so apt an image of suffering'[76] in the innocent pregnant woman. In fairness, it must be said that his descriptions of contemporary Sudratisudra suffering are those of men, but this first, most elaborate, and most sustained – that is, the *exemplary* – description is that of the ancient native women pursued by the conquering Brahman chieftain.

Phule's prose is excessive but owes its effectiveness to the relentlessness of its exorbitant imagery. Each unit of description borders on naivety, but strung together they comprise a canny device for producing solidarity-sympathy-crime.

Phule's exemplary image of suffering acts as a mirror in which Sudratisudras see themselves and, by seeing, *feel* solidarity; for they are 'virtually torn asunder at the thought of the suffering undergone by their ancestors whose blood flows through their veins'.[77] It allows the British to witness in their minds' eyes Brahman crimes and feel undeniable sympathy for their victims; for, once Sudratisudra suffering is described, the British will 'undoubtedly' find that the Sudratisudras 'symbolize' the very 'agony of any oppressed and tormented people'.[78] And once Sudratisudra solidarity and British sympathy solidify, then Brahman 'heroism' and ritual purity will finally be seen for the crimes that they are.[79]

However, the light of truth can only pierce obscurity with the aid of a sentimentality that Phule seems to assume is simultaneously natural and irrepressible yet must be educed, even cultivated. If Brahmans, as conquerors, had not divided Sudratisudras from each other, and if, as intermediaries, they had not insinuated themselves between the British governors and their most humble subjects, then perhaps a single representation of victimage would suffice to provoke natural sentimentality. But because Brahmans occupied a position from which they distorted others' experiences of the world, excessive, unrelenting representation was necessary to chip away at intermediate distortions.

What this suggests is that supplication and the project of sentimentality that here supports it are linked to the danger of intermediation. Whether the intermediary be political (Brahmin as imperial clerk) or religious (Brahmin as priest), his positioning prevented humble subjects' direct access to higher authorities (whether of the Raj or the divine) and vice versa. As intercessor he also impeded others' ability to know the world by the evidence of observation and experience.[80] One of the most profound effects of Phule's early intellectual formation in mission schools supported by the Free Church of Scotland may be his consistent distrust of intermediation as a cause of distortion. Distrust of 'popish' priestcraft and the high valuation on the personal profession of faith springing from a universal faculty of judgement and common sense were enduring intellectual legacies of the European Reformation, characterizing not only many Protestant sects most active in proselytizing in Asia and Africa, but also the work of Enlightenment thinkers like Paine. Certainly, many Enlightenment philosophers disapproved of scriptural evangelism. 'Search not the book called the Scripture, which any human hand might make,' Paine advised in *The Age of Reason* 'but the scripture called the Creation.'[81] Nevertheless, whether the source of 'experiential knowledge'[82] be the universality of the Word, made accessible by the teaching of European vernaculars and translation into non-European vernaculars, or the universality of Creation, made accessible through the study of rigorously ordered nature and the demystification of sensibility, both Protestant missionaries and Enlightenment philosophers agreed in emphasising personal (though not individualistic) faith achieved through direct, unmediated experience.

The common inheritance of an esteem for unmediated personal experience of universal truth thus hardly made it a 'paradox', as O'Hanlon suggests, that Phule and his circle could admire, and take inspiration from, both Protestant 'missionary efforts' and Enlightenment 'religious radicals'.[83] Indeed, Phule's own profession of faith in *Slavery* echoed Paine though with notable deviations:

> I denounce all the main books of the *bhats* which decree us their slaves ... and embrace that book (which may have been written by a person belonging to any other country or religion) which propounds that all human beings have a right to enjoy human rights in equal measure.[84]

Whereas Paine had rejected all books that pretended to revelation because of the fundamental inability of *particular* languages, so prone to problems of translation, to convey a *universal* theology,[85] Phule did not deny that the universal theology of Baliraja could indeed be conveyed through the local and temporal variability of words because it pervaded and transcended them. While Paine rejected words in rejecting the Word for Creation, Phule rejected only the Brahmans' sacred Word but not words. However, Phule did seem to believe that Creation itself, like Paine's natural right, could be rendered inaccessible.

The confluence of Protestant missionary and radical Enlightenment philosophical influences in Phule helps explain why he emphasizes both the organically spontaneous expression of human nature and its deliberate cultivation. Education, especially in the basic skills of literacy but also in practical knowledge (for example, agricultural methods), was a critical safeguard against the power of intermediaries to distort, to denature and to deculturate. Hence, although moral sentimentality was universal and spontaneously natural, it nonetheless benefited from training, and although the humble Sudratisudras were the organic fount of political power, because it was their labour upon the fecundity of nature that founded and grounded society, the restoration of their power could not proceed without education because Brahman intermediation had altered the very culture of power.[86] Facility with words − literacy − would protect Sudratisudras against exploitation, allowing them to observe, judge, and circulate judgements about the world without being dependent on intermediaries who would distort direct experience of that world. As Phule noted in *Cultivator's Whipcord*,

> [M]an has a natural and peculiar intelligence, ... and it is with this intelligence that he invented the wonderful skill of putting down his thoughts on paper ... to note the errors they had made and their experiences, and now there is an immense storehouse of such experiential knowledge in the world.[87]

Cutting their dependence on intercessors, Sudratisudras would be able once again to accumulate and transmit the experiential knowledge that would reauthorize them and reconnect their restored authority to legitimate sources of higher authority, the Raj and the Creator, from which the Brahmans had blocked them. Higher political and religious authority could only qualify *as* legitimate by

actively affirming that reconnection. The performative quality of legitimacy is ultimately what animated Phule's sometimes harsh assessments of British complicity
in injustice (hence, *Slavery in the Civilised British Government* ...). Sentimentality
was thus crucial to Phule's strategy because its powerful images of suffering could
render the Sudratisudras' lot too startling to ignore, compelling the British to
prove the legitimacy of their rule de facto.

Two parties alone Phule exempts of injustice: the sovereign authorities themselves, 'our Creator'[88] and Queen Victoria (and, once upon a time, Baliraja). The
former he excuses by definition. Being the Creator and 'Sustainer' of all humans
equally, God was therefore superior, nominally above all in the empire of creation.[89] Likewise, Queen Victoria, too, stood above it all: within her empire, she
occupied no intermediate position. Consequently, she could never have been
mired in Brahman obfuscations and therefore could never be distrusted. Her
remoteness preserved her impartiality as judge but also impeded her capacity for
rendering judgement. An appeal to her, could she but hear it, would immediately
access two dimensions of justice, social and legal. Superior to the doings of her
subjects and therefore never substantially implicated in them, she retained the
greatest natural sympathy to suffering and, at the same time, was most available
to a straightforward, unsentimental juridical accusation. Therefore, in her, the pair
sympathy-crime would encounter least interference. If she could but be made to
notice, she would certainly feel the pain of the victims and ascertain instantly the
unjust acts that caused them, and in turn her sovereign recognition would con-
solidate Sudratisudra solidarity.

Thus, a claim directed at the queen is directed not at just anyone but at the
most politically responsible person, responsible in the sense not of culpability
but of most responsive for justice: queen, soon to be empress, Victoria was
superlative in responsibility for all her subjects because she was the sovereign.
The problem, though, was her distance: how could a humble appeal be made
to reach one who surveyed a vast empire of many subjects daily reactivating
long, complex histories of interaction with one another? The inaccessibility of
Queen Victoria differed from her own local agents: proximate, their percep-
tions were mediated; remote, hers would nonetheless be immediate. The only
mechanism Phule seems to envisage for overcoming this remoteness is, I would
argue, by making Sudratisudra slavery a world-historical claim. The constant
comparisons to African-American slaves functionally amplify the Sudratisudras'
plight so that it is not a problem of provincial backwardness relative to the rest
of the British Empire but British imperial backwardness relative to the globe.
Phule mentions British abolition as an event only twice[90] but references to the
American emancipation of slaves pervade *Slavery* from its opening dedication
to nearly its final page. Of course, the emphasis on American slavery had to do
with contemporaneity, but what is more important is that the American comparison made injustices in Maharashtra an *extra*-imperial – not a merely technical, local, intra-imperial – concern. The globality of scandalous comparison,

and not the belatedness of British abolition internal to the empire, was the thing wherein to catch the conscience of a queen surveying her far-flung domain.

Between critique and catachresis

More so than other records of naive monarchism, *Slavery* is split between surreality and a sense of reality. Although the distance of the just monarch provided the occasion for subalterns to fall victim to intermediaries' crimes, the same remoteness supported subalterns' projection of a surreal embodiment of justice, with which the 'real' sovereign in question could almost never compete. Hence, the 'real' Victoria might not have lived up to her surreal counterpart. *Slavery* effectively identifies Victoria with King Bali and implicitly places her at a high point of Baliraja's prophesied second coming to 'establis[h] God's kingdom on earth'.

> Thus the prophecy of our ancient women, that one day Bali's kingdom will be established on earth once again, was realized at least to some extent. Millions became the followers of this Baliraja in Europe where he had brought about a tremendous upheaval.[91]

As Christian sovereign, the Queen would necessarily embody this comprehensive social justice.

Fortunately, for both Phule and Victoria, the Queen's geographic remoteness preserved her from any actual test of Sudratisudra sympathy. For in the annals of naive monarchism, subalterns sometimes rejected 'real' empirical sovereigns as impostors, tricksters, or even antichrists in favour of their more just avatars. Daniel Field notes, for example, that, in 1831, Nicholas I of Russia had tried to calm, *in person*, a community rebelling in his name. Nicholas 'suffered an embarrassing failure': legends of a tsar-deliverer would inevitably defeat any tsar who would not deliver.[92] The corollary, of course, is that any 'real' monarch would deliver justice to the downtrodden; therefore, any sovereign who would not, was not real. In traditions as differently rooted as those of Europe and South-East Asia, notes James Scott, 'there are long traditions of the return of a just king or religious savior'.[93] Because the just sovereign was always to come and the justice she embodied always in the future tense, subalterns' complementary vision of redemption need never be articulated as a closed set of fixed demands. As Scott explains: 'Perhaps the most remarkable feature of the [sovereign-deliverer] myth was its plasticity in the hands of its peasant adherents.'[94] Thus the grievances to be redressed could mutate, could be inconsistent from moment to moment. In short, the sovereign-deliverer was surreal because her acts of redress were a forever-open set and could therefore defy the principle of non-contradiction. She embodied the pure potential of redress. Hence, the 'justice' that her acts ratify seemed vague, perhaps, but, in Scott's assessment 'politically incendiary'.[95]

For this reason Scott finds naive monarchism very canny indeed, and, strongly disputing the attribution of 'false consciousness' to it, he interprets it as quasi-deliberately tactical.[96]

Following Scott, but rejecting the trap of false/true (qua deliberate) consciousness, I venture to say that this subaltern vision of justice is incendiary precisely because of its vague surreality. Phule's naive monarchism, aligning Victoria with Baliraja, is interesting, though, because it is not only surreal. *Slavery* had implied that the strategy of supplication could succeed, that it would really, irresistibly provoke sympathy. The combined elements of the text – its linking of sentimentality to sympathy and crime, its critique of intermediation – had made it seem indubitable that, were she to hear the supplication, the queen would deliver the Sudratisudras from injustice. In addition to what I consider Phule's actual faith in the empirical efficacy of the technologies of sentimentality and immediacy that his text constructed, he also made powerful claims for redress which were not the usual vague demand for justice. Based on Phule's study of the idiom of British imperial governance, *Slavery* was a supplication that, almost jarringly, specified mundanely realistic policy proposals.

The way to make 'the hearts and minds of the Sudras ... happy and contented', the way 'the British Government' can ensure 'their loyalty in the future',[97] Phule averred, is to incorporate them in administrative offices. The way to counteract the abusive partiality that the high-caste 'monopoly'[98] on office surely guaranteed was not to refuse Brahmans office – which would constitute an equal and opposite monopoly – but to insist on proportional representation in all offices. 'And if the government is unable to obtain [an] adequate number of people from all castes in proportion to their population,' Phule elaborates, 'then only Europeans should be employed to work on these posts.'[99] In a political context of hereditary prejudices, entrenched privileges, and historic partialities, Phule was not naive to think that greater oversight by outsiders – guaranteed by the queen's sympathy – could improve the lot of Sudratisudras. If Sudratisudras could not yet represent themselves in office, then justice called for a more thorough penetration of India by British officials who would personally visit the villages.[100] Imperial administrators' more pervasive superintendence locally would thwart the wily ability of Brahmans to cloud British vision.

Phule specified another point within the vast machinery of imperial administration at which Sudratisudra insertion was critical. In order to accelerate Sudratisudra emancipation geometrically, Phule recommends that the British train and hire more Sudratisudra teachers for Sudratisudra communities. Doing so would ensure that education itself not be prejudicial. Education undistorted by caste prejudice would have both affirmative and negative effects. If the Sudratisudras were to become again the constitutive power of Maharashtrian society, they would need positively to rebuild their capacity as a people. Sudratisudras educating themselves with the initial aid and oversight of the British would slowly renature and reculture themselves for freedom. In addition, developing practical knowledge and overcoming illiteracy would negate their dependence on Brahman intermediaries.

How might we try to understand *Slavery*, this volatile political-theoretical artefact comprised of real and surreal moments, as a whole? In my view, Phule's real–surreal monarchism mixes critique and catachresis. By 'critique' I have in mind specifically Michel Foucault's initial definition of critique as a 'way of thinking' whose object was 'the art of not being governed quite so much'.[101] In Foucault's analysis, critique and 'governmentalisation' – the multiplication and spread of systematic practices-knowledges concerning the direction of individuals' conduct from the late medieval period in Europe – challenge and spur the development of each other. Moreover, both ultimately derive from a specifically Christian government of conscience and the critique of this pastoral conduct of conducts, founded in scriptural hermeneutics.[102]

Paine's writings and missionary Protestantism served as transmitters of critique's legacy. Together these influences primed Phule for his encounter with Orientalist scholarship, which gave him access to both philology and hermeneutics. Shut out of Vedic hermeneutic traditions by reason of caste, Phule could probably only have honed critique under European imperialism. Given that, in Phule's view, the dominance and 'cunning' of Brahmanism pre-empted disciplines of textual interpretation from within the more egalitarian traditions of Islam and Buddhism from gaining a foothold in Maharashtra, the confluence of Paine, Protestantism, and Orientalism – with British imperial governance as their common support – provided the only discursive context powerful enough to contradict Brahmanism. The only point of enunciation for a Sudratisudra critique of Brahmans' domination of – and via – truth and power was opened by Britain's imperial presence. Acknowledging that Phule's agency as political thinker-resister was produced in and by subjection helps to account for *Slavery*'s reality-effects, for why it did not veer towards the hyper-radical position that Sudratisudras should not be governed *at all*, by Brahmans, Mughals, *or British*.[103]

Sustaining the mundane specificities of a reality, *Slavery* may therefore seem relatively conservative. However, like much critique historically, the text's audacity is bound up with its seeming conservatism. For what could be more audacious *and* conservative – from the perspective of upper-caste advocates of national unity rebuffing British imperialism in India – than a fellow 'Indian's' effectively uttering, 'A white woman will save brown men from other brown men', against elite Brahmins' position of national unity: 'Some brown men want to remain subordinate.'[104] In a context in which elite Brahmins were conceding that the brutal excesses of 'Hinduism' should be reformed to promote cross-caste national unity in favour of greater Indian autonomy from Britain, Phule's surreal statement that the Sudratisudras 'will never forget the obligations of the Queen, who alone can remove the bond of slavery tied around their necks by the wily Brahmans'[105] is catachrestic, even if it abuses neither syntax nor semantics.[106] Not only did Phule speak impossibly from a de-authorized position, but his speech was nonsense to early upper-caste nationalists who believed that Sudratisudras should want to remain patiently subordinate to Brahmans as the latter reformed themselves, should cherish unity with them as the latter restored self-government. Phule wanted precisely to highlight disunity and amplify impatience.

To argue that a white queen will save the Sudratisudras from other Indians is to advocate something *like* 'humanitarian intervention':[107] an outside power must intervene to redress an inhumane imbalance of present forces. However, humanitarian superintendence seems a better description because, although foreigners like the Brahmans, the British were no longer outsiders. Phule claimed that Sudratisudras once had but now no longer have constitutive power, and, because of the compound structure of their slavery, will never again have it without the superintendence of the only force that could, were it more vigilant, trump Brahman dominance. To the upper-caste nationalist agitation for greater self-government, Phule advocated more rigorous, intensive imperial penetration by administrators who would be answerable only to the queen and accountable primarily to Sudratisudra interests.

Having been rendered thoroughly ignorant, enslaved in body and especially in mind, by centuries of Brahman cunning and force, Sudratisudras cannot yet refill the offices of popular government without tutelage. Thus, what is most surprising about Phule's naively monarchist, patriotically imperialist political theory is that, perhaps unwittingly and certainly paradoxically, he proves himself to be an earnest pupil of J. S. Mill, though for ultimately Painean reasons. Phule asks for the British to be a rigorous and intensive 'tutelary' power in order for Sudratisudras to restore themselves to constitutive power, reconstructing a society that can in due time govern itself in the representative mode. The British imperial presence, driven by the sympathy of the queen, would help Sudratisudras overcome their 'backwardness' and regain the capacity for representative self-government, and this capacity would serve Sudratisudras after the eventual departure of the British: 'the English are here today, but who knows whether they will be here tomorrow? They won't be here till eternity. Therefore, all the shudras should make haste to free themselves from the ancestral slavery of these *bhats*.'[108] About this, too, Phule is not naive. Although he could only have made his intervention under the transnational conditions of the British Empire, Phule clearly saw the need to gesture towards a post-imperial – one might even say, vernacularly postcolonial – perspective.

Notes

1   The four positions in the varna system, in 'descending' order, are Brahmin, Ksatriya, Vaisya – the three 'twice-born' groups – and finally the Sudras. The Atisudra or Dalit occupies a position 'underneath' this hierarchy and was formerly known as 'Untouchable'. As G. P. Deshpande notes, however, Phule polemically collapses the social field into two groups only, the Brahmans (consisting of all the twice-born groups) and the Sudratisudras (the Sudras and Atisudras). See G. P. Deshpande, 'Of Hope and Melancholy: Reading Jotirao Phule in Our Times', in G. P. Deshpande,

ed., *Selected Writings of Jotirao Phule* (New Delhi: LeftWord Books, 2002), 8. In order to distinguish what I judge to be Phule's references specifically to members of the priestly varna from his references to the class of twice-born persons as a whole, I use 'Brahmin' for the former and 'Brahman' for the latter. Finally, when he wrote in English, Phule capitalized 'Brahmin' and so on; however, the Marathi translators do not capitalize these terms. Hence, my quotations reflect their choices.

2   Jotirao Phule, *Slavery*, trans. Maya Pandit, in *Selected Writings of Jotirao Phule*, 87.

3   *Ibid.*, 25.

4   Daniel Immerwahr, 'Caste or Colony? Indianizing Race in the United States', *Modern Intellectual History*, 4: 2 (2007), 275–301; Nico Slate, *Colored Cosmopolitanism: The Shared Struggle for Freedom in the United States and India* (Cambridge, MA: Harvard University Press, 2012).

5   Ranajit Guha, *Elementary Aspects of Peasant Insurgency in Colonial India* (Durham, NC: Duke University Press, 1999), 113, 271; Steven Hahn, *A Nation under Our Feet: Black Political Struggles in the Rural South from Slavery to the Great Migration* (Cambridge, MA: Belknap Press of Harvard University Press, 2004), 59–61, and 'But What Did the Slaves Think of Lincoln?', in William A. Blair and Karen Fisher Younger, eds, *Lincoln's Proclamation: Emancipation Reconsidered* (Chapel Hill: University of North Carolina Press, 2009), 108.

6   Guha, *Elementary Aspects*, 251–77; Hahn, *Nation*, 57–60, 149–57.

7   Phule, *Slavery*, 40.

8   *Ibid.*, 28.

9   Phule, *Cultivator's Whipcord*, trans. Aniket Jaaware, in *Selected Writings of Jotirao Phule*, ed. Deshpande, 147.

10 Phule, *Slavery*, 31.

11 *Ibid.*, 40.

12 Phule, *Cultivator's Whipcord*, 150, 170, cf. 193.

13 Phule, *Slavery*, 36.

14 *Ibid.*, 27.

15 Devendraswarup, 'Genesis of the Aryan Race Theory and Its Application to Indian History', in S. B. Deo and Suryanath Kamath, eds, *The Aryan Problem* (Pune: Maharashtra Mudran-Shala Press, 1993), 35. See also Megan C. Thomas, 'Orientalism and Comparative Political Theory', *Review of Politics*, 27: 4 (2010), 653–77.

16 Madhav M. Deshpande, 'Aryan Origins: Arguments from the Nineteenth-Century Maharashtra', in Edwin F. Bryant and Laurie L. Patton, eds, *The Indo-Aryan Controversy: Evidence and Inference in Indian History* (New York: Routledge, 2005), 410.

17 *Ibid.*, 419–20.

18 *Ibid.*, 421.

19 Rosalind O'Hanlon, *Caste, Conflict, and Ideology: Mahatma Jotirao Phule and Low Caste Protest in Nineteenth-Century Western India* (Ranikhet: Permanent Black, 2002), 150.

20 Phule, *Slavery*, 27.

21 *Ibid.*, 28, 41.

22 *Ibid.*, 41.

23 *Ibid.*, 28, 69.

24 *Ibid.*, 28, 54.

25 Orlando Patterson, 'Slavery and Slave Revolts: A Sociohistorical Analysis of the First Maroon War, 1665–1740', in Richard Price, ed., *Maroon Societies: Rebel Slave Communities in the Americas*, 3rd edn (Baltimore: Johns Hopkins University Press, 1996), 287.

26 *Ibid.*

27 Phule, *Slavery*, 29, 31, 46.
28 *Ibid.*, 37, 98.
29 *Ibid.*, 66.
30 Rochana Bajpai, 'Liberalisms in India: A Sketch', in Ben Jackson and Marc Stears, eds, *Liberalism as Ideology: Essays in Honor of Michael Freeden* (New York: Oxford University Press, 2012), 70–1.
31 Deshpande, 'Of Hope and Melancholy', 2; O'Hanlon, *Caste*, 111.
32 As there is little direct evidence of influence of Paine's writings on Phule's writings, and only anecdotal evidence of Paine's writings' inspiration on Phule the person, Phule's best commentators, above all O'Hanlon, tread carefully in interpreting intertextual debts. In avoiding making strong claims about what *Slavery* owes to Paine, I follow O'Hanlon's lead here, though I claim more intertextual parallels than she does.
33 O'Hanlon, *Caste*, 198.
34 Thomas Paine, *Rights of Man*, in Bruce Kuklick, ed., *Political Writings*, rev. student edn, (Cambridge: Cambridge University Press, 2000), 90, 87–8.
35 Paine, *Rights of Man*, 89.
36 *Ibid.*, 150.
37 *Ibid.*, 190.
38 *Ibid.*
39 *Ibid.*, 166.
40 *Ibid.*
41 *Ibid.*
42 *Ibid.*, 198.
43 Phule, *Slavery*, 39.
44 Paine, *Rights of Man*, 171.
45 Phule, *Slavery*, 35.
46 *Ibid.*, 44.
47 *Ibid.*, 78–9.
48 *Ibid.*, 31.
49 Phule, *Cultivator's Whipcord*, 167.
50 Phule, *Slavery*, 45.
51 *Ibid.*, 38; cf. 31–2.
52 *Ibid.*, 45.
53 *Ibid.*, 75.
54 *Ibid.*, 88.
55 *Ibid.*
56 *Ibid.*, 76, 94.
57 Jotirao Govindrao Phule, *Slavery (in the Civilised British Government under the Cloak of Brahmanism)* in *Collected Works of Mahatma Jotirao Phule*, vol. I, trans. P. G. Patil (Bombay: Education Department, Government of Maharashtra, 1991), 26. The Pandit translation seems inconsistent, possibly incorrect, here (*Selected Writings*, 67).
58 Phule, *Slavery*, 88.
59 Phule, *Cultivator's Whipcord*, 167.
60 See Phule, *Cultivator's Whipcord*, 175, 177; *The Book of True Faith*, trans. G. P. Deshpande, in *Selected Writings of Jotirao Phule*, ed. Despande, 235.
61 Phule, *Slavery*, 27.
62 *Ibid.*, 37.
63 *Ibid.*, 72.
64 *Ibid.*, 55.

65 *Ibid.*, 50–1.
66 *Ibid.*, 73, 74.
67 *Ibid.*, 74, 75.
68 *Ibid.*, 32.
69 *Ibid.*, 67.
70 Cf. Phule, *Cultivator's Whipcord*, 117, 134.
71 Phule, *Slavery*, 79.
72 *Ibid.*, 44.
73 The classic theoretical representation of Victorian Britain's humanitarian foreign policy is J. S. Mill's 'A Few Words on Non-Intervention', in *The Collected Works of John Stuart Mill*, vol. 21 (Toronto: University of Toronto Press, 1984), 109–24.
74 Phule, *Satsar*, Number 2, trans. Urmila Bhirdikar, in *Selected Writings of Jotirao Phule*, ed. Deshpande, 222.
75 Phule, *Slavery*, 41–2.
76 *Ibid.*, 40.
77 *Ibid.*, 41.
78 *Ibid.*, 40.
79 *Ibid.*, 41.
80 *Ibid.*, 53, 82.
81 Paine, *Age of Reason*, in *Political Writings*, ed. Kuklick, 287.
82 Phule, *Cultivator's Whipcord*, 176.
83 O'Hanlon, *Caste*, 197–8.
84 Phule, *Slavery*, 98.
85 Paine, *Age of Reason*, 286–7.
86 Phule, *Slavery*, 30.
87 Phule, *Cultivator's Whipcord*, 176.
88 Phule, *Slavery*, 98.
89 *Ibid.*
90 *Ibid.*, 39, 47.
91 *Ibid.*, 74.
92 Daniel Field, *Rebels in the Name of the Tsar* (Boston: Houghton Mifflin, 1976), 23; cf. 6–8.
93 James C. Scott, *Domination and the Arts of Resistance: Hidden Transcripts* (New Haven, CT: Yale University Press, 1990), 101.
94 *Ibid.*, 97.
95 *Ibid.*, 98.
96 *Ibid.*, 102–3.
97 Phule, *Slavery*, 35.
98 *Ibid.*, 34.
99 *Ibid.*, 87.
100 *Ibid.*, 87, 96.
101 Michel Foucault, 'What Is Critique?', trans. Lysa Hochroth, in *The Politics of Truth* (New York: Semiotext(e), 1997), 29.
102 Foucault notes that 'critique is biblical, historically'. Foucault, 'What Is Critique', 30.
103 In Foucault's rendering, critique is historically specific – not 'we do not want to be governed *at all*', rather, 'how not to be governed *like that*': 'What Is Critique?', 28.
104 These utterances I assign to Phule and early upper-caste nationalists rewrite Gayatri Chakravorty Spivak's pair of ideological sentences – 'White men are saving brown women from brown men.' 'The women wanted to die' – by which Hindu patriarchy and British imperialism interlock around *sati*/'suttee.' For Spivak, their tight

interlocking rendered it impossible for the subaltern woman to speak in a way that could be heard. See Gayatri Chakravorty Spivak, 'Can the Subaltern Speak?', in Cary Nelson and Lawrence Grossberg, eds, *Marxism and the Interpretation of Culture* (Urbana: University of Illinois Press, 1988), 271–313.

105 Phule, *Slavery*, 87.
106 On catachresis, see Spivak, *Outside in the Teaching Machine* (London: Routledge Classics, 2009), 70.
107 I thank Lynn Zastoupil for suggesting the relevance of 'humanitarian intervention'.
108 Phule, *Slavery*, 89.

4

The New World 'sans-culottes': French revolutionary ideology in Saint-Domingue

Johnhenry Gonzalez

In February 1794, two and a half years after slaves in the French colony of Saint-Domingue initiated the Haitian Revolution by taking up arms against their former masters, the Jacobin-controlled National Convention in Paris issued the first ecumenical decree of slave emancipation in modern history. While the Haitian and French Revolutions occurred contemporaneously, scholars of the period have long been at odds with regard to the extent and the nature of the ideological connections between the two events. The most parsimonious inter-pretations suggest that the disruptions and conflicts of the French revolutionary era destabilized colonial Saint-Domingue and the broader Caribbean creating a strategic opportunity for slave insurgents to rise up – but that any ideological parallels were of a superficial nature and were quickly wiped away by reaction in France and Napoleon's eventual decision to legally restore chattel slavery in the colonies. French historian Yves Bénot exposes the many limitations of the idea that revolutionary Haitian slave emancipation was innately linked with met-ropolitan France, whose massive eighteenth-century commercial profits were based in no small part on the especially intensive plantation slavery of colonial Saint-Domingue – the eighteenth century's leading global supplier of sugar and coffee. Bénot points out that many of the most prominent French revolutionar-ies opposed emancipation, or strategically evaded the question.[1] In addition, the same French Republican officials who first proclaimed emancipation in Saint-Domingue in 1793 within a context of military crisis, immediately attempted to restore plantation production on the basis of a state-directed system of sharecrop-ping that historian Laurent Dubois has characterized as 'Republican racism'.[2] And yet it is neither coincidental nor inconsequential that from the earliest days of the Haitian insurrection, French republican language of liberty, equality, and 'resistance to oppression' appeared prominently in the pronouncements of the island's ex-slaves in arms.

Aimé Césaire writes that it is 'the worst error to consider the Revolution of Saint-Domingue purely and simply as a chapter of the French Revolution'.[3] Representing the opposite viewpoint C. L. R. James emphasizes both the adoption of liberal-democratic ideology by Caribbean slave insurgents and the radical universalism of the French Jacobins' February 1794 act of slave emancipation in claiming that Saint-Domingue and revolutionary Paris briefly constituted two allied wings of a fully transatlantic revolutionary movement.[4] At stake in this debate are weighty claims regarding the nature of both the Haitian and French Revolutions. Haitian nationalist authors keen on celebrating the autonomous origins of their nation's unprecedented struggle for independence tend to emphasize the non-European origins of the country's independence and the political role of creole, maroon, and African-born leaders.[5] Haitian historians have long argued against the improbable but strangely persistent claim that the original slave insurrection of August 1791 was incited by white royalists who believed that the threat of a slave rebellion would advance their faction in its struggle against white republicans within the colony. To explain the Haitian Revolution merely as a New World offshoot of Parisian radical republicanism would also be to disregard the autonomy and initiative of the slaves who ignited Haiti's revolutionary process. And yet it would be impossible to decipher the complex trajectory of the Haitian Revolution without considering the political upheavals that upended French society during the 1790s. By discussing both the adoption of European liberal-democratic rhetoric by Caribbean insurgents as well as the language of universalism that accompanied the 1794 French emancipation decree, this chapter explores some of the strongest examples of direct ideological linkages between the French and Haitian Revolutions as well as the underlying disjunctures that limited the influences of metropolitan political thought in the former colony.

The revolutions in Saint-Domingue and France

A Jamaican-born slave named Boukman Dutty was the principal organizer of the great rebellion of August 1791 that initiated the Haitian Revolution. Three months later Boukman was killed in battle and the French prominently displayed his head on a pike. In November 1791 the remaining rebel leaders Jean-François, Georges Biassou and Toussaint Louverture sued for peace, promising to usher former slaves back to the plantations in exchange for general improvements in working conditions and freedom for a small group of leaders. Unwilling to entertain demands made by people who they still considered their property, the white colonists refused to negotiate. In 1792 as the rebels battled the French and consolidated their position in the island's rugged interior they first launched the historic demand for universal slave emancipation. In July 1792 Georges Biassou, Jean-François, and a young insurgent leader named Charles Bélair issued what was probably the Haitian Revolution's first published demand for general slave emancipation.[6] After Biassou and Jean-François' attempt to negotiate for more limited changes had been rebuffed, they adopted new and much broader demands. Their letter of July 1792 culminated in a call for 'general liberty for all the men held in slavery'. The letter was addressed to the Saint-Domingue General Assembly, the French National Commissars in the colony, and all of 'the citizens of the French part of Saint Domingue'. Bélair and his co-authors invoked the natural rights of the enslaved 'citizens' of Saint-Domingue regardless of race. They also reminded the then-rulers of Saint-Domingue that they were formally bound by the *Déclaration des droits de l'homme*. The authors quoted from the declaration, stating that 'men are born free and equal in rights and that the natural rights are liberty, property, security, and resistance to oppression'.[7]

The 1792 letter signed by Bélair, Jean-François, and Biassou, represents strong and early historical evidence in support of C. L. R. James' claim of a historic connection between the plantation labourers of the Caribbean and the revolutionary masses of France.[8] The authors saluted the 'joyous revolution that has taken place in the mother country and that has created the path that our courage and our efforts will cause us to climb'. These three rebel slave leaders were making a clear statement about the direct political connections between the Haitian Revolution and the French Revolution. They wrote that their goal was to 'arrive at the temple of liberty like those brave Frenchmen who are our models'.[9] The insurgents' 1792 letter made its way across the Atlantic and was reprinted in the 9 February 1793 issue of the *Créole Patriote*, a Jacobin-affiliated journal published in Paris by the Saint Domingue-born journalist Milscent-Créole. By February 1793, a year before the National Convention's decree of universal emancipation, the Haitian rebels' demands for general liberty had already been published in France.

Perhaps the most remarkable thing about Biassou, Jean-François, and Bélair's historic demand for general emancipation is that it was soon granted by the revolutionary French officials, first in Saint-Domingue and later in Paris. In August 1793, faced with British invaders, monarchist French rivals, and powerful bands of black insurgents, the French Republican ruler Léger Félicité Sonthonax made a desperate bid to preserve Republican rule in Saint-Domingue by abolishing slavery in an attempt to win the support of the island's black majority. Sonthonax's decree of 29 August 1793 reflected total acquiescence to the published demands of Biassou, Jean François, and Bélair. While Biassou and Jean-François ignored the French decrees of abolition and remained loyal to the Spanish crown, which had commissioned them as generals, Bélair switched his allegiance to the French Republic along with his fellow black officers Toussaint Louverture, Henri Christophe, and Jean-Jacques Dessalines. In February 1794, the revolutionary leaders in Paris ratified Sonthonax's decision by issuing a general decree of slave emancipation that covered all of France's colonies.

How radical were the French revolutionaries?

In order to investigate the limits and failures of French revolutionary republicanism in Saint-Domingue, it is useful to employ the language of 'the masters' tools' as it has emerged in the literature on American slave resistance. Did the eventual collapse of radical Jacobinism and Napoleon's historic decision in 1802 to reverse the 1794 emancipation decree prove that republicanism was another of the 'master's' tools'? After the National Convention boldly abolished slavery in 1794, French colonial officials – white and black – spent the next decade locked in a losing struggle to keep newly freed black citizens bound to the same colonial plantations where they had toiled as slaves. By 1802, white supremacy and slavery again triumphed in the French colonies following Thermidor and the rise of Napoleon.

Perhaps the overall racism of the French revolutionaries was evident from the start. Some historians have emphasized the 'deafening silence of the Montagnards' with regard to the troublesome question of colonial slavery.[10] The Jacobins had a mixed record on the question of slave emancipation, and some of the leading lights of the Jacobin Club and the Committee of Public Safety did not have a record of clear opposition to slavery. As Yves Bénot has pointed out, 'with regard to colonial questions, differences of political opinion did not mirror the political divisions of the metropolis'.[11] The fact that many of revolutionary France's most committed abolitionists were Brissotins and Girondins meant that once the Montagnards had turned on them and denounced Brissot and his associates as traitors, the cause of slave emancipation became associated in some circles with the ever-looming threat of counterrevolutionary conspiracy. Robespierre himself denounced the Girondists in November 1793 in the National Convention, saying that 'the same faction that in France wants to reduce the poor to the condition of miserable servants and to submit the people to the aristocracy of the rich, wants at the same time to set loose and arm the *nègres* in order to destroy our colonies'.[12] But by 1794, the evident contradiction between the incendiary social egalitarianism of the Jacobins and their lingering support for slavery and French colonialism was resolved by the successful armed mobilization of black insurgents in Saint-Domingue, which set the stage for an unprecedented form of cross-racial, transatlantic emancipationist politics among the radicalized sansculottes of France.

The revisionist school of French Revolutionary historiography, concerned with exploding Marxist arguments about the 'progressive' and 'popular' character of the Jacobin dictatorship, have tended not to investigate the National Convention's support for revolutionary slave emancipation. Jean-Daniel Piquet offers an excellent explanation of this phenomenon. Piquet observes that the National Convention's 1794 decree of slave emancipation is conspicuously absent in the more conservative, anti-Jacobin interpretations of the French Revolution, writing that they 'would not dare to recognize that the origins of the most beautiful event in the history of humanity can be attributed to a group of criminals, fanatics, or tyrants'.[13] For historians who have striven to explain the Jacobin dictatorship as a violent cabal that used a radical ideology of equality and social emancipation as a cynical cover for their own ambitions and depredations, it remains somewhat cumbersome to have to explain why the Jacobin-controlled National Convention approved and actually moved to enforce a decree that ended slavery in all of France's colonies and granted the former slaves the rights of French citizens.

Recent years have witnessed a welcome proliferation of new research on the history of France's overseas possessions during the period of the revolution. Nearly all subsequent historians writing on these matters have recognized their debt to the work of C. L. R. James. Perhaps the boldest argument that James makes about the Haitian Revolution is his claim that its success was in large part a result of the short-lived but extremely important political alliance between the ex-slave insurgents of Saint-Domingue and the revolutionary urban labourers and peasants of France. James' claims to this effect had no precedents in the previous historiography and deserve to be quoted at length:

> Paris between March 1793 and July 1794 was one of the supreme epochs of political history. Never until 1917 were masses ever to have such powerful influence – for it was no more than influence – upon any government. In these few months of their nearest approach to power they did not forget the blacks. They felt towards them as brothers, and the old slave-owners, whom they knew to be supporters of the counter-revolution, they hated as if Frenchmen themselves had suffered under the whip.[14]

James also writes that:

> The workers and peasants of France could not have been expected to take any interest in the colonial question in normal times, any more than one can expect similar interest from British or French workers to-day. But now they were roused. They were striking at royalty, tyranny, reaction and oppression of all types, and with this they included slavery. The prejudice of race is superficially the most irrational of all prejudices, and by a perfectly comprehensible reaction the Paris workers, from indifference in 1789, had come by this time to detest no section of the aristocracy so much as those whom they called 'the aristocrats of the skin'.[15]

On 2 February 1794, the Jacobin, and prominent member of the Committee of Public Safety, Barère spoke in the Convention against the intrigues of Saint-Domingue colonists and said that 'it is well known that the whites are the aristocrats of the colonies, while the *hommes de couleur* and the *nègres* are the patriots and that they were right to rise up against the whites'.[16] The words of Barère represented the rising tide of Jacobin anti-slavery, which would unleash the decree of 16 pluviôse at what was arguably the period of greatest radicalization and mass political involvement of the entire revolution.[17]

Since the publication of *The Black Jacobins*, many historians have followed the example of C. L. R. James by writing dramatic descriptions of the National Convention session of 16 pluviôse of year II. The environment in the National Convention on this day seems to have had nothing to do with lawyerly calm or parliamentary routine. All surviving accounts of the formal abolition of slavery record an absolutely raucous session dominated by a mood of revolutionary enthusiasm for the lofty ideals of racial equality and universal liberty. Many of these accounts have included the intervention of R. Levasseur (de la Sarthe) who in arguing that the Convention should 'repair the wrong' of slavery and 'proclaim the liberty of the Negroes', asked the president of the session not to 'suffer the Convention to dishonour itself by a discussion'.[18] Rather than a parliamentary manoeuvre to bypass opposing voices, Levasseur's request for immediate passage of the decree seems to reflect the overwhelming mood among the representatives of the Convention and the throng of observers in favour of universal abolition. The decree passed by acclamation amid shouts of '*Vive la République! Vive la Convention! Vive la Montagne!*'.[19] The fanfare and overt enthusiasm of the moment has been recorded in the 1794 ink and gouache drawing by the renowned historical painter Nicolas André Monsiau, which depicts dramatic embraces on the floor of the National Convention, black and white onlookers rejoicing, and a black infant being held up dramatically in the direction of the president.[20] The official records of the session record that an elderly woman of colour who was observing the proceedings actually fainted from joy and excitement.

There is reason to believe that this abolitionist enthusiasm was not merely confined to the halls of the National Convention but that it thrived for at least a short period in the faubourgs of Paris and in at least some of the provincial towns. Yves Bénot, one of the most knowledgeable historians to have written on the questions of slavery and colonialism during the French Revolution, has written an appropriate summation of the fairly ample support that antislavery received among the French masses during the period of the terror. Bénot writes that 'the spirit of the sans-culottes, animated by an ideology that was somewhat vague but that was at least inspired by the great slogans of justice and equality – read happiness for all – was naturally favourable to the call for general liberty'.[21] An article by the historian Jean-Claude Halpern first published in the 1995 collection *Les abolitions de l'esclavage* summarizes his excellent research on the variety and extent of state-sponsored celebrations of emancipation that occurred in France in the aftermath of the decree of 16 pluviôse. Through examining parliamentary, municipal, and departmental records from the winter and spring of 1794, Halpern has identified over twenty official festivals that were called together to celebrate the abolition of slavery. Rather than small stuffy ceremonies, some descriptions survive which indicate that the festivals were lively affairs with large processions and graphic symbolism including the Goddess of Liberty and people of colour having their chains removed. The message of revolutionary slave emancipation seems to have been made fairly clear. Helpern reports that 'at Bourg-sur-Rhône (Bourg-Saint-Andréol) in the Ardèche … the sugar islands were symbolized by an island in the Rhône where people went to search out young citizens loaded with chains, representing black slaves, in order to free them'.[22] In *A Colony of Citizens*, Laurent Dubois' recently published monograph history of revolution and slave emancipation in Guadeloupe, he cites the research of Helpern to support his claim that the abolition of slavery was celebrated as a 'dramatic transformation' within France itself by 'thousands of Parisians' and others 'throughout France' who attended public events to herald the liberation of the slaves.[23]

Evidence of this revolutionary generosity and mass sympathy for the newly anointed black citizens of the colonies appears in radical newspapers that enjoyed a fairly wide circulation in Paris during the terror. During the time of the decree of emancipation, the press of the Hébertistes and of the radical Jacobins expressed positions that were sometimes even more radical than the decrees and pronouncements made in the Convention. Whatever may have been the true opinions of the leading Jacobins with regard to questions of race and slavery, the readers of the *Père Duchesne* and *le Sans-Culotte Observateur* as well as readers of the official *Feuille de Salut Public* were presented with an enthusiastic outpouring of anti-slavery that connected the struggle for emancipation with the struggles that the revolutionary Parisian journalists were urging against tyranny, clericalism, and aristocracy. In a chapter of Piquet's book *L'Emancipation des Noirs* entitled *Les militants révolutionnaires*, Piquet cites a series of the most interesting articles on slave emancipation, which appeared in the radical press of Paris in the aftermath of 16 pluviôse. The issue of the *Sans-Culotte Observateur* of 2 ventôse included a lengthy description of the festival that was held in Paris in honour of emancipation:

> Of all the republican festivals, this one has the greatest character, because it brings more than half of the human race in contact with liberty … With what pleasure were the sweet chants of equality and independence repeated … With what sacred curiosity did one contemplate the representatives of all the aggrieved peoples of Africa and America in beautiful triumph, honored by the august presence of the representatives of the entire people of France, proclaimed free like the people of France and called upon to share and defend their rights.[24]

For the most politicized sectors of French society, the insurrection in Saint-Domingue was not passing unnoticed, and debate and discussion on slavery was almost certainly more widespread than at any previous point in French history. By the beginning of 1794, the dominant opinion had become revolutionary emancipationism. The discussion of slave emancipation in issue 347 of Hébert's *Le Père*

Duchesne even concluded with a wishful form of eighteenth-century political internationalism:

> The time will arrive, I hope, when all peoples after having exterminated their tyrants, will form a single family of brothers. Perhaps one day we will see Turks, Russians, French, English and Germans reunited in the same senate, to compose a great convention of all the nations of Europe. When the other nations see the fruits that this union will have produced, when under wise laws we will all be content, then men with even a little blood in their veins will try to imitate us, and we will offer help to any who want to escape from slavery.[25]

Hébert seems to have been fairly excited at the idea that the people of France were able to offer a *coup d'épaule* to help a distant people free itself from slavery. Although the mobilized enthusiasm for slave emancipation dried up quickly in France with the onset of Thermidor, and although the official reintroduction of colonial slavery under Napoleon failed to stir up any major domestic opposition, at the height of the Jacobin terror French abolitionism reached an unprecedented crescendo.

Nearly every historian to have commented on the 16 pluviôse decree has acknowledged the importance of the accomplished fact of the Saint-Domingue slave insurrection and Sonthonax's historic decree of 29 August 1793 in the National Convention's decision to abolish slavery. Many have also cited the fact that after the decree of abolition, Danton was supposed to have pronounced that 'The English are done for.' These historians have correctly pointed out that the National Convention's decree of abolition had something to do with their desire to thwart the British invasion of Saint-Domingue and perhaps even to spread the flames of slave rebellion to Britain's valuable Caribbean colonies. In Saint-Domingue the French decree of abolition was indeed used as a guarantee against English attempts to conquer the colony by restoring slavery with the support of the plantation owners. In parts of the Lesser Antilles things were taken even further, and the decree was used as a weapon of war under Victor Hugues, who led the reconquest of Guadeloupe from the British by assembling an army of emancipated slaves and who used this decree to bring war against the British in neighbouring islands and on the high seas. Some historians might be tempted to explain away these events as examples of a cynical and expedient recourse to slave emancipation as a tool for imperial warfare. Of course this tactic had its precedents, as in Lord Dunmore's Proclamation of 1775 or in the early enlistment of Saint-Domingue slave rebels including Jean François, Biassou, and Toussaint Louverture as officers of the Spanish Crown. However, this argument does not apply perfectly to Republican France's programme of abolition throughout the Caribbean. It certainly does not apply to France's small South American colony of Cayenne (French Guyana), which the English did not have particularly eager designs for (and which Yves Bénot has somewhat dismissively referred to as a *colonie qui n'intéresse personne)*.[26] The fact that French Guiana was not a vital piece on the imperial chessboard did not stop the National Convention from ordering the abolition of slavery there. The Jacobin-appointed governor of Cayenne, Jeannet-Odin (who happened to have been the nephew of Danton), implemented the decree of 16 pluviôse and officially liberated the roughly 10,000 slaves living in the colony. Legal slave emancipation at both Guadeloupe and Cayenne in 1794 demonstrated the universal intentions of the Jacobin legislators in abolishing slavery in all colonies in February of that year.

The original impetus and probably the most significant factor behind France's 1794 abolition of slavery were the successful slave rebellions, particularly in Saint-Domingue. However, some historians have taken this observation so far as to ignore or forget the political conjuncture in France that made the decree of 16 pluviôse possible. An example of this error comes through clearly in the claim by the French intellectual Louis Sala-Molins that the 1794 abolition of slavery was 'wrested by the slaves and initialled without enthusiasm by the great nation'.[27] Sala-Molins, for all of his sophistication of thought and familiarity with the events of the period, is simply unwilling to acknowledge the fact that no word besides enthusiasm better describes the political mood and the publicly-expressed sentiments that accompanied the 1794 decree. The fact that enthusiasm in and of itself was not enough for the Montagnard leaders and the masses of the radical sans-culottes to preserve their hold on power and spread their universalist, egalitarian vision to the ends of the Earth, does not mean that an immense abolitionist enthusiasm did not animate many of the Montagnards, Hébertists, and sans-culottes of year II. A gentler version of Sala-Molins' outright dismissal of Jacobin anti-slavery appears in the most recent edition of the *Oxford History of the French Revolution*, in which the author William Doyle writes that the National Convention abolished slavery 'reluctantly and belatedly'.[28] Like Sala-Molins, in this passage Doyle seems to be considering the French Revolution as a single, massive and abstract historical entity responsible for the events of the entire decade 1789–99. Instead of participants in a pitched battle between political forces defending the often radically opposed interests of different social classes, the sans-culottes of Paris and the Committee of Public Safety are somehow expected to answer for the colonial policy of the Legislative Assembly, the Directory, or even of the Consulate. The distinction between different periods and different ruling groups is made quite clear in *The Black Jacobins* when James explains the reversal of the 16 pluviôse decree by arguing that 'the passionate desire to free all humanity which had called for Negro freedom in the great days of the revolution now huddled in the slums of Paris and Marseilles, exhausted by its great efforts and terrorized by Bonaparte's bayonets and Fouche's police'.[29] In this case, James' Marxist framework offers the advantage of analysing the French Revolution not as some sort of unified entity, but more as it actually was: a period of political transformations in which power was traded violently between different political currents representing distinct and antagonistic social groups. It was neither the Bourbon monarchs, nor the Saint-Domingue planters, nor the Bordeaux merchant elite who abolished slavery in 1794 – any more than it was the labouring masses of France or the Committee of Public Safety who legally restored it in 1802. It was in the very nature of the French Revolution that one group accomplished its goals over the objections and often over the bodies of the other.

1802, the fall of Charles Bélair and the rise of Dessalines

When Napoleon sent an expeditionary force of 20,000 French troops to Saint-Domingue in February 1802, the French generals carefully denied and concealed their plans to legally reinstate the slave system. But as the French arrested leading black officers such as Toussaint Louverture and struggled to return former slaves to the sugar plantations, the local population became increasingly convinced of the rumours that the French intended to re-enslave them. In August 1802, as revolts against the French expeditionary force broke out throughout the colony, signatory to the 1792 letter, Charles Bélair, and hundreds of soldiers under his command joined the rebellion. French forces in the region, including those led by the former slave General Jean-Jacques Dessalines, quickly mobilized against Bélair. On 6 September, less than three weeks after beginning his rebellion, Charles Bélair and his wife Sanite Bélair were captured and sent before the firing squad. While French Republican concepts of liberty clearly shaped the early course of the Haitian Revolution, Napoleon's decision to forcefully reimpose slavery eroded French ideological influence in the nascent nation of Haiti. And yet even as the metropolitan authorities turned away from the radical egalitarianism of the early 1790s, the revolutionary language of equality had left a lasting impression on the black masses of Saint-Domingue. In 1802, as Bélair led his final daring rebellion against the French, insurgent leaders in Saint-Domingue would continue to invoke the French revolutionary slogan of '*resistance à l'oppression*' – using it against a French state that had itself betrayed its earlier project of slave emancipation.[30]

Although General Dessalines obeyed his French superior officers by arresting and executing the rebel Charles Bélaire, Dessalines himself was biding his time, serving his French superiors while waiting for the right moment to turn against Napoleon and his occupying army and take over the island for himself. In September 1802, as Napoleon's dwindling expeditionary force in Saint-Domingue struggled to corral a restive black population back into slavery, the French General staff anxiously speculated about the loyalties and ambitions of General Dessalines. The French General Quantin wrote to the colony's military Governor General Rochambeau claiming that Dessalines feared the wrath of his '*sans-culottes*' and that, because of this political pressure from below, might be planning to turn against France.[31] Quantin's prediction was borne out several months later when

Dessalines, after having used his position under the French expeditionary force to get rid of domestic rivals, performed a volte-face and decided to lead the growing rebellion against the French. Quantin's otherwise unremarkable battlefield dispatch is interesting because it may represent the only contemporary application of the term 'sans-culottes' to the rebel slave masses of the Haitian Revolution. The use of French revolutionary categories by combatants in the Haitian Revolution offers some of the strongest evidence of the ideological interconnections between the two cotemporaneous events.

Haiti and the problem of institutional teleology

If the Haitian Revolution has been silenced or otherwise denied its proper place in the history of modern social revolutions, it is not only because its leading participants were former slaves of African descent. It is also because the revolution's outcomes do not conform to teleological narratives of liberal-democratic nation building, or of revolution as a necessary force for ushering in economic and technological progress. In today's history curricula the Haitian Revolution is increasingly grouped in with the American and French Revolutions as part of the early-modern 'Age of Revolutions'. But Haiti's founding revolution was profoundly different, especially in the sense that it never lived up to the schema by which revolution functions as a modernizing force catalysing technological advancement and the emergence of new, more sophisticated and efficient modes of capital accumulation. Whereas the colonial slave system involved capital-intensive, proto-industrial methods of production, nineteenth-century Haitian society became profoundly decentralized and historically averse to large enterprise. In a reversal of Whiggish chronologies of advancement through capital accumulation, technological innovation, and economies of scale, the nineteenth-century Haitian economy was made up of a growing patchwork of small farms that were far smaller, less capitalized, less technologically advanced, and less efficient than the colonial plantations.

Academics have been attracted to the intellectual history of the Haitian Revolution because of the unprecedented universal application of citizenship rights to former slaves. The formal emancipation of slaves in colonial Saint-Domingue in 1793 and their inclusion as citizens of the revolutionary French Republic in 1794 represented a historic triumph of Enlightenment principles over slavery, colonialism, and nascent racial ideology. But while it may be appealing to view the Haitian revolutionaries as early champions of a kind of democratic, Western liberalism, these categories do not easily fit the social realities of early Haiti: a society characterized by *caudillismo*, *marronage*, and class conflict over forced labour. To be sure, ideologies of liberty, republicanism, citizenship, equality, and '*resistance à l'oppression*' were on the lips of the former slave insurgents and they appeared in official state discourse. But so too there arose the reactionary systems of empire, monarchy, and feudal aristocracy. The Empire of Dessalines and the Kingdom of Henri Christophe recalled both the princely lineages of West Africa as well as the absolutist monarchies of Europe. On the other hand, David Geggus's provocative assertion that the Haitian Revolution was 'authoritarian from beginning to end',[32] does not sufficiently convey the radical, emancipatory politics of the revolutionary Haitian masses. While the early republics, kingdoms and empires that ruled Haiti were largely modelled after European state systems, the countryside experienced the flourishing growth of African-derived religious congregations and quasi-political secret societies. The resilience and growth of maroon communities and religious secret societies in early Haiti demonstrates that an anti-colonial movement that incorporated European political rhetoric and institutional forms could also give rise to the growth and spread of non-European cultural, ideological, and political institutions. The post-emancipation legacy of *marronage* encapsulates popular political practices of clandestine and irregular forms of class struggle that were neither authoritarian nor liberal-democratic but which profoundly shaped the new nation.

Faced with oppressive rulers and denied the protection of official laws and rights, the early Haitian masses pursued land and liberty by extra-legal means. While some academics are inclined to associate the term 'democracy' with the early Haitians' struggles for freedom, the strategies and systems that they devised to avoid post-emancipation confinement and exploitation do not easily map on to European, liberal-democratic discourses of legal rights or participatory politics. Rather than struggling to express their collective aspirations through participating in nascent public institutions, early Haitian labourers avoided the repressive reach of the state and carved out semi-autonomous rural farms and communities that partially recalled the evasive strategies of colonial-era maroons. Rather than toiling for an enlightened patriotic bourgeoisie and helping to create a powerful new nation-state with robust institutions, the Haitian masses resisted their haughty rulers by creating a separate and parallel system of economic and cultural institutions. These included a form of extended family-farm compound called the *lakou*, a bustling network of decentralized public marketplaces, and a host of African-derived religious assemblies and secret societies. The post-revolutionary decades represented a formative era for Haiti's religious secret societies. None of these institutions closely resembled a formal democratic political party and they never allowed the masses to fully free themselves from an entrenched commercial elite and a series of corrupt military regimes. But they are enduring and important institutions that have survived to the present day and that remain as evidence of the early Haitian masses' underlying yearning for economic and social autonomy.

Judged against the plantation slavery that persisted in the rest of the Caribbean, and even the lives of serfs or free-born peasants and labourers in early nineteenth-century Europe, the former slaves of Haiti achieved a great deal. By the 1820s, a substantial percentage and perhaps even a majority of Haitian families in all regions of the country had acquired small farmsteads, usually between three and twenty acres. Depending on the location and characteristics of the particular parcel, as little as five acres of Hispaniolan farmland was sufficient to provide an early Haitian family with food for domestic consumption and surplus crops for sale on the local market. In addition, many post-emancipation farmers had access to stands of coffee and dyewoods, which were early Haiti's primary export commodities. Some could also harvest secondary export commodities including hardwoods, long-staple cotton, cacao, leather, beeswax, and tortoiseshell. Instead of intensive plantation cultivation, the coffee, dyewoods, hardwoods, and animal products that the Haitian peasants harvested and sold were either the remnants of colonial-era plantations or the products of spontaneous, natural growth. By periodically extracting these commodities from the landscape and selling them to cash-crop speculators, Haitian peasants made money with which they supplemented their independent subsistence production.

Even though Haiti emerged from the revolution with a comparatively even distribution of land, the society was neither egalitarian nor democratic. All of the early Haitian governments were military dictatorships. Even as the masses rejected forced labour and the plantation economy withered away, the countryside never became a paradise of social equality. Absentee landowning, sharecropping, and domestic servitude all thrived in post-emancipation Haiti. Oppressive relations of production in the rural sphere never disappeared following the fall of the plantation economy; they just became so splintered, unstable, and small scale that they could not support significant efforts towards capital accumulation or state building.

The history of nineteenth-century Haiti demonstrates that social progress, like beauty, exists in the eye of the beholder. Excepting a few abolitionist Haiti promoters such as Thomas Clarkson, who wrote guardedly optimistic accounts of the Haitian experiment, nearly every nineteenth-century European or North American observer decried the new nation as hopelessly barbaric and backward. But for the early citizens of Haiti, their new nation offered innumerable advantages over their previous condition of enslavement. At a time when slavery persisted in all neighbouring societies of the Caribbean, ordinary Haitian labourers had a chance to achieve dignity and economic independence as landowners, tradespeople, or soldiers. Under Dessalines and Christophe thousands of Haitians still felt compelled to illegally flee forced labour, but they had a far easier time escaping and creating their own independent communities than did fugitive slaves in the days of the French colony. By 1820 forced labour on the plantations had fully given way to smaller-scale systems of independent farming, sharecropping, and domestic servitude. Early Haiti never emerged from the shadow of dictatorship and poverty, but for black people in the nineteenth century it was the closest thing to a free country that existed anywhere in the New World.

If Haiti's history is judged against the ideal of liberal democracy and European or North American standards of institutionality and statecraft, the founding revolution will be inevitably portrayed as an abject failure much as it was by the country's early nineteenth-century white detractors. However, the experiences of the country's former slave citizens offer another framework with which to conceptualize and judge the revolution: as a prolonged, collective, popular campaign of escape from the confinement of plantation labour and from the repressive hand of the state. Judged in this light, whatever the corrupt nature of the country's weak official institutions, the rise of partially autonomous rural communities in nineteenth-century Haiti represented an unprecedented triumph for former slaves and their descendants.

Notes

1 Yves Bénot, *La révolution française et la fin des colonies, 1789–1794* (Paris: La Découverte, 2004).
2 Laurent Dubois, *A Colony of Citizens* (Chapel Hill: University of North Carolina Press, 2004), 278.
3 Aimé Césaire, *Toussaint Louverture: La Révolution Francaise et le problème colonial* (Paris: Le Club français du livre, 1960).
4 C.L.R. James, *The Black Jacobins* (New York: Vintage Books, 1989).
5 The term 'creole' refers to island-born people. Maroons were runaway slaves who created unauthorized settlements on the remote margins of plantation regions.
6 Recent scholarship has cast doubt on the exact identity of the third figure, identified by signature only as 'Bélair'. This may have either been a very young Charles Bélair or a subordinate of Biassou named Gabriel Bélair. For the purposes of exposition, this chapter will assume the former rather than the latter. Charles Bélair was by far the youngest of the prominent black generals of the Haitian Revolution. Little is known about Charles Bélair's life and background before the outbreak of the Haitian Revolution except that he most likely began life as a creole or island-born slave. Bélair was a trusted favourite of Toussaint Louverture. He is best remembered as the martyred leader of a failed revolt against the French expeditionary force during the final phase of the Haitian revolution.
7 Piquionne, Nathalie. 'Lettre de Jean-François, Biassou et Bélair, juillet 1792', *Annales Historiques de la Révolution française* 311 (Jan-March 1998), 132–4. '*la liberté général de tous les hommes détenus dans l'esclavage*', '*les hommes naissent libres et égaux en droit et que les droits naturels sont la liberté, la proprieté, la sureté, et la résistance a l'oppression*'.
8 James, *Black Jacobins*, 120, 134.
9 Piquionne, Lettre de Jean-François, 133, '*heureuse révolution qui a eu lieu dans la Mère Patries et qui nous a frayé le chemin que notre courage et nos travaux sauront nous faire gravir*', '*arriver au temple de la Liberté comme ces braves Français qui sont nos mo dèles*'.
10 Claude Wanquet, *La France et la première abolition de l'esclavage, 1794–1802: le cas des colonies orientales, Ile de France (Maurice) et la Réunion* (Paris: Éditions Karthala, 1998).
11 Bénot, *La révolution française*, 80, '*sur les questions colonials, les differences d'opinion politique ne recoupaient pas les clivages politiques de la métropole*'.
12 Quoted in Bénot, *La révolution française*, 81, '*C'est ainsi, que la même faction qui en France voulait réduire tous les pauvres à la condition d'ilotes, et soumettre le peuple à l'aristocratie des riches, voulait en un instant affranchir et armer tous les nègres pour detruire nos colonies.*'
13 Jean-Daniel Piquet, *L'émancipation des Noirs dans la Révolution Française (1789–1795)* (Paris: Éditions Karthala, 2002), 7. '*On n'osera pas reconnaître que la paternité du plus bel événement de l'histoire de l'humanité fut imputable à des criminels, des fanatiques ou des tyrans.*'
14 James, *Black Jacobins*, 139.

15   *Ibid.*, 120.

16   Bertrand Barère de Vieuzac quoted in Yves Bénot, *La révolution française*, 'Comment la convention a-t-elle aboli l'esclavage en l'an II* in A.H.R.F., *Revolutions aux colonies* 1993.

17   The decree of emancipation was passed in the National Convention on 4 February 1794, 16 pluviôse of year II according to the French Republican calendar. The event remains known to historians as the decree of 16 pluviôse.

18   James, *Black Jacobins*, 140.

19   Jean-Pierre Biondi, *16 Pluviôse An II* (Paris: Éditions Denoël, 1989) 13.

20   Nicolas-André Monsiau, *L'Abolition de l'Esclavage par la Convention, le 16 Pluviôse An II.* (Paris: Musée Carnavalet).

21   Bénot, *La révolution française*, 200.

22   Jean-Claude Helpern, 'Les Fêtes révolutionnaires et l'abolition de l'esclavage en l'An II', in Dorigny, ed., *The Abolitions of Slavery* (New York: Berghahn Books, 2003), 163.

23   Laurent Dubois, *A Colony of Citizens* (Chapel Hill: University of North Carolina Press, 2004), 163.

24   *Sans-Culotte Observateur* 20 February 1794. Quoted in Piquet, 376. '*De toutes les fêtes républicaines, celle-ci porte le plus grand caractère, car elle associe à la liberté plus de la moitié du genre human … Avec quell plaisir on répétait à l'unisson les doux cantiques de l'indépendence et de l'égalité! … Avec quelle curiosité sainte on contemplait dans un si beau triomphe les représentants de tous les peuples inignes de l'Afrique et de l'Amerique honorés par la presence auguste de la representation du peuple français tout entière, proclamés libres comme lui, appelés à partager et à défendre ses droits.*'

25   Jacques Hébert, Le Père Duchesne Number 347. Quoted in Piquet, 378. '*Un temps viendra, j'espère où tous les peuples après avoir exterminé leurs tyrans, ne formeront qu'une seule famille de frères. Peut-être un jour verra-t-on des Turcs, des Russes, des Français, des Anglais, des Allemands, réunis dans le même Sénat, composer une grande Convention de toutes les nations de l'Europe. Lorsque les autres nations verront les fruits qu'elle aura produits, lorsque sous les lois sages, nous serons tous heuruex, alors les hommes qui auront un peu de dang dans les veines chercheront à nous imiter, et nous donnerons un coup d'épaule à ceux qui voudront sortir d'esclavage.*'

26   Bénot, *La Révolution Française*, 59.

27   Louis Sala-Molins, *The Dark Side of the Light* (Minneapolis: University of Minnesota Press, 2006), 116.

28   William Doyle, *The Oxford History of the French Revolution* (Oxford University Press, 2002), 411.

29   James, *Black Jacobins*, 270.

30   Rochambeau Collection, Doc. 1176 '*Extrait d'une lettre ecrite par Cangé*', n.d. In October of 1802, French forces near Petit-Goave in the Southern Province of Saint-Domingue found a letter in the pocket of a 'brigand' who had been killed in battle. The undated letter was signed by the insurgent leader Cangé and was headed with the slogans '*liberté*', '*egalité*', and '*resistance à l'oppression*'.

31   General Quantin to General Rochambeau, 29 September 1802, St Marc, Doc. 1122, Gainesville, FL: Rochambeau Collection, UF Smathers Library Special Collections.

32   David Geggus, 'The Caribbean in the Age of Revolution', in David Armitage, Sanjay Subramanyam, eds, *The Age of Revolutions in Global Context, 1760–1840* (New York: Palgrave Macmillan, 2010), 97.

5

Confronting colonial otherness: the Judicial Committee of the Privy Council and the limits of imperial legal universalism

Bonny Ibhawoh

Empire was premised on an uncertain universalism. The notion of the civilising mission that underpinned nineteenth- and twentieth-century European imperialism assumed a cosmopolitan universality that was constantly in tension with the racialised otherness of those colonised. The idea of the civilising mission gestured towards a tentative inclusivity that made imperial universality conceptually coherent. However, the liberal promise of Britain's 'civilising mission' or the republican ideas behind France's *mission civilisatrice* depended as much on visions of a shared humanity as on a discourse of racialised difference.[1] These notions captured the essence of what may be termed the 'colonial contract'. The metropole's claim to ownership of colonial land, resources, and labour was predicated on the corresponding duty to promote the welfare and development of the colonial inhabitants. The Act of the Berlin Conference of 1884 by which European powers negotiated the political partitioning of West Africa expressed this paternalistic impulse of the civilising mission. The Act referred to the 'development of trade and civilisation' in Africa, and declared the aim of 'instructing the natives and bringing home to them the blessings of civilisation'.[2] French officials claimed that French civilisation was not only superior to anything that existed in the colonies but also had universal applicability. As the imperial narrative went, France had an obligation to export those aspects of its own culture from which all humanity could potentially benefit.[3]

British colonialism was likewise underpinned by a civilising and universalising vision which was conveyed in the notions of the 'sacred trust' and the 'dual mandate'. The 'dual mandate of Empire', wrote British colonial administrator Frederick Lugard in 1922, was defined by the intersecting interests of Britain and her colonies. Britain was in the colonies for the mutual benefit of her own industrial classes, and of the 'native races in their progress to a higher plane'.[4] Britain's

role was to bring the 'gains of civilisation' with as little interference as possible
with native customs and mode of thought.[5] However, understandings of what
constituted the 'civilising mission' were varied and complex. In the interpretation
of some British officials in India, for example, the goal of the civilising mission was
not to necessarily convert the heathens, but to return India to its 'natural' path of
historical development towards a more civilised society. In the British imagination, this entailed the restoration of the social and political standing of enlightened
indigenous rulers, the definition of liberal property rights, and the revival of customary legal systems such as the *panchayat* village tribunals.[6]

Herein lies the great paradox of the imperial project. The mandate to civi-
lise the native and raise him or her to a higher plane required the extension of
certain normative standards to the colonies. In this sense, the civilising mission
mandated a deliberate universalism. Within the broad rubric of the civilising mission, European norms, practices and institutions were reconstructed as universal
and extended to the colonies on a scale conducive to colonial interests. But
this had to be done in a way that did not fundamentally disrupt the indigenous
customary order because a disruptive universalism would have unsettled social
order from the start. What was required was a supple, yet hegemonic notion of
the universal, one that would require constant tinkering and reinterpretation.
If the language of civilisation and modernity represented a universalist fulcrum
of Empire, the language of race and custom pointed at the essentialised otherness of the colonised that was crucial to maintaining imperial hierarchies. This
bounded universality of the civilising mission points at another basic tension of
Empire: otherness was always unstable, and social boundaries had to be constantly redrawn and re-legitimised.[7]

Nowhere was this tension between the imperial universalist impulse and the
practicalities of everyday colonial Othering more evident than in the realm of law
and the administration of justice. Within the British Empire, as in other European
empires of the nineteenth and twentieth centuries, colonial legal and judicial
discourses were shaped by notions of native difference. However, these notions
of colonial difference were tempered by a cosmopolitan and universalist idealism
that was perhaps less evident in other spheres of the colonial enterprise. Native
otherness had to be responsively accommodated within the larger homogenising
agendas of the Empire. The logic was self-evident: although different, colonised
natives somehow had to be brought within the fold of 'civilisation' in fulfilment
of the universally redemptive promise of the liberal Empire.

Recent studies have drawn attention to the complicated and contested history of the construction of colonial legal knowledge and the political and intellectual influences that shaped it.[8] Scholars of law and empire have challenged
British claims to establishing a universal rule of law in the Empire, arguing instead
that colonialism was fundamentally based on stressing the difference between
the coloniser and the colonised, usually in terms of racial and ethnic identities.[9]
Maintaining colonial difference in the realms of law-making and administration

of justice was essential to sustaining Empire. A truly uniform and consistent rule of law would have profoundly threatened the power dynamic that distinguished coloniser from the colonised, and abrogated the very foundations of the imperial project.[10] Thus, in spite of its universalist aspirations, the pragmatics of colonial rule required the construction and maintenance of multiple registers of colonial otherness along racial, ethnic, religious, class, caste, generational, and gender lines. How did colonial officials and institutions and colonial subjects reconcile this apparent paradox in the realms of law and the administration of justice? In addressing this question, the role of the Judicial Committee of the Privy Council (JCPC) offers some unique insights.

The work of the Judicial Committee of the Privy Council (JCPC) epitomised the tension between imperial legal cosmopolitanism and the practicalities of colonial difference. As the highest court of appeal in the British Empire, the JCPC forged a centripetal jurisprudence of Empire that homogenised law across the British Empire, as judges smoothed over local differences by applying precedents from colonies, dependencies, and communities across the Empire.[11] In the nineteenth and twentieth centuries, the JCPC adjudicated thousands of appeals from territories across the British Empire. This chapter examines the universalising impulse in British imperial justice in the work of the JCPC in India and Africa. It juxtaposes the intellectual merits and practical limitations of legal universalism in JCPC jurisprudence. The ideal of the imperial judicial uniformity that the JCPC represented had broad appeal among constituents in both metropole and colony. In adjudicating the cases that came before them from across the Empire, the lords of the JCPC strove to uphold a common standard of British justice. However, everyday conditions in the colonies and the practicalities of judicial governance across the Empire often made it difficult, if not impossible, to fully achieve this cosmopolitan ideal. In the end, the contradictions of imperial legal universalism and persistence of colonial difference would call into question the legitimacy of the JCPC and usher in its decline along with the political structures of Empire in the era of decolonisation.

A hegemonic and contested universalism

The ideal of judicial uniformity and standardisation was deeply held in both metropole and colony. The universalising goal of Empire's civilising agenda fundamentally shaped the ideas and practices of judicial governance in the colonies. In particular, European colonisers found the notion of universalism useful in both the processes of legal codification and judicial standardisation. In British India, a universalist idealism underpinned early utilitarian attempts at legal codification, which often meant the exportation of English law to the colony. This strengthened the legitimating myth of colonial laws and cloaked the need of the state to use law to maintain its authority. The colonial legal system tended to categorise complex religious identities into the monolithic categories of 'English', 'Hindu', and 'Muslim', each with fixed attributes. Hindus were to be governed by Hindu law and Muslims by Muslim law. But in reality, indigenous society was much more heterodox and variegated than such simple categories of colonial legal knowledge and classification allowed. By separating Hindu and Muslim personal laws from public law, which remained largely influenced by the principles of English Common Law, the colonial state sought to harness existing legal structures and to diminish the upheaval thrown up by conquest.[12]

Colonial law and justice often fell short of their liberal and universalist promise. A dominant universalism was consistently mingled with attention to how particularity and difference constrained the applicability of universal principles.[13] This trend has been noted in the extant literature on the history of imperial political thought, which draws attention to the connections between various forms of moral universalism and projects of conquest. Although some studies note the mutually constitutive relationship between liberalism and Empire, others critically assess the sorts of universalisms that accompanied imperial expansions.[14] A central theme in these studies is the tension between a bold civilising and universalising ideology of imperial law, and a much more cautious imperium which sought to preserve local customs and instrumentalise law to maintain dominance and stifle dissent. The tension between the drive for uniformity and centralisation on the one hand, and the variegated legal spaces that made up Empire on the other, challenge the narrative of universalism and cosmopolitanism.[15]

Imperial legal universalism was also a distinctly hegemonic construct that was paradoxically underwritten by a certain Eurocentric parochialism. As other studies have shown, scientific and scholarly attention to global phenomena in the nineteenth-century imperial age was in part driven by, and can be said to have contributed to, European parochialism. European imperialism emerged as Europe came into an understanding of itself as 'an entity with global reach and global significance, both because of its outsized power and because of the apparent uniqueness of European progress in human history'.[16] This parochialism paradoxically fed a universalising impulse. Europe was the world and the world was Europe. Universalism and globality in this sense did not entail the aggregation of local experiences and diverse regional perspectives. Rather, it meant the spread of European ideas, practices, and institutions across empires and the world. In the realm of law and justice, much of what came to be framed as universal were mostly European. For example, the law of nations or international law became both distinctively European and universal. Like the civilising mission, the interpretation of *ius gentium* rested on the fundamental premise that Europe was uniquely in possession of universal moral and political truths.[17]

It is therefore with caution that we must proceed with the notion of *imperial universalism*. Imperial justice was universal in its aspirations towards commonality, cohesion and standardisation. It was less so in its practice or *raison d'être*. Thus, to fully understand British imperial legal universalism, it is necessary to move beyond analysing the spread of English law simply as a vehicle for exporting

British values around the world. It is also important to understand the complex processes and transformative outcomes of the interactions between metropolitan law and indigenous practices in the administration of colonial justice.

The universalist premise of the JCPC

The JCPC was more than a colonial court. It was the quintessential imperial court. One of several standing committees of the British Privy Council, its primary mandate as an appellate court was to uphold overarching British standards of justice in the colonies and dominions. Its jurisdiction went beyond national and regional colonial boundaries, making it a veritable clearing house of conflicting legal codes, demands, and disputes, and hence a gateway to both local processes and imperial regulation.[18] It comprised metropolitan judges who, having limited knowledge of the laws they were expected to interpret and legal customs of the disputants who came before them from the colonies, struggled to find the right balance between promoting common British standards of justice while allowing for some degree of local difference. The revered lords of the JCPC saw themselves less as part of the imperial political order and more as *umpires of the Empire*: impartial arbiters and exponents of the universality of British justice. The image of the JCPC was of a learned, technical body, far removed from the excitement of imperial politics, and therefore, disinterested in the outcome of the cases that came before it. The combination of technocratic excellence and remoteness from politics served it well in maintaining its reputation of an impartial judicial body.[19] Sitting at the metropolitan centre in Westminster, JCPC was less symbolic of the hegemonic power of empire than courts in the colonies. For many colonial subjects, it offered a largely neutral judicial space, beyond the direct influence of colonial officialdom, where they could negotiate and challenge colonial law.

Until the enactment of the Statute of Westminster in 1931, which enabled British dominions to assert more political autonomy and discontinue judicial appeals, the JCPC was the final court of appeal for more than a quarter of the world. It made final rulings and interpretations of a vast variety of laws across the British Empire-Commonwealth, including Roman-Dutch law from South Africa, British Guyana, and Salome; Spanish law from Trinidad; pre-revolutionary French law from Quebec; the Napoleonic Code from Mauritius; Sardinian law from Malta; Venetian law from the Ionian islands; medieval Norman law from the Channel Islands; Muslim, Buddhist, and Hindu law from India; Ottoman law from Turkey, Cyprus, and Egypt; Chinese law from British courts in Shanghai; and diverse indigenous customary laws from across Africa.

Although sitting at the imperial centre, the mandate of the JCPC was to administer locally relevant justice. It typically adjudicated cases based on the prevailing laws in the colonial realm or dominion jurisdiction from which each case

was appealed. However, the lords of the JCPC also took seriously their responsibility of maintaining common judicial standards across the Empire irrespective of
the prevailing domestic laws. Many of these judges traversed the world on administrative postings and promotion within the British legal service. Their precedents
were imperial and their worldviews were distinctly cosmopolitan. Judges with
experience in the colonies were particularly desired on the JCPC bench because
they were thought to possess knowledge of local customs and traditions that
would be crucial to adjudicating colonial appeals that came before the Court.
Lord Watson, a long-serving judge of the JCPC, was extolled for his acumen
in interpreting laws according to the spirit of the jurisprudence from which an
appeal came. 'If it was a Cape appeal from South Africa, he was a Roman-Dutch
lawyer; if it was an Indian case of adoption, he entered into the religious reasons
for the rule to be applied; if it was a Quebec case of substitution under the old
French code, or a Jersey appeal about the customs of Normandy, it was just the
same.'[20] This eclectic approach to judicial governance was considered crucial to
the work of this court of last resort in the Empire. The judges who served on the
JCPC had to be 'jacks of all trades', and adept at adjudicating wide-ranging legal
disputes from across an Empire that was rapidly expanding and encompassed peoples with unfamiliar legal cultures.[21]

Many constituents in Britain and the colonies saw the JCPC an indispensable
link, the central connector between the distant constituents of the British Empire
and a symbol of enlightened association based on English common law. It was
a key agent in the task of judicial standardisation by adjudicating contentious
questions of local law from a detached perspective. In practice, it was involved
more with interpreting colonial statutes and proclamations than with applying the
general common law to the Empire. The diversity of legal systems in the Empire
made this necessary. Although there may have been no ambition to export common law as a monolithic system, there was clearly an intention to uphold some
common standards of judicial interpretation across the Empire founded on fundamental notions of British justice. The JCPC's role in maintaining jurisprudential
homogeneity is demonstrated most clearly in its exercise of the power of judicial
review. The basis of that power lay in the principle that all colonial legislatures
were subordinate to the Crown and that colonial law and justice must conform to
British standards.[22] Colonial English-style courts were expected to serve no lesser
function than the courts in England. Their purpose was to deal with disputes in
terms of clear-cut rights and duties, established by objective investigation of only
those events deemed relevant to each case.

The JCPC forged imperial unity through universalist interpretations of divergent colonial statute laws and indigenous customary laws. In 1879, the JCPC
stated in a landmark judgment: 'It is of the utmost importance that in all parts
of the Empire where English law prevails, the interpretation of that law by the
courts should be as nearly as possible the same.'[23] Writing in 1922, Lord Haldane

stressed the JCPC's quest for judicial uniformity and standardisation even in cases involving non-English law:

> We sit there to administer Buddhist law, or Hindu Law, or Mohammedan Law, one after the other. We administer Roman-Dutch law from South Africa or from Ceylon, or French law from Quebec, or the Common Law of England for Ontario … [We] try to look for the *common principle* underlying systems of jurisprudence of differing kinds. [We] know that the form often veils over a very similar substance. We are constantly finding that, where great broad principles of justice are concerned, you find – veiled, but still there and only distinguished by technicalities – the same substance as belongs to other systems.[24]

Another long-serving judge of the JCPC, Lord Atkin, described the JCPC as 'the only agency for securing any measure of uniformity in legal development over the whole of this vast Empire'.[25] The JCPC's quest for uniformity and standardisation in the adjudication of colonial appeals reflects the Empire's universalist impulse in judicial governance.

There were, however, limits to the JCPC's ability to pursue legal uniformity due to the regular need for the Board to apply unfamiliar non-English law. As Lord Haldane put it, the jurisdiction of the JCPC was a 'very delicate one' and the Crown could not always be safely advised to interfere with matters involving the constitutions or systems of governments of the Empire's colonies and dominations. The object of the JCPC adjudication, Haldane stated, was to 'make the part of the Empire from which the appeal comes, have the sense of seeing that there has been a mistake, if one has been made'.[26] The process of appeals adjudication had to reflect the law and the spirit of the country from which the appeal was brought, as well as adhere to the laws and traditions of that country. In other words, even in its quest for judicial uniformity and standardisation, the exigencies of imperial governance made it necessary for the JCPC judges to accommodate divergence and difference.[27]

Faced with the tenuousness of the imported English law and the resilience of indigenous customary laws, the lords of the JCPC often sought to accommodate both systems of law. It was necessary to temper the initial insistence on imperial unity of the English law with the development of a plural system of laws and with the mixture of common law and indigenous customary law. Although common law was more universal in nature, indigenous customary law varied considerably.[28] In many parts of the British Empire, indigenous customary laws were allowed to exist only in subordination to colonial statute law. Customary laws and practices were generally denied judicial recognition where they conflicted with local statute law or with the presumed universalist standards of British justice.[29]

The JCPC played a decisive role in delineating the threshold for accommodating indigenous customary laws within the judicial system. It was frequently called upon to interpret colonial laws and make decisions on disputes arising from the conflicts between English law and indigenous customary laws. In adjudicating these cases, the Privy Council addressed the central tension in colonial judicial governance – that between upholding uniform standards of colonial justice based on common law traditions and simultaneously allowing for some degree of local divergence based on customary practices. This balance was considered essential to achieving justice. The imperial judges at the JCPC also recognised that in order to achieve justice in the colonies, some flexibility was required in the interpretation of colonial statute law and indigenous customary laws.

Justice, equity, and good conscience

The standardising and universalising role of the JCPC was enabled by colonial statute law. This prescribed the application of English common law and the 'principles of justice, equity and good conscience' were necessary and practicable. The ultimate goal of the civilising mandate in the realm of law was to uphold basic imperial standards of justice while accommodating indigenous law and practice. In British India, this aspiration was expressed in Queen Victoria's Declaration of 1858, which provided that the colonial state would not unduly tamper with the religious and cultural sensibilities of its subjects. Indigenous law would be allowed to prevail in personal law cases concerning marriage, inheritance, and succession. It is significant, however, that the courts were also directed to rule according to principles of 'justice, equity and good conscience'.[30] This phrase appears frequently in early colonial laws and treaties. In the Bengali regulations of 1781 and the Punjab Laws Act of 1887, the maxim of 'justice, equity and good conscience' constituted the residuary source of law. Both required court judges to act according to justice, equity, and good conscience. This principle encapsulated generally accepted notions of justice defined to coincide with English law.[31] It also became a primary means of accommodating and regulating customary law, particularly in India, where British authorities first faced the problems of large non-European communities with their own systems of laws. The basic rule was that in the absence of a rule from statute, written sources of personal law, custom, or case law, a court must decide a case according to 'justice, equity and good conscience'.

In British Africa as in India, local customs and traditions were tolerated and allowed to co-exist with the imported English legal system, to the extent that they were not considered 'repugnant' to the law of England or vaguely defined principles of 'natural justice, equity and good conscience.'[32] Colonial courts were expected to enforce a curious blend of English common law principles, colonial statute law, and local African customary law within a framework of supposedly universal notions of morality and natural justice. Although indigenous customary laws were tolerated, even accommodated within colonial legal systems, the ultimate goal was to create some legal and judicial standards across the Empire that represented British ideals. The Gold Coast Supreme Court Ordinance of 1867, the first of the statues that formally introduced English law to Britain's African colonies, stipulated the enforcement of common law, the Doctrines of Equity, and the Statutes of General Application that were practised in England on the date that the colony received its local legislature. Likewise, the Judicature Act, which introduced English law to East Africa in the late nineteenth century, obligated local courts to apply 'English Common Law, the doctrines of equity and the statutes of general application in force in England as at 12th August 1897' when English law officially took effect in the colony.[33]

The principle of justice, equity, and good conscience gave colonial courts wide discretionary powers in the administration of justice. In India, many judicial decisions relating to the ascertainment and interpretation of customary law were guided by this maxim, which came to represent the idealism of imperial judicial universalism. Invoking the 'justice, equity and good conscience' principle, the courts could bypass local statues and draw instead from a variety of legal traditions including English law, Roman law, laws of continental European countries, and even natural law. Whenever they came across a situation to which no local custom was applicable, colonial judges resorted to deciding cases according to 'justice, equity and good conscience'. In so doing, English judges invariably based their decisions on the rules of English law with which they were acquainted.[34]

The JCPC played a key role in instrumentalising the maxim of 'justice, equity and good conscience' to entrench English legal standards in India after 1833.[35] As a superior court composed of senior judges of England trained in English law, it was natural for them to interject their own notions of justice and equity into the Indian legal system. Thus, the JCPC acted as a channel through which English law concepts came to be assimilated within the fabric of the Indian law. In several Indian cases that came before the JCPC, their lordships based their decisions on the principle of justice, equity and good conscience rather than substantive law. Even in some cases where the parties had explicitly invoked customary Hindu or Islamic law, the JCPC ruled on the basis of evidence and the principle of justice, equality, and good conscience.[36] Delivering judgment on behalf of the Privy Council in one such case, Justice Knight Bruce stated that English-style courts in India, by their very constitution, were obliged to decide cases according to equity and good conscience.[37]

Likewise, in the case of *Varden Seth Sam* v. *Luckpathy*, decided in 1862, the JCPC pointed out that because courts of the East Indian Company did not have any prescribed general law to which their decisions must conform, they had to 'proceed generally according to justice, equity and good conscience'.[38] As reported, this case, which concerned the transfer of property title, involved an Armenian Christian plaintiff and multiple defendants including an Indian Muslim, a Hindu, and a 'Christian British subject'. The case turned on the question of which property law should be applicable because the parties were not of the same race or creed and had not contracted with reference to any particular law. There was, at the time, also no applicable general local law covering the transfer of property that could be applied. In its judgment, the JCPC applied the principle of justice, equity, and good conscience, which was in effect English property law. The JCPC took a similar approach in *Lopez* v. *Muddhu Mohan Thacur* where English law was applied in a property dispute over land that had been submerged and washed away by the Ganges River but later re-formed when the water receded from the original site.[39] It was held that the regained land belonged to the original owner rather than the party laying claim to that land. The applicable legal principle, the JCPC held, was not merely derived from English law but was also founded on 'universal law and justice'.[40]

There was, however, a great deal of judicial selectivity in the JCPC's application of English common law or the principle of 'justice, equity and good conscience' in adjudicating colonial cases. The touchstone for applying a principle of English law was whether it was suitable to the local conditions in the colony from which the case came. The JCPC concluded in a number of cases that many principles of English law were not conducive or adaptable to India and so refused to apply them. For example, the English rule laid down in the famous case of *Tweedle* v. *Atkinson*[41] barring a third party to a contract from suing, was deemed not applicable in India on the ground that the English rule was based on a legal procedure unique to England and irrelevant to India. In the Indian case, which concerned a contract for marriage involving a minor, the JCPC noted that it might occasion 'serious injustice' if the English common law doctrine was applied to agreements entered into in connection with marriage contracts in India where marriages are contracted for minors by parents and guardians.[42] In general, 'justice, equity and good conscience' came to be equated with English justice resulting in the application of English common law principles framed in universal terms. However, in some cases the practicalities of everyday judicial governance required a focus on the local and the particular, rather than the universal, in the interpretation of justice, equity, and good conscience.[43]

The limits of judicial universalism

Nineteenth-century British utilitarians pledged rule of law based on universal principles. But even they recognised how much the particularity of colonial societies undercut this universalism and how effectively various groups and interests unsettled the universalism of colonial legal and normative assumptions.[44] The key constraint on imperial universalism was the persistence of local difference. In the end, the management of difference was as much a device of imperial control as Empire's insistent universalist idealism. Maintaining colonial otherness in the realm of law-making and administration of justice was also essential to sustaining the Empire. Within the British imperium, the political economy of difference centred on claims of cultural authenticity and supremacy. It also involved the recognition and accommodation of a multiplicity of peoples and their varied customs. This meant drawing boundaries between coloniser and colonised, civilised and uncivilised, modern and traditional, Christian and heathen. Imagery of the native Other reinforced these colonial boundaries and shaped modernising agendas. The legal spaces of the Empire, especially the courts, were the key arenas where these social and identity boundaries of colonial difference were fashioned and sustained. These boundaries, however, which were socially constructed and inherently unstable, were continually contested and subverted. Because it operated beyond the direct purview of local colonial officialdom, the JCPC was a fitting site for contesting and negotiating colonial difference. It was crucial not only to the construction of colonial difference but also to managing the tensions between native exceptionalism and imperial universalism. In adjudicating in the Empire, the JCPC manifested the contradictions of British law and served as a venue for conflicting discourses of inclusion and exclusion, of power and restraint.

It is evident from the jurisprudence of the JCPC that the civilising and modernising agenda of Empire was everywhere mediated by assumption about the essential difference of the colonised Other. Colonial law, even in the aspiration towards universalist British justice, departed from the common law in its ascription of privileges, immunities, and distinctions between colonisers and colonised. The overriding otherness of race was certainly evident in the judicial work of the JCPC. But beyond racial otherness, the JCPC was also a site for forging and reinforcing other forms of difference along ethnic, religious, cultural, and gender lines.

The ideals of judicial universalism, widely shared within colonialism officialdom and among the lords of the JCPC, could not always be upheld amid the exigencies of colonial governance. The JCPC's misunderstanding and misapplication of local religious and customary law sometimes wreaked havoc in the political economy and social order of the colonies. For example, by drawing an analogy between English trusts and Muslim endowments (*wakf*) in one Indian case, the JCPC overruled the legality of a *wakf* set up for private benefit, upsetting hundreds of financial arrangements and sparking a political campaign by the Muslim League in India.[45] In Kenya, where the distinction between the practice of Islamic law in East Africa and in India had long been understood, local Muslims and colonial officials voiced strong disagreement with a JCPC ruling that was based on Indian precedents.[46] The JCPC judgment was perceived as a simplistic and homogenous view of Islamic law, ignorant of the cultural contingencies and complexities of Kenya. Moreover, the Indian case that had provided the grounds for the JCPC decision in the Kenyan case was also severely criticised in India and eventually overruled by Legislative Act. Local critics of the Kenyan judgment argued that the JCPC did not consider, and apparently did not have evidence for, the different course of historical development of Islamic law in India and East Africa. According to one contemporary legal scholar, the JCPC's ruling in the case amounted to applying judicial precedent in such a way that extended the judicial errors of one part of the British Empire to make them law in another.[47]

This exemplifies the practical limitations of the JCPC's approach to imperial judicial universalism.

The decision to appoint indigenous judges to the JCPC in the late nineteenth century had a paradoxical effect on imperial judicial universalism. On the one hand, it gave the JCPC, which had long been criticised for its unrepresentative bench of mostly English judges, a more cosmopolitan outlook. On the other hand, the appointment of indigenous judges further revealed the limitations of the JCPC quest for judicial uniformity and imperial standardisation. In his memoirs, Sayed Ameer Ali, the first Indian and first Muslim judge on the JCPC, noted his frequent disagreements with his English colleagues on the JCPC because of their limited knowledge of local conditions in the colonies. As he put it: 'those unquestionable legal experts lacked basic knowledge about the customs and institutions of India and ended up applying English doctrines to Indian situations'.[48]

The paradox of upholding imperial standards of justice while still accommodating native difference was not easily resolved. The lords of the JCPC seemed acutely aware of the practical constraints on judicial standardisation and uniformity. Although the idealism of exporting English law to the colonies prevailed in the nineteenth century, by the 1920s experiences across the Empire convinced London of the need to adapt law to local conditions and defer to local authorities in the administration of justice. This reinforced the longstanding principle of the JCPC of not interfering in local judicial proceedings 'unless it is shown that, by a disregard of the forms of legal process, or by some violations of the principles of natural justice, or otherwise, *substantial and grave injustice* has been done'.[49] In several colonial cases that came before them, the lords of the JCPC took the position that the universalist ideals of British justice would be better realised not by judicial uniformity but by recognising and upholding local difference and exceptionality. Upholding the common law or maintaining uniformity in the judicial process could not be an end itself. The ultimate goal of judicial governance was to ensure that justice was served in each case. The JCPC took this position in the Indian case of *Narendra Nath Sircar* v. *Kamal Basini*, when it cautioned against using English cases to interpret legal wills in India. It stated: 'To search and sift the heaps of cases on wills which encumber our English Law Reports, in order to understand and interpret Wills of people speaking a different tongue, trained in different habits of thought and brought up under different conditions of life, seems almost absurd.'[50]

One case that clearly illustrates the practical limits of judicial universalism even within the framework of the principle of justice, equity and conscience is the Nigerian case of *Yisa Dawodu* v. *Suwebatu Danmole*.[51] This case arose from a family dispute over the division of the estate of the patriarch of a prominent Yoruba family, Suberu Dawodu, who died intestate in 1940. First heard at a local high court, the case was ultimately appealed to the JCPC in 1960. One of the questions before the courts was determining the validity of African customary law in sharing the estate of the deceased among his nine children from four wives. Evidence was tendered at trial that, under the local customary law applicable to the litigants, the division of estates among the children of the deceased could be done in either of two ways. The first custom was division *per stirpe* among the deceased individual's four wives. Under this customary rule, known as *Idi Igi*, each wife would respectively receive one-fourth of the estate, irrespective of how many children she had with the deceased. Under this rule, an only child from a wife got the same share as many children from another wife, the children consequently not receiving equal shares of their father's estate. In contrast, under the second customary rule, known as *Ori Ojori*, the estate would be divided equally among the children of each wife. In this case, division into fourths favoured the plaintiffs, whereas division into ninths favoured the defendants.

At the high court it was decided that the customary law of *Idi Igi* (division by stirpes) was inequitable 'repugnant to justice and good conscience'. The presiding judge accordingly made an order for division of the estate into nine parts to be shared equally among the children. The case was subsequently appealed to the Supreme Court, which held that the custom of *Idi Igi* was *not* contrary to natural justice, equity, or good conscience, and reversed the earlier judgment of the high court. The Supreme Court issued a counter-order for the division of the contested estate into four parts shared among the wives, rather than nine parts shared equally among the children. This led to a further appeal to the JCPC, which upheld the position that the customary rule of division of estates by stirpes among the wives, though unfamiliar to English legal traditions, was not contrary to natural justice, equity or good conscience. In a judgment delivered by Lord Evershed, the JCPC held that the native family law of *Idi Igi* (division among wives rather than individual children) was a valid part of the local African native law and custom on succession, even though it might not be considered so in other communities. Lord Evershed stated: 'The principles of natural justice, equity and good conscience applicable in a country where polygamy is generally accepted should not in a matter of this kind be readily equated with those applicable to a community governed by the rule of monogamy.'[52]

What this case so clearly shows is that the lords of the JCPC were themselves cognisant of the perils of judicial universalism. Notions of justice and good conscience could not always be universalised. The principle of 'justice, equity and good conscience' sometimes served effectively as a tool with which colonial courts, and specifically the JCPC, could uphold judicial uniformity and common standards across the Empire. But in order to do justice, it was not always practical to construe this principle in truly universal terms. In some cases, the principle allowed the lords of the JCPC to accommodate local difference when it perceived that substantial injustice would be done if they applied uniform legal and judicial standards.

Universality, representation, and legitimacy

The main challenge that confronted the JCPC in the age of decolonisation was making the transition from its historic task of managing colonial differences to the new mission of managing national differences. In adjudicating colonial differences in the British Empire, the JCPC operated within a framework of imperial, political, and normative cohesiveness. Colonial otherness could easily be accommodated and managed within the context of imperial hegemony. Within this imperial framework, the contradictions of imperial universalism and native otherness did not pose a serious threat to the legitimacy of the JCPC. Colonial subjects could express dissatisfaction with judgments considered unjust by local standards, but such complaints often did not seriously threaten the legitimacy of colonial courts. However, as the British Empire disintegrated in the second half of the twentieth century, the political and normative framework for maintaining legal and judicial conformity also fell apart. The notion of universal imperial justice could no longer provide constraints on metropolitan and local expressions of difference. Without the homogenising power of the Empire, the JCPC became increasingly seen as insular and unrepresentative, falling into irrelevance amid the varied and autonomous judicial systems of the newly independent nations of the Commonwealth.[53] Attempts to reforms and transform it into a Commonwealth Court of Appeal failed as India and most colonies in Africa, following the precedent of Canada and the Irish Free State in the 1930s, abolished appeals to the Privy Council upon gaining independence. By the 1960s, the jurisdiction of the JCPC had shrunk to a few dependencies and former colonies.

The question of colonial representation on the JCPC is relevant to the debate over its imperial legacies. In spite of the JCPC's universalising aspirations, there were no serious attempts to make its bench more representative of the constituent parts of the Empire for much of its history. A judicial body of last resort composed exclusively of English judges, critics argued, was ill equipped to effectively adjudicate appeals from different legal systems within the expanding Empire.[54] Although the most persistent calls for reforming the JCPC came from the colonies, there was also domestic pressure for a more representative JCPC or in some cases, an alternate Imperial Court of Appeal. Questions over colonial representations in the JCPC echoed longstanding debates over judicial unity and cohesiveness within the British Empire. It was frequently pointed out, for example, that few judges on the JCPC had any training in the Roman-Dutch law that was applicable in Ceylon and the Cape Colony. This raised further concerns about judicial incompetence and miscarriage of justice. The main complaint was that, being composed almost entirely of British judges, the JCPC could never match local practitioners in their knowledge of local law and conditions.

Beyond the question of representation, however, there was also the general perception that the JCPC, regardless of its agenda of fostering imperial uniformity, was ultimately a parochial second-class court. It was, after all, an appellate court constituted exclusively to adjudicate colonial cases; an imperial court situated in the imperial centre but with limited jurisdiction over metropolitan cases. The reluctance of British officials to contemplate having British appeals heard by anybody else other than the House of Lords was taken as evidence that, with the Privy Council, the dominions and colonies were being subjected to an inferior court to which Britain did not subject her own citizens. Critics often made reference to the landmark case of *London Joint Stock Bank* v. *McMillan*, in which it was held that the decisions of the JCPC were not theoretically binding in English courts, even if they might be deemed influential.[55]

Nationalists in the colonies also drew attention to key procedural differences between the judicial work of the House of Lords and the Privy Council. The judgments of the House of Lords took immediate effect, whereas JCPC 'judgments' were, in fact, merely recommendations, upon which the Crown made the final decision in an Order in Council. This gave rise to doubts about the character of the Judicial Committee as a true court. The view that the JCPC was an inferior adjudicatory body designed for the colonies persisted in spite of assurances by officials in Whitehall that the Judicial Committee was indeed a court, and that the King in Council had no constitutional power to interfere in any way with its judgments.[56]

The image of the JCPC as a court for the colonial underclass was not easily shaken. If the JCPC was good enough for colonial subjects, why was it not also considered good enough for British citizens? This became a key argument against the retention of the right to JCPC appeals in the colonies or the establishment of a successor Commonwealth appeal court. At a time when the assertion of national sovereignty and claims about universal human rights and the equality of nations were key messages of nationalist anti-colonial politicians, the idea of subjecting citizens of newly independent nations to selective and inferior justice struck a chord in the colonies, and was strongly rejected. For much of its history, the JCPC was a vital link of the Empire, connecting the distant constituents of the British Empire through the administration of appellate justice. In the end, however, the universalising and homogenising role of the JCPC was constrained as much by its structure as it was by the practicalities of administering justice in a diverse and fragmented Empire.

Notes

1   For a discussion of the tensions in colonial universalism and the construction of native difference see F. Cooper and A. L. Stoler, eds, *Tensions of Empire: Colonial Cultures in a Bourgeois World* (Berkeley and Los Angeles: University of California Press, 1997). For a more specific discussion on the paradox of French republicanism and the colonial othering see A. Conklin, *A Mission to Civilize: The Republican Idea of Empire in France and West Africa 1895–1930* (Stanford, CA: Stanford University Press, 1997).

2   'Berlin Act 1884', in E. Hartslet, ed., *The Map of Africa by Treaty* (New York: Routledge, 2012), 473.

3   Conklin, *A Mission to Civilize*, 94.

4   F. D. Lugard, *The Dual Mandate in British Tropical Africa* (London: Frank Cass, 1922), 570.

5   F. D. Lugard, *Political Memoranda: Revision of Instructions to Political Officers on Subjects Chiefly Political and Administrative, 1913–1918* (London: Frank Cass, 1970), 9.

6   J. Jaffe, *Ironies of Colonial Governance: Law, Custom and Justice in Colonial India* (Cambridge: Cambridge University Press), 9.

7   A. L. Stoler and F. Cooper, 'Between Metropole and Colony: Rethinking a Research Agenda', in Cooper and Stoler, eds, *Tensions of Empire*, 3–7.

8   For example, Jaffe, *Ironies of Colonial Governance*.

9   P. Chatterjee, *The Nation and Its Fragments* (Delhi: Oxford University Press, 1993); K. Parker, 'The Historiography of Difference', *Law and History Review*, 23: 3 (2005), 685–95.

10   E. Kolsky, 'Codification and the Rule of Colonial Difference: Criminal Procedure in British India', *Law and History Review*, 23: 3 (2005), 631–84, and Chatterjee, *The Nation and its Fragments*, 9.

11   R. De, '"A Peripatetic World Court": Cosmopolitan Courts, Nationalist Judges and the Indian Appeal to the Privy Council', *Law and History Review*, 32: 4 (2014), 822.

12   S. den Otter, 'Law, Authority, and Colonial Rule', in Douglas M. Peers and Nandini Gooptu, eds, *India and the British Empire* (Oxford: Oxford University Press, 2012), 170, 173.

13   Otter, 'Law, Authority, and Colonial Rule', 176.

14   See, for example, Jennifer Pitts, 'Empire and Legal Universalisms in the Eighteenth Century', *American Historical Review*, 117: 1 (2012), 92–121.

15   De, 'A Peripatetic World Court', 823.

16   Pitts, 'Empire and Legal Universalisms in the Eighteenth Century', 92.

17   *Ibid.*, 94.

18   N. Chatterjee and C. Smith, 'Communities-in-Law: Self, Sociality and the Legal Process in the British Empire, 1790–1950' (Communities of Law Research Network Paper, University of Plymouth, 2011), 2.

19   De, 'A Peripatetic World Court', 824.

20   R. B. Haldane, 'Lord Watson', *Juridical Review*, 9 (1899), 279.

21   B. Ibhawoh, *Imperial Justice: Africans in Empire's Court* (Oxford: Oxford University Press, 2013), 29.

22   A. Todd, *Parliamentary Government in the British Colonies* (Boston: Little, Brown, 1880), 14.

23   *Trimble* v. *Hill* [1879] 5 Appeal Cases 342 at 345.

24   Lord Haldane, 'The Work for the Empire of the Judicial Committee of the Privy Council', *Cambridge Law Journal*, 1: 1 (1923), 154; emphasis added.

25   G. Lewis, *Lord Atkin* (London: Butterworth, 1983), 94.

26   Haldane, 'The Work for the Empire', 143.

27   Ibhawoh, *Imperial Justice*, 43.

28   J. N. Matson, 'The Common Law Abroad: English and Indigenous Laws in the British Commonwealth', *International and Comparative Law Quarterly*, 42: 3 (1993), 753.

29   P. Fitzpatrick, 'Terminal Legality: Imperialism and the (De)composition of Law', in D. Kirkby and C. Coleborne, eds, *Law, History, Colonialism: The Reach of Empire* (Manchester: Manchester University Press, 2001), 21.

30   Otter, 'Law, Authority, and Colonial Rule', 171.

31   J. D. M. Derrett, 'Justice, Equity and Good Conscience', in L. Benton, ed., *Law and Colonial Cultures: Legal Regimes in World History, 1400–1900* (Cambridge: Cambridge University Press, 2002), 139.

32 For a detailed discussion of the repugnancy doctrine in colonial law in Africa, see B. Ibhawoh, 'Stronger than the Maxim Gun: Law, Human Rights and British Colonial Hegemony in Nigeria', *Africa: Journal of the International African Institute*, 72: 1 (2002), 55–83.

33 Colony and Protectorate of Kenya, 'Report of Legislative Council Debates', 86 (1960), 384. Also see M. Bwonwonga, *Procedures in Criminal Law in Kenya* (Nairobi: East African Publishers, 1994), 24.

34 M. P. Jain, *Outlines of Indian Legal History* (2nd edn) (Bombay: Tripathi, 1966), 75.

35 *Ibid.*, 103.

36 See, for example, *Sree Narain Rae* v. *Bhya Jah* [1839] in P. Saraswati and B. Banerjee, *Privy Council Judgments on Appeals from India*, vol. 1 (Calcutta: Sreenath Banerjee, 1880), 179–86.

37 *Hunooman Pandy* v. *Mussumat Koonweree* [1856], in Saraswati and Banerjee, *Privy Council Judgments on Appeals from India*, vol. 1, 554.

38 Reported in E. Moore, *Reports of Cases Heard and Determined by the Judicial Committee*, vol. 9 (London: V. R. Stevens and Haynes, 1864), 303–23.

39 *Lopez* v. *Muddun Mohan Thakur* (1870), 13 *Moore's Indian Appeal Cases* (hereinafter MIA), 467.

40 *Ibid.*

41 *Tweedle* v. *Atkinson* (1861), 121 *English Reports*, 762.

42 *Khwaja Muhammad Khan* v. *Husaini Begum* (1910) 12 Bombay LR 638.

43 D. Swinfen, *Imperial Control of Colonial Legislation, 1813–1865: A Study of British Policy towards Colonial Legislative Powers* (Oxford: Clarendon Press, 1970), 44.

44 Otter, *Law, Authority, and Colonial Rule in India and the British Empire*, 170.

45 De, 'A Peripatetic World Court', 830.

46 *Fatuma binti Mohammed bin Bakhshuwen* v. *Mohammed bin Salim Bakhshuwen* [1952] 1 Appeal Cases 1.

47 G. W. Bartholomew and J. A. Iliffe, 'Decisions', *International and Comparative Law Quarterly*, 1: 3 (1952), 392.

48 N. Chatterjee, 'Law, Culture and History: Amir Ali's Interpretation of Islamic Law', in J. McLaren and S. Dorsett, eds, *Legal Histories of the British Empire: Laws, Engagements and Legacies* (London: Routledge, 2014), 46.

49 Re: Dillet (1887) 12 Appeal Cases 459 [Privy Council].

50 *Narendra Nath Sircar* v. *Kamal-basini Dasi* (1896), 23 *Indian Law Reports, Calcutta Series*, 563.

51 *Yisa Dawodu and Others* v. *Suwebatu Danmole and Others* (1962) United Kingdom Privy Council 20.

52 *Yisa Dawodu* v. *Suwebatu Danmole*, 20. This case has been examined in detail in B. Ibhawoh, *Imperial Justice*, 61ff.

53 B. Ibhawoh, 'Asserting Judicial Sovereignty: The Debate over the Inclusion of Indigenous Judges in the Judicial Committee of the Privy Council', in McLaren and Dorsett, eds, *Legal Histories of the British Empire*, 42.

54 J. B. Nihill to K. Roberts-Wray, Confidential Memorandum, National Archives of the United Kingdom (NAUK) CO/ 1026/114, 20 May 1955.

55 [1918] *Appeal Cases* 777, 25. For an analysis of this case, see H. H. Marshall, 'The Binding Effect of Decisions of the Judicial Committee of the Privy Council', *International and Comparative Law Quarterly*, 17: 3 (1968), 744.

56 K. Roberts-Wray, NAUK CO/ 1026/114, 16 May 1955.

6

The indigenous redemption of liberal universalism

Tim Rowse

A critical historiography of liberalism shows its contingent availability to specific political projects. Bhikhu Parekh has demonstrated, for example, how the work of John Locke and John Stuart Mill was available to colonising authority. Locke judged American Indians according to the extent to which their laws and institutions realised the capacity for reason that was humanity's common heritage. In their application of reason to the use of the natural resources that God had endowed and to the designs of their laws and government, Indians were far less accomplished than the more advanced Europeans who were dispossessing, displacing, and improving them. 'In Locke's view, English colonisation not only did [Indians] no harm, [it] also respected their natural rights and conferred on them great economic, moral, cultural, scientific and political benefits.'[1] Locke was consistently egalitarian, Parekh argues, but his truncated sense of the plurality of human flourishing meant that his 'principle of equality accepted [Indians] and other "savage" people as equal *objects* of concern but not as self-defining *subjects* entitled to equal and full self-determination'.[2] Turning to Mill, Parekh argued that while he saw all of humanity as having the right to liberty, he classified non-Europeans as lacking the capacity to make good use of it. Colonial authority – even when forcefully applied – could be justified to the extent that it developed that capacity. Parekh's critique, while crediting both Locke and Mill with a commitment to a common human capacity for reason and liberty, faults their liberalism for identifying the realisation of those capacities too closely with the forms of life that Europeans had evolved; thus non-European humanity would have to be tutored by liberal colonists.

The idea that all subject peoples – as humans endowed with reason – could and should be instructed in the practice of a liberal way of life can be given a name: liberal universalism. In her paper 'Mill and the Imperial Predicament', Karuna Mantena has argued that the difficulties of colonial rule severely tested liberal universalism, tempting liberal improvers of humankind to revise their assumptions about the susceptibility of those whom they were trying to 'improve'.

As the difficulties of colonial tutelage accumulated, those of fading liberal optimism looked to racially determinist theories of native incapacity that had become scientifically respectable since the mid-eighteenth century inception of racial typologies of humanity. The consequent prescription was that colonial despotism must continue. Mantena's examples – Mill and James Fitzjames Stephen – exhibit the 'instabilities inherent' in the liberal account of 'legitimate empire'.[3]

I want to draw attention to two problematic features of this critical historiography of liberalism. First, the strategy of Parekh and Mantena – typical of postcolonial scholars of liberal imperialism, and undoubtedly illuminating – is to focus on the conceptual and practical dilemmas manifest in the texts and careers of exemplary Western intellectuals; they offer a postcolonial re-reading of a canon. Second, it is possible, when focused on such figures, to produce a narrative of decline. Mantena glosses her account of Mill and Stephen as the 'collapse of liberal imperialism' and 'the decline of liberal ideologies of imperial rule'.[4] The words 'collapse' and 'decline' seem to me to overstate her thesis, which is better glossed as describing an 'oscillation' within liberalism. Indeed, the universalist elements of liberal imperialism seem to have survived until the era of de-colonisation, after the Second World War, to give ennobling narrative to the end of Empire.

There were ways of continuing to believe in a universal human capacity for improvement, and there were other agents suited to sustaining this belief. Certain colonised intellectuals developed forms of liberal universalism that enabled critical commentary on prolonged tutelage. As Bayly has shown, since 1800, Indian intellectuals have fashioned 'historicisms' that project into the Indian past demonstrations of the intrinsic potential of Indians to seize the opportunities arising from modernity and from their contact with British civilisation.[5] Similarly, certain North American and Antipodean indigenous intellectuals cast the colonial conjuncture into narratives that historicised both colonised and coloniser: the colonised have pasts that show their potential, and the colonisers have not yet corrected civilisational weaknesses that compromise their conduct of the civilising project. What such native 'counter-historicisms' imply is a standpoint of observation and historical assessment that is external to any particular culture, from which one can test and measure the progress and flaws of any people claiming to be 'civilised'.

To illustrate the anti-colonial resourcefulness of the liberalisms of the colonised, I will quote from the writings of five indigenous intellectuals: Peter Jones (1802–53), Charles Eastman (1858–1939), Zitkala-Ša (1876–1938), Apirana Ngata (1874–1950) and William Cooper (1861–1941). While each made use of racial terminology to give accounts of their people's specificity, each did so within an underlying framework of universality that was rooted in two powerful strands within European thought: the universal/philosophical history concept that all humans could and would pass through a stage of agriculture; and the Christian idea that all humans were sinful but redeemable souls before God. What makes their work part of the global history of liberalism is that they sustained an idea that was fundamental to liberalism as an imperial, civilising project of government: the presumption or hope that all humans have the capacity for improvement.

Christianity, liberalism, and racism

Christianity has affinity with liberal universalism to the extent that it warrants faith that all humans are capable of improvement, regardless of their 'race'. Coleman's study of Presbyterian missionaries working among US Indians in the nineteenth century is an example.[6] These Presbyterians were sure that Indians, *in their heritage and in their colonised condition*, were inferior, but as no human was beyond the reach of Scripture, they 'saw the failings of their charges as the product of circumstances, not race', and their understanding of Indian capacity remained resolutely 'equalitarian'.[7] To dismiss the Indian capacity to advance under Christ's teaching was to set limits to the power of God; to cast some branches of humanity as being beyond the reach of God's grace was a deeply un-Christian thought. As well, 'the missionaries simply discounted biology' when biological paradigms of human diversity were acquiring authority.[8]

Andrew Porter concedes that the 'exclusivity' of racial thought 'created serious problems' for missionaries because it was 'at odds with Christianity's egalitarianism'.[9] However, while racial explanations of such confronting events as the Indian 'Mutiny', the Jamaica rebellion and China's Boxer Uprising held some appeal for missionaries in the second half of the nineteenth century, 'missionary outlooks continued to rest on the conviction of universality', on biblical authority. Non-Europeans' sin was to be explained by reference to their circumstances rather than to their inherited nature.[10] In the South Pacific, writes Jane Samson, missionaries were anguished in coming to terms with the different forms of humanity. They 'experienced a genuine internal struggle between their abhorrence of island cultural practices and their need to retain faith in the universal message of Christianity.' Missionaries 'close to despair had to force themselves to remember that divine grace made no exceptions and had no favourites'.[11]

Christianity's resistance to racial explanation may be sourced not only to steadfast Biblical literalism but also – paradoxically – to Christian thought's contact with the Enlightenment. Coleman writes that while Presbyterian missionaries' 'intellectual rigidity' rendered them sceptical of racial pessimism, their Scripture-based conviction that humanity is universally sinful was buttressed by 'a characteristically eighteenth-century Enlightenment faith in the unity of mankind, the sameness of human nature, and environmental explanations for human diversity.'[12] Brian Stanley argues that while Christianity up to the early eighteenth century had assumed a distinction between the rational European and the irrational savage, 'what was new about eighteenth-century thought was its increasing tendency to assert the intrinsic unity and equality of all humanity and to explain the manifest differences between "primitive" and "civilized" peoples in terms of the impact of the environment'.[13] He continues that 'on the central question of how the "heathen" were to be civilized', nineteenth-century missionaries were shaped by the eighteenth-century Scottish Enlightenment concern to create 'the conditions for individual and collective virtue through an educational process dedicated to the imparting of rational knowledge, especially knowledge of the history of human social development'.[14]

Among the indigenous writers examined in this paper – all products of Protestant Christianity – we do find concessions of native inferiority, but no concession that this condition was inherent or unredeemable. Indigenous liberal universalism historicised inferiority as a remediable, contingent phenomenon. Confidence in the native future was sustained, in each case, by the writer's own life-experience: if I am the product of my own seized opportunities for self-improvement, do I not exemplify the possible trajectory of my race? The four men and one woman whose writings I describe below found an answer to the racial pessimism into which many liberals were tempted to lapse. Because they could offer (indeed embody) a confident narrative of the propagation of the capacities befitting the liberal subject, they were agents of the survival of liberal universalism.

Peter Jones 1802–53: gaining mastery over fate

Peter Jones (aka Kahkewaquonaby) was born of a Mississauga mother and an English father in 1802. He was raised by his mother's family, according to the traditions of her people; then he attended school. In 1823, he converted to (Methodist) Christianity. His account of his conversion, in speeches to audiences in Leeds in 1831, associated Indians' turning to God with their embrace of agriculture: 'Since my countrymen have found the Saviour in their hearts, they are beginning to plant potatoes, sow corn.'[15] For Jones, if the bounty of nature were a manifestation of God, then to shift from hunting to ploughing – rendering the earth more productive – was to align more closely with God's plan. Civilisation was as much an economic as a moral and spiritual commitment. Thus in his invitation to further mission endeavour among his people, he evoked not only Indians' need for redemption but also the land's fecund promise to the farming Christian.[16] To give in to fatalist pessimism about Indians was wrongly to suppose that 'the Supreme Disposer' had 'decreed that the doom of the red man is to fall and gradually disappear, like the mighty wilderness, before the axe of the European settler'.[17] The Indian destiny was rather to join the European settler in realising the land's goodness.

Devoting himself to missionary work among his people, at a time of rapid Indian depopulation and loss of land to immigrant settlers, Jones became a leader and spokesperson of the Indian community that farmed on the banks of the Credit River, Upper Canada. At the time of his commitment to growing crops and saving souls, the Indians of Upper Canada were witness to Britain's first project of mass settler colonisation since the rebellion of the Thirteen Colonies. These conditions presented three challenges to Indians' previous mode of adjustment to colonial authority. First, from the 1790s, Indian Territory – a borderland in which both British and US authority had been limited – had begun to fall under effective colonial rule either as Upper Canada (British) or as upstate New York and the Northwest Territory (USA). Second, the fur-trading economy (with low European population densities and a relatively autonomous Indian hunting mode of production) was being replaced by an agricultural economy (with small towns, immigrant family farms and a higher European density). Third, British authorities were becoming both more conscious of the cost of gift-based Indian policy and more ambitious to uplift Indians from dependency. In combination, these changes threw down a challenge to Indians coming into adulthood in the 1820s and 1830s: whereas their ancestors had adapted to colonisation as hunters and as warrior allies with claims to British gifts, Indians were now finding it less possible to survive as hunters and were discovering themselves to be less valued as warriors. Peace between the USA and Britain and the settlement of farms on former hunting grounds were changing the options of Indian manhood.

Jones' Christian agrarianism was a project to make Indians new. For those promoting civilising guardianship as the duty and rationale of colonisation, the Credit River community proved that Indians could convert both to Christianity and to agriculture. Jones visited Britain in the 1830s to promote his people's successful adaptation and to lobby the Colonial Office to reject the pessimism of those – such as Lieutenant Governor of Upper Canada (1836–7) Sir Francis Bond Head – who promoted 'removal' as native protection.

In his posthumous *History of the Ojebway Indians: with especial reference to their conversion to Christianity* (1861) – a compilation, by his admirers, of Jones' writings – Jones assays strengths and weaknesses of Indian heritage. On the positive side, the customary economy and polity had stably associated people with place.

> Each tribe or body of Indians has its own range of country, and sometimes each family has its own hunting grounds, marked out by certain natural divisions, such as rivers, lakes, mountains or ridges; and all the game within these bounds is considered their property as much as the cattle and fowl owned by a farmer on his own land. It is at the peril of an intruder to trespass on the hunting grounds of another.[18]

Warfare among Indians, while fierce, manifested admirable qualities: leadership and courage. Jones also credited Indians with knowledge of their country, not merely possession of it: he admiringly describes Indians' plant-based medicines.[19] He evokes precolonial procedures of chiefly authority and decision-making councils; he recalls the effectiveness of chiefs in wars with colonising powers.[20] He describes Indians' rituals of diplomacy and deliberation, their languages, their amusements and their naming customs, giving his own name Kahkewaquonaby as an example.

In Jones' view, while there was much Indian heritage to be proud of, the Indians' lost world had also been blighted by fears and vulnerabilities. Memories of precolonial times must be qualified by conceding that 'the pagan ideas of bliss are almost entirely sensual, and relate to the unrestrained indulgence of the animal appetites'.[21] Indians' susceptibility to the worst influences of the colonists – most importantly 'firewater' – had demonstrated their psychological and moral vulnerability. He quotes an elder who held Indians partly responsible for their current state: 'The Great Spirit has hidden his face from his red children, on account of their drunkenness and their many crooked ways.'[22] Indians' fatal flaw had been, and in many places remained, a culture of fear and unhappiness: 'the Indian in his natural state is not happy.'[23] 'From experience of my early life, I can truly say, that their imaginary bliss is so mixed up with everything that is abominable and cruel, that it would be vain to look for real happiness among savage tribes.'[24] So much of their religion had been fear – 'everything that strikes the dark untutored mind of the Indian with awe and astonishment becomes to him an object of dread and adoration.'[25] He devotes a chapter to describing and lamenting the lingering influence of witchcraft and remarks: 'They [Indians] have neither Heaven to attain nor Hell to escape' – a handicap to their motivation to improve themselves.[26] Jones thus presents Indians as vulnerable to the worst that the colonists offered. He lists five evils introduced by whites: drunkenness; 'the habit of taking the name of God in vain'; 'introduction of contagious diseases'; 'dishonesty, lying and deception'; and 'the loss of their country and game'.[27]

> If it be difficult for the Christian to follow the good he knows, what must be the utter helplessness of the pagan Indian, who is destitute of all Christian privileges? This much I admit – that the state of the red man, previous to the introduction of European vices, and the fire-waters, is superior to what it is now, when the white man's religion has not changed his heart. But the Indian, unhappily, is more prone to follow the evil than the good practices of the white man. This proves he is naturally depraved; and if Christianity has not effected all that is desirable in the suppression of vice, it is the Indian's sin, and not the whiter man's vice, that ought to be blamed.[28]

Jones' presentation of Indians' past, present and future is thus focused on the uncompleted evangelical task of improving the Indian.

Although Jones sees 'civilisation' as largely a Christian achievement, his book offers glimpses of a more secular, materialist understanding: 'civilisation' included science, political structures. 'A civilised state, *even without religion*, is far preferable to paganism.'[29] He hails Edward Jenner's defeat of smallpox.[30] When explaining the decline in Indians' mortality, he points to the demographic benefits of civilisation.[31] Peace – including peace of mind – and good government are features of the civilised condition. Jones values *Pax Britannica* insofar as it enabled a continuing settlement of grievances between the Mississauga and their neighbours and former bitter enemies, the Six Nations. Orderly government, peace and authority over nature were themes of Jones' account of civilisation.

Jones did not renounce Indian government but he sought its reform and codification (particularly in the parental government of children), and its nesting within overarching colonial authority, as a relationship of father to children. Not disputing the transfer of power to the British government, his text includes his own and others' many protestations of loyalty to the Crown. 'The British Government have taken [Indians on the south shore of Lake Superior] under their paternal care; they have been taught to look up with reverence to their great Father, the Governor and the Indian agents. As a consequence the chiefs have yielded their authority into the hands of more wise and powerful guardians.'[32]

Jones' editors included petitions and letters presented in 1840 by the General Council of the Credit River Indian community. The text twice poses the question: are Indians now the treaty partners or the colonial subjects of the British?[33] The book's reproduction of these addresses to the Superintendent of Indian Affairs, to the Governor-General, and to the Governor of Upper Canada convey some Mississauga attempts to persuade British authorities: to secure their rights to their reserved lands; to maintain Toronto as the capital of the nascent Province of Canada, where the Great Father would remain accessible to the Mississauga; to give their children manual arts training; to allow individuals to shift their land entitlements from one tribe to another; and to include fishing among activities banned on the Sabbath.[34] The petitioners also wanted to know their rights to hunt. Thus these documents illustrate a moment of renegotiation, by Jones and his colleagues, of the political terms of certain Indians' co-existence with their colonial masters. Before mass migration, the 'silver chain' of British-Indian friendship had made Indians allies, not subjects, of the Crown.[35] Then settlement on a massive scale made Indians the Crown's children. However, the Crown's protective actions had been deficient, provoking Jones' and his colleagues' recitation of rights desired and withheld.[36] The acts of self-representation reproduced in Jones' *History* thus align a residual Indian capacity for self-government with the welcomed, overarching power and responsibility of the British Crown. The reprinted petitions are both acts of submission and declarations of a degree of autonomous collective presence within the King's realm.[37] They are liberal in the sense that they evoke the capacities of Indian subjects who are augmenting – as Christian farmers – their arts of self-government.

The challenge of 'Social Darwinism'

In the one hundred years after Jones' death, indigenous intellectuals who projected a future for their people had to contend with an influential perspective on human diversity and human history in which native peoples had no future. This perspective is sometimes called Social Darwinism, though we should not attribute coherence to thoughts gathered under that label.[38] The salient features

of 'Social Darwinism' were that within human history there was a natural tendency for peoples, nations, or races to compete with one another for political
and material ascendancy, and that the weaknesses of certain peoples, nations, or
races doomed them to fail when they came into contention with stronger peoples, nations, or races. One of the most popular expositions of the idea that some
branches of humanity were destined to fail was Benjamin Kidd's *Social Evolution*
(1894), 'an immediate and enormous success around the world'. Translated into
ten languages, including Chinese and Arabic, it 'tapped into the apocalyptic sense
of change and crisis that marked end-of-the-century culture'.[39]

For Aborigines, Maori and native North Americans Kidd's prognosis was bleak.

> Whether wars of extermination have been waged against them, or whether they have
> been well treated and admitted to citizenship, they have always tended to disappear
> before the more vigorous incoming race.[40]

> [D]espite the great consideration shown for the rights of the lower races, there can be
> no question as to the absolute ascendancy in the world today of the Western peoples
> and of Western civilisation.[41]

In Kidd's view, such ascendancy should not be explained as the effect of racial
superiority but as proof of the relative 'social efficiency' of certain races. To be
socially efficient was abundantly to possess 'strength and energy of character,
humanity, probity and integrity, and simple-minded devotion to conceptions of
duty'.[42] Anglo-Saxon peoples blessed with these qualities were now in possession
of North America, Australia, New Zealand and South Africa, having exterminated the inferior peoples of those lands either by violence or by 'mere contact'.[43]

It was possible for an indigenous intellectual to write from within Kidd's perspective – that is, to see human history as contention between the more and the
less socially efficient – without conceding that one's own people were doomed to
be uncompetitive. When the Society of American Indians (SAI) formed in 1911,
it stated as the first of its aims: 'To promote and cooperate with all efforts looking to the advancement of the Indian in enlightenment which leave him free, as a
man, to develop according to the natural laws of social evolution.'[44]

Charles Eastman 1858–1939: the Indian renewed

The writer quoting the SAI's aims was the Sioux Charles Eastman. Eastman's
father had converted to Christianity after being captured during the wars on the
Plains in the early 1860s. After being reunited with his son, he urged Charles
to embrace Christianity and education. Eastman followed his father's word to
the extent of attending Knox School, graduating in medicine, working for the
Bureau of Indian Affairs (BIA) as a reservation doctor, and serving as an agent of
the Young Men's Christian Association.[45] He flourished also as an author, drawing

on his own bicultural experience to present Indian civilisation in positive terms to non-Indian American readers. He was pleased for his Indian names to be known: Hakadah and Ohiyesa. Eastman argued that his 'race' (a term he used repeatedly) was equal to the challenge of social evolution and that it should be 'allowed to retain its own religion and racial codes as far as is compatible with the public good, and should enter the body politic of its own free will, and not under compulsion'.[46] That Eastman's race had not yet been given that opportunity was a defect of the USA's Indian administration, Eastman insisted; the Indians' problems did not reflect their capacity.

Indian policy since the beginning of the republic had included the provision of reserves, and the purpose of the *Dawes Allotment Act* 1887 was to change the social, economic, political, and cultural meaning of land to the reserves' Indian residents. The Act authorised the government to assign allotments of 160 acres to heads of families and lesser amounts to younger persons and orphans. Reserves were to be surveyed and rolls of tribal members prepared. Indians listed on the tribal rolls were to select their own lands, but if they failed to do so, the Indian Agent would make the selection for them. Then the government would hold title to the land in trust for 25 years; during that time allottees were supposed to acquire the competence to deal in their land as personal property, that is as real estate. Any surplus reservation land could be sold. In 1906 further legislation allowed for allotment without the 25-year waiting period: an allottee would be entitled to sell his/her land as soon as he/she gained title. Becoming an allottee and giving up tribal ways were intended to qualify each Indian for citizenship. It was assumed that most allottees would farm their land.

Frederick Hoxie argues that early optimism about the assimilation of Indians and about the dissolution of the reservation/BIA complex could not be sustained. Assimilation at the beginning of the twentieth century was becoming a more pessimistic and less ambitious programme, in which Indians were thought to continue to need tutelage and protection/regulation. Thus both the reservation and the BIA persisted as instruments for governing Indians. The notion of state as guardian remained plausible to those who wished the Indian well, including to Indian intellectuals such as Eastman who worked for the Bureau. Other Indians in the SAI were more critical of what they saw as the BIA's persistent paternalism. That Indians were distinct from other Americans in heritage and status also continued to be plausible, and the persistence of the notion of Indian difference undermined or qualified the policy goal of formal equality of Indians as citizens. Indians were thought to be vulnerable in their land dealings and in their consumption of liquor.[47]

In *The Indian Today* (1915) Eastman was sympathetic to the aims of assimilation policy but critical of its execution. 'The typical red man of today is a rancher on a large or small scale,' he was pleased to note.[48] However, he thought that this development was in several ways retarded: by the poor quality of land (relative to whites' holdings), by the continued rationing of Indians (their residual treaty right), by the inadequacy of instruction in agriculture, by the government's corrupt management of reservation forests. Nonetheless, Eastman saw progress in 'the average present-day Indian' – 'a man who earns his own living, speaks the language of the country, wears its dress and obeys its laws.'[49] He quoted Bureau data to show that more than half the nation's 330,000 Indians had been allotted and that the allottees were increasing by 5,000 per year. However, the United States did not offer good training in citizenship, Eastman argued, referring to 'the pauperizing and demoralizing agency system'.[50] BIA officials included many who Eastman described as 'the political boss and the "little czar"'.[51] 'The prevailing currents of American life' were encouraging Indians of initiative to become 'diplomats of a lower type, quick and smart, but not always sound'.[52] It was tempting for Indians to look upon 'the new civilization as a great, big, grab-bag'.[53] In the administered life of the Indians, the moral frailty of American civilisation revealed itself: the USA, by its military strength, had acquired civilising responsibilities before it had civilised itself. This was the historical conjuncture to which he addressed his book. 'You are suffering from a civic disease, and we are affected by it. When you are cured, and not until then, we may hope to be thoroughly well men.'[54] He mentioned favourably a proposal to place the BIA under the supervision of 'a commission of non-partisan men, half of whom could be Indians'.[55]

Eastman's *The Indian Today* exemplifies the persistence among indigenous intellectuals of confidently universalist notions of guardianship and improvement. Eastman's universalism is particularly interesting because his understanding of human diversity was clearly racial. He referred to 'blood' and to fractions of descent as determinants of Indians' character.[56] When he used the term 'race', it was not merely a synonym of 'people': his commitment to biological inherency is clear. The Indian's heritage included not only virtues such as loyalty, honour, and service that struggled to be enacted in the new civilisation.[57] It was also physical – a strong, healthy, athletic body whose prowess is the theme of several admiring passages in *The Indian Today*.[58] Eastman's 'counter-historicism' included narrating the corruption of that fine body and ethos by the government's inept management of Indians' transition from hunter to reserve-dweller. 'In their state of deep depression, disease had its golden opportunity.'[59] Indian depopulation had been a contingent incident of a corrigible state of affairs, he argued, but now the census showed population recovery.[60] Eastman considered his people's future partly in eugenic terms. Although the reserve system had produced an Indian who had been 'against racial type', the Indian race was fundamentally sound, and it was benefiting from intermarriage with whites.[61] Eastman's sense of Indians' racial continuity transcends physical criteria. The Indian is facing 'the extinction of his race as a separate and peculiar people; but as a type, an ideal, he lives and will live!'[62]

These eugenic thoughts were situated within a framework of racial equality. Eastman's Christianity sustained a conviction that while humanity consisted of different races, no race had a firmer purchase on 'civilization' than another. In *From the Deep Woods to Civilization*, Eastman recalled his first contact with 'the great-ness of Christian civilization, the ideal civilization'.[63] In both *The Indian Today* and *From the Backwoods to Civilization* he invoked Christianity – in essential continu-ity, he said, with Indian ideals – as the standpoint for evaluating what Americans called their civilisation: he found it excessively materialistic and rewarding of self-interest. As he wrote in 1915, '[W]e want the best in two races and civilizations in exchange for what we have lost.'[64] This sentence succinctly relativises all races and civilisations from the standpoint of a position of judgement that is external to them all. While his Christian convictions fortified Eastman's confidence that such an external position really existed, an anecdote from his appearance at the First Universal Races Congress (London 1911) illustrates his willingness not to label that ethical vantage point as necessarily Christian. He recalls himself saying: 'We who are met here are not all of that religion, and I would suggest that we substi-tute a term to which we can all subscribe, since we meet here not in the name, but in the spirit, of Christianity, of universal brotherhood.'[65] He reported with satisfaction the pleasure that this argument gave to the Congress non-Christian delegates.

The argument of this paper so far is that while certain European liberals surrendered their universalism to what seemed a realistic and scientific apprecia-tion of the stubborn plurality of humanity and of the unanticipated difficulty of advancing some peoples, it was possible for indigenous intellectuals to sustain universalisms that worked for them in two ways: by upholding their innate capac-ity for acculturation (as attested in their own life courses); and by giving grounds for indigenous evaluation of their self-appointed tutors in civilisation. While erst-while European liberal universalists could look to racial science and to anthropol-ogy for intellectual accounts of native failure to 'improve', indigenous intellectuals could draw on Christianity as the framework of a robust universality. Should belief wane in the literal truth of such New Testament propositions as 'God hath made of one blood all nations of men for to dwell on all the face of the earth' (Acts 17:26), indigenous intellectuals could point to empirical demonstrations of their own people's survival capacities: native population recovery. Vaccination and agriculture gave Jones hope that Indians could become less vulnerable to Nature; Easton cited recent US Census data.[66] Both could point to their peoples' accul-turation to 'civilisation'. The second decade of the twentieth century presented another testing and proving ground for indigenous acculturation: war service.

Warriors for empire and democracy: Apirana Ngata and Zitkala-Ša

Indigenous peoples in Australia, Canada, New Zealand, and the USA gener-ally supported their nation-state's mobilisation in the First World War with land, money, and warrior labour. In this section I will compare what Apirana Ngata (Maori) and Zitkala-Ša (aka Gertrude Bonnin, Sioux) each said about their peo-ple's commitment to the New Zealand and US war efforts.

By 1914, Maori and Native Americans were subject in different ways to state and church policies of assimilation. In New Zealand, though subject to distinct legislation about their lands and their municipal government, Maori were citizens: males had been enfranchised in 1867, females in 1893; four seats in the House of Representatives were elected by Maori. Although Maori land-ownership had been recognised by treaty in 1840, their estate had diminished rapidly in the nineteenth century through pressure to sell or lease acreage for Pakeha use, and some land had been punitively confiscated after the 'New Zealand Wars' of the 1860s. To arrest such alienation and avoid extinction as a people, Maori modernisers sought new uses of the remnant estate. Espousing a programme of Maori self-reform, Apirana Ngata, a Maori Member elected to the House of Representatives in 1905, began to promote commercial agriculture to Maori and to advocate public policy that would ease their transition from warriors to settlers.

In the United States, Zitkala-Ša faced the situation that I have already described in contextualising Eastman. That is, assimilation had been intensified and made more systematic by the *Allotment Act* of 1887. Indians were being inducted into citizenship through programmes of education and land tenure reform managed by the BIA. In contrast with Maori, citizenship for Indians was conditional on their embracing prescribed changes in land tenure and in way of life. By 1914 their leaders – having formed the SAI in 1911 – were increasingly critical of what they saw as the neglectful, corrupt intrusion of the BIA. In short, by the time of the First World War, the Maori were citizens beginning voluntary experiments in new forms of land title and land use, while the Indians of the USA – many not yet citizens – were caught up in a prolonged programme of supervised change in land tenure and land use.

In addition, the two nation-states inserted themselves into the First World War in different ways and in different terms. Whereas New Zealand was a loyal Dominion of Britain with troops and diplomacy deployed within an Imperial war effort from 1914, a more ambivalent United States did not commit troops until April 1917, and President Woodrow Wilson's war aims espoused 'democracy' and 'self-determination' in terms that gave hope to peoples under European (including British) Imperial rule. Both Britain and the United States presented themselves as fighting for liberal government against despotism, but whereas for Wilsonian liberals Imperialism was among the Old World obstacles to the world march of Democracy, for British liberal imperialists, the Empire would, in the long term, propagate liberal political institutions wherever the Union Jack flew.

In speeches to the New Zealand House of Representatives Ngata presented Maori as warrior-subjects of the British Empire. Thus he spoke from his lineage: his paternal great uncle and mentor Ropata Wahawaha had led Ngati Porou troops allied to the Crown in the 1860s Land Wars. 'I have no doubt that as soon as the Maori understand that their services will be accepted …then the offers that will be made to the government will be sufficient, I think, to fill one troop-ship,' said

Ngata on 1 September 1914.[67] The four Maori MPs formed the Maori Contingent Committee, promoting the deployment of a distinct Maori unit, and appealing to each tribe's pride in contributing volunteers. At first limiting the Maori contingent to garrison duty, the British command eventually sent them to Gallipoli and the Western Front. At the war's end, Ngata celebrated a triumph for the Polynesian race. He thought it

> romantic ... that the scattered native populations of Polynesia who were under the mana [authority] of New Zealand – a race which little more than a century ago were savages or half-savages – should have realized their responsibility as citizens and responded to the call from the Mother-country of the British people of these Islands ... [For their contribution], something was due to the Polynesian people that a distinct record should be made of the organization of the contingent, their training, and the part they took in the fighting at Gallipoli and later on in France and Flanders.[68]

The war's toll raised the issue of conscription and in 1916 Parliament debated whether Maori should be exempt. Ngata's long-time political ally Dr Maui Pomare (Western Maori) opposed Maori exemption, for conscription should 'treat every man alike', no matter what his creed, wealth or colour.[69] The Northern Maori member Mr Tau Henare supported exemption 'because the Maori people is one of those small races on earth that will vanish altogether if most of the men go to the front and leave only a few behind'.[70] The following day, Ngata explained why he wanted Maori included in conscription: it was to ensure the continuing viability of the Maori Contingent and to oblige the tribes that had not yet demonstrated loyalty with a high volume of volunteers. That the Maori Contingent must remain an identifiable unit within the Imperial deployment was so important to Ngata that it overrode fear for Maori population recovery: he declared Henare's 'declining race' argument to be 'sentimental'. He then added an argument which related fighting to social evolution.

> That race [i.e. Maori] has declined largely because it gave up fighting ... I have seen hapu after hapu and tribe after tribe declining in numbers because they could not fit themselves into a scheme of life where there was no fighting – fighting with their hands and bodies, not fighting with their minds. Your civilization requires fighting with brains; it requires special equipment for the battle of life. It takes more than half a century for some of these warrior tribes to accommodate themselves to these new conditions. They pine away, they die, largely because there is no fighting.[71]

When Mr C. H Poole interjected at this point 'there is an Irish element in them', Ngata agreed. He went on to say that Maori enlistment had not at first been patriotic; they had enlisted because 'the spirit of their fathers ... called them to fight, and they went to fight. Patriotism and those other things came afterwards as excuses'. As a result of the Maori war effort, 'Many misunderstandings that exist at present between the two races will disappear.'[72] Had they let the Pakeha do all the fighting for New Zealand, Maori would have lost their self-respect, and this same consideration now warranted their inclusion in conscription.[73]

Thus Ngata interwove three representations of Maori: as loyal subjects of the British Empire; as a race in perilous transition from their warrior past to new, unfamiliar principles of social organisation; and as fellow citizens of Pakeha, equally obliged to serve, and on the threshold of better mutual understanding. What is the relationship of such evocations of Maori to the universalist confidence of liberalism whose fortunes I am considering in this paper? Here, we need to be clear about what was at stake when liberal universalism faltered in the second half of the nineteenth century: whether civilising imperialists could continue to postulate non-European educability. When native peoples served effectively in the armed forces of settler colonial societies, they could be understood as demonstrating their loyalty to the nation and their aptitude for acculturation. It was the latter — their competence to be part of a more complex social organisation — that made native war service a vindication of liberal universalism: with the right treatment, such as fair opportunity for war service, natives were capable of rapid improvement. Ngata presented soldiering as an opportunity for Maori development: to serve Empire and nation would discharge, in a contemporary way, their inherent proclivity to be warriors, and it established a bond of shared sacrifice with Pakeha.

Ngata's speeches about Maori war service in World War One did not articulate a political bargain.[74] While his project of Maori modernisation required concessions from Pakeha authority — about land tenure and development finance in particular — he did not present war service as an item of exchange for Pakeha political concessions. Rather, Maori war service, as Ngata presented it, enacted a status already achieved and further proved the potential of Maori for racial self-development; he bargained for Maori nothing more than Pakeha respect.

In 1917 over one-third of the Indians in the USA were non-citizens; although such people (if male) were obliged to register for armed service, they could not be drafted. Nonetheless, Indians volunteered in substantial numbers. 'Of the 11,803 Native Americans who registered for the draft prior to September 1918, the federal government inducted 6,509 into the service.'[75] More Indians enlisted and were inducted after September 1918, but the total number in war service is unknown. For Zitkala-Ša and her Indian associates, to the extent that Indians remained non-citizens and victims of a stifling program of tutelage, there was a bargain to be argued: with such Indian war service, the USA could no longer withhold citizenship.[76]

Born on the Yankton Sioux Reservation in 1876, Zitkala-Ša had persuaded her mother in 1884 to allow her to attend a Quaker Boarding School. Ambivalent about her experience there, she nonetheless accepted further education and for a few years taught at the avowedly assimilationist Carlisle School. Buoyed by recognition as a writer, speaker, and musician, from 1900 her writing — both autobiographical and political commentary — had presented her uneasy mediation of white American civilisation and Indian heritage. While her public identity was unequivocally, theatrically Indian, she advocated not only more respectful treatment of Indians but also a more critical attitude by Indians towards their own heritage. For example, before a 1918 Congressional hearing, she contradicted many Indian activists by denouncing the use of the drug Peyote in neo-traditional Indian religious ceremonies.

Zitkala-Ša wrote for and at times edited the SAI's *American Indian Magazine*. Her Americanism, revealed in those pages, seems to have been influenced, at times, by the terms in which Woodrow Wilson projected his country's historic role. Her editorial in the July–September 1918 issue of *American Indian Magazine* declared that Indians were conscious of the blood that they were shedding as part of 'a great united American brotherhood fighting in a common cause, the defense of world democracy'.[77] America, 'the greatest of democracies' was in this way shining its light on Europe, but 'as America has declared democracy abroad, so must we consistently practice it at home … If [the Indian] is good enough to fight for American ideals he is good enough for American citizenship now'.[78] In the same issue, her article 'Indian gifts to civilized man' celebrated the decision to integrate Indian volunteers and conscripts, rather than to segregate them in an Indian unit. She presented Indians as intensely patriotic, and she pointed out the high stakes: 'when we realize that the only future hope of the Red Man is in his educated, physically strong men, we marvel at his heroic response.'[79] She thus presented Indian war service as creating an obligation to Indians of which the United States had to be reminded in the post war world. 'In the defense of democracy his utter self-sacrifice was unequalled by any other class of Americans. What now does democracy mean to him and his children?' she asked in her 1921 article 'Americanize the first American'.[80]

However, in two pieces written during the 'Wilsonian moment', Zitkala-Ša evoked Indian war service less as a provocation to reciprocity between Indians and government and more as Indian participation in a new internationalism.[81] At the Paris Peace Conference:

> Little peoples are now to be granted the right of self determination! Small nations and remnants of nations are to sit beside their great allies at the Peace Table; and their just claims are to be duly incorporated in the terms of a righteous peace.[82]

The 'ten thousand Indian soldiers swaying to and fro on European battlefields' were 'mingling their precious blood with the blood of all other peoples of the earth, that democracy might live'.[83] Indians were defending not only the USA, she pointed out, but also 'its democratic ideals. The Red Man of America loves democracy and hates mutilated treaties.'[84] In his 'Four Points' speech on February 1918 Wilson presented the 'democratic ideal' as 'self-determination' – a phrase that SAI activists could understand to include what they were already demanding: the withdrawal of BIA administration and the granting of citizenship to Indians.[85] 'Belgium is leading a historic procession of little peoples seeking freedom!', she wrote, and the American Indian grievance was among the 'divers human petitions' that 'daily ascend' to the 'peace table' of the Paris Conference.

> Actions of the wise leaders assembled in Paris may be guided ostensibly by temporary man-made laws and aims, dividing human interests into domestic and international affairs, but even so those leaders cannot forget the eternal fact that humanity is essentially one undivided closely intertwined fabric through which spiritual truth will shine with increasing brightness until it is fully understood and its requirements fulfilled. The universal cry for freedom from injustice is the voice of a multitude united by afflictions. To appease this human cry the application of democratic principles must be flexible enough to be universal.[86]

Thus the *American Indian Magazine* aligned Indian war service not only with US diplomacy but also with the aspirations of 'a multitude united by afflictions'. Indians' promotion of their US citizenship was one of the many global resonances of the 'Wilsonian moment'.

William Cooper: British Aborigines?

In the 1930s letters, petitions, manifestoes, and newspaper interviews of the Australian Aboriginal William Cooper, we can see an indigenous intellectual finding terms to name the universal capacities and entitlements of humans, including his innovative and – at first sight – puzzling uses of 'white' and 'British'. Cooper was a Yorta Yorta man whose education in European ways came from Christian missionaries and from being a servant, as a boy, in the Melbourne household of the wealthy pastoralist whose livestock occupied his ancestral land. Cooper's career included the rural manual labouring trades that were common in his lifetime and at which many Aborigines were proficient. He was also a member of the Australian Workers Union and – like many active trade unionists – he read about the wider world. Cooper's political activism on indigenous rights accelerated after his retirement in 1931 when he moved to Melbourne. He organised a petition to the British King (1934–7) and he founded the Australian Aborigines League in 1936.

Transition to agriculture seemed to Cooper – as to Jones, Eastman, and Ngata – to be a way for his people to advance and to survive. As long ago as the 1880s, he and other Yorta Yorta had asked for allotments for families to farm. By the 1930s he was highly critical of government's failures to support Aboriginal farmers with finance, infrastructure, and training. Based on his own efforts at self-improvement, he believed that Aborigines would adapt and learn quickly, if given a chance. Civilisation, he suggested, can be picked up in three generations.[87] He presented his views on Aborigines' aptitude for advancement in terms of a three part 'stadial' schema distinguishing the 'myall [wild] Aboriginals'; the 'partly civilised and detribalised aboriginal' and the 'civilised aboriginals'.[88] Each cohort in each region could claim its characteristic achievements and entitlements. The third stage – 'civilised aboriginals' – was thus not merely an asserted entitlement ('we claim the right to advance to full European culture'), for such advancement was also inevitable: 'the primitive culture [was] destined to ultimately perish.'[89]

Like many Christians, Cooper drew from his religion the conviction that all races were equal in the sight of God.[90] However, there was also a human vantage point from which the claims of all peoples to be 'civilised' could be evaluated. How 'British' were Australians? For Cooper, 'British' – idealised – named a standard of civility. As he stated in his petition to the King and elsewhere, the Crown had charged its colonial officials with high duties towards native people, but Australian governments had not yet lived up to these responsibilities.[91] Because Australian governments had been neglectful, 'the system is pauperizing us and not helping us in any way'.[92] The failure of Aborigines to advance was largely due to the failure of whites to accept the responsibility that the Crown had given them. Native peoples elsewhere, better treated, had flourished. He warmly cited Canadian efforts 'to preserve the Eskimo race'.[93] A journalist quoted Cooper as remarking in 1937 that 'In Fiji, not very long ago, the people were cannibals. Now they have their own doctors and lawyers and professional men. Is it not shameful that Australia should be so backward in training her native people?'[94] His most frequent comparative case was the Maori: they had been enfranchised since 1867 – why not Aborigines?[95] He was also aware that the New Zealand Cabinet included a Minister for Native Affairs and that a Maori (Ngata) had held this position.[96] Maori were being compensated for their losses of land, he pointed out to Prime Minister Lyons, but not Aborigines.[97]

That these comparative cases – Eskimos, Fijians, and Maori – fell within the British Empire and sustained Cooper's repeated invocation of the non-racial status of the British subject. Where the British standard of political conduct was upheld, native potential could be realised. For Cooper, the Empire was a realm of universality, not in the sense that it embraced all of humanity but in the sense that it was not racially exclusive: every native people would have its chance, if British ideals were realised.[98]

Within this universalist framework, Cooper did not deny the reality of 'race'. He saw himself as a member of (indeed a spokesman for) his 'race'.[99] The organisation that he founded in 1936, the Australian Aborigines' League, limited 'full membership' to persons 'with Aboriginal blood in them.'[100] He was proud of his colour, and he wanted whites to acknowledge that he and his people were not 'inferior clay'.[101] He acknowledged that he was himself of mixed descent ('I have European blood in my veins'),[102] but his thinking about race in Australia tended to be dualist: there were Aborigines and there were whites, and 'the coloured person' 'feels more in common with the full blood than with the white'.[103] However, he emphatically opposed the racial determinism of Australian thinking about Aborigines, and he filled racial and national categories with historical and ethical content. Whites could make more effort to 'think black'.[104]

For Cooper, the important distinctions within the human race were cultural not racial. But he was not a cultural relativist either: the differences that mattered to him were distinctions of advancement along a universal path of human improvement. 'Culture' was the term he used to refer to a plane of recognisable and rewardable achievement in civilisation; that is, he referred to 'culture' as if it were something that one could lack and could acquire. He referred to 'those of our race who are as yet uncultured.'[105] He imagined a time 'when Aboriginal people are fully cultured'.[106] When they arose from their primitive condition, 'they would scarcely be recognised as the same people'.[107] While the objects of the Australian Aborigines' League included conserving 'special features of Aboriginal culture',[108] there is little in his writing to indicate what he thought was worth preserving, other than 'certain corroboree dances, in the ways the Old World peoples have retained their folk dances'.[109] Thus when Cooper insisted that the fortunes of races were culturally determined, he was not making a plea for cultural pluralism; he was insisting that British–Australians enable Aborigines to acquire the culture that he understood to be necessary to participate in civilisation. Cooper's idealised 'British' is a signifier for a standard by which all human conduct is to be judged. 'British' was the best form of human civilisation to which all Australians – Aborigines and whites – should aspire.

Cooper was addressing fellow Australians for whom 'White Australia' and 'British' signified racial or descent-based community and shared tradition, the 'crimson thread of kinship' between white Australians and their Mother Country, to which Aborigines were not connected in the ethnically 'imagined community' of Australia's federation.[110] Disturbing this sense of 'British', it was but a short step for Cooper also to use 'white' as a signifier of civilisational, rather than ethnic, characteristics. He did so by intervening in the discussion about the remote regions of the continent. White Australians then feared that they still too thinly populated their vast continent: how to occupy the regions closest to Asia? Combining eugenic and geographical thought, many Australians believed that people of British stock were poorly suited to colonising those parts of Australia with extremes of climate: much of Australia was too hot and humid for 'Nordic' people. Should Australia experiment with non-British immigration, to fill the difficult North? Cooper suggested that Aborigines were adapted to populating the North and Centre of the continent.[111] 'The dark race will prove an asset to Australia', if Australia used Aborigines to fill the continent's Northern spaces.[112] Those who worried that Australia might have to compromise the 'White' Australia policy and resort to populating the North with southern European migrants were assured by Cooper that 'for the purposes of this policy [i.e. using 'civilised Aborigines' to populate the North] *the Aboriginal is white*'.[113]

Conclusion: the mobile signifiers of universality

Mantena has argued persuasively that Mill's liberalism was unstable in a way characteristic of 'the structure of imperial ideology': the 'universalist defence of empire' was easily tempted to infer from the resistance of the colonised to civilising influence that some cultures could not join the universal march of human progress. So liberalism oscillated (and is fated to oscillate) between 'universalist justifications and culturalist alibis'.[114] We can accept Mantena's instability thesis without assuming that it will manifest only in 'oscillation'. While 'oscillate' may describe the trajectory of particular liberal thinkers, other intellectuals remained steadfastly universalist because they found the available 'cultural alibi' both personally repugnant and politically hopeless. While canonical British liberals such as J. S. Mill could be persuaded by colonial experience, by racial science and by the nascent discipline of Anthropology to see humanity as differentiated in capacity for improvement, some native intellectuals adhered to the view that the red, brown, and black peoples of the earth could and would advance if offered respectful, competent, and unselfish tuition by those who presented themselves as the bearers of 'civilisation'. So the instability that Mantena identifies may manifest not only as an oscillation in an intellectual career but also as a polarity among individuals who occupy different positions within the global field of liberalism: staunch indigenous universalists contesting metropolitan invokers of the 'culturalist alibi'.

What intellectual inheritance enabled the figures studied in this paper to imagine history from a universalist standpoint? These native intellectuals drew conviction not only from their own life experience – self-improvement and recognition for it – but also from two universalist ideas that flourished in eighteenth-century Europe: the stadial explanation of human variety as manifesting the sequential development of all branches of humanity; and Christian faith that all humans were fallen souls that could be primed for the redeeming reception of God's word (whether in English or in their own tongue). When racial theories of human diversity began to permeate European thought, and even when racial thought seemed to gain credibility from advances in the biological understanding of speciation, the triumph of the idea of pre-destined racial hierarchy was not assured; notions of racial variety/ hierarchy had to compete with these two deeply entrenched universalisms. That liberalism was contested between universalism and racial or cultural particularism is one of the insights of postcolonial historiography; however, we should not presume that the contest was 'won' by racial science. These New World intellectuals could not afford to believe that being a member of a certain race determined one's destiny. It is not that they denied the reality of racial difference or dismissed the possibility that racial traits were transmitted down the generations. Their concessions to racial notions of human variety were made within a persistent conviction that there are universal standards of human attainment and that every branch of humanity has the right, the capacity and the duty to oblige that standard. How to name the standpoint of the universal was problematic in a world where nations and empires tended to identify themselves as 'civilisation' itself. I have given instances of the inventiveness of Easton (at the 1911 Universal Races Congress) and Cooper (his 'British' and 'white').What was important about liberal universalism was that every branch of humanity, including those that colonised, must be measured against a civilised standard.[115]

Notes

1 Bhikhu Parekh, 'Liberalism and Colonialism: a Critique of Locke and Mill', in Jan Nederveen Pieterse and Bhikhu Parekh, eds, *The Decolonization of the Imagination* (London: Zed Books 1995), 81–98, 88.

2 *Ibid.*, 92.

3 Karuna Mantena, 'Mill and the Imperial Predicament', in Nadia Urbinati and Alex Zakaras, eds, *J. S. Mill's Political Thought* (Cambridge: Cambridge University Press, 2007), 298–318, 301.

4 *Ibid.*, 316, 317.

5 Christopher A. Bayly, *Recovering Liberties: Indian Thought in the Age of Liberalism and Empire* (Cambridge: Cambridge University Press, 2012).

6 Michael C. Coleman, 'Not Race, but Grace: Presbyterian Missionaries and American Indians, 1837–1893', *Journal of American History*, 67: 1 (1980), 41–60.

7 *Ibid.*, 42.

8 *Ibid.*, 58.

9 Andrew Porter, *Religion Versus Empire? British Protestant Missionaries and Overseas Expansion, 1700–1914* (Manchester and New York: Manchester University Press, 2004), 283.

10 *Ibid.*, 286.

11 Jane Samson, 'Ethnology and Theology: Nineteenth-century Mission Dilemmas in the South Pacific', in Brian Stanley, ed., *Christian Missions and the Enlightenment* (Grand Rapids, MI/Cambridge, UK: William B. Eerdmans, 2001), 99–122, 122.

12 Coleman, 'Not Race, but Grace', 59.

13 Brian Stanley, 'Christian Missions and the Enlightenment: a Re-evaluation', in Stanley, ed., *Christian Missions and the Enlightenment* (Grand Rapids, MI/Cambridge, UK: William B. Eerdmans, 2001), 1–22, 11.

14 *Ibid.*, 17.

15 Peter Jones, *The sermon and speeches of the rev. Peter Jones, alias, Kah-ke-wa-quon-a-by, the converted indian chief, delivered on the occasion of the eighteenth anniversary of the Wesleyan Methodist missionary society for the Leeds district, held in Brunswick and Albion street chapels, Leeds, September the 25th, 26th, and 27th, 1831, taken in short hand, verbatim as delivered* (Leeds, undated), 15.

16 Peter Jones, *History of the Ojebway Indians: with especial reference to their conversion to Christianity* (London: A.W. Bennett, 1861), 54–6.

17 *Ibid.*, 29.

18 *Ibid.*, 71.

19 *Ibid.*, 152.

20 *Ibid.*, 39, 105–10, 130.

21 *Ibid.*, 28.

22 *Ibid.*

23 *Ibid.*, 93.

24 *Ibid.*, 28.

25 *Ibid.*, 85.

26 *Ibid.*, 101–2, 143–52.

27 *Ibid.*, 167–9.

28 *Ibid.*, 92–3.

29 *Ibid.*, 93, emphasis added.

30 *Ibid.*, 142.

31 *Ibid.*, 240–1.

32 *Ibid.*, 110.

33 *Ibid.*, 116, 127–8.

34 *Ibid.*, 123–8.

35 *Ibid.*, 216–17.

36 *Ibid.*, 217, 242.

37 *Ibid.*, 243–4.

38 John Wyon Burrow, *The Crisis of Reason: European Thought 1848–1914* (New Haven, CT and London: Yale University Press, 2000), 92.

39 Paul Crook, 'Historical Monkey Business: the Myth of a Darwinised British Imperial Discourse', *History*, 84: issue 276 (1999), 633–57, 644.

40 Benjamin Kidd, *Social Evolution* (New York: Macmillan & Co., 1895), 327.

41 *Ibid.*, 335–6.

42 *Ibid.*, 349.

43 *Ibid.*, 50.

44 Quoted in Charles A. Eastman, *The Indian Today: the Past and Future of the First American* (New York: Doubleday, Page & Co., 1915), 133.

45 For a survey of the forms of Sioux Christianity and an explanation of its firmer hold among Sioux than other Indian nations see D. Lindenfeld, 'The Varieties of Sioux Christianity, 1860–1980, in International Perspective', *Journal of Global History* (2007) 2: 3, 281–302.

46 Eastman, *The Indian Today*, 106.

47 Frederick E. Hoxie, *A Final Promise: the Campaign to Assimilate the Indians, 1880–1920* (Lincoln, NE: University of Nebraska Press, 1984).

48 Eastman, *The Indian Today*, 82.

49 *Ibid.*, 94.

50 *Ibid.*, 106.

51 *Ibid.* Eastman left the BIA in December 1909. According to one biographer, his 'statements on the corruption, graft, and inefficiency of the Bureau of Indian Affairs primarily surfaced after 1910. By that date, Eastman had had two bitter confrontations with white agents while serving under them as a government physician.' R. Wilson, *Ohiyesa: Charles Eastman, Santee Sioux* (Urbana: University of Illinois Press, 1999), 144. He rejoined the BIA in 1923.

52 *Ibid.*, 105.

53 *Ibid.*

54 *Ibid.*, 106.

55 *Ibid.*, 114.

56 *Ibid.*, 120, 124.

57 *Ibid.*, 175–6.

58 *Ibid.*, 129.

59 *Ibid.*, 140.

60 *Ibid.*, 1, 12, 135–6, 165–6.

61 *Ibid.*, 43, 147.

62 *Ibid.*, 165–6.

63 Charles A. Eastman, *From the Deep Woods to Civilization* (Boston: Little, Brown & Co., 1916), 57.

64   Eastman, *The Indian Today*, 120.

65   Eastman, *From the Deep Woods*, 190.

66   Refutation of the settler colonial myth of the 'Dying Native' had commenced in the United States in the 1870s. Brian W. Dippie, *The Vanishing American: White Attitudes and U.S. Indian Policy* (Middletown, CT: Wesleyan University Press, 1982), 130–2, 135. I have discussed the place of demographic knowledge in US discourses of settler colonial 'guardianship' in Tim Rowse, 'Population Knowledge and the Practice of Guardianship', *American Nineteenth Century History*, 15 (2014), 15–42.

67   *New Zealand Parliamentary Debates* (NZPD) 1 September 1914 vol 169, 662. In some regions – Taranaki, Waikato – enduring Maori hostility to Imperial Britain weakened Maori enlistment.

68   NZPD 29 November 1918, vol. 183, 579.

69   NZPD 30 May 1916, vol. 175, 519.

70   NZPD 31 May 1916, vol. 175, 573.

71   NZPD 1 June 1916, vol. 175, 612.

72   *Ibid.*

73   *Ibid.*, 613.

74   In contrast, arguably, with his stance in his 1943 pamphlet *The Price of Citizenship*: 'Has he proved a claim to be an asset to his country? If so he asks to be dealt with as such. An asset discovered in the crucible of war should have a value in peace.' Quoted in E. Ramsden, *Sir Apirana Ngata and Maori Culture* (Wellington, NZ: A. H. & A. W. Reed, 1948), 61.

75   Thomas A. Britten, *American Indians in World War One: at Home and at War* (Albuquerque: University of New Mexico Press, 1997), 58–9. This amounted to 13 percent of the estimated Native American adult male population.

76   Zitkala-Ša, *American Indian Stories, Legends, and Other Writings* (New York: Penguin, 2003), 244. Eastman also used Indians' World War One service as an argument for citizenship. See Wilson *Ohiyessa* 141, 161.

77   *Ibid.*, 181.

78   *Ibid.*, 182.

79   *Ibid.*, 185–6.

80   *Ibid.*, 243.

81   E. Manela, *The Wilsonian Moment: Self-determination and the International Origins of Anticolonial Nationalism* (New York: Oxford University Press, 2007).

82   Zitkala-Ša *American Indian Stories*, 191.

83   *Ibid.*, 193.

84   *Ibid.*

85   *Ibid.*, 191.

86   *Ibid.*, 191–2.

87   Cooper to Patterson 31 October 1936, in Bain Attwood and Andrew Markus, eds, *Thinking Black: William Cooper and the Australian Aborigines' League* (Canberra: Aboriginal Studies Press, 2004), 56.

88   Cooper to Lyons 16 January 1937, in Attwood and Markus, eds, *Thinking Black*, 65.

89   Cooper to Harris 16 March 1937, in Attwood and Markus, eds, *Thinking Black*, 69.

90   Cooper to Gribble 31 October 1933, in Attwood and Markus, eds, *Thinking Black*, 38.

91   *Herald* (Melbourne) 15 September 1933; Notes on meeting with Paterson 23 January 1935; Cooper to Lyon 31 March 1938, in Attwood and Markus, eds, *Thinking Black*, 35, 43, 94.

92   Notes on meeting with Paterson 23 January 1935, in Attwood and Markus, eds, *Thinking Black*, 45.

93 Cooper to Lyons 23 October 1933, in Attwood and Markus, eds, *Thinking Black*, 36.

94 Cooper to Lyons 26 October 1937, in Attwood and Markus, eds, *Thinking Black*, 80.

95 Cooper to Lyons 28 July 1934; Notes on meeting with Paterson, 23 January 1935, in Attwood and Markus, eds, *Thinking Black*, 41, 44.

96 Cooper to Lyons 26 October 1937, in Attwood and Markus, eds, *Thinking Black*, 81.

97 Cooper to Lyons 31 March 1938, in Attwood and Markus, eds, *Thinking Black*, 94.

98 For a Black South African parallel see Vivian Bickford-Smith, 'African Nationalist or British Loyalist? The Complicated Case of Tiyo Soga', *History Workshop Journal*, 71 (2011), 74–97. Soga, celebrated by the ANC as a 'black nationalist', wrote: 'The more I know of good English people, the greater is my admiration of them as a race ... I know nothing of the justice of other nations; but I know something of the "fairplay" of an Englishman' (84). Bickford-Smith employs the distinction between 'ethnic' and 'civic' nationalism to make sense of Soga's anti-colonial ideology and of the ways it has been remembered.

99 Cooper to Perkins 13 January 1934, in Attwood and Markus, eds, *Thinking Black*, 39.

100 Cooper to Minister for the Interior 22 February 1936, in Attwood and Markus, eds, *Thinking Black*, 48.

101 Cooper to Editor of *The Ladder* 5 November 1936, in Attwood and Markus, eds, *Thinking Black*, 58, 62.

102 Cooper to Menzies 31 August 1940, in Attwood and Markus, eds, *Thinking Black*, 127.

103 Cooper to Editor of *The Ladder* 5 November 1936, in Attwood and Markus, eds, *Thinking Black*, 58.

104 Cooper to McEwen 17 December 1938, in Attwood and Markus, eds, *Thinking Black*, 109.

105 Cooper to Selby 1 February 1937, in Attwood and Markus, eds, *Thinking Black*, 67.

106 Cooper to McEwen 19 February 1938, in Attwood and Markus, eds, *Thinking Black*, 90.

107 Cooper to Paterson 18 February 1937, in Attwood and Markus, eds, *Thinking Black*, 68.

108 Cooper to the Minister for the Interior 22 February 1936, in Attwood and Markus, eds, *Thinking Black*, 48.

109 Cooper to Paterson 15 June 1936, in Attwood and Markus, eds, *Thinking Black*, 52.

110 D. Cole 'The Crimson Thread of Kinship: Ethnic Ideals in Australia 1870–1914', *Historical Studies*, 56 (1971), 511–25.

111 Cooper to Paterson 31 October 1936; Copper to Paterson 18 February 1937; Cooper to Harris 16 March 1937; in Attwood and Markus, eds, *Thinking Black*, 57, 68, 69.

112 Cooper to Paterson 25 June 1937, in Attwood and Markus, eds, *Thinking Black*, 75.

113 Cooper to McEwen 19 February 1938, in Attwood and Markus, eds, *Thinking Black*, 90, emphasis in original.

114 Mantena, 'Mill and the Imperial Predicament', 299–300.

115 I would like to thank Sarah Irving, the participants of the 'Global History of Liberalism' seminar (University of Sydney, July 2012) and two anonymous referees at *Modern Intellectual History* for comments that helped me improve this paper.

7

Troubling appropriations: Pedro Paterno's Filipino deployment of French Lamarckianism

Megan C. Thomas

Pedro Paterno causes trouble as a historical figure. On the one hand, he is sometimes considered a national hero of the Philippines. The son of one of the early
critics of Spanish colonial practices, Paterno worked to raise the profile of the
Philippines in elite European circles, which was one of the strategies of the late
nineteenth-century Filipino reform movement that preceded the Philippine
Revolution of 1896. His writings extolled the virtues and riches of the Philippines,
and he himself joined the later Revolutionary government of Malolos in 1898,
in the Revolution's second phase, against the American occupation. On the other
hand, he is also the original turncoat, the Janus figure who offered his services to
Spain and negotiated the truce with Revolutionary forces in 1897, and after the
fall of the Malolos government and with the establishment of American colonial
rule, he pursued positions within the American government.[1]

His intellectual work is no less troubling. He wrote pieces that neither vindicated Spanish colonialism nor called for revolutionary change, but that promote
the Philippines as the home of civilizational achievement. At the same time, they
engage with and translate into a Philippine context some troubling theories of
racial purity and mixing. Paterno's writings of the 1880s illustrate the ways that
emerging nationalist thought in the colonial world breaches the kinds of political
fault lines along which we often evaluate it. His writings highlight indigenous
agency in the story of civilizational advancement in the Philippines, but they also
embrace ideas of civilizational destinies connected to racial types, and endorse the
idea that some races are retrograde and destined to be extinguished.

Ideas travel from one context to another all the time, transformed in the process. But the stakes of these transformations seem higher when the ideas are about
racial superiority and inferiority, and the ideas are travelling from a European
context to a colonial one. Studying political thought in the colonized world can
be heady and inspiring. Many students of the history of political thought, which

is often still conceived of as a series of great thinkers that span the ages, have become attuned to the ways that many of its great thinkers have articulated, if not invented, ways of knowing that have underwritten some of the most egregious regimes of global political domination.[2] Scholars who aim for a more politically thoughtful and also more global view of the history of political thought may be inclined to seek in the past some kind of redemptive moment. Concerned with the way that ideas of racial superiority and inferiority persist in the present day, and inspired by the way that people have resisted forms of domination, scholars can find exciting material in the writings of colonial subjects who took up and challenged ideas about racial superiority and inferiority; ideas that in direct and indirect ways underwrote the colonial domination under which they lived. These histories of how travelling ideas have been transformed and challenged by colonial subjects are an essential corrective, in more than one sense, to a Eurocentric canon of political theory.

The trouble comes with a thinker like Pedro Paterno, a colonial subject who takes up and takes on ideas of racial superiority and inferiority, transforming them to the benefit of those he claims as his people, but in ways that do not neatly or directly challenge the presumptions generally underwriting colonial domination. What do we do with the colonial thinker who appears to be not so much reproducing European ideas of racial superiority and inferiority, but instead transforming them into his own unique account of racial superiority and inferiority? His thought is not a duplication of European thought, but neither is it clearly oppositional to the presumptions of European colonialism in the ways that we might desire. His thought can teach us much, not just about the subjects on which he writes, but also the ways that thought can travel and be transformed in what might seem the oddest ways. His writings demonstrate how colonial appropriations of European thought can unsettle our expectations of them; they invoke political claims that are neither repetitions of European supremacism nor challenges to presumptions of racial inequality. They teach us about the way that one ambitious, creative young man addressed the ways that his homeland and people had been denigrated or at best ignored by the more powerful of the world, and saw an opportunity to address that wrong by wielding some of the most ideologically potent tools of colonial domination. His writing invokes political claims that are neither repetitions of European supremacism nor challenges to presumptions of racial inequality.

This chapter shows how Paterno, an elite young Filipino living in Europe in the 1880s, incorporated some of the latest French social Darwinist thought into his writing about Philippine ethnology. As he translated ideas from one context to another, he also combined them in unique and sometimes unsettling ways. The result is writing that asserts the position of the Filipino at the head of civilization alongside and not behind 'advanced' European peoples. It accomplishes this, however, through constructing 'Filipino' in a way that paradoxically both incorporates and excludes those thought of as the 'primitives' of the Philippines.

In contrast with intellectual production elsewhere in the colonial world as it has generally been studied, Paterno's writings and those of his compatriots demonstrate that intellectual travel in the colonial world does not always follow the lines of colonial rule, travelling from a metropole to its colony. In India, of course, a long and deep history of British scholarship about India's religions, languages, etc. meant that late nineteenth-century Indian intellectuals often engaged with these British accounts, and even with British intellectual currents that were not directly related to India. Indian intellectuals used British sources in ways too broad to be collectively characterized, but in this book we have one example in Inder Marwah's work on Indian appropriations of Spencer, and another in Lynn Zastoupil's work on 'flows and counterflows' of Indian thought. These Indian intellectuals regularly retooled and transformed scholarship and ideas from India's English colonizers, and even the Germans via an English link. But when we turn to the Philippines, the picture changes a bit. Ideas and scholarship from the Philippines' colonizers – from Spain – are only sometimes the main European point of reference for late nineteenth-century Filipino intellectuals. In this chapter, we will see how one of Paterno's pieces in particular engaged directly in contemporary racial debates in France. Paterno's appropriations of French racial theories are not appropriations of the thought of the colonizer of the Philippines, but they are appropriations of the authority of advanced European science and civilization. The power of Paterno's appropriations lay in part on the authority of European science and civilization, authority that he was not contesting, but to which he was laying claim.

Paterno's use of then-contemporary French social thought shows one way that social and political arguments have been transposed from one context to another in ways that also transform them. When this young Filipino referenced French social thought, he used claims made by social scientists and commentators who themselves were deriving their models from biological theories of evolution. Just as Darwin's ideas were appropriated in the English-language world by social theorists and commentators, in France, Lamarck's theory of evolution became a resource for people thinking about human life and its organization. Thus, at one level Paterno is appropriating French thought and applying it to a Philippine setting to narrate the evolutionary history of peoples in the Philippines. But the transformation is more profound than a change in scenery or subject. Paterno referenced with approval figures who were at odds with each other in the French context.

These French social thinkers borrowed from Lamarck a framework that focused on the use versus disuse of organs or characteristics as the mechanism of adaptation to environmental factors, and that also posited a general principle of increasing complexity; some of them also incorporated more Darwinian principles of natural selection.[3] Within these parameters, however, there was wide variation and vociferous contestation. Specialists in the anthropological sciences differed, sometimes vehemently, over significant points, such as what constituted a racial trait or how to gauge the racial purity of a population versus its racial mixing. And beyond the specialist scientific community, everyone was weighing in on how such purity or mixing should be interpreted. These arguments over scientific principles were complicated by the fact that they were also arguments about pressing social issues in France of the day. Arguments over scientific principles were sometimes thinly veiled and other times explicit references to how to understand the place of Jews in the French nation. The body of the French nation was increasingly understood in biological terms, yet it was also presumed Catholic (or secular, but never Jewish). Lamarckian arguments about racial purity versus mixing, health versus decay, and advancement versus stasis, might be opportunities to speak either in defence of French Jews as an integral part of the vitality of the French nation, or as an attack on them as foreign and inferior bodies polluting French stock. Transposed to the social context of the Philippines, the scientific arguments did not apply in the same way. The roles that arguments about racial destiny, purity, and mixing played so prominently in French ethnological theories, and their popularization, as part of an anxious conversation about the French nation, were replayed in this Philippine production as part of a different plot. In the Philippine production, the anxious conversation was about the racial capacities of peoples of the Philippines, with consequences for how one evaluated the possibilities for a future without Spanish tutelage.

Ilustrados' worlds

Paterno's writings are a part of a broader story of the political lives of turn-of-the-century French racial thought. They are also part of a broader story about social thought in the late nineteenth-century Philippines. In the 1880s, a flowering of writing about the Philippines was produced not by the colonial Spaniards, but instead by highly educated elite youth of the Philippines, who are often referred to collectively as the *ilustrados* (enlightened).[4] These young men were frustrated by the hypocrisies of Spanish colonial rule in the late nineteenth-century Philippines – for example, by the official and unofficial power that friar orders had in the government and over the everyday lives of the people of the islands, when the friars exerted no comparable influence in the Spanish peninsula. These young men were frustrated, too, by the official and unofficial limits to locals' ascent up the ladders of government institutions, no matter what their education or talents. At the same time, these young men benefitted from the fact that they could attend secondary schools in the provinces and even a (Dominican) university in Manila, which offered degrees in principle comparable to those of institutions in the peninsula.

Fuelled by their families' ambition and wealth, many of these young men took the relatively quick and reliable routes to Europe, via steamship and the Suez Canal, to pursue advanced training and degrees. Once in Spain, many experienced a sort of disillusionment when they found that the mother country whose praises were sung so loudly in Manila was actually straggling at the rear of Europe's march of scientific progress rather than leading the way. As a result, many of these young men looked beyond Spain to wider Europe to partake of scholarly work and insert themselves into elite society, often navigated via Masonic networks. Some of these young men also found an opportunity in the Spaniards' underachievement; they were able to use the latest scientific theories and techniques to illuminate the history and ethnology of the Philippines, adapting disciplinary knowledges that are often associated with colonialism but that were only occasionally mastered by their Spanish colonizers. Many of these young men were also politically active, seeking reforms in the colonial administration of the Philippines and rights as Spanish citizens. It was in this context that many, like Paterno in his own way, sought to raise the profile of the Philippines in European circles via their artistic, scholarly, journalistic, and (what we might call) social networking and lobbying efforts.[5]

Some of these same young men who wrote and worked in the 1880s to promote the possibilities of political reforms in the Spanish colonial administration would go on to be significant figures during the Revolution and early Philippine Republic. When the Republic was cut short by the United States' colonial aggression, those who survived found different ways of living with and under American rule, and Paterno was not the only *ilustrado* to take a leadership position with the American colonial government. For those with moderate, liberal political aims, personal ambition, and who had perhaps seen their home provinces decimated by war, American colonial rule held some promise for a state free of the influence of the friar orders, a state in which progress, education, and economic prosperity were supposed to be central concerns.

Paterno was one of these young men. He was born in Manila in 1857 to a *mestizo* family of mixed Chinese and Tagalog heritage. His family had become wealthy and prominent through its business interests, and the young Paterno was educated at Manila's esteemed Jesuit school the Ateneo before leaving for Madrid to pursue higher education, where he completed a law doctorate in 1880 at Madrid's Central University. Paterno's family had been among those caught in an earlier era of repression of the 1870s, when liberals in the Philippines who had clamoured for reforms were imprisoned or exiled. Pedro's father was deported for alleged conspiracy in 1872, although he was later able to return to Manila. The young Pedro Paterno spent most of the 1870s through 1890s in Spain, where he practised law, lived well off the pension his family sent to support him, and in general promoted himself in social circles, somewhat to the exasperation of some of his compatriots. He had a reputation among his peers of being a pretentious climber and had ambivalent relations with many in the group. Despite their reservations about him, the fact that Paterno wrote and published in Spain during the 1880s and early 1890s was politically significant for them. This was before the Revolution of 1896 that aimed to end Spanish rule in the country and would establish its first republic, during a period when many forward-thinking Filipinos sought to push for significant reforms under the mantle of Spanish sovereignty. They sought rights as Spanish citizens equal to those of Spanish citizens from the Spanish peninsula. Thus the fact that Paterno was publishing in Spain was significant for other young Filipinos who sought to raise their collective profile in the metropole and on the broader European stage.[6]

In what follows, I focus on two of Paterno's writings, *Ancient Tagalog Civilization* (1887) and *The Itas* (1890).[7] These writings use French evolutionary thought, as it was being taken up in French anthropological circles and was refracted through the lens of contemporary social and political issues. Elsewhere I have written about how *ilustrado* writings used methods and presumptions of ethnological sciences in order to find commonalities across some of the numerous ethnolinguistic boundaries in the Philippines, commonalities that suggested the existence of a cohesive 'people' that predated and was independent of their Spanish civilization and so was proto-national.[8] The methods of ethnological sciences were able to recover and reconstruct elements of what appeared to be a prehispanic history and culture, making it possible to see value in what had hitherto been a devalued past. The idea of a unified prehispanic past of diverse contemporary peoples was expressed in part through the language of race, a language that naturalized commonalities as well as difference. Race discourse, Michel Foucault observed, 'has a great ability to circulate, a great aptitude for metamorphosis, or a sort of strategic polyvalence' by which it can be and has been taken up in markedly divergent and often opposed political projects.[9] As we will see, the different nuances of 'race' and of related conceptions of 'people', 'civilization', and 'culture' reveal how various were the meanings and associations of 'race' at this time, and in particular, how these variations contained both opportunities as well as challenges for those who wrote about the Philippines.

Although the idea that 'race' marks difference and hierarchy is more familiar as a twenty-first-century idiom, we need to understand, too, how it marked commonalities and equivalence in order to understand its use and operation in this case. On the one hand, 'race' as a category, like 'people' or 'nation', could have what Anthony Milner has described in the context of colonial Malaya as 'egalitarian overtones', in that 'concern about the condition of the race is a concern not for an aristocratic elite but rather an entire community'.[10] In this mode of thinking, members of a race were of equal status, in relation to that race, in a way that members of a nation were in principle of equal status with respect to that nation. As Milner argues, the formal equivalence of members of a 'race' was reflected in how 'race' concerned 'the interests of the common people' and 'possesse[d] no necessary hierarchical implications'.[11] In this sense, the history of races was a kind of effort at history from below: the subject was collective and common, not individual or exceptional. This history of races, as divisions of human groupings, was the science of ethnology.

Of course, ideas about 'race' were not universally democratic. The vocabulary of race was often employed with a grammar of hierarchy, according to which some races were taken to be more advanced than others. Borders that marked racial difference could be drawn around the Philippines but also within it, marking some peoples of the Philippines as more advanced than others. The hierarchical grammar often employed with the vocabulary of race worked both for and against these intellectuals in their efforts to authorize the civilization of some peoples of the Philippines. On the one hand, some elite Filipinos could claim rights and status for a broader multilingual group on the basis that their 'people' or 'race' was distinct from but approaching the level of advanced European peoples, and distinct from and leaving behind others deemed more barbaric. Yet employing the vocabulary of race with the grammar of hierarchy brought liabilities as well, for the *ilustrados* were sometimes on the receiving end of racial discrimination and deprecation, and their claims to advancement were not always accepted by those invested in racialized thinking.[12] Paterno's writings highlight some of the ways that *ilustrado* writings manifest how ethnological sciences were often laden with a hierarchical politics that reinforced established narratives of civilization in contrast with the primitive.

Paterno's ways of conceiving of civilization as successive eras

Paterno's *Ancient Tagalog Civilization* (1887) and *The Itas* (1890) both purport to be works of scientific enquiry that treat the prehistory of the Philippines in terms of the cultural and racial groupings that Paterno (and others) thought existed among the then-contemporary Philippine population.[13] The distinction that was of most concern to Paterno in these works, and on which I focus in this chapter, is that which marked a difference between most of the lowland Catholic peoples of the Philippines on the one hand and the '*Negritos*', or darker-skinned animist peoples of the highlands on the other. The '*Negritos*' were viewed as primitive not only by the Spaniards but also by lowland Catholics. The latter, of which there were and are many different language groups aside from Tagalog, were referred to by Spaniards generically as '*indios*' (Indians) or '*indígenas*' (natives). The word '*indio*' at this point had come to have a particularly racist ring to it. When they sought administrative reforms and equal rights as Spaniards, most of the young *ilustrados* had in mind others like them – the *indígenas* whether Tagalog, Ilocano, Cebuano, etc., but not those they thought of as primitive '*Negritos*'. Though they would at times articulate solidarity with and concern for '*Negritos*', they expressed outrage when Spaniards conflated them with those whom they thought of as primitive.

In these two pieces of writing, Paterno engaged in complicated and innovative appropriations of scholarly and theoretical discourses, combining ideas from distinct traditions in novel ways. To better understand the distinctive nature of his use of French appropriations of evolutionary thinking, it is helpful to have a sense of some of the other discourses in which he wrote these narratives of the natural history of the Philippines. In addition to French evolutionary thinking, he used frameworks of 'universal' history (invoking at least two different formulations: one Catholic and another secular) and invoked Orientalist research (especially emphasizing spiritualist and mystical readings), bringing these scholarly discourses into conversation with migration-wave theories of prehispanic Philippine history. By doing this, he performed a complicated action of intellectual appropriation and innovation to theorize the relationship between peoples of the Philippines as well as their respective places in history.

The language of Paterno's writings shows his attachment to both contemporary scientific theories and Catholic models of history, an older idiom of universal civilization. Paterno confidently cited 'the law of progress', confirmed by 'the Philosophy of History', 'ethnological theory', and 'geographical theory' in support of his outline of Philippine history.[14] He used the outlines of 'universal' history, a concept and practice by which all of the world's peoples were placed within a grand historical schema that marked the rise and fall of successively advanced civilizations, to interpret ethnological data of Philippine history. Although the richly named 'universal' history was typically written from a particular perspective that was clearly European (the writings of G. W. F. Hegel come to mind), Paterno sought to rewrite it to incorporate the Philippines. His universal history sometimes sounded quite Catholic – as when he wrote that the study of Philippine 'prehistory' could show 'the progressive march of that Archipelago in the ways of Providence' – yet sometimes sounded secular.[15] In seeking and interpreting the data of 'prehistory', he wrote,

> it is necessary ... to study [the data] one and a hundred times, searching for their relations, similarities, and union amongst themselves or with those characteristic of other peoples, as the modern sciences demand; since in this mode those same data, etc. will rise to the heights where only Universal History is written, to the purest regions where only the spirit of Humanity lives and works. It matters a great deal to us that the Philippines is not excluded from the Universe.[16]

Paterno craved a history that was normative, a history that described not just descent and relation, but also progress and advance.

Paterno put together the outlines of universal history and explicitly racial theories to ennoble Philippine history and also to connect its peoples in a way that avoided tainting them all with primitiveness. He wanted to connect those peoples of the Philippines whom he and others marked as primitives to those whom he saw as 'advanced', without erasing the contrast between them that he took to be important. In this vein he concentrated in particular on the Ita (now generally called 'Aeta' – 'Negrito' people of the highlands of Luzon) as the primitives, and the Tagalogs as the advanced.[17] Paterno placed the Ita at the centre of Filipino *history*, though he contrasted *contemporary* Ita with 'advanced' Filipinos, and predicted the Ita's future extinction. He portrayed the Tagalogs as having incorporated the ancient Ita but also as having overcome them, because as a 'civilization' and 'race' the Tagalogs, he wrote, were inclined towards progress. The 'Tagalog' for Paterno was characteristically *filipino*, as in 'of the Philippines', but also ambiguously marked as the ontological centre of a broader 'Filipino' civilization-race. This greater Tagalog was both the culmination of prehispanic Philippine history as well as the agent of future Philippine advance. Paterno told a story in which the Ita were racially and culturally both 'other' to the more 'advanced' peoples of the Philippines, but also connected to them; the Tagalog people, in turn, were the epitome of the advanced peoples of the Philippines and inherently progressive.

Writing in a speculative mode, Paterno conceived of three eras of Philippine history, characterized in turn by 'the aborigines', 'the Tagalog civilization', and finally 'the Catholic civilization'.[18] In general terms, Paterno followed a theory, then widely accepted, according to which the Philippine islands had been peopled in prehistoric times by successive, racially distinct waves of migration from neighbouring land masses: first, dark-skinned peoples from Australia or New Guinea, and then lighter-skinned peoples, referred to as Malay or Malayan, from the Malay peninsula and neighbouring islands. The descendants of these distinct waves were thought to be identifiable as the dark-skinned 'Negritos' of the Philippine highlands on the one hand, and the lighter-skinned lowland (and Catholic) groups referred to by Spaniards as *indios*.[19] The basic framework of this account was already an old narrative that upheld a familiar-sounding hierarchy, in which the most-recently-arrived Spanish Catholic civilization was at the top, followed by the now-Catholic *indígenas* (who were taken to be racially Malay), and at the bottom were the dark-skinned, animist peoples supposed to have descended from the islands' earliest inhabitants. This account also purported to explain why the dark-skinned animist people lived in the highlands, effectively out of the reach of the Spanish colonial state – they had been pushed there out of the better lowland and coastal areas, it was thought, by the conquering superior peoples who came later. Notice that in this story the history of progress in the Philippines is driven by colonization, and its best qualities come from the most recent arrivals. No wonder, therefore, that by Paterno's time, this account was widely accepted among European scientists, and was also captured in a prominent Jesuit account of Philippine history written for use in the colony's secondary schools. Paterno borrowed the exact wording of this textbook, describing the 'Aetas, Etas or Itas, or as the Spanish call them, the Negritos' as the 'aborigines' of the Philippines who, of all 'the diverse races that are found in the Archipelago', seemed to be 'the first settlers of the country'.[20] In this account, race and racial traits were conceived in both biological and civilizational terms: the Malay invaders had a 'more robust constitution' and were 'endowed with a higher degree of culture', which explained and validated their successful conquest.[21]

Paterno's telling of this story of migration was distinct from others, however. He distinguished the Ita wave or era from the later Tagalog by characterizing the latter as those who had first achieved an actual 'civilization', whereas the former's historical era had no civilization. For Paterno, it was via civilization and culture that a race was superior or inferior, and so thrived or languished as a result. In this distinction, he may have been inspired by French formulations. French ethnology was especially concerned with and inflected by the language of civilization (by way of illustration, consider that the secretary general of the French Society of Anthropology from 1887 to 1902 had a chair in the history of civilizations).[22]

Paterno dedicated the bulk of his earlier work, *The Ancient Tagalog Civilization*, to interpreting the secrets of the titular civilization, which he referred to as the second epoch of Philippine history. The Tagalog epoch and Tagalog civilization were general terms in his arguments, of broad scope. On the one hand, the title phrase of the work 'Tagalog Civilization' connoted the ethnolinguistic group who often considered themselves, and were considered by many foreigners, to be the most advanced of the Philippines (and to which not coincidentally Paterno himself belonged). But for Paterno the Tagalog civilization was also a civilization broader than just Tagalog-speaking people, a civilization that he thought was common to many groups. Contrary to the practices of ethnological science, he did little to document the relationship between what might appear to be distinct groupings, and instead made broad claims about the Tagalog civilization, which he said had dominated the Philippines during this era.[23] Though he excluded '*Negritos*' from this civilization – which we will consider in greater detail below – he otherwise used the idea of the Tagalog civilization to unite the ancestors of Catholic Filipinos in all of their manifest ethnological diversity. Thus, his ancient Tagalog civilization, though specifically and narrowly named, was in his conception quite broad.

Most of his focus was on a rich and somewhat fanciful explication of this Tagalog civilization and in particular its religion, which he called alternatively 'Tagalism' (*Tagalismo*) or 'Bathalism' (*Bathalismo*), the latter deriving from Bathala, a prehispanic Tagalog divinity.[24] Arguing that prehispanic Tagalog religion was not animist, 'spiritist', or pantheist, he wrote that Bathalism was a religion on par with Catholicism, equally inspired by truth. He proved this by finding in Bathalism institutions, concepts, and figures that paralleled those of Catholicism, including the Catholic idea of God (Bathala) but also equivalents for Catholic saints, priests, cathedrals, heaven, hell, bishops, confession, friar orders, and even the virgin mother.[25] Paterno's attempts to show the equivalence between Catholicism and Bathalism (or Tagalism) went so far as to argue not just that Bathalism was as good as Catholicism, but also that Bathalism *was* Catholicism. Catholicism, he said, was present in the Philippines before the arrival of the Spaniards, albeit in a subtle, Oriental form.[26] Though he noted that Spaniards had, 'with arms in hand, brought to us knowledge of the True God', he posited that the seeds of Catholicism had indeed already been planted in the Tagalogs.[27] In arguing that Bathalism looked like Catholicism, Paterno drew on similar arguments made by seventeenth- and eighteenth-century Jesuit missionaries in China, who thought they found in Confucianism concepts similar to Catholicism's and even saw evidence of ancient

Christianity, of which contemporary practices were perversions.[28] These interpretations, written in an earlier century to show the great potential for Jesuit success in converting in their Asian territories, had been strongly disputed by Dominicans and Franciscans. Paterno took the claims that had been made earlier for Jesuits' purposes and translated them into the idiom of his own concern, which was to secure the position of the Tagalog civilization among the great civilizations of world history. In the process, these Jesuits' texts, which were written to burnish their organization's reputation in Rome, became part of an argument to enhance the reputation of the Tagalog civilization.

Paterno found not only Catholicism in Philippine prehistory; he likewise associated other grand traditions with the Tagalog civilization, which had the effect of further ennobling and placing it at the centre of universal history. He explained the presence of prehispanic proto-Catholicism by amassing evidence of the influence of Catholicism in other Asian cultures, and the influence of other Asian cultures in the Philippines. In amassing this evidence, he tended towards quantity rather than coherence. For instance, he wrote a section on Christian doctrines in China before the Christian era, and other sections connecting the Tagalog civilization or Tagalism with Brahma, Buddha, China, Persia, and Egypt, composing a somewhat cacophonous and oddly ahistorical account.[29] His sources here were largely French, of the Orientalist tradition of which he partook, a tradition with more narrow scholarly strands and also more broadly diffused in fashionable society. He positioned the Philippines, in particular the prehispanic Tagalog civilization, as a kind of missing link between the great civilizations of the West and the ancient ones of the East, and also as being the culmination of them all.

We have seen how Paterno re-purposed or revised narratives of successive and progressive civilizations in the Philippines, Jesuit accounts of latent Christianity in Asia, and Orientalist associations of the East with ancient grandeur. Now we will turn to look at how his writings incorporated French versions of arguments about race and evolution and, again, in the process transformed their purposes.

Paterno's race thinking and its French antecedents

The ancient Tagalog civilization was in Paterno's account central to the unfolding of the world's ancient history, showing by association that contemporary Tagalog civilization was noble, distinguished, and glorious. Paterno portrayed contemporary 'Tagalogness' not only in terms of great civilization, but also – and significantly – in terms of biological race. The greatness of the contemporary Tagalog was due to the people's racial quality of being able to change and progress, rather than by its continuity with a great ancient past. Finally, the Tagalog race was for him importantly a mixed race. Paterno's ideas reflect his creative appropriations of what was at the time cutting-edge French thinking about social history that was drawn from theories of evolution.

As with Social Darwinism, Social Lamarckianism appropriated creatively and selectively from a theory of biological evolution in order to explain contemporary social struggles. Whereas Darwin identified natural selection as the mechanism by which species changed over many successive generations, Lamarck theorized that there was a natural drive towards increasing complexity and refinement, and that species' behaviours, in response to their environment, changed the traits of their bodies in ways that would be passed on to successive generations. This theory gave particular importance to the effects of use versus disuse. That is, disused organs would atrophy and disappear; those that were exercised would become more robust. In France, these theories from the natural sciences were taken up and developed by theorists of human life, behaviour, and diversity to explain what they thought were the racial divisions of humans and the qualities supposedly inherent in those racial groupings. Ideas of racial hierarchy had been long established in France, but in the 1870s and 1880s those ideas had become particularly complicated and internally contested. Specialists argued about which kinds of markers were the significant 'racial' ones. Many believed physiological and biological traits were the significant ones for marking race (and here, the shape of the head was a particularly fashionable index, but the more familiar hair colour, skin colour, and eye colour were data points as well). Others held that a race was defined by cultural or civilizational traits. And though everyone seemed to agree that humans were divided into races and therefore that one could speak in terms of whether a race was pure or not, they disagreed about whether such purity itself was a benefit or liability to the population that exhibited it.[30]

At one level, these debates were in form like any scientific controversy in a time of theoretical innovation and contestation. But the timing mattered politically, too. In France of the 1870s and 1880s, stung by defeat in the Franco-Prussian War and eyeing a rising power in newly united Germany, anxieties about Frenchness mapped very neatly on to arguments that analysed data which purported to measure how racially mixed France was, what its racial components were, and whether any of them, or mixture itself, was a reason for France's apparent weakness. Many of these arguments did not explicitly address whether French Jews were racially the same as other French people, or whether or not they were inferior, but such questions and their contemporary political consequences lurked not too far behind.[31] In Paris, these arguments were likely carried beyond the academies and into society's parlours. Even as far away as Madrid, an ambitious and pretentious young man such as Paterno might be conversant with such ideas, particularly if he wanted to associate himself with the grandeur of French society and the relative sophistication of French science. With this quick sketch in mind, we will now turn back to Paterno's writing.

In order to arrive at his account of the Tagalog as a mixed race, Paterno began with a story of benevolent conquest. In this account, one race did not just conquer the other and push it out. This was a kinder, gentler kind of conquest – a conquest of peaceful and progressive mixing. The invaders 'learned the language and the habits of the country on which they set foot, with enthusiasm and the desire to please'. They 'solicited [its] women, and acquired family and friendships' 'quickly blending among the diverse established tribes'. The result was 'a new race that was mixed in peace with the ancient settlers [*antiguos pobladores*]', so in this account the conquest inaugurated not just a new era, but also a new race.[32]

This new Tagalog race was dynamic and therefore superior *because* it was mixed, and it was with this emphasis that Paterno's work took a markedly specific but creative derivative turn. In Paterno's account, the Tagalog were the robust and progressive mixed race of the Philippines, on par with those of Western Europe. He explained,

> it is known that races that do not mix degenerate in the course of time, and then disappear. On the contrary ... those that mix – the mestizo races, like the Spanish, the French, the German, the English, in general 'those of the western countries of Europe' – that ... 'are found to be so intermixed that none could claim an authentic genealogy' – [those races] live [to be] robust and powerful.[33]

Here Paterno began quoting extensively from a work published just the previous year in Paris, Yves Guyot's preface to *Problems of History*. Guyot was a classical economist who found in evolutionary ideas the basis for the laissez-faire economic principles that he favoured. As a local politician and later a member of the national legislature, he had been a member of the radical faction of the Republicans. However, his economic ideas increasingly widened a gap between himself and most on the left.[34] He also wrote contemporary socioeconomic analyses, and although he was not an anthropologist nor did he write extensively about race, he was one of many French figures who used Lamarckian evolutionary language to treat social, historical, or political questions, and whose ideas Paterno found useful for his own purposes.

Paterno continued his extended quotation from Guyot, which itself illustrates Guyot's appropriation of Lamarckian evolutionary thought: 'The most complicated organs are perfected through the accumulation of innumerable variations, slight though they may be; the same thing happens in social organisms'. Here, Guyot (and so Paterno) connected the particularly Lamarckian idea of evolutionary progress as an inevitable force towards increasing complexity and perfection to the idea of racial progress through the dynamism of mixture. The biological language that describes such *mestizo* races as 'robust and powerful' is more than metaphorical – the idea of race being invoked here is one both civilizational and biological. Paterno continued to quote Guyot's words approvingly as the latter turned to another way to illustrate the value of dynamism, progress, and mixed races, by way of contrasting them with their opposite, 'the static civilizations of Asia'. Drawing on a classic Orientalist conception of Asian societies as unchanging, Guyot (and so Paterno) wrote that 'it is a disgrace for the Chinese, the Arabs, and the sects inhabiting Indostan, to have conserved their hegemony'.[35] Although

Paterno quoted Guyot approvingly and at length, these statements about the virtues of mixed races and their contrast with 'static civilizations of Asia' meant very different things in the contexts of Guyot's and Paterno's writing.

Guyot was engaged in an ongoing general argument in France about whether it was or should be a racially pure nation. For those worried about French racial stock, the anxieties in the 1880s would have been the threat of the Germans on the one hand (Were they of superior stock? They had more blond people with longer, narrower heads!) and French Jews on the other (Such dark hair and round heads!). One way Guyot criticized the position of those calling for racial purity in France was by characterizing their position as essentially Oriental. 'Heterogeneity is one of the causes of the strength of France, and the men that work to destroy it, take on not only an impossible task, but also a retrograde one. No doubt they seek to take us [back] to the static civilizations of Asia.'[36] By characterizing his opponent's position as 'Oriental', Guyot's call for France to embrace its mixedness was positioned as a conservative call to make France more like itself – to make itself more purely French, if you will, by abandoning the idea of purity.[37] We might read this as one form of racist thinking opposing another.

Guyot cast aside anxieties of national inferiority by appealing to the sense that France was of course at the forefront of the world. He used this sense to argue, for his French audience, that racial mixture was good and essentially French, and that calls to purify France racially were a danger to the French race. Paterno, on the other hand, in translating these ideas from French to Spanish also translated them from one political context to another. In his formulation, the idea that European races were advanced in turn supported the idea that racial mixture was good, which therefore vindicated the Tagalog race as a robust and superior race. Unlike their 'disgraced' Oriental neighbours, Tagalogs had not 'conserved their hegemony' – they were a 'robust and powerful' race like the French, German, English, or Spanish and therefore on par with the European. Thus, when taken along with Paterno's earlier work extolling the greatness of the ancient Tagalog civilization, we see Tagalogs emerging as the best of both worlds: they were connected to distinguished ancients, but they were also robust and mixed.

Again, we might read this as one form of racist thinking opposing another, though the logic is different from the way in which Guyot deployed Orientalist ideas to disparage racial purity. Unlike the Frenchman, Paterno most strongly contrasted the robustness of racial mixture not with reference to 'the Chinese', 'the Arabs', or 'the sects inhabiting Indostan', but with the present-day Ita people of the Philippines. The contrast between the Tagalog race and the contemporary Ita was the most dramatic of his work, even though his theory attributed the origins of the Tagalog race to a mix with the ancient Ita. Whereas some of the ancient Ita had mixed with the superior invaders to beget the new mixed race, others had instead 'retreated, appealing to arms', and who 'vanquished … took refuge in the harshness of the mountains'.[38] This Ita people, 'abhorring union or mixing with others, wastes its existence in the most degenerate isolation', and this was the patrimony of the contemporary Ita.[39] In contrast to the dynamism of the mixed-race legacy that had its apex in the Tagalog language and culture, 'the pure Ita race has remained resting in [its] path, and its language has remained stationary'.[40] Contemporary Ita were not 'the surviving remains of cultured ancestors, but rather peoples who have fallen behind, who, because of particular circumstances, have remained arrested in one of those stages through which humanity passed in the infancy of its life, a ship of civilization that dropped anchor in the ocean of life.'[41]

In characterizing the contemporary Ita as the racial and cultural opposite to the Tagalog – pure as opposed to the Tagalog's mixed, and static in contrast to the Tagalog's dynamism – Paterno also borrowed other formulations from French evolutionary social thought. He wrote of the contemporary Ita as an ailing, decaying body whose natural death approached:

> By continuous isolation during long centuries ... [this people has] not felt the necessity of modifying its type of life, has not acquired the aptitude of transforming itself, has become accustomed to sloth, stasis, inaction, petrifaction, in other words, to not progressing in the moral order, to perishing in the physical order; it is a people that has nourished itself for a long time with a few unchanging and poor ideas, leaving it very weak, and now it is difficult for it to move, to work, to carry out any effort or regenerative project, and is therefore condemned to disappear before the peoples that know how to progress, that live, work, and march forward.[42]

In this formulation, the Ita were condemned not by their contemporaries (be they Tagalog or Spanish) but by their cultural inability to transform themselves, by their atrophy as a people. Paterno's language of atrophy and decay versus regeneration and progress derived from French Lamarckian social thought, but also incorporated Darwinian elements that had an affinity with other French evolutionary thinkers.

Most prominent and controversial among such thinkers was Vacher de Lapouge. Lapouge went on to publish a controversial work on the Aryan during the Dreyfus Affair, but as early as 1886 gave a series of lectures, published shortly thereafter, in which he predicted the inevitable death of entire races, drawing on Larmarckian ideas of adaptation and incorporating Darwinian principles of natural selection. In one of these lectures, he asserted that in the future 'superior races will substitute themselves by force for the human groups retarded in evolution'.[43] Paterno had no direct connection with Lapouge as far as we know, but not long after, he too envisioned the inevitable death of entire races. For Paterno, it would be a product not of force but of internal atrophy, again echoing the theme of use and disuse in Lamarckian thought. The trope of the inevitable death of an inferior, retrograde race suggested an inevitability that allowed Paterno both a romantic attachment to the ancients as well as utter abandonment of the contemporary: the contemporary Ita were one of those inferior races 'retarded in evolution', and the Tagalog, the superior, was capable of adaptation.

Paterno borrowed with seemingly equal approval the frameworks of French writers who were part of the same general argument, but not on the same page, in the French context. Recall that Guyot, who claimed that robust races were mixed, criticized those who championed the idea of a racially pure France. Guyot's explicit target was, as indicated in a footnote, Joseph-Arthur de Gobineau, the famous author of modern racist thought, whose *Essai* had just come out in a second edition in 1884.[44] Gobineau had conceived of human history as a series of contests between races in which the victor was always diminished by mixing with the vanquished, and thought France's major threat was its internal racial impurity.[45] Lapouge, who later became a champion of Gobineau, was probably already the most prominent and provocative advocate of the idea that some races were superior to others and that France's future was compromised by its mix of inferior stock with the superior. Guyot argued, contra Lapouge and Gobineau, that *mixed* races were more vital and robust than pure ones. What is of particular importance is the way that the antagonisms between these two different versions of French social evolutionary thought – Guyot's on the one hand, and Lapouge's on the other – are smoothed away in Paterno's refashioning.

Not ancestors, but specimens

Paterno's 1887 work *The Ancient Tagalog Civilization* focused on his beloved civilization, whereas his 1890 work *The Itas* was an exercise in demonstrating his familiarity with scientific theories, a string of references in his footnotes listing works whose erudition he hoped to associate with his own work. By characterizing his own Tagalog and Filipino self as indubitably modern, accomplished, and scientific, he could expose what he thought to be primitive in the Philippines without risk of contaminating the country's reputation. The Ita were the primitive other of the Philippines, safely consigned to historical death, and so it was as a scientific hero that he offered his study documenting what he predicted would soon disappear.

Though Paterno stressed the difference between the ancient ancestral Ita and contemporary Ita, he thought that study of the latter could reveal something about the former and, so, about the Tagalogs' own past. It was important for contemporary advanced peoples to understand the contemporary primitive, for 'the condition and customs of savage life [*vida salvaje*] are similar in many aspects ... to those of our own ancestors in an age now very distant [and] the studies of stationary peoples illustrate and explain many customs and ideas, particularly those nebulous and occult, encrusted in the spirits of advanced peoples like fossils in rock'.[46] The Ita were analogous to an inanimate specimen for the study of natural history, which could be studied 'as a geological medal with the date rubbed out, buried among the evolutions of humanity, and its study will awaken us, as if it were the Prehistory of the Filipino people [*pueblo filipino*]'.[47] Thus, the living Ita were not exactly the 'Prehistory of the Filipino people', but they were something like that: isolated elements of their 'customs and ideas' remained buried deep in the 'spirit' of advanced Tagalogs, the 'Filipino people'. Paterno used here a narrative of progress and the metaphors of archaeology both to lay claim to a past and also to affirm its distance from the present.

Sometimes, Paterno would write in more benevolent if equally paternalistic terms about the ancient Ita's value. Though progress was the overall shape of history, every stage in that history had its own particular contribution (cf. Hegel or Herder). Like other 'simple and first civilizations', Paterno wrote, the Ita had 'something of value in itself, and always something new that is not found in any other'.[48] In this vein, Paterno enjoined his reader to appreciate primitive peoples' contributions to human history:

> [F]ar from disdaining inferior civilizations in view of the superior ones, we look at them with interest and we study them with love, as new and original examples of human activity, following the steps of the learned naturalist, who does not disdain moss and lichen in view of the slender palm or the sturdy pine; since true History does not consist so much in the succession of facts, as in the manifestation of human activity, in the universality of the investigations, extending to all thought, all language, all tradition of man, or rather his beliefs, customs, laws, sciences, arts, letters, in all places and all times.[49]

Paterno employed a plural conception of what we today might call 'cultures' but which he called 'civilizations' – a conception that admitted both difference and equivalence, even if it also retained the patronizing tone of confident superiority. This was a smaller-scale and more intimate version of the more general sort of claim that a European scholar might make with regard to the patrimony of an earlier and 'other' civilization without risking taint by association. Paterno attempted to claim the more primitive Ita as the patrimony of the advanced Filipino people, simultaneously confirming their primitivism and their value, and underscoring both connection and distance. The Ita belonged to another time and had to be judged accordingly: 'in order to understand them ... it is necessary for us to cast off all our customs and habits, and to approach [them] with no ... preoccupations of any kind'.[50]

The distance between the 'us' and the 'them', and the relativist bent of the model that he adopted, allowed Paterno to criticize 'European civilization' ever so gently in the voice of an imagined other. His criticisms of 'European civilization' are fleeting but powerful; perhaps more interesting is the way that he carefully wrapped these criticisms in a bed of qualifications that distances him from them. He began this passage by acknowledging that 'for those born in and accustomed to European civilization, there is nothing superior to it in any place or time', establishing from the outset the primacy of this position, and only gently qualifying it by casting it as an insider view.[51] The relativism of such qualitative judgements becomes more prominent as the passage proceeds, and the reader is asked to shift perspectives: 'on the other bank of the river ... the fundamental laws change'.[52] Inviting his reader to imagine along with him what the world looked like from the perspective of the Ita, he wrote that '[t]he Itas have looked at Christian civilization through their own lenses; and under their color, our civilization has nothing admirable nor appealing'.[53] Instead, in the view of the Ita from the opposite riverbank, 'the great European civilization appears as a deceitful siren ... Its morals are hypothetical; its justice ... rests on brute force, and its theoretical preachings of liberty, progress and wellbeing produce only slavery, anarchy, and tribute [*tributo*, compulsory payments to a ruler]'.[54] Here Paterno voiced a criticism of 'European civilization' as being hypocritical and indeed the author of violence. Taken on its own, this criticism would make a powerful case for Paterno as a more radical critic of colonialism. However, Paterno articulated these strident criticisms of 'our civilization' by placing them in the mouths of those understood as primitive, distancing himself from such perspectives. It is perhaps a paradox that he also cemented his position as among those truly 'of' the superior European civilization precisely through demonstrating his ability to see the primitives' point of view sympathetically and with a patronizing condescension. By evaluating the 'other' and understanding though not accepting its point of view, he performed the superiority of the truly civilized.

Finally, the study of the Ita was valuable for the progress of the advanced peoples of the Philippines because it would help the latter to recognize what needed to change or be left behind. Here, Paterno returned to distinctively Lamarckian tropes. For the advanced Filipino peoples to fulfil their promise, he wrote, they had to 'know to adapt their ancient traditions to Progress' and 'succeed in harmonizing their ancient habits and customs with new ideas'.[55] The Philippines was well-suited to this, not only because it had '*the faculty of adapting itself* to the new conditions of existence with which it is presented.' Calling again on theories of racial strength through mixing, Paterno explained that in the Philippines, 'ancient races are gathered in its bosom, like races rejuvenated by active and hardworking blood', which have a 'powerful action of advance'.[56] In order for that active and powerfully advancing blood to complete the natural progress against the 'hereditary influences [of the ancient races] that work in the contrary sense', advanced peoples of the Philippines needed 'knowledge of their traditions [*tradiciones*]; in obeying them and knowing when to get rid of them in time, when they have become useless or prejudicial, lies the secret of giving life and advance[ment] to that numerous people [*pueblo*]'.[57] This art or skill – knowing when to obey tradition and when to abandon it – was precisely what the descendants of mixed race had demonstrated. Through study of their own primitive past, the advanced people of the Philippines could ensure that their trajectory continued upward, and ultimately they could arrive at the 'brilliant, glorious future' to which they were 'called'.[58] The story of the Tagalog-Filipino people is one of historical and future triumph, with the present marked as a key and urgent moment in which the correct decisions must be made to hasten the (right) future.

Conclusion: futures of the past

Paterno embraced the concept of race-as-culture. Like others who found in models of evolutionary biology tools for thinking about social and political life, he saw 'race' as a meaningful unit of analysis. But it was a race's cultural features – its civilization – that were most meaningful for him. Those cultural features were for him biological, in a sense – remember his language about the 'active and hardworking blood' with 'powerful action of advance'. But this was a biology not particularly attached to physiognomy, and it was a cultural biology that was also at times (selectively) mutable and adaptable.[59]

It is tempting to attribute Paterno's praise for racial mixing to his own family's *mestizo* status. However, in his writing he never referred to Chinese patrimony in the Philippines, the most prominent manifestation of *mestizaje* in Manila. Whether one reads this as a lack of interest or as studious avoidance of an uncomfortable subject, it is a notable absence. Yet to read *mestizaje* in Paterno's text too exclusively in these terms would be reductive, for Paterno was also responding to and using French scholarly arguments about racial mixing and racial purity that were infused with political significance, in addition to the outlines of 'universal history' and its attendant validation of colonial rule.

Paterno took debates in French anthropology, sociology, and economics and used them to make an argument about the Tagalog 'race', which accommodated the idea of Ita ancestry and overcame a sense that primitive ('*Negrito*' or 'black') ancestry was a liability. It did so, of course, by insisting that primitive *cultural* traits had already been exterminated. Thus, this is an example of how 'universal' principles (of natural selection and racial strength), articulated in and out of local political configurations (ideas of race and fitness in late nineteenth-century France), became available, precisely through their articulation as universal, to quite different and distinct local arguments (about race and fitness in the Philippines). Although the model was the idea of the French as a race of mixed-race origins that was superior in civilization to its ancestors, the idea, stated in general terms, could be applied by Paterno to the Tagalogs.

Paterno's appropriations of contemporary French ethnological and anthropological writings may be an uncomfortable reminder that the political history of race thinking is as complex as it is troubling. This colonial subject used the idioms of civilizational advance and racial thinking to promote the 'advanced' peoples of the Philippines in order to put them at the helm of the ship of history alongside the 'robust' races of Europe. It troubled one set of colonial and racialist hierarchies, but it deeply underscored others. Paterno's opinions that veered towards natural genocide – that is, the idea that retrograde races would naturally die off and disappear – resonate particularly strongly with the way indigenous Americans were being thought of by many white Americans around the same time, especially in the United States. Probably most white Americans of the 1890s envisioned the future of their country as one in which indigenous Americans had disappeared, whether via genocide, cultural genocide, or because (as Paterno thought of the Ita) they were simply destined to collectively wither and die. Perhaps no wonder, therefore, that Paterno saw opportunities for affinities between the civilized peoples of the Philippines and the new American colonizers. Early American administrations in the Philippines pronounced on what to do with the uncivilized highland peoples, and American anthropologists scrambled to categorize and catalogue these new additions to the collection of tribes under American control, inspection, and tutelage. But the affinities between Paterno's and American ideas have limits. Although Paterno predicted a future extinction of those whom he took to be indigenous primitives, and narrated their coming extinction in disturbing terms, his vision involved no deliberate state-sponsored violence like that which had long been practised in the United States against American Indians. In comparison to that large-scale racial genocide, his vision in these works of the extermination of racial primitives was one in which there were no aggressors.[60]

Paterno's peers sometimes privately mocked his pretentions and derided the dilettantism of his scholarship. Many of his peers also wrote critically of Spaniards' racial prejudices, and sometimes even mocked the idea of racial superiority or inferiority. But more often, like Paterno, they countered racial prejudice with evidence of the civilization and advancement of the 'cultivated' people of the Philippines. Paterno set himself off from his peers by his appropriation of French evolutionary thought and the stridency of his conviction that the primitive peoples of the Philippines were doomed to extinction. But like him, most of his peers also drew contrasts between themselves, as exemplars of Philippine advancement and readiness for political rights, and the primitives of the Philippines, whom they characterized as needing a paternal guiding hand.

Notes

1 Resil Mojares's *Brains of the Nation: Pedro Paterno, T. H. Pardo de Tavera, Isabelo de los Reyes and the Production of Modern Knowledge* (Quezon City: Ateneo de Manila University Press, 2006) is the most comprehensive study of Paterno's life and work to date, as well as the most important work on *ilustrado* thought more generally. Mojares also nicely encapsulates the historiography assessing Paterno (see esp. 3–4).

2 Barbara Arniel, 'The Wild Indian's Venison: John Locke's Theory of Property and English Colonialism in America', *Political Studies*, 44: 1 (1996), 60–74; Vanita Seth, *Europe's Indians: Producing Racial Difference 1500–1900* (Durham, NC: Duke University Press, 2010); Uday Singh Mehta, *The Anxiety of Freedom: Imagination and Individuality in Locke's Political Thought* (Ithaca, NY: Cornell University Press, 1992).

3 On the uptake of Darwin and the Lamarckian versions of social evolutionary theory in France, see Linda L. Clark, *Social Darwinism in France* (Tuscaloosa: University of Alabama Press, 1984); Freeman G. Henry, 'Anti-Darwinism in France: Science and the

Myth of the Nation', *Nineteenth-Century French Studies*, 27: 3/4 (1999), 290–304; and Jean Gayon 'Darwin and Darwinism in France before 1900', in Michael Ruse, ed., *The Cambridge Encyclopedia of Darwin and Evolutionary Thought* (Cambridge: Cambridge University Press, 2013), 243–9. A helpful primer on Lamarck and Darwin is Michael Ruse, 'Evolution before Darwin', in Michael Ruse, ed., *The Cambridge Encyclopedia of Darwin and Evolutionary Thought* (Cambridge: Cambridge University Press, 2013), 39–45.

4 For more on the *ilustrados* and their scholarship in general, in addition to Mojares's *Brains of the Nation* and my *Orientalists, Propagandists, and Ilustrados*, see Benedict R. O'G. Anderson, *Under Three Flags: Anarchism and the Anti-Colonial Imagination* (London: Verso, 2005); and the foundational work by John N. Schumacher, S. J., *The Propaganda Movement, 1880–1895: The Creation of a Filipino Consciousness, the Making of the Revolution*, rev. edn (Manila: Ateneo de Manila University Press, 1997).

5 For more on the *ilustrados*, their propaganda work, and the late nineteenth-century Spanish colonial context, see the works referenced in note 4, above.

6 This biographical sketch is drawn from Mojares, *Brains of the Nation*, 3–12; Mojares also treats Paterno's writings extensively, 43–102.

7 Pedro Alejandrino Paterno, *La antigua civilización tagálog* (Madrid: Manuel G. Hernández, Impresor de la Real Casa, 1887); Pedro Alejandrino Paterno, *Los Itas* (Madrid: los Sucesores de Cuesta, 1890).

8 For a broader discussion of *ilustrado* writings and the ethnological sciences, see Thomas, *Orientalists, Propagandists, and Ilustrados*, ch. 3.

9 Michel Foucault, *Society Must Be Defended: Lectures at the Collège de France, 1975–76*, trans. David Macey (New York: Picador, 2003), 76. Foucault refers to 'race struggle', but I find the formulation helpful for thinking about race discourse in general.

10 Anthony Milner, *The Invention of Politics in Colonial Malaya: Contesting Nationalism and the Expansion of the Public Sphere* (Cambridge: Cambridge University Press, 1994), 52.

11 *Ibid.*, 53.

12 I build on others' work here; in particular, see Filomeno V. Aguilar, Jr., 'Tracing Origins: *Ilustrado* Nationalism and the Racial Science of Migration Waves', *Journal of Asian Studies*, 64:3 (2005), 605–37; Mojares, *Brains of the Nation*, esp. 83–8, 298–300; and Paul A. Kramer, *The Blood of Government: Race, Empire, the United States, and the Philippines* (Chapel Hill: University of North Carolina Press, 2006), esp. 51–73.

13 Paterno, *Itas*; Paterno, *Antigua civilización*. Concerning these two works in particular, see also Mojares, *Brains of the Nation*, 46–52, 56–9, though he analyses their significance along with Paterno's other works (69–102), and the significance of *ilustrado* works more broadly (383–505).

14 Paterno, *Itas*, 64.

15 *Ibid.*, 65. Though the more secular 'Universal History' was still deeply Christian (e.g. Hegel or Herder), the Church was hostile to it.

16 *Ibid.*, 2–3.

17 I will follow Paterno and use the term 'Ita' in this chapter.

18 These are listed originally under headings referring to the three epochs: 'La de los aborígenes', 'La de la civilización tagala', and 'La de la civilización católica'. Paterno, *Antigua civilización*, 2.

19 For more on the racial wave migration theory, see Thomas, *Orientalists, Propagandists, and Ilustrados*, 61–2, and Aguilar, 'Tracing Origins'.

20 Paterno, *Antigua civilización*, 3. Translations are my own unless otherwise indicated. Paterno quoted here (without specific attribution but with a footnote) from the introduction of the Jesuit text for secondary education: P. Francisco X. Baranera,

Compendio de la Historia de Filipinas (Manila: Imprenta de los del Pais, 1878). Smita Lahiri has shown that this narrative was adopted in friar writings at least as early as 1874. (Smita Lahiri, 'Rhetorical Indios: Propagandists and Their Publics in the Spanish Philippines', *Comparative Studies in Society and History*, 49: 2 [2007], esp. 262). Paterno followed the prologue of the Baranera textbook, which he would have read as a student at the Jesuit's secondary school in Manila. Baranera's Spanish-Jesuit story had used a racial-civilizational rubric (of successive migration waves as advancement) to posit Spanish-Catholic civilization as the culmination of Philippine history; in Paterno's modification, the Tagalog people were both the ancient apex and those destined to bring a new height to Filipino-Catholic civilisation.

21 Paterno, *Antigua civilización*, 4, taken verbatim from Baranera, *Compendio*, VIII.

22 Clark, *Social Darwinism in France*, 140. For more on the rifts in French ethnological and ethnographical theory, see also Emmanuelle Sibeud, 'The Metamorphosis of Ethnology in France, 1839–1930', in Henrika Kukulick, ed., *A New History of Anthropology* (Malden: Blackwell, 2008), 96–110; and Joy Harvey, 'Evolutionism Transformed: Positivists and Materialists in the *Société d'anthropologie de Paris* from Second Empire to Third Republic', in David Oldroyd and Ian Langham, eds., *The Wider Domain of Evolutionary Thought* (Dordrecht: D. Reidel, 1983), 289–305.

23 In another work, for example, he referred to the Bagobos, an animist people who lived on the slopes of Mount Apo in Mindanao, as 'Tagalogs of Mindanao (tagálos de Mindanao)'. Pedro Alejandrino Paterno, 'El cristianismo en la antigua civilización tagalog (continuación)', *La solidaridad*, 15 September 1892, 803.

24 Paterno, *Antigua civilización*, 53, 77.

25 *Ibid.*, 35, 41, 67–8, 72, 143–5, 147–8.

26 *Ibid.*, 145–51.

27 *Ibid.*, 31.

28 Paterno cited the example of Father Tachard, a seventeenth-century French Jesuit in Siam who had sought to convert the Siamese court (and thus the Thai people). His source was Luis de Estrada, *Cuadro geografico, histórico, administrativo y político de la India en 1858* (Madrid: Imprenta y Estereotipia de M. Rivadeneyra, 1858). Writing in the wake of news of the 'Sepoy Mutiny' (Indian uprising, rebellion, revolt, or revolution, in 1857–58), Estrada stressed how little had been published in Spanish about India. On the Jesuits in India and China and the 'Chinese rites' controversy, see Lewis A. Maverick, *China, a Model for Europe* (San Antonio: Paul Anderson, 1946); Jonathan Spence, *The Question of Hu* (New York: Vintage, 1989); Joan-Pau Rubiés, 'The Spanish Contribution to the Ethnology of Asia in the Sixteenth and Seventeenth Centuries', *Renaissance Studies*, 17: 3 (2003), 418–48. The best known of these Jesuitical texts was Du Halde's; his audience was broad, and he was a significant source for both Montesquieu and Voltaire when they wrote about the East. Voltaire, *The Philosophy of History* (1765) (New York: Philosophical Library, 1965); Montesquieu, *Spirit of the Laws*, trans. Thomas Nugent (New York: Macmillan, 1949).

29 Paterno, *Antigua civilización*, 53–81, 152–68, 175–6, 182–206.

30 Clark, *Social Darwinism in France*, esp. 138; Chris Manias, *Race, Science, and the Nation: Reconstructing the Ancient Past in Britain, France and Germany* (New York: Routledge, 2013), esp. ch. 6.

31 In general, this sketch is drawn from Clark, *Social Darwinism in France*, esp. 139, 144–5 (on Lapouge), 147–51 (on anxieties about the race of Frenchmen), 138–40, 152 (on *l'Homme* and criticism of Lapouge); Manias, *Race, Science, and the Nation*, esp. 215–16 (on Lapouge); and Henry, 'Anti-Darwinism in France'. A later example of French evolutionary-anthropological race thinking was articulated in 1900 by Paul Topinard,

already a prominent French anthropologist during the 1870s and 1880s, who 'stated explicitly that Jews were not a separate race and called the "French race" a mixture of three "peoples"'. By 1900, the Dreyfus Affair had dramatically brought these issues into the mainstream French political discourse. Clark, *Social Darwinism in France*, 140; see also Manias, *Race, Science and the Nation*, ch. 7.

32 Paterno, *Itas*, 226.

33 Paterno, *Antigua civilización*, 3–4. My translation derives from Paterno, but he translates from Yves Guyot, 'Préface', in Paul Mougeolle, *Les problèmes de l'histoire* (Paris: C. Reinwald, 1886), xi. Paterno follows most closely Joseph Montano's formulation of three (as opposed to two) racially distinct successive waves: Negrito, Indonesian, and Malay. Paterno, *Itas*, 27; cf. J. Montano, 'Rapport à M. le Ministre de L'instruction Publique sur une Mission aux Îles Philippines et en Malaisie (1879–1881)'. *Archives des missions scientifiques et littéraires, 3e serie* XI (1885), 308.

34 On Guyot, see Clark, *Social Darwinism in France*, 62–4, 159, 165, and Harvey, 'Evolutionism Transformed', 301–2.

35 Guyot, 'Préface', xi, as quoted in Paterno, *Antigua civilización*, 4.

36 *Ibid.*

37 In this formulation I am inspired by and indebted to Joyce Zonana's argument that Western feminism has often portrayed patriarchy as Eastern, therefore rendering radical demands for its abolition in the West as conservative calls for the West to be more like itself. Joyce Zonana, 'The Sultan and the Slave: Feminist Orientalism in the Structure of Jane Eyre', *Signs: Journal of Women and Culture in Society*, 18: 3 (1993), 592–615.

38 Paterno, *Itas*, 228.

39 Paterno, *Antigua civilización*, 3. Paterno probably borrowed from an earlier work by Montano the idea that the Ita were racially pure; Montano had noted that some Negritos, having successfully fled from the invading races, had conserved their pure blood. Montano, 'Rapport', 310. Elsewhere Paterno borrowed nearly verbatim from J. Montano, *Voyage aux Philippines et en Malaisie* (Paris: Librairie Hachette et Cie., 1886), 310.

40 Paterno, *Itas*, 229.

41 *Ibid.*, 63.

42 *Ibid.*, 46–7.

43 Lapouge, quoted in Clark, *Social Darwinism in France*, 145.

44 Guyot, 'Préface', x–xi.

45 Clark, *Social Darwinism in France*, 148; Michael D. Biddiss, *Father of Racist Ideology: The Social and Political Thought of Count Gobineau* (New York: Weybright and Talley, 1970), 112–31.

46 Paterno, *Itas*, 5.

47 *Ibid.*, 65.

48 *Ibid.*, 5.

49 *Ibid.*, 5–6.

50 *Ibid.*, 59.

51 *Ibid.*, 58.

52 *Ibid.*

53 *Ibid.*, 59.

54 *Ibid.*, 58.

55 *Ibid.*, 4.

56 *Ibid.*, 3–4; emphasis in original.

57 *Ibid.*, 3, 4.
58 *Ibid.*, 4.
59 cf. Bankimchandra's conception of Hindu culture as valuable but also mutable: Partha Chatterjee, *Nationalist Thought and the Colonial World: A Derivative Discourse?* (Minneapolis: University of Minnesota Press, 1986), 57, 62, 64–6.
60 On American period racial thinking, and in particular as it resonated with US racial politics, see Kramer, *The Blood of Government.*

8

Colonial hesitation, appropriation, and citation: Qāsim Amīn, empire, and saying 'no'

Murad Idris

In a weak and servile nation, the word 'no' is little used.

– Qāsim Amīn[1]

Saying 'no' and colonised thought

The above epigraph appears in *Aphorisms* (*Kalimāt*), a posthumously published collection of notes and maxims by Qāsim Amīn (1863–1908). An Egyptian jurist, political theorist, social critic, and supposed feminist, Amīn bemoaned the absence of the word 'no'. Its absence, he implied, emblematised Egypt's weakness and servile acquiescence, whereas its presence would constitute a powerful refusal and reversal of impotence. As a wealthy Egyptian with an aristocratic Ottoman background, Amīn studied for four years in France and soon after became a judge in Egypt. He went on to help found Cairo University, establishing his legacy as a thinker who drew a theoretical and practical connection between education and civilisational progress.

The one who says 'no' claims the authority to reject and the power to negate. The colonised's refusal might negate particular colonial prohibitions or the colonial relationship as a whole. As Frantz Fanon writes in *Black Skin, White Masks*, 'man is a *yes*', an affirmation of life and dignity, and 'man is also a *no*. *No* to scorn of man. *No* to degradation of man. *No* to exploitation of man. *No* to the butchery of what is most human in man: freedom.'[2] Previously unable to say 'no', or prevented from saying it, the colonised becomes powerful and free. Such an utterance would be an opposite of what James C. Scott calls the weapons of the weak; farting silently as the emperor passes by, or shuffling one's feet to slow down a march, do not fundamentally alter the political structure.[3] Instead, saying 'no' can be a weapon that calls its speaker's will and power into being. It would represent one form of colonised agency that resonates with idealised constructions of anti-colonial resistance.

This is not the case with Amīn. He calls for 'no', but his writings do not contain a direct refusal of colonialism. Even when he is critical of European commentators and practices, he is far from a subversive, anti-colonial intellectual who directly confronts the metropole. Amīn's call for 'no' is directed at Egyptian, Arab, and Muslim audiences. In his other Arabic texts, he aggressively demands that Egyptians reform themselves and negate their own customs, not European domination. Like the coloniser, he says 'no' to the colonised. But Amīn also wrote for European audiences, and his tone there differs; he defensively argues against those who see Islam as inherently inferior and problematic. Common across these writings is a civilisational critique of Egyptian practices and a modernist reformulation of Islam; little surprise then that Amīn's writings, especially on the liberation of women and the veil, have been read as marking the success of colonial Orientalism, the introduction of a fifth column in the colony, and as vehicles for colonial interests in the guise of feminism.

The first of Amīn's major texts was in French: *Les Égyptiens: Réponse à M. Le Duc d'Harcourt* (1894), which responds to a polemic about Egyptian backwardness, *L'Egypte et les Egyptiens* (1893), by Duc d'Harcourt. His most famous Arabic writings are *The Liberation of Women* (*Taḥrīr al-marʾa*, 1899) and *The New Woman* (*al-Marʾa al-jadīda*, 1900). His other Arabic works are the posthumous *Aphorisms* and two collections of articles, *Causes and Effects* (*Asbāb wa natāʾij*, 1895–8) and *Manners and Exhortations* (*Akhlāq wa mawāʾiẓ*, 1895–8).

Amīn's emphasis shifts across these works. This chapter argues that central to understanding colonised thought, as well as political thought from the margins in general, are the shifts entailed by speaking to different and multiple audiences, as well as these audiences' own responses to such shifts. Colonised thinkers such as Amīn adapted their claims to different readers and populations, and each of these audiences responded to these texts and, sometimes, to Amīn's reception elsewhere. These two layers of audience and reception frame this chapter.

First, colonised intellectuals navigate their entanglements in layered webs of power. They write to persuade other marginalised people in their immediate vicinity *and* European thinkers abroad. Subtle shifts, alterations, and outright contradictions across Amīn's writings reflect their intended audiences, as well as the reactions these writings anticipate or invite. Such shifts reflect how a colonised thinker might navigate colonial discourses in the colony, writing a work either for the coloniser or for the colonised, but not both. Although some of his contemporaries and a number of current scholars read shifts in Amīn's thought as revealing his 'true colours' and his alliance with European colonialism,[4] the first half of this chapter identifies these shifts, clarifications, and restatements, and discusses their attendant politics of *colonised hesitation*. This first half considers Amīn's references to thinkers like Jean-Jacques Rousseau, John Stuart Mill, Herbert Spencer, and Charles Darwin, and to places such as Europe and the United States. These comparisons, I suggest, are selective appropriations, colonial hesitations, and performances for particular audiences.

On the other hand, attempts to address distinct audiences across different works, or to appeal to multiple audiences in one work, may not succeed. Authors can fail to calibrate their arguments to their intended audience. Different audiences can interpret one or many texts in numerous ways. And a thinker's reception in one city can affect his work's reception in another. The political legacy of colonised intellectuals is constituted around the globe, across multiple audiences. Some scholars have studied the polarised reception of Amīn's work in Cairo, particularly his polemical exchanges on the veil with the business entrepreneur Muḥammad Ṭalʿat Ḥarb. Building on this scholarship, the second half of this chapter will consider the polemical responses by Muḥammad Farīd Wajdī and ʿAbd al-Majīd Khayrī. I also turn to Amīn's reception in Europe, to argue that it affected his reception elsewhere. Audience and reception comprise the social life of colonised thinkers and texts. Thus, this part of the chapter focuses on the selective appropriation and citation of Amīn's own work by his contemporaries in Cairo and in Europe, including the intersection of Cairene and European responses.

Theorising colonised reception

Contemporary Anglophone scholarship has neglected these double dynamics of adaptation and reception. Instead, Amīn has been understood either as a mouthpiece for colonialism or as a feminist. This either/or emerges out of Leila Ahmed's important and germinal intervention in 1992, a time when many had celebrated Amīn as the father of Arab feminism. Ahmed argues that Amīn's patriarchal politics should not be mistaken for feminism. But in addition to describing how Amīn substitutes Egyptian patriarchy with European-style patriarchy, Ahmed reduces him to a middle-man of colonial discourse. She stresses that he only and simply mimics: his writings feature the 'wholehearted *reproduction* of views common in the writings of the colonizers', and his 'assault on the veil represented not the result of reasoned reflection and analysis but rather the *internalization* and *replication* of the colonialist perception'. His book on the emancipation of women 'represents the *rearticulation* in native voice of the colonial thesis of the inferiority of the native and Muslim and the superiority of the European'. He describes Muslim marriages, she observes, in a way reminiscent of missionary discourse, and 'only the British administration and European civilization receive lavish praise' in his work. He 'only becomes intelligible … by reference to ideas *imported* into the local situation from the colonizing society'. She repeats, 'The ideas to which Cromer and the missionaries gave expression formed the basis of Amin's book', and his call 'was *essentially the same* as theirs'. She declares: 'Under the guise of a plea for the "liberation" of woman, then, he conducted an attack that in its fundamentals reproduced the colonizer's attack on native culture and society'. She concludes her own attack: 'Far from being the father of Arab feminism, then, Amīn might more aptly be described as the son of Cromer and colonialism'.[5] What use is it, Ahmed seems to ask, to say 'no' to one kind of patriarchy if one assents to another? And more deeply, what use is it to say 'no' to the colonised if in the language of the metropole, and so as a structural 'yes' to the epistemic, political, and discursive terms of the coloniser? How are such prescriptions and prohibitions traded and refashioned across colonial repetition?

There is a widely and correctly held consensus that Amīn is not a feminist. As Albert Hourani put it in the 1960s, Amīn 'is scarcely what a later generation would call a feminist'.[6] Amīn turns the education of women into a civilisational litmus and the removal of the veil into a marker of modernity. Any benefits to women, in this schema, are in the service of the nation and incidental to women.[7] As Ahmed and others have indicated, Amīn's acts of moral legislation about women's internal constitution and about their dress code, appearing in the name of 'the nation' and 'progress', are part of Amīn's modernist technocratic ideology, not feminism.[8] Ahmed's thesis is distinct in casting Amīn as a parrot: not that he adapts colonial discourse nor that his reformist modernism can promote the interests of the coloniser, but that he reproduces, replicates, and rearticulates, that he is the 'son of Cromer', and so his is a necessarily imperial discourse repeating the coloniser's words. Ahmed's argument elides the power dynamics and subtle navigations of colonised intellectual production. The problem of Amīn's relationship to colonialism is not a simple 'yes' or 'no'. To reduce it to the either/or of mimicry or authenticity runs the risk of misunderstanding the workings of colonialism, engaging in intellectual guilt-by-association, and defending a politics of authenticity.

Amīn's modernist technocratic views on the household and women have a deep affinity to European discourses about civilisation, gender, and Islam, but the affinity does not render what he writes repetition without a difference. Postcolonial theorists such as Partha Chatterjee and Megan Thomas have considered dynamics of repetition, imitation, and selective appropriation between colonised and coloniser. As Chatterjee notes, more than a mere reproduction, the politics of nationalist, anti-colonial thought 'impels it to open up that framework of knowledge which presumes to dominate it, to displace that framework, to subvert its authority, to challenge its morality'.[9] Although the anti-colonial thrust of the thinkers Chatterjee and Thomas study is evident, this is not the case with Amīn. His apparent 'reproductions' are more troubling and uncomfortable. Indeed, whereas Thomas helpfully points out that intellectual borrowings by the colonised from Orientalist and colonial discourses are not necessarily 'validations of a political order',[10] Amīn's borrowings might be read as offering precisely such a validation, not of the existing Egyptian regime and society, but of Europe as dominant power and model, and European discourses as dictating the future.

Amīn and other colonised thinkers are caught in networks of repetition through practices of citation. Amīn is accused of parroting European discourses and assumptions. He calls on Egypt to become a reiteration of European success.

And arguments about Amīn's intellectual legacy reproduce the polarisation of his context. His work is constituted by these layers of reiteration and citation. Just as Edward Said observed that 'Orientalism is after all a system for citing works and authors', colonial exchanges are a nested network of such citations.[11] As a set of techniques and discursive practices, the author's citations and the networks of citations surrounding his work are woven through colonial exchanges. Amīn cites European thinkers and Euro-American contexts, re-inscribing their privileged status. He, in turn, is cited by Arab thinkers, who sometimes comment on his citations. He responds, arguing against those who claim he engages in 'Western imitation', treating imitation as a discursive artefact. At the same time, Amīn himself was read and cited by Europeans, who cite his citations and citations of his work.

The politics of audience and persuasion

Common wisdom today is that Amīn's three major works represent three different approaches. In the first, he responded to d'Harcourt by noting that Islam and Egyptians were not the essential problem, but that the root cause lay in education generally and in the education of women specifically. He mobilised Qur'ānic verses to this effect and defended against charges that Islam supports unthinking obedience and oppression, demonstrating the benefits of some of the Muslim practices that d'Harcourt condemned while noting that others were un-Islamic. The second book, *The Liberation of Women*, is usually regarded as Amīn's attempt to elaborate using Islamic principles the rights that should be given to women. Readers often see Amīn's third book, a response to his critics, as revealing his 'true colours'. In *The New Woman*, Amīn appeals not to Islamic sources, but to the authority of a smattering of European thinkers like Rousseau, Darwin, Spencer, Mill, and Schiller. The three stages of this narrative arc would be: defending Islam, using Islam, and abandoning Islam in favour of the West. Thus the idea is that Amīn defended what he took to be contemporaneous Islamic practices, then criticised them on Qur'ānic and Islamic grounds, and finally criticised them by referencing European thinkers.

Defensive postures and blaming others: a Francophone audience

There is some truth to this reading. However, Amīn is actually more consistent across his writings. He delivers variations on his platform that shift in response to audience and reception. His first work, written in French and not translated into Arabic until 1976, was intended for a Francophone and predominantly European audience. The other two works are written in Arabic and are explicitly addressed to Egyptians. It is not surprising that Amīn modifies his tone and presentation depending on his intended (or expected) readership.

Such modifications, in which a colonised thinker's tone and position shift when appealing to different centres and forms of power, and when an argument, its implications, or all its parts are sometimes withheld, are the thinker's colonial hesitations. Amīn's approach to d'Harcourt's critiques in *Les Égyptiens* is defensive. He responds to criticisms of Egypt by pointing to problems in Europe.[12] However, he also calls for a middle way when he accepts but reframes many of d'Harcourt's claims. The book contains a defence of Islam as such rather than Islam in practice, together with an indictment of Egyptian practices.

Consider the philosophy of history embedded in Amīn's defensive response to d'Harcourt. The latter's claims about Egyptian despotism and cruelty, he notes, are ironic in light of the Louis XIV's absolutism and his profound contempt for his subjects. 'Are there many examples in Egypt of similar cruelty'? he asks.[13] Such comparisons abound in the work; they seek to silence d'Harcourt by shaming him, while eliciting the support of European reading publics. He explains that Egypt is the past of France, and that if d'Harcourt would only have seen this, he would have had more faith in the unfailing law of perfectibility, progress, and evolution:

> In condemning the current situation in Egypt, he does not realize that he also condemns the condition that had been that of France before being that of Egypt. Honestly, I do not see why our past, in my view, or even our present, in Mr. d'Harcourt's view, however bad it is, should prevent that we evolve according to the law of perfectibility that governs the entire universe. And in the past, was not the France of the nineteenth century like us?[14]

Amīn enumerates the obstacles that feudal France confronted, then exclaims: 'Well! If all of this did not prevent the French from becoming a beautiful and great nation today, why does Mr. Harcourt want it to be the case that our past is a perpetual obstacle to our recovery'?[15] If progress is the rule, why does d'Harcourt not extend the same logic and courtesy to Egypt, Amīn seems to ask, that France's history demands?

In *Les Égyptiens*, Amīn introduces the idea that governance and foreign powers can inhibit the flow of the overarching law of evolution and progress. D'Harcourt is right, he says, that Egypt is poorly governed. Egypt's conditions under the rule of Mehmet Ali, he writes, have improved; d'Harcourt should give Egypt credit for its development and for the people's willingness to improve themselves and cultivate the sciences. Egypt's history prior to this moment, however, had been peculiar. According to Amīn, it had been 'exploited by monsters in human form, from all countries and all types. It was the theatre of the most dramatic scenes. I know all the horror stories, the unspeakable acts, and I suspect far more terrible things; and truly, I cannot comprehend how our unfortunate people could resist such cruel oppression.'[16]

Amīn does not say who these monsters who exploit Egypt are. The scope of the claim leaves it ambiguous whether he has in mind the Ottomans, the French, the British, or other Arab powers. This ambiguity shifts the responsibility for Egyptian weakness on to others, perhaps on to those with whom Amīn's European readership might identify. Given the expansiveness of his claim, he would be presenting France as a monster, an enemy, and a traitor to its own ideals; France has forgotten its past and prevents others from advancing, but it is nonetheless the model of freedom. This perspective, simultaneously praising Europe while subtly suggesting that it is monstrous, represents an important difference across his works. All three works feature a generally positive disposition towards Europe, but *Les Égyptiens* and *The New Woman* are the least overtly critical, if in different ways. In other words, where some have seen his second work, *The Liberation of Women*, as being grounded in a reinterpretation of the Qur'ān and the third work as adulation for European thought and progress, I propose that the difference runs deeper; his discussion of European empire shifts. The ambiguity and ambivalence of *Les Égyptiens*, which places the blame on others, becomes a more explicit observation of European domination and hypocrisy in *The Liberation of Women* – but for which Amīn places the blame on Egyptians.

Aggressive postures and aggression by nature: Cairo I

If in *Les Égyptiens* Amīn notes that Egypt had been exploited by monstrous outsiders – perhaps including European powers – *The Liberation of Women* suggests that exploitation is the natural course of history. Scholars have understated the degree to which Amīn adopted a zero-sum mentality based on a confrontation among nations and civilisations – a popular rendition of a social Darwinian struggle for survival.[17] Such elements are, I argue, actually central to his thinking and rhetoric.

Amīn reads European imperialism as an existential threat. He writes, this time in Arabic, 'we have never faced as much danger as we do now', because 'Western civilisation' has 'expanded from its origin to all parts of the earth', leaving no place untouched. He continues: 'Whenever Western civilisation enters a country, it seizes the wealth and resources of that country including agriculture, industry, and commerce. In doing so, Western civilisation uses every method of achieving its goals, even though some of these methods are harmful to the inhabitants of the regions concerned.'[18] Searching for earthly happiness, the nations of the West 'resort to every possible method'. When confronted with obstacles or 'potentially harmful situations, Westerners have resorted to force and violence'. Whereas *Les Égyptiens* portrayed the past and despotism as the obstacles and dangers that confronted Egyptians, against which they sought to reform and innovate, this later description presents the West as violent; not for the sake of justice, peace, or other lofty ideals, but in order to attain their material goals.

According to Amīn, 'Western civilisation' has two strategies for dealing with others, though the outcomes are comparable. On the one hand, 'When Western civilisation encounters a primitive nation – however miserable its condition – it either destroys the inhabitants or evicts them from their own land, as was the case in America and Australia'. This pattern, he points out, is also found in the European advances in Africa. On the other hand, 'a country like ours', which was once civilised and comes with 'historical traditions, religions, laws, and customs and with some form of elementary organisation' is dealt with differently. After 'intermingling' with the people, and on account of their scientific, economic, and other sources of power, Western powers 'acquire their most important sources of wealth'. In the process, 'the status of the outsiders improves while the status of the indigenous inhabitants deteriorates'. In this 'struggle for survival' – which he ascribes to Darwin as natural selection – the weak members of the species 'are eliminated', while the victorious multiply.[19]

Instead of identifying how 'natural selection' operates in political discourse or informs European policy, Amīn's scientific realism redeploys its lesson to an Egyptian audience. A political theory that justified to those in power how and why they were dominating the globe through their natural superiority became, in Amīn's second book, a call by the colonised to the colonised, to cease being the object of domination by the powerful – and to join their ranks. Although he does not call European residents in colonies the agents of empire, Amīn nevertheless identifies how their particular motivations feed into a larger process of global economic domination: 'the driving motive that prompts an Englishman to live in India, a Frenchman in Algeria, a Russian in China, or a German in Zanzibar is profit. All these nations are interested in acquiring resources from people who neither appreciate the value of their treasures nor use them'.[20]

Travellers from European states go to their respective colonies for profit, but the problem, he says to Egyptians, is the attitude and behaviour of those who are dominated. Amīn hovers between condemning how European states behave across the globe and the existential threat they pose to all peoples, including Egyptians, and the scientific realism of 'the way things are', beyond moral judgement.[21] He fails to see how such discourses are performative, that one actor – one European state – with this belief can change the dynamics of relations. Instead, the lesson he extracts from this struggle is that 'preparing for this battle is the only way by which a country can avoid elimination and destruction'. He implicitly identifies the European advance on Egypt as a form of aggression or attack, and calls for Egypt to 'arm itself for the struggle *with the same armour*' in order to 'survive alongside its competitor': 'Every country needs to be on the alert, assembling capabilities equal to those of whoever is attacking it, especially those intangible intellectual and educational capabilities that are central to every other of power'. If it follows this path, Egypt will 'gain control over its own wealth, and the land will justifiably belong to its inhabitants rather than to strangers'.[22]

And yet, in this text, the 'obstacles' to progress are not Europe, imperialism, or foreign monsters: the 'only obstacles that can hinder us from proceeding on this path are those we may create ourselves'. Within the frame of global struggle, Amīn presents Egyptians with absolute control over their future. If anything, European control provides the necessary conditions for advancement: 'Today we enjoy a form of justice and freedom that I believe has never before been experienced by Egyptians.'[23]

Egypt's way forward, Amīn writes, is to take advantage of the opportunity afforded by imperial justice and colonial freedom in order to 'discard all unacceptable habits and eliminate every undesirable trait that hinders their progress'. It is to 'depend upon themselves for any necessary reforms', instead of relying on weak and ineffective governments. He elaborates in *Aphorisms* that reform does not consist of new laws, governments, or institutions, but that curing the nation's ailments requires the reform of the people themselves.[24] When speaking to Europeans in *Les Égyptiens*, Amīn emphasises that a great deal of progress had taken place in Egypt, and asks for giving due credit to Egyptians and placing blame on foreigners. When speaking to Egyptians, however, Amīn notes that European exploitation of other nations generally occurs by nature, and then sidesteps the implications of this context to demand that Egyptians adopt a do-it-yourself mentality in the Darwinian struggle, giving them a nearly impossible degree of control over their futures. Even as these distinct perspectives navigate different centres and networks of power, Amīn's appeals to autonomy and choice, on the one hand, and to the natural course of history, on the other, elide fundamental questions of power.

Inventing Islam, disaggregating Europe: Cairo II

The active reform of the people, Amīn explains in *Liberation*, requires reconsidering religion. Rather than calling for a secular separation of church and state or a 'decrease' of Islam, as some commentators have mistakenly claimed, Amīn calls for something more radical: to see that all the habits, customs, and beliefs that people place under the rubric of Islam are historical and 'historicisable' artefacts that have been attached to Islam.[25] With this view of Islam in history and what is essentially Islamic outside it, Amīn sketches out the history of Egypt, Arabs, and Islam and its relationship to Europe. On the one hand, he suggests that the history of Islam is written into the history of Europe, but that contemporary Muslims have become pre-Islamic. Presenting a civilisational philosophy of history, he argues, 'The Arab state disappeared from Spain, Islamic knowledge was transferred to Europe, and Muslims returned to the condition of pre-Islamic times.' On the other hand, just as France was the past of Egypt in *Les Égyptiens*, Islam is the past of Europe in *The Liberation of Women*:

History has demonstrated that by the end of the first century of the Hijra, the flag of Islam fluttered over the most important parts of the world. These remarkable expeditions were not intended to force people to adopt Islam, but rather to protect Islamic borders and to expand the sphere of control, the sovereign power, and the benefits from the resulting industry and trade. *These are the same goals that prompt present-day Europeans to expand into Eastern countries.*[26]

Amīn's ambivalence about Europe resurfaces: it threatens the existence of Egypt, but it follows the natural course of history, to such an extent that rather than a condition of coloniser and colonised, Europe is a self-interested rational political actor like early Islamic empires. One cannot, he implies, morally condemn one without the other. Instead of condemning either, Amīn seems to say, Egyptians should focus on self-improvement. This stance is an inversion of the position he adopted when speaking to Europeans about their past.

The either/or that Egyptians face revolves around the reform of women. Egyptians can focus 'on the necessity of living and enjoying life, or else condemning ourselves to death and extinction'. What is at stake, he suggests, is the question of how it is that 'they have become strong and we have become weak'. His response to this question, which most of his contemporaries also confronted, echoes many other non-feminists who advocated for providing women with opportunities to contribute to society in order to strengthen the nation: 'depriving our society of the contribution of women is a major cause of its weakness, and the upbringing of children will be ineffectual unless we provide their mothers with an upbringing first'.[27]

Europe is the past of Islam, but Amīn does not treat Europe as a homogeneous and monolithic entity, and he adds the United States to the comparison. It is not simple Europhilia guiding his diagnoses and prescriptions, nor admiration for the coloniser. He explains that a nation's way of life, geography, culture, and temperament are factors that 'bring about variations among European states', and in this way, they too are in competition with one another.[28] He singles out the United States as the state that has made the greatest advances regarding women. Divorce there is accepted, he writes, because of its laws and because it 'works hard in the search for progress'.[29] With this and other social features, Americans – not Europeans – lead the way in his ranking of progress:

The American woman is in the forefront, followed by the British, the German, the French, the Austrian, the Italian, and the Russian woman, and so on. Women in all these societies have felt that they deserve their independence, and are searching for the means to achieve it. These women believe that they are human beings and that they deserve freedom, and they are therefore striving for freedom and demanding every human right.[30]

The differences between *The Liberation of Women* and *The New Woman* should not obscure this important continuity. Amīn repeats that each European nation and the United States are different from one another in the conclusion of *The New Woman*:

> The training of the American woman, her manners, her customs, and ethical standards are different from those of the French woman, who differs again from the Russian woman. And the Italian woman has nothing in common with the Swedish or the German woman. But all these women, in spite of differences of climate, race, language, or religion, are all the same in one respect: they have their freedom and enjoy their independence.[31]

These advancements, he explains in *The Liberation of Women*, are not due to religion, which he says is evident for two reasons. First, Western nations are not Muslim, but Islam is superior to Christianity. And second, religions are moulded by the specific practices and traditions of each nation, and neither Christianity nor Islam are exempt from this principle. His view of history makes possible a defence of Islamic principles against contemporaneous Muslim practices: Islamic law stipulated the equality of women before Europe did, but it is not practised or implemented properly. Amīn makes this claim more explicit in *The New Woman*: 'Islam, some twelve centuries ago, granted women rights that have only been achieved by Western women during the past couple of centuries.'[32] Islamic law, in this reformist schema, is the surest foundation upon which a nation can compete in natural selection, but only when properly implemented.[33]

Defensive frustration and transnational comparisons

The idea of a competition among nations was implicit in Amīn's *Les Égyptiens* and became an explicit axiom in *The Liberation of Women*. It animates many of the arguments in *The New Woman* as well. Amīn explains that warfare may still occur, but it is no longer the primary means by which peoples compete. The competition remains, but it has become 'more demanding than the clashing of swords or firing off arrows'. Instead of pointing to how Europe conquers either through violence or economic expropriation, *The New Woman* intensifies the earlier text's exaggeration of the pure, autonomous, and context-free agency of the colonised as the antidote to extinction: the negligent, half-hearted, lazy, and ignorant are 'threatened by death and destruction. The door of competition has opened before the human race'. Just as the 'inhabitants of a country compete with one another' with all means available to them, 'all of them compete with the foreigner who has penetrated in their midst through connections and patronage'.[34]

Gone from *The New Woman* is the idea that European aggression, no matter how natural, puts a burden on Egyptians to transform themselves. Instead, echoing the linear temporality he had presented to d'Harcourt, Amīn tells Egyptians that Egypt is the past of Europe: 'we are moving in the same direction taken by Europe at an earlier time in its history.'[35] And again, prioritising the observation from *Les Égyptiens* that foreigners had dominated Egypt but that it had nonetheless survived, he appeals to the universal competition of *Liberation*: 'Even after Egypt lost its independence and was overwhelmed by oppression, injustice, and disaster, it was able to maintain its existence and its uniqueness. Egypt had the constitutional make-up to maintain it through its competitive struggle with other nations.'[36] The linear path of civilisational progress is 'driving humanity along a single path', and so all Egyptians, like Amīn, are impelled to 'take Europeans as our example', to imitate their customs, and 'to pay attention to European women'.[37] Amīn is blind to how colonial discourses require colonised subjects to take the metropole as their future and model. He does not treat the idea that Europe is a model and ideas like 'progress' as weapons in the competition among nations. They are, he implies, universal and neutral. He also does not see that such ideas are historical; 'the family' as a historical artefact and sociopolitical unit arises out of particular modern conditions. Instead, he takes fourteenth-century historians and philosophers such as Ibn Khaldūn to task as obsolete: he 'does not mention one word about the family, which in effect is the foundation of every human society'.[38]

The United States' superiority is a recurring theme in *The New Woman*. Americans are to Europe in development, he writes, as Europe is to the Middle East; only the Americans have nearly abolished divisions between the sexes, particularly in employment. They accuse Europeans of oppressing women in the way that Europeans accuse Eastern men of sexist despotism.[39] After describing how women in the United States top the list and 'have gained a large share of public rights', Amīn turns to Europe, ranking the various states again, and also indicating how their laws about women are transferred to their colonies. Egypt, he notes, is in 'the third stage of that historical development', for Islamic law regards women as free persons but Egyptian families in practice do not.[40]

Amīn does not simply condemn Egypt nor does he simply idolise Europe. He presents the United States as superior to both. And he goes beyond Euro-America. Consider his discussion of India, as he contrasts Indian progress with Egyptian immobility: 'Indian Muslims ... have advanced their ideas through extensive research and have developed an awareness of the condition of women in human society, as well as grasping the importance of her roles in society.'[41] After quoting extensively from several activist-thinkers, he demands that the reader compare what Indian theologians and legal theorists say with those from Egypt, who demand that men intensify the seclusion of women and refrain from educating them. The excuse Egypt's theologians give, he writes, is that to do otherwise is 'blind imitation of Western customs'.[42] With his appeal to India, Amīn presents himself as part of a transnational movement that is *not* exclusively European or Western and in which Muslims from other parts of the world do participate. And yet, at the same time, he presents India and Indian Muslims as responding to local conditions, effacing any link between them and colonialism.

Terms of imitation and colonial hesitation: Cairo III

In an echo of what he had written to d'Harcourt seven years prior, Amīn claims that the situation in Egypt is 'completely changed' from the despotism of the past. 'We have become free, and we love freedom.' If *Les Égyptiens* and *The Liberation of Women* were clear that Egypt needed to reform itself, *The New Woman* identifies a domestic attitude that stands in the way of this reform. *Liberation* had presented the threat of Europe and natural selection as an impetus to work on oneself in order to become superior. *The New Woman* reacts against a local defensive posture that asserts that Egypt is *already* superior: 'When Europeans discussed their sciences and arts, we boasted about the past Islamic civilisation, and when contemporary Western civilisation was mentioned, we bragged about past Arab civilisations. This is like an old woman who in her senility consoles herself with the memories of her youthful beauty.'[43]

It is right to feel sadness and despair, he suggests, at the prospect that 'the life of the Islamic nations had approached its end, eliminating them from any competition with other nations'.[44] It is, he also explains in *Aphorisms*, the same impulse that makes Arabs obsess over the past of the Arabic language as the *lingua franca* of science, the arts, and philosophy in ages past. Arabic had become stagnant and was displaced by European languages. They became 'the required model in simplicity, clarity, precision, movement, and flow … in spite of this, our people agree that our language continues today to hold the highest rank, claiming that it is the master of all languages – just as they claim that Egypt is the mother of the universe'.[45]

Amīn finds this fear of imitation in how his contemporaries approach ordinary language. He writes,

> I do not know what the aim is for those writers who, should they want to express a new invention, expend their energies in the search for an Arabic word equal in meaning to the foreign word. For example, they use the word *sayyāra* [car; previously, caravan; literally, (frequent) traveller] instead of the word automobile [*ūtūmūbīl*]. If the goal is to make the meaning accessible to one's mind, then the foreign word that people are accustomed to does the desired job more completely than the Arabic word. If their goal is to prove that the Arabic language does not need other languages, they have tasked themselves with something impossible, for there is not nor will there be a language that is independent of others and self-sufficient.[46]

He goes on, railing against those who obsess over the superiority and completeness of Arabic – often through an appeal to the completeness of the Qur'ān – and attempting to give the people their agency, not from the coloniser, but from their past:

In order for this opinion to be correct, we must suppose that this language is the result of a miracle, having emerged perfect the moment it came to exist in the world. The evidence says otherwise, for all languages are beholden to rules of change and mass use. We are the legatees of Arabic; whatever we invent through our aptitude [*malaka*; natural disposition] should naturally be considered Arabic.[47]

And so he explains the problem with the way the language itself is practised and taught, as though its reader always faces diglossia:

In other languages, a person reads in order to comprehend. But in Arabic, one comprehends in order to read. If he wants to read a word made up of the letters *'-l-m*, he could read it as *'alima, 'ulima, 'ilim, 'alam, 'allama,* or *'ullima* [knew, was known, learned, flag, taught, was taught]. He cannot choose one until he understands the meaning of the sentence, since that dictates the correct vowelling. This is why reading is one of our most difficult arts.[48]

The problem extends even to common phrases, words that have been conjoined together for so long that they have ossified and their meaning has been lost.[49]

As a response to critics of *The Liberation of Women, The New Woman* specifically calls out those who disagreed with the earlier work, some of whom presented him as a mindless imitator. Scholars at al-Azhar, the Islamic university in Cairo, had objected to Amīn's work – something that Europeans commenting on Amīn's work also recognised, as I take up in later sections. Amīn confronts one of their arguments, namely that women never contributed to human knowledge or progress, even in Europe. He retorts that the innocent reader would be entitled to think that the author 'and others like him have never seen a history book, a scripture, or a journal', and reminds the unnamed scholar of 'the venerable ancestors of his country, and of the many women who had a positive role in his religion'.[50] Later in the work, he again refers to those who critiqued *Liberation* by accusing them of having 'exaggerated our proposals' to mean 'the elimination of seclusion, which in their view is an imitation of Western behaviour'.[51]

In two of the three instances where Amīn responds to his critics, he highlights their objection to the imitation of Europe or the West, but then also responds by citing non-Egyptian sources. One of those citations is to the Muslim Indian theologians, mentioned above. But in the other case, he presents – without much analysis or discussion – a series of quotes drawn from a plethora of European thinkers to defend women's contributions to society. John Stuart Mill acknowledges his debt to his wife after her death.[52] Spencer claims that education is experience, not merely knowing what others have written.[53] Condorcet claimed that whoever deprives another of their rights based on creed, colour, or gender has tramped on his own rights.[54] A few sentences from each of Simmel, Schiller, Rousseau, Fenelon, Lamartine, and others follow one another – a bombardment of 'Western' thought that would seem to confirm to Amīn's readers the charges of Europhilia that his critics levelled.[55] This is how Orientalism's citations operate: European philosophers become symbols of truth, their works moral maxims and witty one-liners.

But when Amīn responds to d'Harcourt, he is critical of some remarks he attributes to European philosophers. He writes, using an argument against d'Harcourt that some of his adversaries in Egypt would adopt against him years later: 'Without going so far as to support the idea that women are intellectually inferior, as in the theories of European philosophers like Spencer and Lambroso ... I do not see what women have to gain by engaging in masculine careers, and I see all that they have to lose.'[56] In his Arabic writings for Egyptians, however, he does not present any such criticism of European thinkers. This is because he seeks, in part, to convince Egyptians that European thinkers are, counterintuitively, already part of Islam. At the same time as he recognises that the 'ancient animosity between the people of the East and the West that has continued for many generations as a result of religious differences was and still is today the cause of mutual ignorance and suspicion', he elsewhere indicates a more complex relationship between Islam and Europe, Arabs and Christianity. Recall that he had presented Islam as the past of Europe. He also presents Europe as the continuation of Islam. He writes, 'The Europeans, who had inherited the sciences from the Greeks, the Romans, and the Arabs in as complete a form as possible, were able to identify the true fundamentals of science in a very short period. And from these they did in two hundred years what others could not do in thousands.'[57] And again, as a history of transfer: 'Historians have acknowledged Egypt's civilisation and have recognised that it was transferred from Egypt to Greece, then to Rome, to the Arabs, and eventually to Europe.'[58]

Amīn goes even further, treating European scholars as authorities of truth. He writes that he is 'not aware of a single European scholar who has proposed changing the existing status of their women'; he treats their agreement that the 'seclusion of women is the primary cause of the backwardness of Eastern societies' not as a political statement to be scrutinised, but as a neutral truth.[59] 'In sum', he proclaims his faith, 'I believe that European civilisation is not exclusively a perfect society, because perfection does not exist in our world of imperfection. It is, however, the best achievement of human beings.' Because of the ability to progress, he continues: 'They have been able to address through it some of the imperfections, and have advanced a step closer to perfection. We must acknowledge this achievement, even if it is minimal in comparison to the desired perfection of the human spirit. The challenge for future generations is to continue this process and to attempt to reach even higher.'[60]

Amīn cites European thought and takes it as the standard of progress, and he indicates the contempt with which Europe is treated across the Middle East. Its scientific and technological superiority, he explains, are accepted, because their worth is self-evident. Meanwhile, there is a prevalent belief that Europeans are morally inferior.[61] The Egyptian 'claim of moral superiority over the West', he writes, 'is like the lullabies sung by mothers when putting their children to sleep'.[62] The soothing fiction prevents a closer look at internal conditions and the reasons by which one's competitors, enemies, or foreign rulers come to dominate them.

Amīn ends this work on a polemical note, one in which Europe no longer figures as a threat in the competition of nations at all. His previous book, he writes, was condemned and labelled un-Islamic by many jurisprudents. He insults other critics on grounds of education and class: 'Many *school graduates* thought it an *excessive imitation of Western life.*' Some of these critics, he notes, are 'simple souls' who had spread silly 'fantasies' when they 'suggested that the emancipation of Eastern women was one of the goals of Christian countries, who intended by this to bring about the destruction of Islam, and that Muslims who supported this were not Muslims'.[63] Ignoring that his work was in fact used by missionaries – as I discuss in the final section – and forgetting his own argument about the competition among civilisations, nations, or religions, he declares aggressively, 'if the Europeans intended to harm us, they would leave us in our present condition, because there would be no better way to achieve their goals. This is without a doubt the truth, and it will inevitably reveal itself, as truth always does, no matter what people may do to conceal or ignore it.'[64]

Faith in progress, extinction, and colonialism: Cairo IV

Amīn went from expressing nearly absolute certainty and faith in the march of progress in *Les Égyptiens* and evolution to terror in the face of possible extinction in *The Liberation of Women*. The two tenets of social evolution – progress and natural selection – are not necessarily in tension. In Amīn's thought, however, they are, because of the status of Europe. He responds to criticism by doubling down: his more defensive posture – against the Orientalist d'Harcourt, against various Cairene responses – emphasises linear progress. Meanwhile, the second work turns the threat of extinction into a motivating call for action. But what is one to make of the return in *New Woman* of the argument of linear progress that he had previously presented to d'Harcourt, or of the sudden *exclusion* of Europe from the competition for survival in this third text, when it had animated *Liberation*? What do these shifts and hesitations say about the political thought of the colonised?

Amīn published *The New Woman* because of responses in Cairo to *Liberation*, and it is because of these responses that this text casts Europe as a neutral model and draws on European sources. But Amīn has a troubled relationship to mimicry. On the one hand, he is blind to the class biases embedded in his critiques of Egyptian life. For example, when he discusses appropriate behaviour in funerals, he explains how embarrassed he feels at Muslim funerals. They are too loud, disorderly, filthy, and cacophonous, more like 'a children's game' or 'a carnival'. He prescribes 'respect for the dead with silence and calm'. He admires the funeral rites of a certain Turkish household, specifically the efficiency, quiet, and privacy of their mourning, for 'when they finished burying him, the deceased's family returned to their home and shut the door the way they usually did'.[65] He applauds the middle class for sanitising mourning and funerary rites in public, and condemns the working and lower classes for their mannerisms and habits.[66] The reform of society is the dominance of the middle class and aristocracy against the other classes.

On the other hand, he hesitates. Simply mimicking the coloniser is not the way forward. Both Egyptians and their former rulers the Turks, he writes, have found a more 'refined humanity' that has 'intermingled with both very deeply': both are 'imitating Europeans in all aspects of their lives. But I do not see that will have a commendable influence with regards to saving our nation from the state it is currently in.'[67] Imitation is not enough, for it makes the people docile. And it is actually ordinary Egyptians who are already engaging in terrible mimicry: the minds of 'our poets, writers, and scientists' are only 'repositories' for storing what they read or hear, 'storehouses' for the thoughts of others; they 'sell these products that are not theirs in the first place, without additions or commentaries of their own'. Their work is 'confined to the repetition of others' ideas, which they've memorised in the way that a child memorises the Qur'ān. If the many hear them or read their words, they applaud, compliment, and yell, "Wow! So-and-so is great! There's no one like so-and-so in the whole world!"'[68] Too easily impressed and lacking independent thought, the printed word appears to ignorant imitators like 'magic', through their blind faith in what they read.[69] Such a reader is only a spectator and follower.

This frustration animates Amīn's claim in *Causes and Effects* that Egypt had become nothing but 'a spectator' in the competition among nations. He explains:

> All the nations of Europe directed their attention toward economic issues, tending to them to the utmost. They established administrative units for commerce, manufacture, and their colonies, and they established many schools for trade and manufacturing; they rushed into the means of colonialism, each jostling the other in this way. The competition between them over this was intense, reaching the point of battle and war. Not a single one of them delayed in spending money and lives to expand its commercial sphere, opening doors to selling its products, until even men of politics became convinced that there would be a war someday between England and Germany because the competition between the two nations, in all parts of the world, had brought each to the point of considering that one of them cannot continue along its path without annihilating the other.[70]

As mere spectators, Egyptians express admiration or contempt for the various powers, 'as though we are aliens, here to observe and then go back in peace'. The reality of the matter, he warns, is that 'we are the object over which they are fighting, and we are the cause of their troubles. We are that big, juicy bite that each of them wants to swallow right up'.[71] He compares Egypt to European powers and the United States; the capitalist empires are both examples and threats.[72]

As mere spectators, various Egyptian figures, he writes in *Manners and Exhortations*, stand in the way of progress. The *bey* acts like he loves the British and their colonial work in their presence, but tells the French the opposite, and repeats this hypocrisy with every group.[73] He singles out the 'political employee': Europeans consider him wonderful because he wants them to rule Egypt. Englishmen consider him alert and able to complicate or solve issues as necessary. Egyptians consider him clever and able to trick the English in ways no one else can. In fact, Amīn writes, his 'methods are those of a silly muppet [*ḥiyal qara kūz baṣīṭa*]'.[74]

Such figures, and this last one in particular, respond to the gaze of empire by seeking to impress colonial powers and deceive all those around, without contributing to the welfare of the people. It would seem that it is this figure, too, that others have associated with Qāsim Amīn – a figure who could not properly respond to the fact of the imperial gaze, or for whom the gaze was beyond control.

Colonised intellectuals and the gaze of the empire

Cairene exchanges

A flurry of books appeared in Cairo in response to Amīn's work. A good number seethed with vitriol. Juan Cole has masterfully dissected one such series of class-inflected exchanges, between Amīn and Muḥammad Ṭalʿat Ḥarb, a business entrepreneur. Cole indicates that Ḥarb seized on one of Amīn's shifts from *Les Égyptiens* to the Arabic texts; for Ḥarb, Amīn's shifts demonstrated Amīn's hypocrisy and he 'bitterly denounces him for switching positions'.[75] Ḥarb argues against the idea that Amīn is a 'Luther of the Orient', mocking the label with which his admirers praised him.[76] Others, especially the anti-British Egyptian nationalist Muṣṭafā Kāmil, saw in Amīn's writings a betrayal of the national cause, a British imperial plot, and a foreign conspiracy to defame Islam and subvert Egyptian habits, Muslim morals, and the course of nature. In addition to polemicising against Amīn, Kāmil, as the editor of the newspaper *al-Liwā*, created space for others to do the same; *al-Liwā* became a 'fierce opponent' of Amīn and his ideas, 'an arena for the most intense vilifications against him'.[77]

Other Egyptians across the political and economic spectrum responded to Amīn. Their range spanned those like Muḥammad Farīd Wajdī, a philosopher and student of the reformer Muḥammad ʿAbdū who would become affiliated with al-Azhar as a journal editor, and the math teacher ʿAbd al-Majīd Khayrī. Such responses to Amīn share a fundamental point of agreement, namely that Amīn is only mimicking Europe, parroting their discourses and calling for their imitation. They reject his ideas because of their apparent inauthenticity. To do otherwise, they imply, would be to play into the hands of a colonial scheme.

Wajdī published his attacks on Amīn in *al-Liwā*. His book-length response, *The Muslim Woman*, responds to Amīn's *The New Woman* (hence the title).[78] As Albert Hourani notes, although 'Abdū sought to resolve any contradiction between Islam and civilisation 'by saying that true civilisation is in conformity with Islam', Wajdī's polemical apologetics leave the reader with 'an implication that the *true* Islam is in conformity with civilisation'.[79] Whereas Amīn cites Mill and Darwin, Wajdī cites Pierre-Joseph Proudhon, Auguste Comte, and Charles Fourier with equal frequency. He explains that he is 'against those who consider perfection to be only where there is domination and might'. He frequently calls Amīn super-ficial and criticises his admiration for Europe as no more than awe in the face of might.[80] Other nations, particularly in Europe, had reacted against their centuries of oppressing women by going too far in the opposite direction and, in the pro-cess, mandating what is harmful to women; and even further, those who seek to liberate women actually seek cheap labour that is destructive of women's bodies.[81] Wajdī explains that he is concerned with the veil because, although it takes away some freedoms from women, and although women are 'closer to purity and perfection' than men, it is an irreplaceable safeguard against corruption. He echoes Amīn's classist presumptions, but turns them on their head: women veil when outdoors because their interactions are not with respectable doctors, but with people on the streets – the domain of 'sinfulness [*al-fasāq*]' and the 'riffraff [*ghawghā*]'.[82]

Wajdī shares other writers' disdain for imitation, but he also shares Amīn's fear of extinction. He writes about the dangers of civilisational imitation, implicitly adapting Ibn Khaldūn:[83]

> After a great deal of research, analysis, and investigation into the course of histori-cal events, we conclude that there must be correspondence [*tanāsub*] between the imitating and the imitated nation in their primary constituent elements [*ḥāfiẓatihimā al-ra'īsiyyatayn*]; this correspondence would guarantee and safeguard that the stronger does not vanquish the weaker and eradicate its components [*taḥlīl 'anāṣiri-hā*]. In the science of civilisation, I only know imitation as the weaker nation's readiness to accept the influences of the stronger nation, yielding to abide by its movements.[84]

Wajdī's adaptation of Ibn Khaldūn limits the conditions under which imitation can be beneficial. By inserting Qāsim Amīn's writings into an Arabo-historical and sociological discourse grounded in Ibn Khaldūn, Wajdī turns his 'science' against Amīn while claiming greater authenticity. He participates in the construc-tion of a scientific Islamic heritage with contemporary relevance.[85]

For Wajdī, foreign influences cannot have their desired effect without a req-uisite correspondence. What's more, he recognises that stronger nations present themselves as the model to be imitated. The stronger denies that there is a struggle (*tanāzu'*) and casts the adoption of its features as posing no danger to the other's existence. Stronger nations engage in a performance that denies the political basis of their claims. 'Whoever considers our conditions through a detailed civilisational lens will find that our nation's primary constituent elements are not similar in any way to the primary constituent elements of any of the nations whom we are called upon to take as our model in our vital issues. The advice to imitate, based on what we have presented, is advice for servility toward annihilation.'[86] Imitation, he explains, should be limited to the economic sphere. Too many Arab thinkers, he warns, parrot what European philosophers say 'word for word' – a critique not unlike Amīn's criticism of rote memorisation.[87] Like Amīn he cites the 'extinction' of the natives of the Americas; rather than describing it as a military conquest with mass atrocities, colonisation, and structural violence, Wajdī attributes the natives' defeat to 'social causes [*asbāb ijtimā'iyya*]'. It is because of these social causes that, after their 'intercourse [*ikhṭilāṭ*] with Europe's civilised people since the fifteenth-century', the natives were 'unable to take advantage of their proximity to civilized nations' and of Europeans' luxurious lifestyles. Immigrants of European descent inhabited the Americas 'while the original inhabitants remain savages, embracing deficiency day after day, until they number only a few hundred thousand'.[88] With the same civilisational framework as Amīn, he points to unveiled women among 'Egypt's rural peasants, the Bedouins of the deserts, and the Negroes of Africa' as evidence that unveiling does not result in civilisational progress.[89]

The final kind of response to consider is emblematised by a neglected book from 1899 by one 'Abd al-Majīd Khayrī, a teacher at a local school. This book is in response to *The Liberation of Women*. It is titled *A Firm Rebuttal to Mr Qāsim Amīn Bey on the Liberation of Women* (al-Daf al-matīn fī al-radd 'alā ḥaḍrat Qāsim bayk Amīn 'an taḥrīr al-mar'a). The book paraphrases and then attacks nearly all of Amīn's book, section by section. Khayrī rails against Amīn for discussing religious matters in a non-religious way, for imitating the West, and for calling for any change whatsoever. He writes, for example,

> It is incumbent upon a Muslim to hold steadfast to the belief that there is neither change nor transformation in the habits and manners provided in religio-legal [*shar'iyya*] texts and laws like these. He must follow them until he knows that it is outside human power to present better ones. It is incumbent upon him to safeguard them forever. For the laws of the noble [Islamic] legislation [*al-shar' al-sharīf*] require obedience for all time and in all places until Judgment Day.[90]

Perhaps more important than Khayrī's book is a review of it. The review indicates the extent to which responses to Amīn's work in Cairo were not entirely negative; the terms that his defenders drew upon are important for addressing the gaze of empire more directly. The modernist and scientific journal *al-Muqtaṭaf* (*The Digest*) ran a very brief review of Khayrī's response to Amīn, in a section at the end of each issue titled *al-Tarqīẓ wa-l-intiqād* ('Acclaim and Critique'). Khayrī, the review notes, had presented so many gems about Christians, both European and non-European. It cites his assertion that any woman who unnecessarily interacts with men without a veil on her face lacks manners and is unchaste. It quotes his claim that Europeans are not so culturally advanced, because they did not ban slow-dancing between non-spouses (because, he says, extra-marital bodily contact is something that no human or animal can approve of). The two-paragraph review concludes:

> The good author has done well to retain all translation rights [of his book] for himself. If someone were to actually translate these pearls of wisdom into even one European language, Europeans would conclude that our contact with them for the last hundred years has not changed a single thing in our opinions about women.[91]

Al-Muqtaṭaf silences Khayrī with a modernist (and somewhat humorous) putdown: if word of this text got out, the Europeans would think we have not progressed. One can hear the anxiety in their ridicule: what *do* Europeans think, and what if it is true that we have not progressed? The remark takes Europe as arbiter and judge of progress. It is immediately aware of Europe's role as an intense gaze overlooking and intervening in colonial discourse.

These labels and manoeuvres, from Ḥarb's claim that Amīn postured as the 'Luther of the Orient' to Wajdī's claim that Europe presented itself as a benign and innocuous model in order to exercise mastery, and to *al-Muqtaṭaf*'s response to Khayrī, indicate the degree to which competing understandings of imperial politics intersected with Amīn's reception in Cairo. Fear and suspicion of empire shaped the colonial exchange.

Reading Les Égyptiens in Europe, or, can the Muslim speak (of Islam)?

European and American journals frequently mentioned Amīn's three major works. Although his *Les Égyptiens* was written in French and for a Francophone audience, the other two major works were written in Arabic, for an Egyptian audience. Some of Amīn's contemporaries in Cairo read *Les Égyptiens* and attacked Amīn for apparent inconsistencies between it and his Arabic works, and European commentators cited his *Liberation of Women*, though it was not addressed to them. And just as responses in Cairo attacked Amīn for the generally positive response in Europe, some European responses considered progress in Egypt (or 'in Islam') to be unlikely because of the criticisms Amīn's work faced in Cairo, including some of those discussed in the previous section. He was presented by some Europeans as a hopeful Luther of Islam, a reformist, a liberal, and a beacon of hope. For others, Amīn remained deficient, because of his place in historical progress relative to European civilisation. As a Muslim, some implied, he could not speak of Islam objectively. In European readings of Amīn's works, his concerns with extinction and the competition among nations disappear. All that remains is progress, albeit its possibility is uncertain.

The discursive terrain, however, was such that Amīn's work was put to various ends through highly selective readings. For example, an anonymous writer in *The Contemporary Review*, under the pseudonym 'A Coptic Layman', appealed to Amīn and his *Les Égyptiens* as a representative of 'all enlightened Muslims'. By virtue of their enlightenment, Amīn and company apparently 'admit' that the Coptic Church's 'inveterate enemies' are 'the Muslims', who are in fact 'the descendants of her own children', and who only converted because they were unable to withstand the social pressures, contempt, and disadvantages.[92]

Other responses that focused on Amīn's French text, *Les Égyptiens*, tended to be positive but patronising. Armin Vambery wrote as he travelled across the Near East and the Ottoman Empire:

> We can hardly expect the disciples of Mohammed's doctrines, after living in seclusion for hundreds of years, wrapt in ecstasy and admiration of their own world of faith, which they regarded as the highest ideal of human existence, and condemning everything outside as wicked, despicable, and deceptive, all at once to admire, praise, and receive a culture to which hitherto they have been altogether antagonistic. This indeed is asking too much. Against such a sudden transition the proud self-esteem of the Moslem must rebel, and does rebel. However much of the Mohammedan may be convinced of the superiority of our culture, he will always find points in Islam by which to prevent the entire putting on one side of the Koran.[93]

Vambery goes on to ascribe this wilful blindness and obstinacy to Amīn in *Les Égyptiens*. When Amīn had responded to d'Harcourt that 'In chemistry, mechanics, astronomy, medicine, etc., Europeans now have a very wide view, they say; but they stand on our shoulders, and that is why they can see so much further; without the preparatory work done by our investigators of past ages, they would not easily have reached such a height', Vambery sees Amīn's reminder of the entwinement between Islam and Europe as a refusal to put the Qur'ān aside. Although he is encouraged by Amīn's admiration for Europe, he takes Amīn's references to Arabic science to be a defensive obsession with the past.[94] Muslims, however, should be praised for taking the smallest steps, he asserts, for although Europe had it 'easy' to pass from 'centuries' of 'black darkness of medieval barbarism' because of the Renaissance and the legacies of Greece and Rome, the 'Islamic world' has the burden of overcoming its past with 'the traditions of a glorious period of native culture'. It would be like asking 'European society' to 'renounce its old ideas and culture' and adopt 'say, Chinese culture, which is culture of a certain sort'. He continues:

> I have found that the self-control and the strength of purpose of the Moslem pioneers of the reform movement really deserve admiration, and we Europeans are wrong when, ignoring the obstacles connected with all stages of transition, we accuse the Mohammedans of negligence, or, what is worse, of animosity, with regard to modern culture.[95]

Whereas Amīn had concluded his *The New Woman* with a bit of rhetorical flair – 'if Europeans wanted to harm us, they would abandon us to our state of affairs' – Vambery makes the same point in discussing Amīn's French text, but as a calm observation rather than a provocative attack: 'If left to themselves, the nations of Islam will undoubtedly continue in their present state of indolence', he writes, justifying European 'guardianship'.[96] Meanwhile, Amīn's own argument from *Les Égyptiens* about foreign monsters impeding Egyptian progress is nowhere to be found. Vambery instead argues that people like Amīn are evidence that 'Moslem Asia' and the 'Mohammedan under the beneficial influence of Europe' are not as fanatic, obstinate, or averse to reform as many believe. He cites Amīn, and the thinkers and professionals whom Amīn cites, as evidence of small steps in enlightenment and learning.[97]

The problem, Vambery indicates, is neither Islam nor Christianity, but 'religion in general'. He cites philosophers who critiqued the negative role of Christianity in European development and cites Amīn that 'It was not Islam which prohibited intercourse with Europe' or 'forbade its followers to seek knowledge in the West'. Like Amīn, he cites Qur'ānic injunctions to learn, travel, trade, and mingle. Drawing on the temporal trope of a 'Moslem East' still stuck in Europe's Middle Ages, he claims that the 'procrastination' of Islam takes place as religion's absorption of 'vital strength' and 'taking possession of all human thought and aspirations', of everyday life and activities; and he bemoans the authorities' concern with their own interests rather than those of their subjects.[98] Written doubly as a critique of the European powers' approach to the cultivation of virtue among Muslims and as a call for greater European patience with lagging Orientals, Vambery's writings offer Amīn as a source, as a litmus for civilisation (much as women are for Amīn's writings), and as a small sign of progress – the existence of which affirms the need for further European guardianship.

The problem of progress also figured as the question of whether Muslims can speak of Islam, and whether they can reform it. This controversy appears in a European reflection on Amīn's own response to d'Harcourt, and in turn, a reply to that reflection. Whether the Muslim can speak appears in a review of Adolf Harpf's *Morgen- und Abendland: Vergleichende Kultur- und Rassenstudien*. Harpf characterises Amīn as a '*mohammedanische Jurist*' and accepts Amīn's argument that scriptural interpretation is at the heart of the conflict over women. He writes that it was easy for Amīn to show in his reply to d'Harcourt that the Qur'ān can be interpreted as neither more nor less hostile to culture than the Bible, for 'it just depends on how the sacred books are understood [*es kommt nur darauf an, wie die heiligen Bücher verstanden werden*]'. For Harpf, 'Islam' at its peak of intellectual production was in a better condition than Western Christendom in the Middle Ages. And yet, he finds Amīn almost by nature lacking:

> What he did not see, and what from his point of view *he could not and did not want to see*, was that these believers are hostile to knowledge because of the innate inertia of

the chaos of the current Oriental race, and only thereby have they indeed made Islam into the religion most hostile toward knowledge.[99]

Harpf's book was reviewed by Martin Hartmann, one of the leading Arabists of the time. What is most ironic, and also iconic, about this review is the status of 'local' thinkers and activists. Although Hartmann's mission was primarily dedicated to advancing a sociological approach to the study of the contemporary Middle East, he seems in this review to have been committed to the idea that Muslims, by virtue of Islam, are ignorant of Islam's essence. He writes:

> The self-righteous blabber of the rector of al-Azhar (178) and the shallow writing of the 'jurist Kassem Amin' [qāsim amīn] (206) are no substitute for one's own study of the history and essence of Islam, which the Muslims themselves almost always remain ignorant of in truth, when they can inundate us with an overwhelming amount of detail. H[arpf] falls surprisingly and naïvely to the known trick that the Muslims employ, namely to uncover and reveal the weaknesses of French culture.[100]

Just as, for Harpf, Amīn did not, could not, and would not see why Muslims have made Islam hostile to knowledge, Harpf's critic, Hartmann, agrees that to be Muslim is to be ignorant, albeit here of the 'essence' of Islam, which apparently only people like Hartmann as a European scholar of Oriental and Islamic studies can know. That Amīn responded to a Frenchman's critiques by pointing to problems in France, Hartmann suggests, is an easy trope.

The Liberation of Women: *between silence and progress*

Although Hartmann disapproved of Harpf's reliance on Amīn as a source for understanding Islam, Hartmann cited the importance of Qāsim Amīn in a lecture he delivered four years later, at the Munich Oriental Society, on the topic of 'Women in Islam'. He describes Amīn's emergence in the public sphere of Cairo, noting that his *Liberation of Women* calls for 'a complete change in the standing of the Islamic woman as urgently necessary' and that it 'proved that such a change would be more in accordance with the true teachings of Islam than current custom [*nachwies, daß solche Änderung mehr in Übereinstimmung mit der wahren Lehre des Islams sei als die bisherige Sitte*]'. Amīn, he notes, had two kinds of critics, both in the Middle East and in Europe, namely those who wanted to hold on to tradition and others who agreed with him but thought he was reaching too far. Hartmann ultimately finds in Amīn positive evidence of progress because even conservative forces in Egypt had to contend with his claims; he had successfully opened the debate.[101]

If the disagreement between Harpf and Hartmann revolved around whether the Muslim can speak of Islam, a different perspective reacts to *The Liberation of*

Women by pondering whether Muslims can speak – to one another. Henry Noel Brailsford (1873–1958) – an erstwhile philosophy lecturer turned journalist, who volunteered against Turkey in its war with Greece, and who authored *A League of Nations* a few years before its creation – invoked Amīn in an article titled 'Modernism in Islam' in the September 1908 issue of *Fortnightly Review* as a sign of progress. After disavowing that the seclusion of women was required by Islam – 'I doubt whether Mahomet has really much more influence in locking the doors of the harem than has St Paul in delaying woman's suffrage' – he explains that the problem in Egypt is middle and upper-class customs, and 'not so much religion as a primitive sense of property in women'.

Brailsford builds an opposition premised on temporal lag and substantive lack: Galileo, Newton, and Darwin were eventually accepted by the Western Church, whereas the 'Eastern Church and Islam' have yet to face 'Western science'. The Western Church apparently welcomed the Renaissance and made space for thinkers such as Luther, whereas neither Islam nor Eastern Christianity were 'touched by the Renaissance' until it was so late that 'compromise and adaptation were now almost impossible'. For Brailsford, Islam's Europeanised reformers fill the discursive gap provided by the absence of Luther. Through Qāsim Amīn, he ends on an optimistic note: 'But progress there is. A very able Egyptian judge, the late Kassim Bey Amin, wrote a brilliant book on the emancipation of women. The demand for education is growing …'.[102]

Brailsford's critiques echo Amīn's: a stagnant Arab world, simultaneously perfectly decipherable and trapped by its language and alphabet, in need of a reformation like Europe's, but unlike Europe's in that it is to be ushered in by outsiders. Brailsford ponders whether a planned pan-Islamic congress might address 'the propriety of using Arabic, the Latin of Islam, as the language of prayer in countries where Arabic is not the vernacular'.[103] While Amīn was concerned with whether Muslims can *read*, Brailsford ponders whether Muslims can *speak* to one another. If they cannot, one must wonder, who can speak for them, and who should mediate among them?

The general tone of optimism surrounding Amīn's *Liberation*, as a small sign of progress and hope that affirms the success and further need of the civilising mission, was quite common at this point. The different appropriations of Amīn's work, and his incorporation into a network of Orientalist citations, demand attention to the asymmetry, or dissymmetry, in the relationship of coloniser to colonised. The political agency of the colonised and the colonised's appropriations of colonial thought do not take the form of a simple 'yes' or 'no', for in turning back to Europe and the continued life of Amīn's work there, one sees how the appropriation is itself appropriated for numerous ends. For example, a 1908 article, 'Woman in Egypt', in the magazine *The Englishman* describes Amīn as 'founder and leader' of the movement to abolish the 'slavery' of women in Egypt, misattributing to him a position against veiling in its entirety; his *Liberation of Women* (incorrectly transliterated as *Cahrir Al-Mar'ah*) is 'the gospel of liberty for Mohammedan womanhood'.[104] J. Desormeau canonises Amīn as a reformer in the German journal *Dokumente des Fortschritts*; he reviewed Amīn's *Liberation of Women* (and Amīn's life), noting that Amīn presented a 'middle way' between full veiling and unveiling based on Qur'ānic evidence, and spoke European truth to the power of Oriental tradition. Amīn's reforms 'naturally would cancel out any real significant difference between the customs of the Mohammedan and the European', and although enthusiastically received by the youth, his movement was at odds with conservative nationalist forces in Egypt.[105] Roland Knyvet Wilson, in his *Anglo-Muhammad Law*, describes Amīn's writings on marriage and gender as those of a Mu'tazalite.[106] The Reverend Ernest Bourner Allen called one of Amīn's Arabic books in the *Bibliotecha Sacra* 'epoch-making and epoch-marking', and he marks the way that the texts were received in a civilisational framework: he wonders whether in titling his Arabic texts, Amīn had '*borrowed the title from our own civilisation*, I do not know.' Allen explains that he had learned of Amīn's proposals after consulting with 'a missionary of great scholarship, who has been fifty years in the Levant, who is now translating the book'.[107]

The Liberation of Women *and* The New Woman: *between gospel and empire*

In his important study of the intellectual history of sexuality discourses in the Middle East, Joseph Massad describes Qāsim Amīn as having adopted a 'defensive posture against Orientalist representations of Arab and Muslim sexual desires'. In this reaction, Amīn refuses d'Harcourt's claims about Arab sexual desires and instead reverses the charges about sexual appetite to Europeans. Massad makes the compelling case that 'Qasim Amin's reaction did not dictate subsequent discussions of sex in modern Arab intellectual history', and it would be a century before the debate would be, like d'Harcourt and Amin's, focused on the sexual life of contemporary rather than ancient Arabs. The instigators of the new debate, he observes, are 'a group of Western missionaries'.[108]

Taking the Reverend Allen's reference to missionary interest in Amīn's work, and extending Massad's argument about different missionaries or groups that perform the function of missionaries, this chapter concludes by considering how one prominent missionary used Amīn's *Liberation of Women* in his diatribes against Arabs and Islam. For this missionary, Amīn represented a force of Europeanised reform that could not stand in the face of the perverse forces of Islam. By way of confronting the appropriation of Amīn's writings by colonisers, this preliminary account of Amīn's transnational reception will consider the extent to which Amīn is to be held responsible for his readers, or rather, what about his internal critique made it so easy for external enemies to mobilise him in their own service.

Orientalist discourses had an intimate relationship with colonial ends and with European Christianity. The Christian evangelical missionaries who travelled to the Middle East were often foot-soldiers of European imperialism. In their attempts to win the hearts and minds, or rather souls, of Arab Muslims, they were central to the dissemination of such discourses and the shifts in them. At the same time, this particular Orientalist's use of Qāsim Amīn's writings also indicates, on the one hand, the sponge-like nature of Orientalism's reactionary arguments, able to digest and absorb thinkers like Amīn precisely through the kinds of selective appropriation that Chatterjee ascribes to anti-colonial thinkers. On the other hand, the differences between Amīn's European readers and his Cairene reception indicate that he was consistently made to fit two distinct frameworks, each of which refused to take up the tensions, contradictions, and blindness to empire in his own. Central to one was the refusal of the idea that the European can speak of Islam, and to the other, the refusal of the idea that the Muslim can speak of Islam.

Samuel Marinus Zwemer was a Christian missionary of the Reformed Church in America, later professor of missions and professor of the history of religion at the Princeton Theological Seminary, and founder of the then-evangelical Muslim-Christian relations journal *The Moslem World* (now *The Muslim World*). Zwemer, the 'Apostle to Islam', spent years in the Middle East preaching gospel and empire.[109] He cites Qāsim Amīn numerous times. If Amīn argued that women had to be Westernised in order for Egypt to survive, and if self-styled traditionalists argued that women had to be secluded in order to maintain Egypt, Zwemer argues that women must be targeted in order to acquire the whole of Egypt. In *Moslem Women*, which he co-authored with his wife, Zwemer cites what one John R. Mott reported from the 'General Conference for the entire Moslem World' in Jerusalem, 3–7 April 1924. For Zwemer, as for Mott, in a world arranged of competing religions rather than competing nations, women are the mediums, receptacles, and vehicles for the reproduction of nation and belief:

> Owing to the fact that the mother's influence over the children, both boys and girls, up to about ten years of age, is paramount, and that women are the conservative element in the defense of their faith, we believe that missionary bodies ought to lay far more emphasis on work for Moslem women as a means for hastening the evangelization of the Moslem lands.[110]

The hearts and minds of women, or rather their souls, represented for missionaries the way to unmake Islam. The missionaries also approached women as the weak link, and the beliefs of women became the battleground.

In this battle, Zwemer found in Amīn's writing a useful source and tool. 'One of the epoch-making books of the last decade of progress', he writes, is Amīn's *The Emancipation of Woman* (i.e. *The Liberation of Women*), alongside his *The New Woman*. He exudes admiration: 'This brilliant author and judge was one of the lights of the New Egypt, and was a broad-minded, liberal man', and his works 'show that the Moslem world is going to be roused from its slumber of ages by its own sons'. On the topic of the seclusion and veiling of women, Zwemer quotes Amīn, 'Why do we never trust one another or trust our women? Is it because we are inferior to the Christian nations of Europe and America, whose women go unveiled and are trusted and honored? Are we so degraded that no one can trust another?'[111]

On the evening of 2 January 1920, Zwemer delivered a speech to his fellow missionaries. That evening's talks were devoted to the general topic of 'The Worth and the Failure of the Religions of the World'. Instead of actually assessing what Christian missionaries can learn from their religious others, the talks were flat-footed polemics directed at Hinduism, Islam, and non-Christian approaches to women as public failures, followed by a talk on Christianity's private successes and failures. Zwemer's speech, 'The Worth and Failure of Mohammedanism', focused on the failures of Islam. He lists five failures (which remain in currency in many circles in Europe and the United States today):[112] Islam is against children, women, reason, democracy, and the soul. Islam provides nothing for 'the little child', it fails 'in its treatment of womanhood', it 'has failed and utterly failed because it has degraded and dwarfed the human intellect', it has been 'the age-long foe of democracy' that is 'any form of democracy'; and finally it 'has failed spiritually'. Zwemer approvingly cites Hartmann for the fourth failure, Islam's hostility to democracy, noting:

> Dr Hartman[n] of the University of Berlin wrote before the war. (Perhaps he is the greatest German authority on comparative religion as regards Islam). He says, 'Islam is a religion of hate and of war. It must not be suffered to be the ruling principle in any nation of the civilized world. Islam has destroyed cultural possessions and has created nothing, absolutely nothing, in the way of cultural values that have been permanent'.[113]

The unstated irony in this set of statements is rather stark; Zwemer draws attention to Europe's world war when it is Islam that is supposed to be a religion of war.

It is, however, with the second failure that Zwemer invokes Amīn's work. He turns to his go-to passage from Amīn's writing, which appears in Amīn's introduction to *The Liberation of Women*.[114] Zwemer appears to have been obsessed with the passage – though it is unclear from his writing how much else of Amīn he had read – as it also appears in his other works and in slightly emended form as an epigraph to a chapter in his *Childhood in the Moslem World*.[115] It reads as follows:

> Man is the absolute master and woman is the slave. She is the object of his sensual pleasures, a toy, as it were, with which he plays and then tosses away as he pleases. The firmament and the light are his. Darkness and the dungeon are hers. His to command, hers to blindly obey. His is everything that exists and she is an insignificant part of that everything.

Zwemer strategically takes Amīn's polemical rhetoric as the gospel truth. He reads Amīn's rhetoric and hyperbole naively, or hyperliterally, as neutral and native observation about an essential Islam, when its likely purpose had been to elicit indignation in its Egyptian readers and thereby stimulate reform. And so, Amīn's speech matters only if his words can be made to encourage religious conversion instead of social reform.

In 'The Worth and Failure of Mohammedanism', Zwemer mobilises Amīn to represent what 'the Mohammedans say about this failure', a native voice to show that even among the unintelligent Muslims there is recognition of this failure. Reactions to a position like Amīn's further indicate a deeper failure, in the inability of Muslims to confront truth. He then commends the man's credentials, describing him as 'a Mohammedan judge' whose disciple was 'ostracized and excommunicated' because he 'dared to speak the truth about the continued and increasing degradation of Mohammedan womanhood in Mohammedan theology and literature, down the centuries'.[116]

Zwemer's *The Disintegration of Islam* quotes the same passage about man as master and woman as slave, with additional selections.[117] He places Amīn in the company of those whom he labels 'the new Islam' and who believe Islam needs to be reformed or 'reconstructed'. Employing modernism's temporal linearity, the 'new Islam' of which Amīn is a part is a 'revolt against tradition because of its ritualism and medieval beliefs and practices' and a 'moral revolt against the ethical standards of Mohammed and his companions, as recorded in tradition'.[118] Amīn and company are 'leaders in social reform', and Amīn their exemplar: 'The Moslem press in Calcutta, Teheran, Cairo, Bagdad, Constantinople, and Algiers has given similar testimony', evidenced in Amīn's 'plea for the emancipation of the womanhood of Egypt'.[119] He claims Amīn as his own: 'There is no doubt that in social reform, policy, education and all the ideals of democracy, educated Moslems are our allies and not our enemies. They are as anxious as are the missionaries for the uplifting and enlightenment of the masses.'[120]

Two years earlier on 2 January, in an address at the Kansas City Volunteer Convention, Zwemer had repeated the same line about internal Muslim allies, approaching the modernist reformers in the same way as their critics in Egypt, that is, as Islam's fifth column: as 'our allies in all questions of social reform and in the raising of ethical standards', Amīn and those like him 'are all of them engaged in adjusting the old Islam to the standards of the Sermon on the Mount'. The key difference, Zwemer insists, is the opening afforded to evangelism, or the 'new attitude toward Christianity and the Bible', namely a 'willingness to listen and investigate' instead of 'arrogance and fanaticism'. Zwemer's mark of progress and his openness to Amīn stem from his belief that Amīn's critiques of contemporaneous Egyptian institutions might serve Zwemer's missionary ends. He praises Amīn's *The New Woman* and Amīn himself as 'the most outstanding figure' for the position of womanhood among Muslims, quoting extensively from the book.[121] Indeed, when a different version of the talk appeared two months later in the

Missionary Review of the World, Zwemer discusses Amīn and the modernists under the heading 'The social and intellectual crisis in the Moslem world is a present-day call'.[122]

Shields and daggers of colonial orientalism

Amīn's contemporaries in Egypt were aware of an imperial gaze. They inserted his work into a simplistic either/or frame that can be schematised as Islamic/un-Islamic, indigenous/foreign, and coloniser/colonised, thereby eliding the network of citations at work. But first and foremost, it was those readings of Amīn's work that were presented by missionaries and European commentators – be they optimistic, hostile, or strategic – that turned Amīn into the Arab discursive equivalent of an Uncle Tom. It was not, in other words, only Amīn or his local interlocutors who did this. The force of his critiques and hesitations, or the potential for seeing them in terms of the workings of colonialism, was closed off by European responses, not simply by who Amīn admired, cited, or critiqued. Such networks of citation and their histories – locally and globally, between the coloniser and the colonised, among the coloniser reading the colonised and other colonised's responses, or the colonised reading the coloniser's reactions – are central to understanding the navigations of colonial exchanges when a simple 'no' does not prevail.

In James Scott's description of the weapons of the weak, those in power might be inconvenienced but in general need not and do not respond. The weapons of the weak are important for understanding what keeps the weak held down, for these weapons do not alter the dominant structure. Instead, they can soothe the weak and allow them to vent, channelling, expending, and quarantining their energies. These weapons are easily deflected and incorporated into that power structure.

The colonised elite also possessed weapons. These weapons could be neutralised, but in a different way. Amīn's weapon was the written word. He used science, philosophy, and rhetoric to forward his modernising agenda. And he attempted to appeal to multiple groups. Although some of his writings indicated that European powers were expropriating the colonies and that Egyptians faced the possibility of extinction, these claims were not enough for Egyptian audiences and they went unheard among European readers. His writings became, for some Arab readers, evidence of the degree to which imperial powers had successfully indoctrinated colonised intellectuals into betraying their own 'heritage'. These same writings became, for some European and Arab readers, evidence of the kind of progress for which Amīn called. For others, Amīn's books were a weapon in the hands of colonisers, missionaries, and Orientalists.

One of the coloniser's weapons is the ability to silence, interpret, and selectively appropriate what the colonised elite say. The distinctive features of such sets of weapons require that we situate colonised thought in a network of exchanges, appropriations, and citations, and in their relationship to Orientalist knowledge production. After all, what the colonised elite says is, predictably, often framed by the European discourses to which they respond, be they Francophone or Anglophone. The colonised elite may selectively appropriate Euro-American thinkers and ideas, creatively remaking their moral and political force. But it is not only the colonised that writes back. The coloniser can respond, and, as was the case with Amīn's transformation in the hands of Zwemer, the colonised's writings can be strategically appropriated for the colonisers' ends. In turn, the colonised's attempt at grafting a weapon of the coloniser's writings in order to ensure survival, might, or reform is under watch. The colonised performs a kind of authenticity, and is aware of the colonisers' own performances, and might read other colonised's claims as performances for the sake of the coloniser. The colonised elite's daggers are therefore more like defensive shields, whereas it is the colonisers' ability to adjudicate among colonised intellectuals, and to absorb their criticisms and positions into their own particular ends, that refashions these shields into something akin to cloaked daggers. In such a space, saying 'no' to power – to the coloniser, to local authority, or to entrenched customs – is more than an either/or.[123]

Notes

1 Qāsim Amīn. *Kalimāt* (Aphorisms) in Muḥammad ʿAmāra, ed., *al-Aʿmāl al-kāmila (Complete Works)* (Cairo: Dār al-Shurūq, 1988). Amīn's French text is Kassem-Amin, *Les Égyptiens: Réponse à M. Le Duc d'Harcourt* (Cairo: Jules Barbier, Imprimeur, 1894). Two of Amīn's works have been translated, namely *Taḥrīr al-marʾa* (*Liberation of Women*) and *al-Marʾa al-jadīda* (*The New Woman*) in Qāsim Amīn, trans. and ed., Samiha Sidhom Peterson, *The Liberation of Women; The New Woman; Two Documents in the History of Egyptian Feminism* (Cairo: American University in Cairo Press, 1992, 2000). Citations to Amīn's work are as follows: *Kalimāt* = K; *Asbāb wa-natāʾij* = AN; *Akhlāq wa-mawāʿiẓ* = AM; *Les Égyptiens* = E; *Taḥrīr al-marʾa*, *Liberation of Woman* = LW; *al-Marʾa al-jadīda*, *The New Woman* = NW. The epigraph comes from K 148: *fī al-umma al-ḍaʿīfa al-mustaʿbada, ḥarf al-nafī <lā> qalīl al-istiʿmāl*.

2 Frantz Fanon, *Black Skin, White Masks* (London: Pluto Press, 1986), 173.

3 James C. Scott, *Weapons of the Weak: Everyday Forms of Peasant Resistance* (New Haven, CT: Yale University Press, 1985) and *Domination and the Arts of Resistance: Hidden Transcripts* (New Haven, CT: Yale University Press, 1990).

4 For example, in an immensely hostile and conservative history of these debates titled *ʿAwdat al-ḥijāb* (*Return of the Veil*), two of the headings in the chapter on Amīn's *New Woman* are titled 'Qāsim Amīn Uncovers [*yarfaʿ al-niqāb ʿan*] His Face and Unveils [*yusfir ʿan*] His True Nature in this Book' and 'Qāsim Amīn's Attack on the Islamic City.' See Muḥammad Aḥmad Ismāʿīl al-Muqaddam *ʿAwdat al-ḥijāb* [*Reappearance of the Veil*], vol. 1: *Maʿrakat al-ḥijāb wa-l-sufūr* [*The Battle of the Veil and Unveiling*], 10th printing (Riyadh: Dār Ṭayba li-l-Nashr wa-l-Tawzīʿ, 2006), 62, 67.

5 Leila Ahmed, *Women and Gender in Islam* (New Haven, CT: Yale University Press, 1992), 149–63; emphasis added.

6 Albert Hourani, *Arabic Thought in the Liberal Age, 1798–1939* (Cambridge: Cambridge University Press, 1983 [1962]), 166.

7 Consider the parallel with the advantages Plato gives women in the *Republic* for maximising Kallipolis's resources.

8 There is a related set of important studies that identify how calls for liberating Muslim women from 'Islam' emerge out of liberal imperialism; this would not capture Amīn's position, however, as he neither calls for saving Muslim women from Islam nor for Western intervention. See Joseph A. Massad, *Islam in Liberalism* (Chicago: University of Chicago Press, 2015); Anne Norton, *The Muslim Question* (Princeton, NJ: Princeton University Press, 2013); Saba Mahmood, 'Feminism, Democracy, and Empire: Islam and the War on Terror', in Hanna Herzog and Ann Braude, eds, *Gendering Religion and Politics: Untangling Modernities* (New York: Palgrave Macmillan, 2009), 193–215.

9 Partha Chatterjee, *Nationalist Thought and the Colonial World: A Derivative Discourse* (Minneapolis: University of Minnesota Press, 1986), 41–2; Megan C. Thomas, *Orientalists, Propagandists, and Ilustrados: Filipino Scholarship and the End of Spanish Colonialism* (Minneapolis: University of Minnesota Press, 2012), 28–33.

10 Thomas, *Orientalists*, 28.

11 Edward Said, *Orientalism* (New York: Vintage Books, 1979), 23. Also see Jacques Derrida, *Limited Inc.*, trans. Samuel Weber and Jeffrey Mehlman, ed. Gerald Graff (Evanston, IL: Northwestern University Press, 1988).

12 Amīn discusses inconsistencies in d'Harcourt's account, or rather, how its arguments are overdetermined and unclear. For example, on the perpetual imprisonment of the Egyptian woman, Amīn points out that d'Harcourt ascribes this to Egyptian men's jealousy, to the insecurity of the country and of the East more generally (including Copts), and to Islam: 'It is impossible that his readers are not struck by the inconsistency of these ideas and find with me that Mr. Harcourt judged our manners without having studied them [*Il est impossible que ses lecteurs ne soient pas frappés de l'incohérence de ces idées et ne trouvent avec moi que M. d'Harcourt juge nos mœurs sans les avoir étudiées*]' (E 100).

13 E 94.

14 E 26.

15 E 27.

16 E 81–2.

17 An important exception is Marwa Elshakry, *Reading Darwin in Arabic, 1860–1950* (Chicago: University of Chicago Press, 2013), 87, 90, 196–7, 216.

18 LW 62.

19 LW 62–3.

20 LW 63.

21 When Amīn compares the environment in which women are subordinated to men with Europe's foreign relations, he portrays European power politics and deceit in a negative light, calling them out for their hypocrisy:

> The poison of cheating, deceit, and evil will penetrate their hearts, and its influence will appear at every opportunity. This is like those European nations which give the *appearance of peace when in reality they are preparing for war*, and which, when the opportunity arises, leap on their neighbors, tearing them apart.
>
> (LW 84, emphasis added)

On the one hand, the similarity between the subordination of women to how Europeans speak of peace while waging war is a clear call for reforming the status of women in Egypt. He seems to expect his readers to see as a problem what he has identified as an undeclared war on women *because* of its similarity to European deceit and war. On the other hand, Amīn does not call for transforming European powers, or even for condemning them, treating this as the natural course of history.

22 LW 63–4, emphasis added.

23 LW 64.
24 K 159–60. Amīn's related elitism appears in his discussion of genius. An idea is best when expressed by a praiseworthy writer (K 145): his virtue is the measure of the best expression, though genius and madness are similar to one another (K 173). The problem with the Egyptian public sphere is the uniformity of opinion and lack of creativity: 'no strange ideas, no new expressions, no new innovations' and 'no genius who surprises and attracts you with the wonders of his madness' (K 145). Also see K 138, 145–6, 149. He explains in *Causes and Effects* that nations have control over their destiny:

> a nation's condition with regards to happiness and misery, or progress and delay, is not a condition caused or changed by the rule of chance [charity; *ṣadaqa*], for it is a necessary effect that only changes if one changes what is inside that nation. If the nation is active, educated, and civilized, it will have good fortune in this world; if it is lazy, ignorant, and with bad manners, it will have misery.
>
> (AN 171)

25 LW 65.
26 LW 66, emphasis added.
27 LW 46–7. But he also questions whether nationalist sentiment makes much sense, noting that the word 'national' is appended to all institutions: 'Love of the nation has become a new religion; whoever embraces it profits, whoever distances himself from it loses. It is like a tomato blender: everything can be put inside to give it a sour flavour that makes eating it up easier and more acceptable!' (K 157).
28 LW 51.
29 LW 88-9. Amīn expresses admiration for the American ethic of labor (AN 173).
30 LW 7.
31 NW 204–5.
32 NW 118.
33 LW 7.
34 NW 152–3.
35 NW 155.
36 NW 170.
37 NW 190.
38 NW 187.
39 NW 147.
40 NW 124–6.
41 NW 174.
42 NW 176.
43 NW 142.
44 NW 142.
45 K 144. Egyptians, he notes in *Causes and Effects*, 'are in a slumber akin to death' (AN 176).
46 K 142.
47 K 142–3.
48 K 143.
49 K 152.
50 NW 166–7.
51 NW 182.
52 NW 186.
53 NW 183.

54 NW 127.

55 Amīn also points out that critics of his 'admiration for European society' engage in hypocrisy when 'their replies resorted to the opinions of European scholars and writers, and have used resources written by both men and women!' (NW 190).

56 E 107–8.

57 NW 185.

58 NW 170.

59 NW 197.

60 NW 196.

61 NW 190.

62 NW193.

63 NW 200, emphasis added.

64 *Ibid.* He elsewhere expresses his frustration with the many and scorn for the uneducated, calling public opinion 'this stupid multitude [*jumhūr*], the enemy of change, servant of falsehood, and supporter of the unjust? Should reformers always wait for the approval of public opinion, nothing in the world would have changed since the way it was in the age of Adam and Eve' (K 151). In another entry, he expresses frustration at those who refuse to even read *The Liberation of Women*: 'One man asked, "What do you think of *The Liberation of Women*?" "It's filthy!" he replied. "You've read it?" "No." "Isn't it necessary to take a look at it before you judge it to be filth?" "I have not and will not read something that contradicts my opinions!"' (K 155).

65 K 158–9.

66 He likewise describes a trip to the Louvre Palace, where the other Egyptians on the trip were unable to appreciate what he describes as invaluable treasures: worth more than anything money can buy, his companions could not appreciate their beauty (K 150).

67 K 150.

68 K 144. This passage may appear ironic in light of accusations that Amīn treats European sources as a child might.

69 K 152.

70 AN 172–3.

71 AN 173.

72 AN 175. He prescribes a number of 'Western' education reforms, but how 'Westernized' this education actually is not so obvious; it includes things like providing positive and attainable examples of adulthood for children and not instilling superstitious fears in children (AN 193–5, 205–6).

73 AM 209–14.

74 AM 215.

75 Juan Ricardo Cole, 'Feminism, Class, and Islam in Turn-of-the-Century Egypt', *International Journal of Middle East Studies*, 13: 4 (1981), 387–407, 402.

76 Muḥammad Ṭalʿat Ḥarb, *Faṣl al-khitāb fī al-marʾa wa-l-ḥijāb* [*The Final Word about Women and the Veil*] (Cairo: Maṭbaʿat al-Taraqqī, 1901), 6, 7.

77 Muḥammad Ḥussayn Haykal, *Tarājim Miṣriyya wa gharbiyya* [*Egyptian and Western Biographies*] (Cairo: Muʾassasat Hindāwī li-l-Taʿlīm wa-l-Thaqāfa, 2014 [1929]), 100; also see al-Muqaddam, *ʿAwdat al-ḥijāb*, 56–7.

78 Muḥammad Farīd Wajdī, *al-Marʾa al-muslima: radd ʿalā Kitāb al-Marʾa al-jadīda* [*The Muslim Woman: Reply to* The New Woman], reprint (Cairo: Maṭbaʿat Hindiyya: 1912 [1901?]). On Wajdī's writings and life, see Muḥammad al-Hājrā, *Muḥammad Farīd Wajdī: Ḥayātuhu wa āthāruhu* (Alexandria: Maʿhad al-Buḥūth wa-l-Dirāsāt al-ʿArabiyya, 1970).

79   Hourani, *Arabic Thought in the Liberal Age*, 162, emphasis in original; also see Elshakry, *Reading Darwin in Arabic*, 180, 297; and Mansoor Moaddel, *Islamic Modernism, Nationalism, and Fundamentalism: Episode and Discourse* (Chicago: University of Chicago Press, 2005), 93.

80   Wajdī, *Muslim Woman*, 23.

81   *Ibid.*, 5–6.

82   *Ibid.*, 13, 23.

83   ʿAbd al-Raḥmān ibn Muḥammad ibn Khaldūn al-Ḥaḍramī (Ibn Khaldūn), *Kitāb al-ʿIbar wa dīwān al-mubtadaʾ wa-l-khabar fī tārīkh al-ʿarab wa-l-ʿajam wa-l-barbar wa mann ʿāsarahum min dhawī al-sulṭān al-akbar* [*The Book of Lessons and Archive of Origins, on the History of Arabs, Non-Arabs, and Berbers, and the Contemporary Major Rulers*].Volume 1 = *al-Muqaddima* (Prolegomena). English: *The Muqaddimah: An Introduction to History*, trans. Franz Rosenthal, 3 vols, Bollingen Series 43 (New York: Pantheon, 1958). Arabic: *Mawsūʿat Ibn Khaldūn:Tārīkh al-ʿalāma Ibn Khaldūn*, 6 vols (Cairo/Beirut: Dār al-Kitāb al-Maṣrī/Dār al-Kitāb al-Lubnānī, 1999). Arabic: vol. 1, ch. 23, 258–9; English vol. 1, ch. 22, 299–300.

84   Wajdī, *Muslim Woman*, 24.

85   On other appropriations of Ibn Khaldūn, see Mohammad R. Salama, 'Postcolonial Battles over Ibn Khaldun', in *Islam, Orientalism and Intellectual History; Modernity and the Politics of Exclusion since Ibn Khaldun* (London: IB Taurus, 2011), 77–101.

86   Wajdī, *Muslim Woman*, 25.

87   *Ibid.*, 26–8.

88   *Ibid.*, 25–6.

89   *Ibid.*, 20.

90   ʿAbd al-Majīd Khayrī, *al-Daf al-matīn fī al-radd ʿalā ḥaḍrat Qāsim bayk Amīn ʿan taḥrīr al-marʾa* [*A Firm Rebuttal to Mr Qāsim Amīn Bey on the Liberation of Women*] (Cairo: Maṭbaʿat al-Taraqqī, 1899), 6.

91   Review of ʿal-Daf al-matīn', *al-Muqtaṭaf* 23,Y. Sarruf and F. Nimr, eds (Cairo: al-Muktataf Printing Office, November 1899), 855. Arabic: *wa qad aḥsana ḥaḍrat al-muʾallif bi-ḥafẓi-hi ḥaqq al-tarjama li-nafsihi li-ʾanna-hu law tarjama aḥad hādhi-hi al-durar ilā lugha min lughat al-ʿūrūbiyīn la-istadallū minhā ʿalā anna ittiṣālunā bi-him mundhu miʾat ʿām ilā al-ʿān lam yughayyir shayʾan min raʾyinā fī al-marʾa.* On this journal, see Elshakry, *Darwin in Arabic.*

92   A Coptic Layman, 'The Awakening of the Coptic Church', *Contemporary Review*, 71 (1897), 734–47, 734. Donald Malcom Reid writes that 'A Coptic Layman' was probably Marcus Simaika. See his *Whose Pharaohs?: Archaeology, Museums, and Egyptian National Identity from Napoleon to World War I* (Berkeley and Los Angeles: University of California Press, 2002), 359 fn12. Simaika founded the Coptic Museum in 1908; for him, Coptic archaeology represented the fount out of which Coptic nationalism would flow. See Reid, *Pharoahs*, 258–9.

93   Armin Vambery [Arminius Vambery], *Western Culture in Eastern Lands: A Comparison of the Methods Adopted by England and Russia in the Middle East* (London: John Murray, 1906), 282–3.

94   Vambery, *Western Culture*, 283. In the German edition of Vambery's text, the 1906 *Westlicher Kulturinfluss im Osten*,Vambery cites Amīn as one among a series of activist-thinkers who argue that European advances 'in chemistry, mechanics, astronomy, medicine, etc.', are standing on 'our shoulders', such that without 'the preliminary work of our researchers in the past', they would 'not have reached there so easily' (307–8). He continues, presenting an abridged view of his English-language discussions of Amīn, citing him for the claim that Islam is not hostile to science since it commands people to pursue science (344).

95 Vambery, *Western Culture*, 284.

96 *Ibid.*, 383.

97 *Ibid.*, 360.

98 *Ibid.*, 314–17.

99 Josef Adolf Harpf, *Morgen- und Abendland: Vergleichende Kultur- und Rassenstudien* (Stuttgart: Verlag von Streder & Schröder, 1905), 206–7, emphasis added.

100 Martin Hartmann, review of Adolf Harpf, *Morgen- und Abendland: Vergleichende Kultur- und Rassenstudien, Zeitschrift des Vereins für Volkskunde*, 16 (1906), 360–4, 362–3.

101 Martin Hartmann, *Die Frau im Islam: Vortrag gehalten am 3 März 1909 in der Müncher Orientalischen Gesellschaft* (Halle a. S.: Gebauer-Schwetschke Druckerei u. Verlag, 1909). He explains (23 n1):

> Ever since Qāsim Amīn has opened the debate on this problem, the Mu'aijad [the Cairo daily *al-Mu'ayyad*, co-founded by Muṣṭafā Kāmil] has repeatedly treated the question. In February 1909 it published an accessible and simultaneously heartfelt article stating how Egypt suffers under the current practice of marriage, how almost nowhere can one find a truly intimate life partnership and how the woman does not, cannot, and does not want to know about the interests of her husband. And, the Mu'aijad is a thoroughly 'positive' and conservative publication. With enchanted praise they celebrated Qāsim Amīn, who died in 1908, in a eulogy for the first anniversary of his death.

On Hartmann, see Ursula Wokoeck, *German Orientalism: The Study of the Middle East and Islam from 1800 to 1945* (New York: Routledge, 2009).

102 H[enry] N[oel] Brailsford, 'Modernism in Islam', *Fortnightly Review*, 90 (1908), 472–82, 480–2. Portions of the article were reprinted a month later in *The Literary Digest* under the title, 'Trying to Modernize Islam', *Literary Digest*, 37 (1908), 463–4.

103 Brailsford, 'Modernism', 482.

104 Anonymous, 'Woman in Egypt', *The Englishman*, 1: 2 (1908), 42.

105 J. Desormeau, 'Frauenemanzipation in der islamischen Welt', *Dokumente des Fortschritts*, 1: 7–12 (1908), 872–4.

106 Roland Knyvet Wilson, *Anglo-Muhammad Law: A Digest*, 3rd edn (London: W. Thacker and Co, 1908), 469.

107 Reverend Ernest Bourner Allen, 'The Outlook in the Orient', *Bibliotecha Sacra*, 63: 261 (1906), 443–59, 448–9, emphasis added.

108 Joseph A. Massad, *Desiring Arabs* (Chicago: University of Chicago Press, 2007), 55–7.

109 On Samuel Zwemer, see Heather J. Sharkey, *American Evangelicals in Egypt: Missionary Encounters in an Age of Empire* (Princeton, NJ: Princeton University Press, 2008), 93–160.

110 Samuel Marinus Zwemer and Amy E. Zwemer, *Moslem Women* (West Medford: Central Mission on the Study of Foreign Missions, 1926), 170.

111 Zwemer, *Moslem Women*, 93–6.

112 For critical studies of how Islam is made to be the antonym of liberal, Christian, secular, or Western ideals through some of these same categories, see: Saba Mahmood, 'Secularism, Hermeneutics, and Empire: The Politics of Islamic Reformation', *Public Culture*, 18: 2 (2006), 323–47, and Mahmood, 'Feminism, Democracy, and Empire'; Talal Asad, *Formations of the Secular* (Stanford, CA: Stanford University Press, 2003), and *On Suicide Bombing* (New York: Columbia University Press, 2007); Norton, *The Muslim Question*; and Massad, *Islam in Liberalism*.

113 Samuel Zwemer, 'The Worth and Failure of Mohammedanism', North American Students and World Advance: Addresses Delivered at the Eighth International

Convention of the Student Volunteer Movement for Foreign Missions, Des Moines, Iowa, 31 December 1919 to 4 January 1920, Burton St John, ed. (New York: Student Volunteer Movement for Foreign Missions, 1920), 165–72, 169.

114 LW 9.

115 Samuel Marinus Zwemer, *Childhood in the Moslem World* (New York: Fleming H. Revell Co., 1915), 158.

116 Zwemer, 'Worth and Failure', 165–72, 169.

117 Samuel Marinus Zwemer, *The Disintegration of Islam* (New York: Fleming H. Revell Co., 1916), 163.

118 *Ibid.*, 171.

119 *Ibid.*, 194–5.

120 *Ibid.*, 197.

121 Samuel Marinus Zwemer, 'The Present Crisis in the Moslem World', *North American Student: Council of North American Student Movements*, 2: 4 (1914), 177–83, 182–3.

122 Samuel Marinus Zwemer, 'The Fullness of time in the Moslem World', *Missionary Review of the World*, 37: 3 (1914), 175–85, 183.

123 I am indebted to Nick Harris, Theresa Krueggeler, Dan-el Padilla Peralta, Elias Saba, and Rebecca Woods for their feedback on this chapter.

9

Marxism and historicism in the thought of Abdullah Laroui

Yasmeen Daifallah

Like many of his generation of Arab thinkers, the Moroccan historian Abdullah Laroui (b. 1933) is often described as a defector from Marxism. In Laroui's case, the defection is mostly described as one to liberalism, or to a state-centred modality of liberalism that Ibrahim Abu Rabi' calls 'liberal étatism'.[1] This purported change of heart is usually explained in terms of Laroui's supposed adaptation to the changing tides of Arab politics that, once sympathetic to leftist critique in the 1950s and 1960s, gave way to increasingly state-centred versions of liberal – and later neo-liberal – reform beginning in the late 1970s and continuing through the 2000s.[2]

What these interpretations miss, however, is Laroui's peculiar appropriation and subsequent development of Marxism for an Arab context throughout his writing career, particularly in his early works, published in the late 1960s and early 1970s. In these works, Laroui explains that he chooses Marxism on pragmatic grounds, and conceives of it less as a political truth, and more as a school of thought that works best to educate Arab intellectuals and political leaders – for him the primary revolutionary agents in postcolonial Arab societies – about historical change in a world that has been fundamentally reshaped by the physical and intellectual violence of colonialism. It is in this sense that Laroui refers to his Marxism of choice as 'Marxist historicism', denoting his emphatic concern with Marxism as a compelling theory of history, above and beyond his belief in it as a political ideology.[3] It is Laroui's enduring interest in, and conviction of, a Marxist variety of historicism throughout his writing career that critics often overlook when they describe him as yet another convert from the Arab Left.[4] That being said, one should note that these critics are correct to point out the disappearance of the 'Marxist' qualifier in 'Marxist historicism' in Laroui's later writings in the 1980s through the 2000s. The mitigation of the Marxist and 'Third-Worldist' tenor of Laroui's early works in favour of the less explicitly ideological referent, 'historicism' or *al-tarikhaniyya*, should be read in the broader political and intellectual context of the Arab Left's attempt to retain relevance in an atmosphere predominated by statist and Islamist idioms in the 1980s and 1990s, and less as an abandonment of his earlier Marxist sympathies.

The apparent distinction between Laroui's early and late works should be seen as symptomatic of the intellectual trajectory of a generation of leftist Arab thinkers born in the 1920s and 1930s who reached intellectual maturity during the late colonial and early postcolonial periods in the 1950s and 1960s.[5] Like other Arab leftists at the time, including the Egyptian sociologist Anouar Abdel Malek (1924–2012) and the Syrian philosopher Sadeq Jalal Al-'Azm (1934–), Laroui started his writing career in the 1960s at a time of heightened political urgency, when the national liberation state was perceived by these intellectuals to be in need of theoretical and practical guidance to deliver on the prom- ise of political independence, military strength, economic development and self-sufficiency, and cultural modernity. Writing in the wake of the military, political, and psychological shock of the defeat of Nasserist Egypt and Ba'athist Syria – and therefore of the main proponents of revolutionary Arab national- ism – in the 1967 Six Day War, these intellectuals conceived their role as one of explaining, critiquing, and helping overcome what they saw as the inability of the decolonisation state to achieve its goals. The pronounced Marxist tone of Laroui's writings in the late 1960s and early 1970s is therefore representative of the radicalisation of critique in the post-1967 period, and the broader quest to reorient and rehabilitate Arab politics that pervaded Arab leftist discourse at the time.[6]

Still animated by a Marxist notion of history, Laroui's later works, most mark- edly his *Concepts Series* published between 1980 and 1996, also exemplify the trend Arab leftist thought took during that time, which witnessed some fun- damental political shifts in Arab politics. These shifts included the onset of the Lebanese Civil War in 1975 (and continuing until 1990), the Islamic Revolution in Iran in 1979, and the Israeli siege of Beirut in 1982 that forced the Palestinian Liberation Movement out of its Lebanese headquarters. These events, respectively, seemed to illustrate the fragmentation of the 'nation' (hitherto the supposed sub- ject of national liberation) into warring sects, the political viability of an 'Islamic alternative' to the socialist-leaning nationalism that had dominated the political and intellectual scenes since the late 1940s, and a serious blow to what was widely conceived as the only remaining revolutionary agent in Arab politics after the 1967 defeat. Amid increasing desperation about the viability of the revolutionary nationalist project, many Arab leftists of Laroui's generation took their critique from the domain of theorising imperialist domination and revolutionary poli- tics to that of cultural critique. In particular, thinkers like Laroui, Al-'Azm, Yassin al-Hafez, and later Mohamed 'Abed al-Jabiri and Hassan Hanafi considered the persistence of 'traditional' (Islamic and sectarian) modes of life and thought as one of the main, if not the main, barriers to a genuine modernity on economic, political, and social fronts.[7] In this generation's estimate, the objective of the intel- lectual therefore became to modernise culture through sustained examinations of the Islamic and modern European traditions of thought, and to popularise these writings as much as possible.

Certainly, Laroui's privileging of cultural and ideology critique over socioeconomic and political critique has always been a primary attribute of his work, in the 1960s and 1970s as well as in the 1980s and 1990s.[8] What distinguished these later works, however, was their notable shift from a concern with theoretically edifying and guiding the revolutionary intellectual and leader, which presupposed a certain amount of knowledge about salient trends in European progressive (especially Marxist) thought on their part, to an emphasis on introducing the general public to the central precepts of modern thought in a pedagogical, jargon-free manner that lacked the 'cryptic' and distinctly polemical quality of Laroui's earlier writings.[9] In that respect, Laroui's later writings represent a broader shift in leftist Arab intellectuals' self-perception away from being a militant vanguard that leads and/or informs political action to the more subdued status of educators of the general public.

This chapter presents a broad overview of Laroui's political thought that turns around the axis of historicism: the notion that the rules of historical change are singular and universal and that their adequate comprehension gives the human subject a measure of control over historical processes.[10] It is, as Laroui simplifies it in an interview, 'the theory of history as a general, objective process that is not specific to this race or that region, to this culture or to that language, and that is governed by laws of change operating independently of human will'.[11] In particular, I examine how Laroui adapts a Marxist variety of historicism – a theory of history based on a holistic interpretation of Marx's *oeuvre* with a particular emphasis on his early writings – as the theoretical framework most adequate to understanding and transforming the Arab condition. This is primarily because, in Laroui's estimate, postcolonial Arab societies find themselves in a situation similar to that of late eighteenth- and early nineteenth-century Germany, which eventually gave rise to Marxist thought: a concern with the economic and political 'backwardness' relative to other nations combined with an aspiration to transcend that state of subordination. These two attributes of the Arab condition, which Laroui conceives of as self-evident and even intuitive to the Arab intellectual, render Marxist historicism as the best lens through which to analyse and situate the Arab social, economic, and cultural condition within a broader historical trajectory, and to provide insight as to the specific ways in which that condition could be changed.

In the final analysis, Laroui does not argue for a blind imitation of European modernity that ignores the specific histories and cultural traditions of Arab societies, nor does he propose a nativism that preserves or revives such traditions. Rather, he advocates 'specificity': a position that inserts the Arab experience (pre-colonial, colonial, and postcolonial) in the (cultural, political) forms universalised through the spread of European modernity. The result, in his estimate, would be a universalism worthy of its name: one that is not Eurocentric but inclusive of other peoples' histories and experiences. Laroui's argument is at its clearest in his consideration of the possibility for an Arab aesthetic specificity, which I discuss at the end of the chapter.

The life and times of Abdullah Laroui

Born to a middle-class family in Azemmour, a small town south of Casablanca, Morocco, in 1933, Laroui had an early education in religious and public schools, later obtaining a grant to attend the *Collège* Sidi Mohamed in Marrakesh, where he and other Moroccan students studied alongside French students between 1945 and 1949.[12] Having obtained the French high-school degree, the *baccalauréat*, in 1952 with a *mention bien*, Laroui qualified for a scholarship to attend university in France, of which Morocco was a protectorate until 1956. Initially intending to study medicine, Laroui later shifted his focus to the humanities because he 'had the idea to write novels … and could not see how I could be a doctor and a writer at the same time'.[13]

Laroui was to spend the next three years, from 1953 till 1956, at the *Institut d'Etudes Politiques* in Paris, which he describes as 'something like the London School of Economics' where his education was 'essentially an introduction in economic and social history'.[14] He considers these years as the time when he 'was formed as an historian' and traces this formative impact of the *Institut* to the influence of two teachers: Charles Morazé, a member of the *Annales* school of French historiography, and the renowned philosopher Raymond Aron, then professor of the history of ideas at the *Institut*.[15] Given the *Annales'* concern with the study of society and economy in the *longue durée* (as opposed to the traditional historiography of great figures and political events) through the deployment of social scientific methods, Laroui's recalls that his primary lesson from Morazé was that 'social history was not historical facts, but the development of social structures'.[16]

In particular, Laroui traces his interest in Marxism to the way it was considered by these two teachers. For Morazé and Aron, neither of whom was a Marxist, Marx was primarily 'a historian, a brilliant journalist, a social theoretician, but not a political leader or a prophet'.[17] Indeed, Laroui concludes his recollection of his time at the *Institut* by asserting that the influence of these two teachers' conception of Marx is perhaps the reason why he never contemplated joining the Communist Party.[18] Laroui's conception of Marxism as less an ideology, and more a method of examining historical processes, seems in large part owed to the way he was introduced to Marx at the *Institut*.

After attaining a *diplôme d'études supérieure* (equivalent to a master's degree) in 1958, Laroui returned to Morocco and worked in the Ministry of Foreign Affairs, where he served as cultural attaché in Egypt (1960–62), and France (1962–63), before resigning to prepare for his *agrégation* (a competitive exam required to teach at secondary and postsecondary institutions in France) in Islamic studies.[19] Having successfully passed the *agrégation*, Laroui was immediately appointed as an assistant professor of history at the University of Mohamed V in Rabat in 1963. In 1967, Laroui was invited by the renowned Orientalist Gustav von Grunebaum, then the director of the Near Eastern Center at the University of California at Los Angeles (UCLA), to join the history faculty at UCLA. Laroui served as assistant professor of North African history for four years at UCLA before returning to Morocco to work on his *Doctorat d'état*, which he received in 1976 from the Sorbonne with a thesis on 'The Social and Cultural Origins of Moroccan Nationalism 1830–1912'.[20] He continued teaching in Rabat till 2000, when he retired.

While serving as a cultural attaché in Cairo, Laroui started writing his first major work, *L'idéologie arabe contemporaine: essai critique* (hereafter CAI), published shortly before the Arab defeat in the Six Day War. First published in French, CAI was translated into Arabic by the Lebanese publishing house *dar al-haqiqa* in 1970, and then again by Laroui (who was dissatisfied by the earlier translation) in 1995.[21] For Laroui, as for other intellectuals in colonial and early postcolonial North Africa such as Dris Chraïbi (1926–2007) and Abdelkabir Al-Khatibi (1938–2009), writing in French was symptomatic of the educational policy of colonial France, which privileged French over Arabic education in North Africa, therefore making French the language of the intellectual elite in colonial and early postcolonial times.[22] In that connection, Jean Jacques Waardenburg notes how post-independence North African intellectuals started a 'new kind of discourse with French society and culture' that articulated Islamic culture – whether as a 'lost past' or a normative ideal – as a constitutive element of North African identity.[23] The usage of French in these writings, he adds, indicated that these authors not only chose to engage their former coloniser but also their own compatriots 'for whom French was the primary vehicle of intellectual discourse'.[24] That having been said, Laroui's subsequent publications were mostly written in Arabic, and, with the exception of his work on the history of the Maghreb,[25] his other French writings were largely based on his published Arabic works.[26]

In 1973, Laroui published an Arabic language volume comprising a set of essays compiled under the title *al-'arab wa al-fikr al-tarikhi* (Arabs and Historical Thought; hereafter AHT). A variation of this volume was published in French and then translated into English in 1974 and 1976 as *The Crisis of the Arab Intellectual: Traditionalism or Historicism?* Together, CAI and AHT first drew attention to Laroui's critique of the central Arab ideologies of his day (Islamic reformism, liberalism, and nationalism), as well as his critique of European Orientalism. Laroui's *oeuvre* solicited a broad range of reactions from his contemporaries. Some like the Moroccan philosopher Mohamed 'Abed al-Jabiri, considered his writing evocative and daring, but critiqued what he saw as Laroui's elitism, his excessively abstract writing, and his 'axiomatic' mode of writing that states rather than argues.[27] Others, like the Moroccan novelist and literary critic Abdel Kebir Khatibi, considered Laroui's identification of the West as the 'Other' of the Arab as reductive, and held that it reproduced a metaphysics of difference that was particularly troubling given French deconstructionism's teachings about identity and difference.[28] In general, Laroui's works in the early 1960s and 1970s were perceived as marking the arrival of a serious and original contender on the Arab intellectual scene. Arabic language accounts of, tributes to, and critical engagements with Laroui's various contributions have abounded since the 2000s, the latest of which was published in February 2015.[29]

Between 1980 and 1996, Laroui published a series of books in Arabic on what he considered to be the central concepts of modernity. This series culminated in six volumes on the concepts of ideology, liberty, the state, history (two volumes), and reason.[30] This chapter will use Laroui's early works, CAI, AHT, and *The Crisis of the Arab Intellectual* to elucidate his notions of traditionalism and historicism and the way they related to political action, although occasionally referring to his later works to show the continuance of his project despite surface changes.[31]

The intellectual context of Laroui's intervention

Like most Arab intellectuals in the early postcolonial period, Laroui assumes an anti-colonial modernist stance:[32] he argues for overcoming cultural and political subordination to the West through a more thorough grasp and implementation of the theoretical and epistemological premises of modern thought, and a simultaneous recognition that 'all our [contemporary Arab] ties with tradition have been severed in all fields and once and for all'.[33] Writing in the late 1960s and the early 1970s, this argument is meant by Laroui as an antidote to claims that genuine decolonisation is best attained by the revival or renewal of Islamic cultural and sociopolitical norms, or through the weaving together of local culture with modern (specially socialist) modes of production and political organisation. Thus, Laroui's early works situate his radical modernism against what he perceives as the pervasiveness of the 'traditionalist' (Islamist) and 'eclectic' (nationalist) ideologies in postcolonial times.

Laroui also sets his argument against what he conceives as the two dominant modes of leftist engagement in Arab politics in the post-independence period. The first considers ideology a mechanical manifestation of socioeconomic reality and its class constitution (e.g. the position that explains persistence of traditionalist thought by reference to the continued influence of feudalists or the rural bourgeoisie),[34] and the second suffers an 'ideological deficit'[35] because it shuns all theorising in favour of immersion in practical politics.[36] Laroui's early works respond to these two trends as follows: first, and most notably, in CAI, Laroui uses ideology critique to illustrate the irreducibility of cultural production to the prevailing socioeconomic structures of colonial and postcolonial Arab societies. Instead, Laroui argues that the constant tendency among Arab social and political reformers to define themselves by reference to the Western Other renders their thought irreducible to a socioeconomic infrastructure or to specific class formations. Although these are relevant, their explanatory power is limited in grasping the content and trajectory of modern Arab social and political thought.[37]

Second, Laroui attempts to persuade his target audience of 'practical progressives' – who he sees as including major political leaders like Nasser (1918–70) of Egypt, Mehdi ben-Baraka (1920–65) of Morocco, and Ahmed ben-Bella (1918–2012) of Algeria – that ideological edification was essential to effective politics. Indeed, Laroui considers CAI, where he discusses, historicises, and critiques major trends in modern Arab thought since the late 1800s, to ultimately be a study 'of the role of revolutionary consciousness and ideological constitution in raising the performance of revolutionary leadership'.[38] It is in this context that Laroui introduces Marxist historicism (and Marxism more generally) as the revolutionary theory that enables the post-independence revolutionary movement to effect a political leadership that simultaneously addresses the diverse needs of various social groups (bourgeoisie, feudalists, petit bourgeoisie, labour, peasants, etc.) while at the same time attending to the holistic national and historical objectives of revolutionary politics. In the absence of the revolutionary consciousness produced by the leadership's commitment to a particular theory, Laroui argues, politics is reduced to the representation of the class interests of only one of the multiple groups that constitute the liberation movement.[39]

In addition to its significance to forming a truly vanguardist party (and here we see a clear Marxist-Leninist influence on Laroui's thought), the adoption of Marxist historicism would provide the progressive Arab intellectual with a comprehensive and compelling school in historical thought.[40] The importance of supplying the Arab intellectual with historical consciousness, 'the true measure of modernity',[41] cannot be overstated in Laroui's thought. Without such consciousness, that intellectual basks in what Laroui calls a state of 'the perpetual present': 'in the perpetual present … that divorces itself from its lived reality and lives in a time past, one which it considers an absolute truth'.[42] So long as this unconsciousness of one's reality dominates Arab thought (which Laroui posits that it does through the pervasiveness of traditionalism and eclecticism), Arab intellectuals will continue to be both irrelevant to, and ineffectual in, their social and political domains.

Thus, Laroui's project is to transform traditionalist (and eclectic) modes of thought by introducing a specific variety of Marxism, Marxist historicism, and persuading the Arab intellectual that it provides the most adequate understanding of the constitutive processes of the modern world, including the Arab social, political, and cultural reality since colonial intervention. Such Marxism would also equip that intellectual with the best ways to engage and overcome imperial domination. Laroui's argument for Marxist historicism is therefore pragmatic rather than dogmatic: it should be chosen, not for its metaphysical merit or the conceit that it will lead to greater human happiness, justice, or emancipation than would rival systems of thought, but because it illuminates the way the modern world operates, and because the coining of a singular ideology (rather than various interpretations thereof, their validity notwithstanding) would unite and guide the revolutionary party. Any genuine attempt to attain 'progress' in the modern world should be led by a cohesive group who understand and play according to the epistemological rules that govern it.[43]

It is to a consideration of the chief Arab intellectual ailment, traditionalism, and its (Marxist) historicist remedy that I now turn.

Identifying the problem: traditionalism and cultural retardation

In Laroui's estimate, historicism (whether Marxist or not) has two main rivals that are linked by their common rejection of ideas about teleological social and political evolution that prevailed in nineteenth- and early twentieth-century Europe. The first lies in the anti-historicist directions in European religious and political philosophy, literary theory, history, linguistics, grammar, rhetoric, poetry, anthropology, and psychoanalysis that became increasingly attractive to Arab intellectuals in the second half of the twentieth century. These new directions in the humanities and social sciences questioned the primacy of 'historical time' as the only legitimate way of organising and experiencing time in the modern West to the exclusion of other possible notions of time, including those that 'subordinate historical time to some higher value' like divine fate or rational metaphysics.[44] For Laroui, what is most alarming about the increasing salience of these views in Arab intellectual circles in the 1950s and 1960s is that they (unintentionally) serve to legitimate a more serious rival to historicism: a 'traditionalist' understanding of history that had persisted since the precolonial period, and that continues to animate much of the Arab intellectual discourse about the sociopolitical world.[45] Laroui's project is more concerned with analysing and eradicating what he conceives as 'traditionalism' than it is with renewing the relevance of ancient notions of time through utilising the latest anti-historicist trends in Western philosophy.

Indeed, Laroui introduces *The Crisis of the Arab Intellectual* with a 'central [historicist] fact' that he considers the premise of his subsequent analyses of Arab culture throughout the book.[46] This fact, Laroui states, is the 'cultural retardation' of Arab society, or, as he elaborates later, the fact that 'Arab culture both in its classical expression and in the most influential aspect of its present day expression is opposed in every particular to liberal culture'.[47] Instead, modern-day Arab culture continues to be 'traditionalist', animated by a desire 'not merely to draw inspiration from classical Arab culture, but to revive and re-actualize it — if not in the totality of its aspects, then at least in its inner logic'.[48] This desire to 'revive and re-actualize' expresses itself in a community's demands to 'organize its economy and political regime, its legal order and individual, familial and social moral codes, its educational system, etc. in the image of [a historical culture]'.[49]

Laroui's most substantive discussion of the distinction between traditionalist and modern understandings of history comes in the context of his analysis of classical Islamic and modern European historiographical practices. Through examining these two modes of narrating the past, Laroui seeks to highlight the relationship between:

> [T]he study of events (the search for facts, and the techniques of historical description), and the attitude that a society has toward the aggregate of experienced events; in other words, the place that such a society accords to the past in the pattern of its present and its future, and hence of its functioning.[50]

Laroui describes classical Arab-Islamic[51] historiography as heterogeneous.[52] It consists of three distinct but related modes of narration that correspond to the different political stages through which the classical Arab-Islamic community passed. The first mode, dating to the seventh and eighth centuries CE, relied on testimony, 'the transmitted accounts of first-hand witnesses' whose authenticity was closely examined before it was verified.[53] Laroui remarks that this mode of recording and narrating events was characterised by its originality compared to that of preceding and contemporary cultures. This originality consisted in the classical Arab conception of history as 'established, controlled knowledge of past and present' as opposed to 'an accumulation of unverifiable legends'.[54] It owes its development, he adds, to the related practice of producing religious knowledge. The honest and careful recording of the unfolding of revelation and the prophetic tradition was crucial to generating 'true' Islamic knowledge, as well as to matters of private and public law in the early Islamic community (e.g. the order of conversion to Islam affected booty allocations, and the details of Muslim conquests affected the treatment of newly conquered regions).[55]

As the early Islamic community expanded, this 'religious component'[56] of early Islamic historiography was supplemented with a 'communal political'[57] one:

> to the nucleus formed by the stories of the prophet were added the titles of glory and antiquity of each [new community]. The pre-Islamic Arabs ... gave their legends; the Persians gave the long gallery of their king of kings; the Rum gave the annals of Byzantium; and so on.[58]

Such additions reflected the increasing capacity of the state to 'realize a *modus vivendi* between the different groups'.[59] Intended to render cohesive an expansive and diverse entity, this historiography added a new criterion to the previous one: 'a new moderation or liberalism in the acceptance of testimonies'.[60] Finally came 'the historiography of minorities' like 'the dynasty, the legal school, or the mystic brotherhood'.[61] Highly political, this mode 'developed in the shadow of communal historiography',[62] employed the same historiographical method (chiefly testimony), and had the same objective as the second mode but with regard to a particular political, legal, or religious group. Due to its concern with raising group members to pre-eminence while excluding outsiders, it made use of 'subtle omission' as well as 'rudimentary rational critique'[63] in relation to rival groups whose history was to be contested. Laroui gives the example of how the

Shi'ite historian Al-Mas'udi (896–956 CE) used rational critique to 'ridicule the claims of the Umayyads [the historical rivals of Ali]', though he continued to rely 'solely on chain transmission when he dealt with Shi'ism'.[64] Laroui concludes that the historiography of minorities added a rational critical component to Islamic historiography around the tenth century, but that testimony remained the dominant form of verification of historical truth in Islamic historiography.

Laroui points to how the amalgamation of these three modes of historiography produced a prototypical narrative form that finds its best illustration in standard narratives of Islamic history, such as Ibn Al-Athir's (1160–1233). Reflecting the heterogeneity of Islamic historiography, these later narratives comprise a 'nucleus' that record the stages of the prophet's life including revelation, proselytisation, persecution, victory, and conquest. This is preceded by an 'antecedent history' of pre-Islamic peoples, which for these historiographers constitutes a 'pre-history', a period of futility that precedes the real history of prophecy. The prophetic nucleus is followed by the history of the successors in which the historian, although relying on testimony, 'accepts anything that may unite the community, but rarely anything that could be utilized by one faction against another'.[65]

Although these modes of narration may differ, Laroui agrees with Orientalist scholarship of Islamic historiography[66] that what all these modes share is their 'objective' and 'impassive' quality. Although 'objectivity' refers to Arab historians' (variously strict) reliance on verified testimonies to offer as accurate a narrative about historical events as possible, 'impassiveness' refers to their 'employ[ment of] the same style for describing the worst reverses of Arab military history as for describing the heights of gladness'.[67] Rather than characterising these qualities as either 'remarkable' or 'baffling', as Laroui notes his Orientalist counterparts do, he explains the Arab historian's objectivity as dictated by a sense of duty towards God and the community when reporting about the prophetic period or as indicating an inability to judge truth from falsity in its aftermath. It is therefore 'identical either with the moral obligation to tell the truth [about the prophet's time], or with the impossibility of knowing the truth [in the post-prophetic period]'.[68] Likewise, the 'almost clinical detachment' with which Arab historians narrate the changing tides of Islamic history does not signify their fatalism, but their conviction that if setbacks occurred during the prophetic period they were of necessity temporary, 'for the historian is assured of the final result'.[69] During the post-prophetic period, on the other hand, the historian assumes a detached attitude towards facts, 'for if truth is no longer given, no longer guaranteed by a present God, the difference between success and failure becomes relative'.[70] In both cases, the objectivity and detachment in question are not of the 'scientific' type that 'considers events to possess a tangible and immediate impact on human lives'.[71] Rather, they are related to the historian's belief in the religious duty to relay facts. Although this duty lay in establishing an accurate record of the prophetic tradition, life, and works for the early Islamic period, in subsequent periods of political strife in the Muslim community when such 'truth' seemed no longer evident, the historian's disposition was one of a detached observer and recorder of events that ceased to possess a particular meaning or to signify a truth. In this context, Laroui mentions the example of the repeated victories of the Umayyads over the supporters of 'Ali ibn Abi-Taleb in the mid-seventh century. The latter 'were unquestionably in the right',[72] whereas the former were considered unjust by the majority of the believers. Speaking on behalf of the classical Arab historian, Laroui rhetorically asks: 'What was one to think? Was one to think that success denotes God's approval and failures to denote his anger? No, they were mere facts, which must be recorded without further comment, for they are meaningless.'[73]

This 'meaninglessness' of events for the classical Arab historian is what Laroui takes to be the defining (and persistent) character of Muslim society's relationship to the past.[74] Laroui infers from his examination of Arab historiography that the Arab historian 'does not see events as positive facts in their own right',[75] as having a palpable 'weight, effect, or meaning'[76] on subsequent events, or for the human condition in general. Likewise, history, conceived as the aggregation of such events, 'does not [for the classical Arab historian] constitute a level of reality possessing autonomous consistency, where actions can fall into place and by their configuration cause other actions to appear'.[77] The classical view, which for Laroui constitutes the premise of contemporary traditionalism, events are neither generative of each other, nor indicative of an underlying process, meaning, or direction. Rather than seeking to record or recover a historical 'truth', the objective and impassive classical Arab historian suspends judgement about the significance of events and refrains from assigning to them a certain unity or direction. For the classical Arab historian, all facts 'were equal and can appear in any order whatsoever ... [and] history appears not as a succession but a juxtaposition of new beginnings', whereby periods featuring the emergence of a new state or leader (Laroui gives the example of Almohads of twelfth-century North Africa) are understood as new beginnings. The chronological order of the prophetic period, or 'kernel' of Islamic history, and the period between prophetic times and the rise of this new state (in this case, a period of approximately five centuries) 'not so much one of decadence as one of inexistence or occultation, during which nothing important took place'.[78] Of central importance to this historiography are the institutions and practices of the prophetic period, whereas other historical periods have no importance, and are in a basic sense less 'real'.

Laroui situates this traditionalism in a broader pattern of harking to the past that could also be seen in the renewed interest of twentieth-century Western humanities in ancient Greece, Rome, Byzantium, and the Christian West. But he makes a crucial distinction between their two modes of interest in the cultural and political past: whereas traditionalist Arab culture seeks to re-actualise a historical social and political order, its Euro-American counterpart views historical cultures as 'sources of aesthetic insights, of problematics to be reformulated within a new framework, and of ethical models'.[79] In the specific context of the post-liberal West, he adds, 'these [historical cultures] serve, dead though they are, to exorcise the specter of an end to history as embodied in liberal reason'.[80] The 'retardation' of Arab culture is therefore distinguished from twentieth-century Western nostalgia by the radical and substantial nature of its claims: a critical mass of the modern-day Arab community and/or of Arab intellectuals[81] hope to resuscitate the inner logic that once governed the classical (medieval) Arab-Islamic community.

Unlike most leftist Arab intellectuals writing during that period, who tend to take 'retardation' and the subsequent necessity for 'modernisation', as givens,[82] Laroui is quick to note the controversial nature of his claim in an intellectual milieu where 'historicism as a way of thinking is as devalued as scientism, positivism, and metaphysical materialism of the nineteenth century'.[83] Although acknowledging the relevance of twentieth-century critiques of historicism, humanism, and liberalism,[84] Laroui insists that the historicist expression 'cultural retardation' is nevertheless the best way to describe the condition of Arab culture today.[85] His justification for this characterisation of the Arab cultural condition is twofold. First, Arab culture expresses the 'retardation' of the relationships of production in Arab society and economy. 'We refer to retardation', Laroui notes, 'simply because we accept the principle that every culture is the expression of a society, itself defined by its material base.'[86] Indeed, Laroui cites colonisation as itself evidence of the 'absolute failure of the dominated society'[87] to maintain its integrity. This is a historicist justification of historicism: it assumes that history is evolutionary and 'unified', i.e. that it moves in one direction for all human societies.[88] Following this logic, the weakness of Arab economy, society, and polity relative to its European counterpart is itself evidence that the former lags behind the latter. Laroui seems to recognise the circularity of his reasoning when, following this justification for historicism, he asserts his commitment to it as a philosophical premise that requires no justification: 'we have already committed ourselves to and given proof of our historicism without in any way adducing reasons, and even refusing to do so; for to accept the necessity for a theoretical foundation is to owe allegiance to philosophy itself.'[89]

Laroui's second and more compelling justification adds pragmatic flavour to his historicist argument. Although noting the rising popularity of anti-historicist trends among Arab intellectuals in the 1960s and 1970s, he explains it as a compulsive rejection of all things liberal due to the perceived association between liberalism and colonialism. It is such rejection that prompts Arab Marxists to reject 'capitalism in economics, representative democracy in politics, utilitarianism in philosophy, materialism in human relationships, and prose in [literary] expression', even as they realise that such rejection defies the principles of the standard Marxist understanding of history.[90] This antipathy to liberalism (and to any Marxism that assumes liberalism as a historical stage) is, Laroui adds, also behind the lure for Arab intellectuals of philosophical trends like existentialism, psychoanalysis, structuralism, and anarchism that contest historicist (i.e. dialectical and teleological) notions of history.[91] Although recognising the reasons for the attractiveness of these trends for the Arab intellectual, Laroui alerts that intellectual to two adverse effects of adapting these trends for a non-Western setting: one theoretical and the other practical.

First, Laroui posits that European critiques of liberal (and classical Marxist) notions of history, attractive as they may be for anti-colonial Arab intellectuals, assume liberal modernity, if in the form of a reaction to it.[92] What Laroui implies here is that such schools of thought could only have emerged in a society, economy, and polity in which an industrialised liberal-democratic system already existed for a long time, and whose ills these intellectual trends come to underline and address. Liberal modernity thereby constitutes the condition of possibility, both philosophically and actually, for philosophical schools that criticise or reject it. In the manner of a dialectically-minded historian, Laroui seeks to draw to the attention of the 'progressive' Arab intellectual in the 1960s and the 1970s that existentialism, psychoanalysis, anarchism, etc. are themselves enabled by, and contain within them, the intellectual, social, and economic gains of liberal modernity. In that sense, European critiques of liberal modernity do not imply a refusal of liberalism, but its transcendence. Thus, Laroui alerts his Arab reader in AHT to the critical distinction between European and Arab (or non-Western) anti-historicism:

> When the Western intellectual rejects liberalism or the Marxism that accepts liberalism [as a historical stage] … he is rejecting an extant and tangible reality that surrounds him, and that his society has experienced for decades … when we reject it [sic], we reject that which we do not possess, and assume that we own it just because we could reject it. We ridicule [what we see as] a narrow, limited, superficial liberal tradition which we have not yet absorbed, all the while leaving the door wide open for traditionalist thought to pervade our public life, in schools, newspapers and magazines, social clubs. We allow that thought to pose as contemporary because non-liberal, while in reality it is more backward than liberal thought.[93]

Thus, when Arab (or Third-World) intellectuals uncritically appropriate these new trends, they are unaware that 'it is post-liberal western culture that is conceding its modernity to Arab culture, which accepts it as a gift, effortlessly'.[94]

Second, along with his historicist argument about the theoretical hazard of embracing critiques of liberalism without having absorbed and/or experienced it, Laroui worries about the pragmatic political effects of such a position: namely, providing traditionalist thought with ready-made proofs of its currency. In the same pragmatic spirit, Laroui points out that, despite their salience among Western intellectuals, anti-historicism and anti-humanism remain marginal to Western society and politics. Rather, the notion of 'history as progress, rationalism in economics, realism in politics, and humanism in literature and the arts' continues to dominate the 'vision of the economic organization, internal and external politics, social morality, the education system, and "popular" literature in the West'.[95]

In conclusion, Laroui's defence of his historicist claim about Arab 'cultural retardation' seems to be that any meaningful theorisation or political action for Arab political change has to reckon with the continued global hegemony of liberal rationality, and with the cost of a premature espousal of critiques to it. Although Laroui's justifications for adopting historicism are themselves mostly historicist (i.e. they flow from the assumption that history develops dialectically according to knowable rules), they also complicate claims about Arab intellectuals' uncritical adoption of modernist notions of historical change. Laroui does this by illustrating that the choice of historicism is a result of a careful weighing of alternatives rather than an unconscious acquiescence to dominant discourses in Western scholarship about the non-West.[96]

Towards a solution: anti-colonial historicism

The context of Laroui's fierce defence of historicism is important to grasping his deep investment in it as a theoretical and political project. As mentioned above, Laroui's assertion about Arab 'cultural retardation' comes in the context of an intensified state of soul-searching and self-critique that pervaded Arab intellectual circles in the aftermath of Israel's decisive victory in the Six Day War, but whose beginnings were also evident among leftist intellectuals before that time.[97] Far from viewing it as a military or political defeat, Arab intellectuals of that period conceived the Six Day War as a blow to the postcolonial nationalist project, and an occasion for a more careful examination of its theoretical and epistemological premises.[98] Indeed, as Laroui explains to his English-language reader in the preface to *The Crisis of the Arab Intellectual*:

> what interested my [Arab] listeners was not so much the positive results as the failure of those [traditional political parties, Nasserism and Baathism, and Arab Marxism] movements. For the question they were asking, given the situation around 1970, was this: Why, in spite of all our efforts, are we facing the same difficulties that our parents and grandparents did?[99]

This sense of a sustained crisis, extending from the onset of colonialism in the late 1800s[100] to the late twentieth century, is what Laroui often refers to as the 'experiential fact' of (cultural and historical) retardation among the Arab public, and, more acutely, among Arab intellectuals.[101]

This state of political urgency partially explains the wide circulation of Laroui's critique of Arab social and political thought during the late 1960s and 1970s; in particular, his critique of Arab nationalism in CAI, published shortly before the 1967 defeat, seemed to presage Arab nationalism's imminent failure to deliver on its promises of genuine independence and political and military strength. In this earlier work, Laroui does not simply characterise traditionalism (in its Islamist or nationalist guises) as a desire to 're-actualise' the classical Arab-Islamic past as he does in *The Crisis of the Arab Intellectual*.[102] Rather, he complicates traditional-ist claims of fidelity to an Arab or Islamic 'origin' by demonstrating that Islamist and Arab nationalist discourses are shot through with a dual desire to respond to Orientalist and colonial charges of irrationality and backwardness, while 'excavat-ing' the European past for inspiration about their current predicament.[103] The result is usually a sort of hybrid ideology in which, for example, Islamic reformist claims that ascribe modern notions of rationality and scientificity to Islam are combined with a traditionalist notion of time and historical change.[104] By stressing tradi-tionalism's preoccupation with reviving a distant past, rather than the peculiarity of its interpretation of that past, post-1967 Laroui probably means to offer fellow Arab intellectuals as stark a juxtaposition as possible between what he takes to be the decisive difference between the 'inner logics' of traditionalism and modernity: their respective notions of history. Hybrid as modern trends in Arab ideology may be, Laroui's central thesis about them is: 'the concept of history – a concept play-ing a capital role in "modern" thought – is in fact peripheral to all the ideologies that have dominated the Arab world till now.'[105] The peripheral status of history to modern Arab thought is one whose stakes are high from Laroui's viewpoint: not only is 'history' required to fend off traditionalism, it is also necessary to overcome the continued Arab subordination to the West in post-independence times.

Laroui defines 'historicism' as a theory of history that perceives the event as a 'fact or an action that determines other facts or actions; so the present is explained by the past, but the past can be judged by the present'.[106] This is what Laroui means by the 'positivity' of events; that is, the notion that events count as such when they are consequential. The second attribute of historicism introduces human agents into the historical scene: 'because not all actions are equivalent', Laroui posits, 'it is possible to pass judgments on historical participants.'[107] Indeed, Laroui believes that contrary to what its opponents assert, Marx's conception of history maintains a crucial role for agency, for it 'goes beyond the internalization of objectivity – the classical attempt to master nature by submission to its laws – and strives to make a leap towards liberty'.[108] It is precisely the possibility for making such 'leaps' that distinguishes Marxist historicism for Laroui, and is also what makes it most fitting for the Third-World intellectual. What is most telling is that the definition of historicism that Laroui finds most compelling is one that he quotes from Marx's preface to *Capital*:

And when a society has got upon the right track for the discovery of the natural laws of its movement … it can neither clear by bold leaps, nor remove by legal enactments, the obstacles offered by the successive phases of its normal development. But it can *shorten* and *lessen* the birth-pangs.[109]

Laroui juxtaposes this understanding of historicism, which accounts for both con-text and the possibility of human intervention – or, in more philosophical terms, that account for 'structure' and 'agency' – to a 'liberalism [that] believes in fiats'[110] in the agency of an autonomous self-unencumbered by history or context. He also contrasts it to a 'traditionalist historicism [that] denies the necessity for cutting short the period of gestation',[111] therefore condemning the Third World to a prolonged, and supposedly mechanical, process of development. In contrast to both these (equally) modern understandings of history, Marxist historicism posits a historically situated and conditioned subject whose understanding of its own boundedness by 'natural laws of development' makes it possible for that subject to engage in conscious action to 'lessen and shorten' society's movement from one historical stage to the next. This is precisely why Laroui describes historicism as constituting 'the inner logic of political action'.[112] Although giving its subject the parameters of its context (its constitution by past 'events' and its standing in relation to a broader historical trajectory), Marxist historicism provides for a margin of human intervention in that trajectory, for the possibility of an exercising of political will, which, having understood the rules of the historical game, is at a better position to hasten its proceedings.

Laroui confirms this understanding of the relationship between history and its subject in a much later work, *mafhoum al-tarikh* (The Concept of History) where he writes:

> It [the determinism of the historicist] is not a natural determinism, but a voluntary one. This determinism signifies that a society has decided to enter the realm of history, and to persist in the direction [which historicism dictates]. Put more specifically, the rules of historicism become fixed insofar as the human subject is aware that he or she is a historical being. When this happens, history becomes identical to politics, and consciousness to will and initiative. Determinism in this case is a subjective law, not a fate imposed on the subject by an external force.[113]

The subject of historicism (in this case, society as a whole) is therefore one whose entry into the historicist mode of consciousness happens through a conscious decision. But this decision only takes place when that subject becomes aware that it exists in 'historical time', i.e. a time defined by the imperativeness of particular historical stages for all human societies. Thus, for the human subject to be properly historical, it needs to first become aware of its backwardness in relation to others who exist on the same 'historical plane', and to recognise that only a movement along that same plane, in the same direction, could effect historical progress.[114] Only when such a 'decision' is made on the part of subjects aware of their 'historical nature', or their backwardness in relation to others, can history become the realm of political activity, the space where historical knowledge about patterns of social behaviour informs daily political practice and determines the exercise of human will in favour of a particular goal.[115]

In addition to assigning a positive weight to historical events, and to rendering it possible to hold historical agents responsible for their actions, historicism has one more crucial attribute: it understands history as a 'continuity in which knowledge of the past informs the present and the present transforms the past, i.e. makes a new picture of the same material'.[116] This has two implications: first, because our understanding of the present is informed by the past, 'objectivity is guaranteed by history itself'.[117] Whether the historicist accurately reports an event or she or he does not, 'you cannot obliterate it, and it revenged itself precisely by informing your present in spite of you'.[118] Second, because of the constant contention between the past and present (the past informs the present, but the present passes judgement upon the past based on the latter's results) 'truth' is necessarily understood as becoming.[119] It is not accessible or achieved through the exercise of an autonomous reason or the interpretation of scripture. Rather, historicist 'truth' can only be revealed by the workings of history, and is therefore not fixed but mutable and contextual. Thus, what appears as 'truth' at a particular historical moment and within a specific historical context is never absolute or perennial, but a 'truth' that is specific to a particular time and place, and therefore bound to change. In this vein, Laroui highlights how the historicist notion of truth-as-becoming lies at the heart of democratic political practice:

> Democracy as a system of civic rule is based on the assumption that no one owns the political truth (i.e. the route to attaining the happiness, well being and development of society). This truth is formed gradually through continuous deliberation, mutual persuasion, and, ultimately, the voting system, all of which are ways of providing a consensual truth momentarily conceded to [by members of society] until changing circumstances prove otherwise.[120]

In contrast to this context-specific notion of 'truth' and its deliberative political subject, Laroui conceives of traditionalism as breeding a subject loyal to a fixed 'truth' represented by the 'golden age' of Islamic history during the prophetic period. Though Laroui understands this truth itself to be an interpretation conditioned by the sociopolitical context of colonial and postcolonial Arab societies, he ultimately characterises traditionalist thought as 'static, ossified, and nostalgic',[121] and as therefore lacking in historical consciousness.

Laroui's justifies his argument for historicism as the mode of historical and political consciousness that most befits the Arab condition on two grounds. First, an assimilation of historicism could enable a proper and accurate understanding of the social, political, and economic reality of Arab societies because it has continued to shape these conditions since colonialism. The alternative is that not attaining such an understanding comes — and, historically, has indeed come — at great costs in all these areas.[122] The second objective has to do with the potential benefits of adopting historicism, and here is where Laroui's argument for a distinctly Marxist historicism (rather than a liberal or a traditionalist one) could be situated. Historicism, Laroui asserts, would enable political action based on an understanding of history as a process comprised of successive stages, the movement from one to the next being conditioned upon the exercise of human will within the bounds of historical circumstance. The latter renders possible what Laroui terms 'leaps', that is, the ability to compress historical time to include the fruits of a historical stage without fully passing through it. Laroui regards the possibility of 'shortening and lessening the birth pangs' of historical change that the Marxist notion of history provides as the reason why it is the most compatible with the aspirations of the Third-World intellectual and with the latter's intuitive sense that such compression was indeed possible.[123]

Bypassing liberalism

Laroui's works show a consistent objective throughout, and a clear understanding of how a Marxist theory of history could serve to achieve it. This objective is best expressed in the opening lines of AHT:

> Upon rereading a set of lectures and articles about politics, culture, and methods of conducting historical research that I had prepared for various occasions in the past, I realized that the main problem I have been trying to tackle for years is the following: How can Arab thought absorb the achievements (*muktasabat*) of liberalism, before (and without) going through a liberal stage?[124]

What Laroui means by the 'achievements of liberalism' are the set of Enlightenment concepts that underlie the project of European modernity as a whole, including rationalism, humanism, objectivity, and liberal democracy.[125] He identifies the problem of comprehending and transcending this historical stage as one that has long haunted Marxist thought in general, and that has defined the lasting tension between its 'liberal wing', which stipulates the passage through a liberal democratic revolution (à la the French Revolution) to achieve a veritable intellectual transformation, and a 'voluntaristic wing' that argues for bypassing the 'liberal stage' of historical development by enforcing a set of social and economic changes that try to incorporate these Enlightenment principles (through rationalisation, industrialisation, urbanisation, etc.) without a thorough embourgeoisement of society.[126]

The genealogy of this tension notwithstanding, Laroui's broader point seems to be that the assimilation of liberal values is key to effecting genuine and durable political and cultural change in Arab societies, especially the overcoming of liberalism itself, whether that change awaits an organic democratic revolution or is to be voluntarily instilled by a vanguard. A correct understanding of Marxism, Laroui insists, would recall that it seeks to 'transcend the objectives of liberalism after *preserving* them, rather than simply dismissing those objectives'.[127] Basic as this point seems to be, Laroui thinks it has been lost on anti-colonial Arab intellectuals due to their consideration of liberalism as 'the associate, ally, and justifier of colonialism'.[128] Laroui's intervention in the late 1960s and 1970s is therefore chiefly meant as a reminder and a rejoinder to postcolonial Arab intellectuals who seek genuine political and economic independence from their former colonisers and a more egalitarian social and economic order[129] that the only way to achieve these goals is the acceptance and enactment of some measure of liberalism, but also, and more crucially, a grasp of the concept of historical change upon which European modernity was founded. The insertion of the concept of history into Arab social and political thought assumes a particular urgency for Laroui because his analysis of Arab ideological discourse since the late 1800s illustrates the marginality of historical (or, put more accurately, historicist) thought to that discourse, and the problematic results of that absence.[130]

It is crucial that Laroui frames this acceptance of historicism less as an uncritical testimony to the truth of liberal, enlightenment, or even Marxist, thought, and more as an acute recognition of the social, economic, and political reality that postcolonial Arabs face in a present that continues to be shaped by Western hegemony. What Marxism presents here is less a political truth, and more a pedagogy to educate Arab intellectuals and political actors of various persuasions about historical change and to provide them with the tools to effectively engage with hegemonic players in a world which has been fundamentally remade by the physical and intellectual violence of colonialism. As such, and as Laroui continues to assert, the choice of Marxist historicism is primarily a utilitarian rather than a principled one. The guiding logic of the choice is not whether it presents its adherent with a 'true' understanding of history, society and politics, but its political effectiveness: that is, the ability of its adherents to produce favourable results given the constraints of their condition.[131] Indeed, Laroui casts his utilitarian choice of Marxist historicism as not only fundamental to his objective of offering the best political guidance for the intellectual and political leader, but to historicism itself. Commenting on his earlier advocacy of Marxism as a political ethos in CAI, he writes:

> After re-examining some of the critiques that were leveled at my earlier work, it became clear to me that the Marxism I have tried to describe there was a historicist Marxism, if not a Marxist historicism. The premises of [CAI] were: the centrality of political action to theoretical thought, [the use of] utilitarian logic, the choice of Marxism as a pedagogy that could best clarify to non-Europeans the trajectory of the modern world since the Enlightenment and the beginnings of capitalism, and to connect the reality of the individual to that of society on the one hand, and those to historical change on the other. These premises are also the ones that constitute the historicist impulse (*al naz'a al-tarikhaniyya*).[132]

Although such Marxist language seems to have disappeared from Laroui's writings since the early 1980s, following the eclipse of the Soviet Union and the waning of 'Third Worldism' together with the rising popularity of Islamist discourse, the central message of his earlier works unmistakably persist till the late 1990s. Suffice it to note the titles of Laroui's *Concepts* series to realise his continued commitment to 'clarify the trajectory of modernity' as it developed in European history. It is telling that it is titled *Ideology, History, The State, Freedom*, and *Reason*, and this series provides a simplified intellectual history of each of these concepts as they emerged in European political thought, while formulating insightful historical and conceptual arguments for their convergences with, and divergences from, comparable concepts in the Islamic theological, juristic, and historiographical traditions, as well as their relevance to contemporary Arab society. Addressed to a more general readership, the *Concepts* series continues to advocate a message similar to Laroui's earlier critiques of Arab thought in CAI and AHT, if less polemically. Laroui states this message in the introduction to the last installment in the series, *mafhum al-'aql*, or *The Concept of Reason*:

> The problem of method, the subject of the concepts series … relates to the condition that we [the Arabs] have been living in for the past two centuries, one in which the relationship between us and the logic and achievements of our cultural heritage (*turathuna al-thaqafi*), has been severed. The problem that we face today is: does the scholar place himself before or after this rupture – one that has already taken place and had solidified through time.[133]

As such, Laroui seems to conceive of the *Concepts Series* as one attempt to address precisely this problem or challenge, which he variously refers to as 'taking an epistemological leap', 'turning the page', and ultimately 'effecting an epistemological break, *qati'a manhajiyya*'.[134] What needs to be 'leaped over' or 'broken with', Laroui posits in the late 1990s as he did in the late 1960s, is the 'logic of traditional thought', which has persisted since precolonial times. Whereas the early Laroui was concerned with assimilating the gains of liberalism into Arab thought and society through convincing Arab intellectuals and political actors of Marxist historicism, the late Laroui seems bent on applying this historicism himself through a theoretical and historical analysis of the fundamental differences between 'modern' and 'traditional' concepts. Indeed, commenting on the entirety of the *Concepts* series Laroui concludes, '[e]verything I have written till now in fact constitutes several chapters of a single text about the concept of modernity'.[135] It is through the elaboration, 'the deconstruction and reconstruction' of these concepts that the 'intellectual system' of which they are part could be truly grasped.[136] This, Laroui adds, has been 'the clarificatory attempt that I, among others in the Western (Maghreb) and the Eastern (Mashreq) Arab world have attempted to perform, though it does not seem like it has brought about the hoped for effect in Arab intellectual production'.[137] For the early Laroui of CAI and AHT, this 'clarificatory attempt' was best delivered through Marxist historicism.

Marxist historicism and the third-world intellectual

Laroui's argument for the suitability of Marxist historicism for the Arab intellectual is two-layered. The first layer refers to the structural and phenomenological similarity between the experience of Marx (and late eighteenth- and early nineteenth-century German philosophers in general) and that of the Third-World intellectual. The second layer identifies the specific Marxism that Laroui considers to be most relevant to the contemporary Arab intellectual's dual concern with maintaining the specificity of his society's culture and modernising it at the same time.

Laroui begins his essay 'Marxism and the Third World Intellectual'[138] by positing that the condition of 'historical retardation' generates a similar experience in its inhabitants. He elaborates on what he refers to as the 'experiential fact' of retardation in his definition of the 'Third World':

> It [does] not simply designate that part of the world distinguished by famine, illiteracy, and passivity – undeniable characteristics of the Third World today. More exactly, it is to a Second World that we are referring: a world conscious and jealous of its separateness, proud of its traditional culture, a world confronted by the First World (it little matters whether we call it imperial, industrialized, developed, etc.)[139] that it can neither wholly reject nor wholly accept ... If it should happen that some part of the world is unaware of its singularity, indifferent to its past; if it had no demands, no pride, no intellectual 'misery;'[140] if by chance or by necessity it is accommodating and without bitterness, then we are not concerned with it here.[141]

The defining character of the 'Third World' in Laroui's view lies not in its poor material condition, but in its subjects' simultaneous awareness of past greatness and present degeneration relative to other societies. Retardation therefore refers to the combination of the 'daily suffering'[142] of the intellectual and the latter's sustained sense of crisis about his society's condition. Laroui understands this experience to be shared among those whose sense of 'historical retardation' preceded the current Third World. For the boundaries of this Third (or Second) World change, 'in the 19th century it [sic] began at the Danube, if not at the Rhine; today it is mainly the area of the eastern and southern Mediterranean: tomorrow it will be Central Africa'.[143] Indeed, Laroui points out that the very emergence of 'intellectuals' as a distinct group – the Jacobins in pre-Revolution France, the philosophers in nineteenth-century Germany, and the 'intelligentsia' in twentieth-century Russia and Slavic countries – is associated with the development of a 'consciousness of [historical] retardation' on the part of that group in a specific historical context.[144]

For the German, Russian, and later, the Arab intellectual, this sense of suffering is generated by the tension between two desires: the first to retain a unique and highly sophisticated national culture, and the second to overcome the state of political and cultural subordination to the 'First World' (Britain and France, and 'the West' respectively). Thus formulated, the intellectual predicament at hand produces a set of assumptions about historical change that converge with historicism, and that historically underlay the emergence of that concept in eighteenth- and nineteenth-century German philosophy. Laroui identifies these assumptions as: the existence of a historical stage more advanced than the intellectual's own; the unity of human history; the progress of history along a single plane or in a single dimension for all human societies; the compressibility of historical stages[145] such that 'the only problem to be analyzed is how to compress historical time, which is compressible by definition'.[146] Laroui describes these assumptions as '*a prioris* produced by the [Third-World intellectual's] will to life', which, 'rather than being a result of a considered analysis, themselves drive that analysis, whether consciously or unconsciously'.[147] The convergence between the '*a prioris*' of the Third World's intellectual experience and (German) historicism is why Laroui posits that '[e]veryday experience militates in favour of historicism which, [when] regarded as the postulation of the direction of history, can be regarded as a primary given for the Third World intellectual'.[148]

Laroui further specifies the Third-World intellectual's conception of 'historical retardation' as follows. This retardation is

> recent (not too recent, or it would be imperceptible; not too remote or the notion would be magnified into total difference [from advanced societies]); is secondary, that is, not impinging upon the essentials that constitute humanity; and finally, it relat[es] to a single domain, and not to all dimensions of social life.[149]

Laroui considers these qualifications significant because they modify his earlier definition of historicism, or the 'historicist *a priori*' as experienced by the intellectual who belongs to the historically-retarded society (German, Russian, or Arab). Consequent to these qualifications, for example, the Third World Intellectual still considers history to be unidirectional across human societies, but as also 'having different depths',[150] that is, as only affecting particular domains of human existence, and not all of them. This produces a sense that overcoming retardation is possible, because 'it is only partial'.[151] The Third-World intellectual is therefore willing to concede a certain superiority to advanced societies, 'because it is postulated that this superiority was bought at a price – the loss, that is, of certain values that the retarded cultures believe they have been able to preserve' such as moral, spiritual, or affective superiority.[152]

These qualifications, Laroui notes, applied to all societies that felt retarded in relation to colonial Europe in the nineteenth century such as Slavic countries, countries of the Near and Far East, and Latin America.[153] Before them, however, it was Germany that first underwent this experience due to its perception of retardation relative to Britain and France. Hence what Laroui terms the 'exemplarity of the German experience',[154] which was first to give 'philosophical, cultural, and political expression to this psychological state'.[155] Per Laroui's qualifications of the meaning of historicism for the Third-World intellectual, German intellectuals understood Germany's retardation to be only relative and partial. 'It had to do with political unification vis-à-vis France, and industrial advancement vis-à-vis Britain.'[156] The combination of this sense of relative retardation, the correlative overestimation of the local society's (German) values, and 'the refusal to admit that the world could be divided into arenas of history and non-history' forms the seeds, Laroui posits, of what came to be known as 'German ideology'.[157] Laroui's point seems to be that the similarity between the late eighteenth- and early nineteenth-century German condition and that of the mid-twentieth-century Third World bestows a particular relevance to 'German Ideology' as a mode of philosophical expression, and on Marxism as the ultimate inheritor of its problematic.

At this point of his analysis, Laroui poses the following questions: What is the specific relevance of Marx to the Arab intellectual? And which, among the available Marxisms, is most relevant to that intellectual's condition?[158] Laroui's responses to the first question are twofold, one general and one specific. Marxism resonates with the Arab (and Third-World) intellectual because it 'logically and necessarily' fits with his concerns.[159] These concerns are less about 'individual happiness, social justice or economic productivity', the reasons that Laroui cites as typical of First-World intellectuals' conversion to Marxism.[160] Rather, like the German philosophers whose ideology Marx explicates and critiques, Marx (especially the early Marx) was haunted by German economic and political 'backwardness' in relation to Britain and France. So too, the concerns of the Arab intellectual are predominantly 'national, cultural, and historical',[161] that is, specific to the perceived historical 'behindness' of a particular nation to others. This, however, is a dimension of (early) Marxist thought that is shared with other German philosophers, including Fichte, Hegel, and the Left Hegelians in the latter's aftermath. What distinguishes Marx for the Third-World intellectual is that he provides a compelling explanation and critique of German ideology, and through flipping that ideology on its head, effectively universalises it.

According to Laroui, the early Marx saw German ideology as concerned with the 'superior level in relation to which German retardation was to be measured; the possibility of making good such retardation; and the means to do so'.[162] Though German ideology had not, in fact, clearly stipulated these concerns, it nevertheless had sought to respond to them by (implicitly) identifying the 'superior level' with Jacobinism; the 'possibility of making good' as consisting in a higher consciousness of the 'objective facts' of retardation; and the agent of change as the intellectual himself.[163] These three concerns corresponded with the defining characteristics of the German ideology: historicism, the notion that 'real history is retarded history in that it alone permits consciousness' of the existence of distinct historical levels;[164] idealism, which manifests itself in the identification of 'real history' with 'the process of becoming conscious of objective facts' rather than with the (Kantian) positivistic postulation about the existence of these facts in themselves;

and dialectic, the notion that the means of effecting historical change is a revolution that would safeguard the essence of retarded and advanced historical levels rather than, like the French Revolution, believing in the possibility of a '*tabula rasa*' or a perfectly 'rational' notion of historical transcendence.[165] In its clarification of late eighteenth- and early nineteenth-century German philosophy (what Marx refers to as the 'German Ideology'), Marxism thus serves a pedagogical purpose. It explains the German experience of retardation when that was otherwise 'virtually unreadable'.[166]

More importantly from Laroui's perspective is the early Marx's contestation of German ideology's depiction of the problem of German retardation as one peculiar to Germany. Laroui suggests that the early Marx does this by taking that ideology beyond its narrowly German confines, by finding 'beyond Jacobinism, the socioeconomic formation; in the stead of historical retardation, the retardation of the relations of production; in the stead of the intellectual or philosopher, the modern proletariat'.[167] In so doing, Marx 'saves it [German historicism] from particularism'. Whereas for Hegel and Fichte 'dialectic could only be discovered by a German, and universal history can be none other than that of the Germanic spirit', for Marx the problem of retardation related to the 'production system'.[168] As such, 'it could not be confounded with a nation or a race'.[169] In addition to critiquing it, Marx removed from German ideology 'its national and local character, and raised it to a level of abstraction that made it ready for adoption by non-Germans'.[170]

Marx's universalisation of the problem of retardation is paired with a move to de-intellectualise it, to make it less about establishing a heightened consciousness of the 'system' (as was the case with German ideology) and more about political action to bring change from within that system. Whereas heightened consciousness is necessary, Laroui notes that Marxist thought sees it as no longer sufficient for overcoming retardation, because 'the means of compensation [for retardation] is not a factor outside the production system, it is itself a product of that system'.[171] Other popular (intellectual) positions about the question of retardation, such as denial or submission, also become unviable within the Marxist worldview. Whereas denial proves inadequate, 'for one may be able to confront an army, but not – if one wishes to maintain relations with the outside world – a production system',[172] absolute submission, 'which chooses to leave responsibility to others and takes no part in a world that continues to change against one's wishes, is equivalent to historical death'.[173] Marxism therefore provides the Third-World intellectual with a clear understanding of the problem of historical retardation (based on the German experience), carves it as a potentially universal problem for a world ruled by the capitalist production system, and casts overcoming it as a problem of consciousness and action at one and the same time.

It is in this sense that Laroui concludes that Marxism has preserved the Third-World problematic, the dual and urgent desire to change society (due to the intellectual's consciousness of historical retardation) and maintain its distinct national culture at the same time. For the Third-World intellectual, as for nineteenth-century German philosophers, and the early (or, as Laroui calls him, the historicist) Marx after them, this problematic gives rise to the question of political action. For Laroui, the Marxist formulation of this question is as follows: How can a pre- (or non-) capitalist society become capitalist? The question, which Laroui argues animates the entirety of Marx's intervention from his early to his late works, is not simply concerned with the study of the historical evolution of productive forces and relations of production, or to an elaboration of the capitalist system, but to identifying how contemporary 'historically retarded' societies could achieve capitalism in a world that is divided into capitalist and non-capitalist sectors.[174]

Though Laroui does not provide a clear response to this imminent question, his discussion of modernising Arab culture offers some insights into what a path that chooses neither submission nor denial could possibly look like.

By way of conclusion

Laroui's discussion of 'specificity' in the context of cultural production is one site to look for what an 'Arab modernity' that was neither submissive nor 'retarded' could mean. Although he never really provides an adequate definition of 'specificity', Laroui juxtaposes it to the traditionalist's 'authenticity', the former being 'dynamic and advanced' whereas the latter is described as 'stagnant and backward-looking'.[175] Laroui does exemplify what that specificity might look like in the context of his discussion of carving a culture (in the sense of the aesthetic representation of human experience) that is both 'national' and 'universal' at the same time. As an example, Laroui depicts eighteenth-century German and nineteenth-century Russian assimilations of modern Western forms of aesthetic expression (e.g. theatre, novels, dance), while endowing them with their own historical experience, thereby broadening the scope of what constitutes modern culture, making it more representative of the human experience as whole.

In particular, Laroui gives the example of how German theatre introduces 'history' as a 'dramatic tool' that determines the psychological make-up of its protagonists, and in doing so, expands the depth and range of human experience that European theatre could depict. (Prior to this, Laroui notes, French theatre depended on the 'traditional human motives' of greed, lust, ambition, etc. as the basis for its character composition.)[176] Likewise, Laroui points out how Russian drama, music, and dance increased the human impact of European theatre by introducing the figure of 'the peasant', and how Russian novelists invented the new temporality of 'heavy time' to describe the nineteenth-century Russians' experience of time as they compared their current sense of void and lethargy to the imagined tempo of activity and productivity of Western Europe.[177]

Put together, these two examples indicate what Laroui means by 'specificity' in the realm of cultural expression. He attempts to persuade Arab intellectuals to

assume a 'third direction' (presumably that of 'specificity') that deepens and per-
fects what Western culture had achieved, rather than insist on self-isolation and
'folklorism'. This third position is one that Laroui finds to feature a 'rejection of
two cultural traditions':

> The one dominates our contemporary world, claims universality and totality, and
> imposes itself upon us such that we are left with no choice but to comply or admit
> shortcoming; while the other is our inherited tradition, one that we once chose to
> express our condition, but that no longer captures the multiple dimensions of our
> psychological experience today.[178]

Instead of accepting the forms of expression offered by a hegemonic Western
culture or an increasingly irrelevant Arab-Islamic heritage, Laroui calls for the
adoption of

> experiment and risk [that] attempt to deepen and expand the realm of Western cul-
> ture and reveal that this alleged universality is in fact lacking. It lacks our experience,
> an experience that if we manage to properly crystallize, will assume a general signifi-
> cance [for all of humanity].[179]

What Laroui presents us with is a conception of modernity that is deeply informed
by the Western experience and discerns in it genuine prospects for human emancipation and well-being. But this conception also entails a critical distinction
between the actual practices of Western hegemony and universalism and the 'principles and dreams' of modern Western culture. Indeed, the distinction amounts
to one between two Wests: the 'real West' and the 'West as a dream'. The former
'seems to impose itself upon us as a homogenous, transcendental unit ... [it] is the
thick, opaque, and arrogant West that we fight and that fights us'.[180] This is the
West that not only enslaved and colonised the non-West, but also exploited its
own people. But this West, the 'apparent West', should not be conflated with the
other West, the West of the sixteenth to early nineteenth centuries, with its sciences
and arts, and the West that in the aftermath of the nineteenth century became
increasingly critical of itself and its actions, 'the West which revokes the selfishness
of economics and its monopolization of resources and calls for self-emancipation
and self-reconciliation'.[181] The 'West as dream', Laroui notes, is no less a stranger
to the 'apparent West' than the non-West is to it. This critical distinction between
the West as exploiter and coloniser and the West as innovator, creator, and critic
is one that Laroui deems crucial in developing a formulation of Arab modernity
that is aware of the variegated trajectory of its counterpart in the West, and that is
therefore always critical of the kind of route it forges for itself. This is a route that
should reject the West as oppressor and coloniser, and discern and embrace the
'West as dream' and as critique. This appropriation will expand, deepen, perfect,
and therefore transform the West and make it human and universal.

Notes

1 For the characterisation of Laroui as a liberal, see Jaafar Akiskas, *Arab Modernities: Islamism, Nationalism and Liberalism in the Postcolonial World* (New York: Peter Lang, 2009), 33–60. Likewise, IBrahim Abu Lughod argues that Laroui turns from being an 'objective Marxist' to a 'Liberal étatist' in the second part of his intellectual career, see IBrahim Abu Rabi', *Contemporary Arab Thought: Studies in Post-1967 Arab Intellectual History* (London: Pluto Press, 2004), 344–69.

2 For more on the development of the political economy of the Middle East in the twentieth and twenty-first centuries, see M. Cammett, I. Diwan, A. Richards, and J. Waterbury. *A Political Economy of the Middle East* (Boulder, CO: Westview Press, 2015).

3 See e.g. Laroui's description of his brand of Marxism in the introduction to *al-'arab wa al-fikr al-tarikhi* (Arabs and Historical Thinking), first published in 1973, in which he writes, 'After examining some of the criticism directed at m[y *l'idéologie arabe contemporaine*], I realized that the Marxism whose broad strokes I attempted to brush there was actually a historicist Marxism, if not a Marxist historicism' (Casablanca: Al-Markaz al-Thaqafi al-'Arabi, 2006), 67.

4 For a discussion of the conversion of many Leftist Arab thinkers in the 1970s and 1980s, see A. Flores, 'Egypt: A New Secularism?', *Middle East Report* (1988), 153, 27–30.

5 For example, Morocco, Laroui's country of origin, attained its political independence from France in 1956.

6 For more on the radicalisation of critique in the post-1967 period, see S. Kassab, *Contemporary Arab Thought: Cultural Critique in Comparative Perspective* (New York: Columbia University Press, 2010), 1–16. Also see Abu Rabi', *Contemporary Arab Thought*, 1–42.

7 For more on the trajectory of Arab leftist thought in the 1970s and 1980s, see F. Bardawil, 'The Inward Turn and its Vicissitudes: Culture, Society and Politics in Post-1967 Leftist Critiques', in Cilja Harders, Anja Hoffman, and Malika Bouziane, eds, *Local Politics and Contemporary Transformations in the Arab World: Governance beyond the Centre* (London: Palgrave, 2013), 91–105.

8 For example, in the introduction to his *Contemporary Arab Ideology* (originally published in French in 1967), Laroui indicates that what prompted him to write this work was the

> evident political and cultural faltering of Morocco ten years after its independence. To understand this phenomenon, one was supposed to describe and analyze [Morocco's] political and social condition. But, at least theoretically, nothing keeps us from introducing such a [sociopolitical] analysis with a study of the cultural condition. And this was my method of choice.
>
> (*al-idyulujiyya al-'arabiyya al-mu'asira* (Contemporary Arab Ideology) [Casablanca: Al-Markaz al-Thaqafi al-'Arabi, 2011], 23)

Notice here that Laroui does not view cultural analysis as either independent of, or more important than, social analysis, but as complementary to them. Indeed, his early writings entwine ideology critique with historical and socioeconomic analysis. As he clarifies later, Laroui undertakes this line of analysis precisely because he considers theoretical insight to be missing from the Arab progressive movement, which in his estimate, has been mostly concerned with praxis and socioeconomic analysis, at the expense of attending to culture and ideology critique and theoretical edification. For Laroui's explication for his motives for writing *L'idéologie*, see the introduction to *al-'arab wa al-fikr al-tarikhi* (Casablanca, Morocco: Al-Markaz al-Thaqafi al-'Arabi, 2006), 45–76.

9   Laroui refers to his writing style as 'cryptic' in an interview with Nancy Gallagher in 1991. The comment comes in the context of commenting on Ralph Manheim's translation of his *History of the Maghreb* (originally published in French) that Laroui considered to be superior to the French original due to Manheim's efforts at deciphering and understanding his writing. Nancy Ghallagher, 'The Life and Times of Abdullah Laroui, a Moroccan Intellectual', *Journal of North African Studies*, 3: 1 (1998), 132–51, 140.

10   This is a paraphrase of Laroui's definition of historicism in *al-'arab wa al-fikr al-tarikhi* (Arabs and Historical Thought), 173. For a more detailed discussion of Laroui's conception of historicism, see the section titled 'Towards a solution: anticolonial historicism' of this chapter.

11   Gallagher, 'The life and times', 138.

12   *Ibid.*, 132, 134.

13   *Ibid.*

14   *Ibid.*, 135.

15   *Ibid.*

16   *Ibid.*

17   *Ibid.*

18   *Ibid.*

19   *Ibid.*, 137.

20   *Ibid.*, 139–40.

21   For Laroui's criticism of the 1970 Arabic translation of *L'ideologie*, see *al-idyulujiyya*, 7–14.

22   For colonial France's educational policy in North Africa, see A. Heggoy and P. Zingg, 'French Education in Revolutionary North Africa', *International Journal of Middle Easter Studies*, 7: 4 (1976), 571–8. In discussing the writings of Driss Chraïbi, Abdelkebir Khatibi, and Abdullah Laroui, Stephania Pandolfo (2000) and Mustapha Hamil (2002) discuss how these authors understood themselves as co-constituted by, on the one hand, Western culture as introduced by French colonial education that also inaugurated French as the language of culture and intellect and, on the other hand, their indigenous culture and tradition (Arab, Islamic, Berber), resulting in what Charibi called the 'forked tongue, *langue fourchue*' (S. Pandolfo, 'The Thin Line of Modernity: Some Moroccan Debates on Subjectivity', in Timothy Mitchell, ed., *Questions of Modernity*, [Minneapolis: University of Minnesota Press, 2000], 119). Hamil and Pandolfo analyse how for these thinkers, this co-constitution was experienced as an effect of colonial violence and resulted in an inevitable (and irresolvable) sense of alienation from both, French and local, cultures these thinkers attempted to confront. See M. Hamil, 'Interrogating Identity: Abdelkebir Khatibi and the Postcolonial Prerogative', *Alif: Journal of Comparative Poetics*, 22 (2002), 72–86, 74.

23   J. Waardenburg, *Islam: Historical, Social, and Political Perspectives* (Berlin: Walter de Gruyter, 2002), 138.

24   *Ibid.*

25   Abdullah Laroui, *L'histoire du Maghreb: un essay de synthese* (Paris: F. Maspero, 1970). This work was later translated by Ralph Manheim into English as *The History of the Maghrib: An Interpretive Essay* (Princeton, NJ: Princeton University Press, 1977). It was also published in Arabic as *mujmal tarikh al-maghrib* (A General History of the Maghreb) (Casablanca: Al-Markaz al-Thaqafi al-'Arabi, 1984).

26   For example, Laroui notes in his interview with Ghallagher that his 1987 French book *Islame et modernité* comprises a summary of his two Arabic language essays on liberty and the state, both of which were published in 1981.

27 Al-Jabiri's published this critique in a series of articles published in the Moroccan *al-moharrar al-thaqafi* in December 1974–January 1975. The essays were later reprinted in Bassam Kurdi's ed. volume: *Muhawarat fikr 'Abd Allah Al-'Arawi* (Engagements with the Thought of Abdullah Laroui) (Casablanca: Al-Markaz Al-Thaqafi Al-'Arabi, 2000).

28 A. Khatibi, *Maghreb Pluriel* (Paris: Denoël, 1983), 31–5.

29 Examples of such engagements with Laroui include: A. Boumashuli, *Alfalsafa al-Maghrebiyya: Sou'al al-Kawniyya wa al-Mustaqbal* (Moroccan Philosophy: The Question of Universality and the Future) (Casablanca: Markaz al-Abhtath al-Falsafiyya, 2007); K. Abdellatif, *As'elat al-Fikr al-Falsafiyy fi al-Maghreb* (The Questions of Philosophical Thought in Morocco) (Cairo: Ro'ya lil-Nashr, 2008); M. Al-Dahy, ed., *Al-Naghama al-Muwakeba* (The Accompanying Melody) (Casablanca: Dar al-Nashr al-Madares, 2015).

30 These were published respectively in 1980, 1981 (both liberty and the state), 1992, and 1996.

31 For purposes of this chapter, I will be mainly using Laroui's Arabic translation of *L'ideologie* (CAI). I will also be using the Arabic language *al-'arab wa al-fikr al-tarkihi* (AHT) and its English translation *The Crisis of the Arab Intellectual*. It is worth noting that AHT and *The Crisis* each contain two essays that are not available in the other. In AHT, the essays titled 'The National Content of Culture', and 'Marxism's Position vis-à-vis Islamic Ideology' are not translated into the French (and hence the English) version. In *The Crisis*, the essays on 'Tradition and Traditionalization', and 'Historicism and the Arab Intelligentsia' are not available in the Arabic original. In addition, the introduction to the Arabic version of AHT is substantially different from its French and English counterparts. Where relevant, I will point to these variations within the body of the chapter.

32 For more on modernist trends in Arab thought during the colonial and early post-colonial periods, see Albert Hourani, *Arabic Thought in the Liberal Age, 1798–1939* (Oxford: Oxford University Press, 1983).

33 AHT, 61.

34 *Ibid.*

35 *Ibid.*, 56.

36 Laroui explains this best in his introduction to AHT, where he discusses the rationale for writing his earlier work, CAI (AHT, 56–66).

37 See e.g. CAI, 49–63.

38 AHT, 56.

39 *Ibid.*, 58.

40 *Ibid.*, 68.

41 *Ibid.*

42 *Ibid.*

43 Laroui explicitly refers to the pragmatic, utilitarian nature of his argument for Marxism in AHT, 63, 67.

44 Abdullah Laroui, *The Crisis of the Arab Intellectual: Traditionalism or Historicism?* (Berkeley and Los Angeles: University of California Press, 1976), 2–3.

45 *Ibid.*, 10.

46 *Ibid.*, 1.

47 *Ibid.*, 2.

48 *Ibid.*, 8.

49 *Ibid.*, 7.

50 *Ibid.*, 14.

51 The qualifier 'Arab-Islamic' rather than simply 'Islamic' is significant in this context because Laroui, following Constantin Zurayq, whose work he repeatedly sites in this essay, emphasises that other Islamic societies like Turks, Iranians, and Pakistanis 'have, and have had in the past, notwithstanding their Muslim faith, a view of history that is completely different from that of the Arabs' (Laroui, *The Crisis*, 13). Whereas Laroui refers to 'classical Arabian' history writing practices, he identifies the period under examination as the eighth and ninth centuries CE, that is, to the second and third centuries after the advent of Islam to the Arabian Peninsula, and adds that 'historiography was motivated … and sustained by religious faith' (Laroui, *The Crisis*, 17). Thus I add the qualifier 'Islamic', to his 'Arab' above.

52 Laroui, *The Crisis*, 21.

53 *Ibid.*, 16.

54 *Ibid.*, 15.

55 *Ibid.*

56 *Ibid.*, 19.

57 *Ibid.*

58 *Ibid.*, 17.

59 *Ibid.*

60 *Ibid.*, 18.

61 *Ibid.*

62 *Ibid.*

63 *Ibid.*, 19.

64 *Ibid.*

65 *Ibid.*, 21.

66 In this context, Laroui mention's Gustav von Grunebaum's *Medieval Islam* (Chicago: University of Chicago Press, 1946) and David Samuel Margoliouth (unspecified text, but likely the latter's *Lectures on Arabic Historians* [Calcutta: University of Calcutta, 1930]) as both remarking on the objectivity of Arab historiography, however neither 'had brought out the character of this objectivity' (Laroui, *The Crisis*, 21). Likewise, Laroui notes E. F. Gautier's inability to explain the 'impassiveness of the Arab historian who employs the same style for describing the worst reverses of Arab military history as for describing the height's of gladness' (*Ibid.*). Here, Laroui is specifically referring to Gautier's *Le Passé de l'Afrique du Nord: Les Siècles Obscures* (Paris: Flammarion, 1937), 37.

67 Laroui, *The Crisis*, 21.

68 *Ibid.*

69 *Ibid.*, 22.

70 *Ibid.*

71 Laroui, *Al-'arab*, 86.

72 Laroui, *The Crisis*, 22.

73 *Ibid.*

74 Laroui, following the liberal nationalist Syrian intellectual Constantin Zurayq (1909–2000), describes the situation of 'contemporary historical practice' as follows:

> One may say that the present situation is characterized chiefly by the fact that there has been added to the classical vision described above an ideological deformation consequent upon the development of nationalist sentiments, and that the two attitudes mutually reinforce each other in a manner that inhibits the slow diffusion of positivist research methods outside and even within modern academic faculties. History still remains subservient, in contrast to the situation in Turkey, for example, where positivist methods have won the day.
>
> (*Ibid.*, 25)

75 *Ibid.*, 23.
76 Laroui, *Al-'arab*, 87.
77 Laroui, *The Crisis*, 23. Laroui comments that the only kind of consistency that exists in Arab historiography is a 'divine consistency', a consistency between the sequence of events and the 'divine truth' which they embody and indicate in the prophet's life (and in the narration of any other historical period that follows the 'stereotype' of the prophet's life) (*Ibid.*).
78 *Ibid.*
79 *Ibid.*
80 *Ibid.*
81 According to Laroui, one could legitimately talk of a society's cultural retardation 'whether this traditionalist point view is shared by all the community or only by the majority of the intellectual elite' (*Ibid.*, 8).
82 See Anouar Abdel Malek's introduction to the anthology *Contemporary Arab Political Thought* (Trans. Marco Pallis [London: Zed Books, 1983]). We see a sophisticated espousal of leftist nationalism that nevertheless does not display the level of self-awareness of European critiques of (liberal and Marxist) modernity that we see in Laroui.
83 Laroui, *The Crisis*, 1.
84 To be sure, Laroui dedicates the introduction of *The Crisis of the Arab Intellectual* to describing the claims of major anti-historicist and anti-humanist trends in the European humanities, and to noting their rising popularity in Arab intellectual circles (3–8).
85 It is worth noting that Laroui's specification of 'cultural' as opposed to economic, social or political, 'retardation' is not meant to deny the expression's applicability to these domains, as Laroui's repeated use of the expressions 'historical retardation' and *ta'akhur* (literally, behindness) signify. Rather, it should be read as an attempt by Laroui to delimit his analysis to cultural critique, as he points out at the outset of his earliest work, *al-idyulujiyya al-'arabiyya al-mu'asira* (Contemporary Arab Ideology), 23.
86 Laroui, *The Crisis*, 2. It is worth noting that Laroui's critique of the major trends in Arab ideology in *al-idyulujiyyah al-'arabiyya al-mu'asira* and elsewhere elaborately complicates the claim that culture, Arab or otherwise, is the transparent expression of society and economy. In this specific context, Laroui seems to be overstating his case in order to justify the use of 'cultural retardation', his point being that Arab culture is retarded precisely because Arab society and economy are themselves retarded, and culture is ultimately an expression of these domains.
87 Laroui, *The Crisis*, 2.
88 *Ibid.*, 129.
89 *Ibid.*
90 Laroui, *Al-'arab*, 46.
91 For Laroui's critique of Arab progressives' adoption of these trends, see AHT, 50–3, and *The Crisis*, 5–10.
92 Laroui, *The Crisis*, 2.
93 Laroui, *Al-'arab*, 52.
94 Laroui, *The Crisis*, 7.
95 *Ibid.*, 10.
96 For an incisive critique of modern Arab intellectuals' uncritical adoption of modernist assumptions about progress and backwardness see Joseph Massad, *Desiring Arabs* (Chicago: University of Chicago Press, 2007), 1–50.
97 See, e.g. Anouar Abdel Malek, *Egypte, société militaire* (Paris: Editions du Seuil, 1962). Laroui's *L'idéologie arabe contemporaine* was published shortly before the June defeat, and was written between 1961 and 1964 (Gallagher, 'The life and times', 137).

98   For more on post-1967 Arab thought, see Abu Rabi', *Contemporary Arab Thought*; Kassab, *Contemporary Arab Thought*.

99   Laroui, *The Crisis*, viii.

100 Algeria being the sole exception to this range, since the French colonised it in 1830.

101 See, e.g. Laroui, *The Crisis*, 10 and Laroui, AHT, 173.

102 Laroui, *The Crisis*, 8.

103 Describing reformist, liberal, and positivist Arab ideologies that were salient in the late nineteenth to the mid-twentieth century, Laroui writes: 'In its attempt to realize itself, we see the East act like an archaeologist, excavating the stages of consciousness through which the West had passed' (CAI, 57).

104 For more on Laroui's critique of traditionalist Arab ideology, see CAI, especially 49–63.

105 Laroui, *The Crisis*, viii.

106 *Ibid.*, 26.

107 *Ibid.*, 27.

108 *Ibid.*, 88.

109 *Ibid.*, emphasis added.

110 *Ibid.* It is worth noting that in AHT, Laroui describes liberal historicism in the same manner that he describes 'traditional' historicism in *The Crisis*. In AHT, Laroui writes: 'Every liberalism, no matter its form, agrees on a singular conclusion that contradicts the aspiration of the Third World intellectual: that there can be no bourgeois culture without the prior establishment of a bourgeois class'; and later, 'it is thus that the liberal interpretation of Marx shuts the door before the Third World intellectual, and asks him to be patient, and to submit to the Iron laws of history' (187–9).

111 *Ibid.*

112 *Ibid.*

113 Abdullah Laroui, *Mafhoum al-tarikh* (The Concept of History) (Casablanca: Al-Markaz Al-Thaqafi Al-'Arabi, 1992).

114 In AHT, Laroui explains the idea of the 'unity of history' as 'historical progress along a single plane, *'ala sath wahed*, or a single dimension, *fi bu'd wahed*' (173).

115 Laroui gestures at this understanding of politics at the outset of his AHT (17) and again in his *Concept of History*, 360.

116 Laroui, *The Crisis*, 27.

117 *Ibid.*

118 *Ibid.*

119 *Ibid.*

120 Laroui, AHT, 93–4.

121 *Ibid.*, 62.

122 Laroui illustrates the magnitude of this cost through setting the Arab-Israeli conflict as an example of the ahistorical logic of the Arabs versus the historicist logic of the Jewish settlers (1948–67). While the former keeps arguing for a right to the land based on the 'absolute truth' of continuous ownership of the land, the Jewish settler colonises, populates, and toils the land in an organised and systematic manner, and by his actions creates a new reality. Laroui lauds Palestinian resistance movements for having understood that logic and for having begun to assimilate it in their actions in the late 1960s–early 1970s (AHT, 60–3).

123 See 'Marxist Historicism and the Third-World Intellectual' (AHT) for an elaboration of the intuitiveness of Marxist historicism to the Third-World intellectual.

124 Laroui, AHT, 45.

125 Laroui, *Al-'arab*, 17.

126 Laroui, AHT, 46.

127 *Ibid.*, 49; emphasis added.

128 *Ibid.*, 48.

129 Note here that the slogan of the Arab nationalist movement from the 1940s till the 1960s (as represented by Nasserism in Egypt and Ba'athism in Iraq and Syria) was 'liberation, unity, and socialism' (*Ibid.*, 12).

130 Laroui, *The Crisis*, viii. See also Laroui, CAI, 99–138.

131 See e.g. how Laroui describes this 'utilitarian logic' as enabling him to converse with traditionalist thinkers be they 'salafist' (Islamist) or 'ideologues of authenticity' (Islamist or nationalist): 'For the purposes of argument, I accept the legitimacy of the salafist's position on the condition that the latter would agree with me that the our ultimate goal is to give the Arab individual – as a living being, as a producer and a consumer, as a reason and a will – the tools that would enable that individual to persist and succeed in today's world, one governed by a particular logic, and a particular ethic'(Laroui, AHT, 60).

132 *Ibid.*, 67.

133 Laroui, *Mafhum al-'aql*, 12.

134 *Ibid.*, 10. A better literal translation for this expression would be a 'methodological break'. However, the expression 'epistemological break' is a more accurate translation given Laroui's definition of what constitutes a *manhaj* which he defines as 'the logic of modern thought as it compares to traditional thought' (*Ibid.*, 12).

135 *Ibid.*, 14.

136 *Ibid.*

137 *Ibid.*

138 Laroui, AHT, 171–203.

139 The interjection about the various names of the 'First World' is found in the Arabic original, but not the English translation of this essay. In the Arabic text, Laroui adds the following explanatory footnote: 'advanced, civilized, imperial, colonial. For Arabs, the First World is the capitalist, imperialist Western world' (Laroui, *Al-'arab*, 172).

140 In the Arabic original, this expression translates into 'spiritual misery' or 'misery of the soul', *albu's al-ruhi*. Laroui footnotes this expression by referring to its common usage among German Romantics, most especially the German poet Heinrich Heine (1797–1856) (Laroui, *Al-'arab*, 172).

141 Laroui, *The Crisis*, 127.

142 Laroui, AHT, 175.

143 Laroui, *The Crisis*, 128.

144 *Ibid.* One possible response to Laroui's claim about the Third-World intellectual's consciousness of his society's retardation with a rejoinder that such 'consciousness' is not a product of an unmediated experience or of the intellectual sociopolitical position, but signals that intellectual's internalisation of Western definition of 'progress' and representations of Third-World 'backwardness'. Laroui is aware that such representations of progress and backwardness do in fact affect the Third World's intellectual's self-understanding of his society's condition. To be sure, CAI is ultimately a study of how modern Arab thinkers' internalisation of European representations of the West and East have served to mystify and distort these thinker's analyses of their societies since the late nineteenth century. However, in the context of analysing the compatibility between Marxism and the Third-World intellectual, Laroui chooses to shift his emphasis from the way representation influences that intellectual's perception of reality to a discussion of how, given that perception (whatever its source), this intellectual finds in the Marxist theory of historical change a natural fit for his concerns.

145 Laroui, AHT, 173.
146 Laroui, *The Crisis*, 129. In another display of his acquaintance with critiques of the modern notion of history, Laroui follows this statement with the following:'Alterity, historical relativism, and challenging the notion of history as a directional flow of time – these will come later.' Ibid. In the Arabic original, Laroui elaborates that these responses are taken up by the Third-World intellectual as a desperate reaction to the perceived failure in overcoming his society's retardation (AHT, 174).
147 Laroui, *The Crisis*, 129.
148 *Ibid.*
149 *Ibid.*, 130, and Laroui, AHT, 174. This passage is mainly quoted from *The Crisis* with some modifications from its Arabic counterpart in AHT. I made such additions/ substitutions where I thought this would clarify the meaning at hand (e.g. I added 'to all dimensions of social life' from the Arabic original), or be closer to Laroui's initial formulation (e.g. I replaced 'what defines man and life' in the English translation with 'what constitutes humanity', which I adapted from the Arabic version).
150 Laroui, *The Crisis*, 130.
151 Laroui, AHT, 174.
152 Laroui, *The Crisis*, 130.
153 *Ibid.* Here, Laroui quotes H. Kohn, *Panslavism* (Notre Dame, IN: University of Notre Dame Press, 1953); H. Kohn, *The Idea of Nationalism* (New York: Macmillan, 1944); and Y. Teng and J. Fairbank, *China's Response to the West* (Cambridge, MA: Harvard University Press, 1954).
154 Laroui, *The Crisis*, 130.
155 Laroui, AHT, 175.
156 *Ibid.*
157 Laroui, *The Crisis*, 131.
158 Laroui, AHT, 171.
159 Laroui, *The Crisis*, 128.
160 *Ibid.*
161 *Ibid.*, 128.
162 *Ibid.*, 132.
163 *Ibid.*
164 *Ibid.*, 132–3.
165 *Ibid.*
166 *Ibid.*, 135.
167 *Ibid.*, 133.
168 *Ibid.*, 135–6.
169 *Ibid.*
170 Laroui, AHT, 177.
171 Laroui, *The Crisis*, 136.
172 *Ibid.*
173 *Ibid.*
174 Laroui, AHT, 182. Rather than classifying Marx's works into 'early' works that bear the marks of German (especially Hegel's) philosophy and 'late' works that scientifically examine the machinations of capitalist production in industrialised societies, Laroui suggests reading the Marxist intervention as an attempt to answer this question. When Marx's works are read this way, Marx's study of the capitalist system in *Capital* is understood as a (partial) response to the questions he raises in the *German Ideology* (1846) or the *Contribution to the Critique of Political Economy* (1859) (K. Marx and F. Engels, *The German Ideology* [New York: Prometheus Books, 1998]

and K. Marx, *Contributions to the Critique of Political Economy* [New York: International Library Publishing Company, 1904]).

175 Laroui, AHT, 62.

176 *Ibid.*, 111.

177 *Ibid.*, 110–11. In CAI, published six years before this work, Laroui underlines the uniqueness of how cultures that perceive themselves as having had a long and distinct past experience the present. These cultures, Laroui tells us, 'live in the shadow of a glorious past, and therefore experience the present as a time of continuous and miserable degeneration' (25). Arabs, like their Greek, Persian, and before them German and Russian counterparts, experience the present in a particular way that is bred by a perpetual comparison between a distinctive past and a present that lacks such distinction. This is one of the reasons why Laroui considers the study of culture (as opposed to economic or political analysis) as particularly significant for understanding the Arab predicament. This is also why he posits that Franz Fanon's writings about the experience of colonised subjects do not capture the essence of the Arab experience, but bespeak the particular historical experience of the Antilles (among other cultures) that do not experience their present (and past) in the same way that Arabs do. Laroui's contention inadvertently refutes Ibrahim Abu Rabi's critique (made in 2003) that Laroui does not take seriously and build upon Fanon's work. As far as Laroui is concerned, Fanon speaks to an experience of colonialism that is very different from that of the Arabs.

178 Laroui, *Al-'arab*, 113.

179 *Ibid.*, 85.

180 Laroui, *Al-idyulujiyya*, 84.

181 *Ibid.*

Index